Andy McSmith has been a senior writer at the *Independent* newspaper since April 2007, having previously been a political correspondent on the same paper, and political editor of the *Independent on Sunday* and chief political correspondent o[illegible]he *Daily Telegraph* and *Observer*. He is the author of four books: bio[illegible]f John Smith and Kenneth Clarke, a collection of short biographi[illegible]*es of Labour*, and a novel, *Innocent in the House*. He has also contri[illegible]merous other books. He lives in London.

NO SUCH THING AS SOCIETY

Andy McSmith

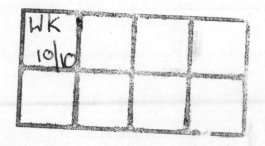

CONSTABLE • LONDON

Constable & Robinson Ltd
3 The Lanchesters
162 Fulham Palace Road
London W6 9ER
www.constablerobinson.com

First published in the UK by Constable,
an imprint of Constable & Robinson Ltd, 2010

A copy of the British Library Cataloguing in Publication Data is available from the British Library

ISBN: 978-1-84901-009-2

Printed and bound in the EU

1 3 5 7 9 10 8 6 4 2

PEFC
PEFC/16-33-111
CATG-PEFC-052
www.pefc.org

To Nick
who was twelve weeks and five days
old when the 1980s ended

CONTENTS

ACKNOWLEDGEMENTS

There are numerous people I should thank for help and information, including Sue Dearie, Nigel Farage, Andy Grice, Adrian Hamilton, Lucy Hodges, Richards Ingrams, James Manning, Amol Rajan, Simon Redfern, John Rentoul, Steve Richards, Belinda Salt, Kim Sengupta, Ben Summerskill, Peter Tatchell, Francis Wheen, the compilers of the excellent Margaret Thatcher Foundation website, my agent Andrew Gordon and publisher Andreas Campomar. Any errors, omissions or misjudgements I may have made are, of course, entirely the responsibility of next door's cats.

INTRODUCTION

THE DECADE OF GREED AND LIVE AID

First, you had to find a ticket. They could fit 80,000 in Wembley Stadium even with a massive stage at one end, but there were many more than 80,000 kids who would have liked to have been there on 13 July 1985. Some queued all night outside the ticket points. Tickets cost £25, at a time when jobs advertised in the local Jobcentre paid £1.20 an hour or less,[1] making it probably the most expensive live show that many in the crowd had ever attended. Yet no one complained, because there was a promise that £20 out of that £25 would go towards famine relief in Africa, and, more to the point, that the precious square of watermarked paper was a pass to the Greatest Gig in the Galaxy.

The crowd began to pour in as soon as Wembley's gates opened at 10 a.m., two hours before the start. Some people had numbered seats in the stands; the rest staked out patches of ground on the tarpaulin-covered pitch. The more ambitious had brought blankets and cool boxes, thinking it was a good day for a picnic, but they were soon disabused as the crowds piled in, pushing everyone forwards, until they realized that they were going to spend the whole day on their feet, with just about enough space to wave their arms. This was a problem for anyone who was hungry or needed the toilet during that long, hot day. Beating a path out of the crowd was difficult enough; the really tricky part was finding the way back to rejoin friends amid a sea of sun-baked bodies. Stewards sprayed the crowd with hoses. The fans begged them to keep doing it. Light rain in the early evening came as a relief.

At last, there was a roar from the crowd as something stirred on the distant stage. It was noon, and to a loud fanfare that day's king and queen of rock 'n' roll had entered the royal box, accompanied by the putative future king and queen of the United Kingdom. First on was Paula Yates, in a jeans suit with close-cropped dyed white hair, carrying her bewildered infant daughter, Fifi Trixibelle. Next, Bob Geldof, scruffy in sweatshirt and jeans jacket. He was hardly still all day, running on adrenaline, rushing from his seat on to the stage to perform with the Boomtown Rats, or to a nearby studio to harangue a live, worldwide television audience, estimated by the BBC at 1.5 billion viewers in 160 countries. At one point in the day, he caused a ripple of disapproval as he swore on live television. He was expected to read out an address to which donations could be sent but exclaimed 'fuck the address', and instead gave out a telephone number. It did not stop the money coming in. He was seen on camera taking a call from the Sheikh of Kuwait, who gave £1m.

By contrast, the man who filed into the stadium beside him had probably never experienced an adrenaline rush in a lifetime in the public eye. Prince Charles looked older than his thirty-six years and quite out of place, in a dark suit with a folded white handkerchief in the breast pocket, striped pale-blue shirt, tie, and perfectly combed and parted hair that left his large ears in view. He endured the music with a fixed smile, apparently feeling overdressed. 'I'll have to buy myself a pair of denims,' he is alleged to have muttered.[2] At one point, he leant over to invite Geldof, in a whisper, to a concert at Buckingham Palace the following week, where they would be playing Bach and Handel.[3] But, the handsome young woman at his side, in a low-waisted, short-sleeved pale-blue dress with padded shoulders, was having the time of her life. Princess Diana was the most photographed woman in the world. To look like Diana was the summit of many a teenage girl's sartorial ambition. Her influence was one reason that padded shoulders had stayed fashionable years after models had walked the Paris catwalk without them; one fashion writer accused Diana of having pads that 'zoom ever further off into the outer limits of Dynastic bad taste'.[4] (Or perhaps the blame should be directed at the boy-kings of fashion, Duran Duran, Diana's favourite band, or at Joan Collins, the grande dame of the American TV soap *Dynasty*.) Diana had lived under the public's gaze for more than four years, but still had a way of lowering her head as if she were trying to hide her face behind her short blonde hair. It was already rumoured that the royal marriage was not the happy-ever-after romance that it had first appeared to be. Their contrasting musical tastes were just one aspect of their incompatibility.

After a few bars of the national anthem, the audience went wild with excitement as those old 1960s rockers, Status Quo, strutted on stage looking like 'a cartoon encapsulation of everything rock 'n' roll is supposed to be

– ordinary blokes with long hair in denims playing 12-bar load',[5] to perform 'Rocking All Over the World'. There were no support acts during this unique concert; every band was big enough to top the bill, almost every number performed was a rock classic. Between the acts, there were sombre interludes as the crowd was shown images of hunger and poverty in Africa. It is a tall order to expect adolescents who have paid money and travelled long distances to hear live rock, to sit patiently through an instructive film about hunger and poverty, but on this unusual day even these bleak messages were received in respectful silence, particularly when 'Drive', by The Cars, which included the line 'Who's gonna pick you up when you fall down?', was played as the soundtrack to a searing video of a child weakened by hunger and struggling to stand up on thin legs. By nightfall, Live Aid had raised £30m, three times what had been expected.

The worst that could be said about that extraordinary day was that most of the people in the crowd had very little idea of the scale and complexity of Africa's problems; £30m was an astonishing sum to raise from one charitable event, but it was nowhere near enough to impact on world affairs. As a comparison, two months after Live Aid, the British government sealed an arms deal with Saudi Arabia that was worth £43 billion, or more than 1,400 Live Aid concerts. The slush fund that the British contractor BAE set aside in Swiss and Panamanian bank accounts to pay commissions, or bribes, to various middlemen involved in the arms deal is thought to have been more than three times the amount raised by Live Aid.[6]

Geldof, to his credit, was quick to realize that if he was to take famine relief seriously he would have to immerse himself in the politics of world trade, because all the energy and goodwill of that summer's day hardly made a ripple on Africa's problems. Even so, Live Aid was one of the greatest displays of generosity that Britain has ever seen, and it is the single most lasting image of Britain in the 1980s – which might seem odd, because the decade is not thought of as a charitable one. In the USA, the 1980s is known as the 'decade of greed' because of the way light regulation and tax changes allowed money to pour into the bank accounts of those who were already wealthy, creating a culture in which the corrupt investor Ivan Boesky told an audience in California that 'you can be greedy and still feel good about yourself'.[7]

There was a similar phenomenon in 1980s Britain, though the phrase used to sum it up was not coined by an investor but by a satirical stand-up comic, Harry Enfield. It was the 'loadsamoney' culture. Salaries were rising, and the higher tax rates had fallen and fallen for those who were paid enough to be affected; the generous cuts came at the start of the decade, but the biggest of all was in 1988, when the top rate went down from 60p to 40p, which put up the disposable income of the well-off by up to one-fifth overnight. It was one of those rare cases when London led the way, and Washington followed. When Ronald Reagan was inaugurated as president of the USA in January 1981, the phenomenon known in Britain as Thatcherism was already almost two years old.

The politics of the 1980s was dominated by Margaret Thatcher – who was prime minister from May 1979 to November 1990 – in a way that no other decade is associated with one individual. And there is no other prime minister about whom opinion is so divided. Her arrival in Downing Street brought hope to people who feared that a sickness had overtaken the western democracies, in which individual liberty was being sacrificed to an obsession with social justice. One of the many messages of congratulation sent to her in May 1979 came from California, from Milton Friedman, the Nobel Prize-winning economist who had developed the theory called monetarism, which hypothesized that the government's first and almost its only responsibility in managing the economy was to ensure that the currency was sound. The orthodox ideas that the state should intervene to keep prices and wage inflation under control, or increase public spending to escape from recession, were rejected by monetarists such as Friedman, who would later take up a post as President Reagan's economic adviser. Thatcher and the new chancellor of the exchequer, Sir Geoffrey Howe, were the first converts to monetarism to hold office in any democracy. Hence the enthusiasm of Friedman's telegram, 'Britain can lead us all to a rebirth of freedom – as it led us all down the road to socialism', and the solemnity of Mrs Thatcher's handwritten reply, 'The battle has now begun. We must win by implementing the things in which we believe.'[8]

The 'we' in that sentence was not meant to be all-inclusive. The beliefs that Mrs Thatcher held with such conviction were minority beliefs. There was not even a majority for them in the Conservative cabinet, but she was very confident that public opinion would rally if she held fast and explained herself clearly. Not for her the middle ground where consensual politicians build their majorities on bland statements with which no one could disagree. So little of what so many politicians say is worth memorizing that the few quotations that people can remember usually turn out to be inaccurate. Thatcher's predecessor, Labour leader James Callaghan, never said 'crisis, what crisis?' Nor did her cabinet ally Norman Tebbit precisely tell the unemployed to get 'on your bike' to look for work. But the things people think Margaret Thatcher said, she did indeed say, including her pronouncement that 'there is no such thing as society'.[9]

When she said this, she was expressing a widely shared view that the welfare state was too bloated, too much of an expense for people who worked hard and paid their taxes, and too easy an option for those who preferred not to work at all, if they could avoid it. When Mrs Thatcher's father was building up his business, it was success or ruin; there was no safety net to catch him if he fell. Necessity made him self-reliant. Mrs Thatcher feared that the welfare state was sapping that self-reliance and she wanted to remind those who fell back on it that they were creating a burden that other people had to carry. It was not something she said on the spur of the moment, but a long-held belief. In 1979, she included a similar sentiment in her handwritten notes for a speech she was preparing. She wrote that there is 'no such thing as a collective conscience, collective kindness, collective gentleness, collective freedom'[10] but was persuaded by advisers not to be so blunt in public. Eight years later, after she had steered her party through three general election victories, there was no need to be so cautious.

It has been said many times that she created a more selfish society, in which the rich flaunted their wealth and the poor were forgotten. Since the Second World War, the United Kingdom had been slowly but steadily becoming a more equal society, as the gap between richest and poorest closed. The Thatcher government reversed that. Between 1949 and 1979, the share of the nation's wealth received by the top 1 per cent fell from 6.8 to 4.7 per cent; in the next ten years, it rose to 7.1 per cent. In 1980, a man in the top 10 per cent of earners would, on average, have been on 2.5 times the weekly income of a man in the bottom 10 per cent, after income tax. By 1990, it was more than 3.5 times.[11] This was achieved partly through tax reductions and deregulation, which allowed net incomes to rise at the top end of the pay scale. Further down, restrictive laws to curb trade unions kept a check on wages. A week after Live Aid, the government turned its attention to the very lowest wages. There were certain groups of workers, such as hotel and restaurant staff and shop assistants, who were protected by the government through agencies known as wages councils, established by Winston Churchill early in the century to set the minimum pay rates for groups of employees who were not protected by strong unions. In July 1985, the government announced that in future no one under the age of twenty-one would be protected by wages councils. Teenagers who had responded to Bob Geldof's call to give to the needy would be repaid with lower-paid jobs. The government believed that lower pay would lead to more jobs, much needed when unemployment was heading up towards the post-war peak of more than 3m that it reached early in 1986.

Nineteen weeks before Live Aid, there was another symbolic image that burned into the memories of those who were alive at the time. The politically minded would say it was more memorable even than the concert in Wembley. Columns of miners marched under their lodge banners back to the pits, defeated, after one of the longest and bitterest strikes in history. The National Union of Mineworkers (NUM) was one of Britain's most politicized unions; its president, the charismatic Arthur Scargill, was a Marxist and its vice-president was a Communist, but the cause for which the miners struck was deeply conservative. They wanted to conserve their way of life. They wanted to go on living in pit villages, working down mines owned by the government, and where there was coal that could not be extracted profitably, they wanted the National Coal Board to keep them open anyway, running at a loss subsidized by the government. But Mrs Thatcher believed that too much industry was owned by the state, that too much was subsidized and that the authority of the elected government was being challenged by an alien organization, the domestic equivalent of the Argentinian junta that challenged British authority by trying to seize the Falkland Islands in 1982. To her, the miners' union was the 'enemy within' – another famous quotation attributed to her that turns out to be wholly accurate.

The miners' defeat was the most serious reverse that the British trade union movement suffered in its long history. The unions had become used to being treated almost as partners in government, with a part to play in setting wage levels, drawing up industrial law and developing economic policy. Mrs Thatcher put an end to that. When she came to power, there were 167 unions affiliated to the Trade Union Congress (TUC) that a combined membership of 12m, plus other professional organizations outside the TUC that did not shy away from industrial action. The Transport and General Workers' Union (TGWU) alone had a membership of more than 2m. That was the high point of union power; from that point onwards it was all downhill. The strikes that broke out in the late 1970s, including those that occurred in the winter of 1978–9, actually had less impact on everyday life than the miners strike of 1972 (which put everyone on a three-day week), or the earlier postal strike that meant everyone went without mail for two months; but too many strikes had worn away public tolerance. Even paid-up union members were declaring that unions should be curbed. Mrs Thatcher's government tapped ruthlessly into the changing public mood by cutting the trade unions out of all decision-making and passing laws to curb their freedom of action. In this confrontation, the government was the stronger side. As the decade ended, major strikes had become almost a thing of the past.

Generally speaking, on economic issues the government succeeded in carrying public opinion with it. Its trade union legislation, the tax reforms, the selling-off of nationalized industries and the attacks on local government spending all provoked ferocious opposition, but the opposition never really had public opinion behind it until Mrs Thatcher overreached herself in 1989 by introducing the poll tax.

In the circumstances, it might be expected that right-wing opinion would also carry the day on other issues, such as sexual morality or race relations. Perhaps surprisingly, this did not happen. People who were basking in the experience of having 'loadsamoney' may have been selfish, but they were not trying to force everyone else to be like them. Race and sexuality were the greatest social issues of the 1980s, and on both counts society was more liberal at the end of the decade than at the start. In the final years of Nelson Mandela's long imprisonment an increasing number of white Britons saw him as a prisoner of conscience, despite the prime minister's unchanging belief that he was the head of a terrorist organization. It is claimed that gays suffered a setback at the government's hands with the introduction of Clause 28, which banned local authorities from 'promoting' homosexuality. Gay men suffered something much worse than a setback in the 1980s, not from bigots, but from the AIDS epidemic, while Clause 28 had almost no effect on them. The only harm it really did was to the Conservative Party, which had to spend years trying to shake off its reputation as a party for bigots.

Though there was a great deal more political activism in the 1980s than in the two decades that followed – more marching, protesting and standing on picket lines – it should not be forgotten that most people did not become involved if they could avoid it, but got on contentedly with their lives. Despite the economic and political upheavals, there were plenty of visible signs that life was getting better, including the arrival of new time-saving or leisure-improving technology. The first video cassette recorders went on sale in 1978, giving rise to the possibility that people could free themselves from the television schedules and watch the programmes of their choice at the time of their choosing. The cheapest VCR advertised in the *Birmingham Evening Mail* in January 1980 cost £172.80, whereas a washing machine or a fridge freezer could be bought for £140, and a black-and-white television for £70. It was during 1980 that the first affordable home computer, the Sinclair ZX80, went on sale; it had no sound or colour, and was very slow, but it cost less than £100. People in the larger towns had recently been introduced to the new machines in the walls of banks, where they could use plastic cards to withdraw cash, but never more than £50 at a time. Shoppers who visited the

Keymarkets store in Spalding, Lincolnshire, would have noticed something unusual. In 1979, this shop was the first in the UK to introduce scanners that read the barcodes on certain products, starting with Melrose tea bags. In 1980, barcodes spread for the first time beyond the grocery trade, when they were introduced by WH Smith.

For male university students, the most interesting innovation of 1980 was the noisy, bulky Space Invaders machines that turned up in every student bar. For teenage schoolchildren, the biggest intellectual challenge of 1980 was trying to solve Rubik's Cube. This new craze was a three-dimensional puzzle, devised in the 1970s by a Hungarian sculptor and licensed by Ideal Toys in 1980, comprising six faces covered with nine stickers in six different colours, which could be turned independently, mixing the colours to one of 43,252,003,274,489,856,000 permutations. The challenge was to turn them back again so that each face was a solid colour once more. By September 1981, 50m cubes had been sold, fifty books had been written about it and there was a magazine devoted specifically to the cube, edited by David Singmaster, a mathematics lecturer from London's South Bank Polytechnic. Children were better at it than grown ups; some could solve it in seconds while an adult could sweat unavailingly for hours. A twelve-year-old boy named Patrick Bossert, from Ham, Surrey, devised a system for solving the cube in thirty-five seconds, which he wrote down on two sides of A4 and sold to other children at his school for 30p a copy; Penguin bought the rights, and *You Can do the Cube* sold 500,000 copies in four weeks, and 1.4m in all, making it the fastest selling title since *Lady Chatterley's Lover*. Its young author had to take action in the high court to prevent pirated copies going on sale.[12] Hobbies such as this were more fun and less divisive than politics.

Even in 1981, when the inner cities were torn apart by race riots, there was a yearning in society to put aside ideology and civil conflict, and muddle along together. In that year, for the first and only time in the twentieth century, a new political party made an impact on national politics. This was the meteoric Social Democratic Party (SDP), formed in reaction to the left-right divide separating Labour and Conservatives, and which looked briefly as if it might be the next governing party, but which had gone out of existence by 1989. The same longing for something uncontroversial and unifying explains the astonishing popularity of the royal wedding of 1981, and the cult of Princess Diana. It also goes a long way towards explaining the phenomenon of Live Aid, which offered the young a way to be involved in one of the great issues of the time, without being divisive or dull.

In 1980, the developed world was cut in two by the military border that ran through Germany, between the communist and capitalist blocs. They had learnt to coexist, but no one knew how long peaceful coexistence could last. The capitalist system was more dynamic and more successful economically than its rival, but once communism took hold of a country, it seemed that nothing could turn it back. No established communist system had ever been dismantled or overthrown from within. People expected this contest between rival systems to continue indefinitely. Instead, they saw it coming to a quick, decisive and non-violent end. As communism rolled out of Eastern Europe in 1989, an American philosopher forecast that the end of history was approaching[13] and that every other political system in the world would evolve into the western model of liberal capitalism.

These developments were mirrored in domestic politics. Since 1945, the UK had edged towards becoming more 'socialist', with free medicine, free schools, state pensions and more than 40 per cent of the country's industrial capacity owned by the state. Within the Labour Party, there was a vigorous movement led by Tony Benn to give the country another sharp push in the same direction. Mrs Thatcher, however, was determined to 'roll back the frontiers of socialism',[14] which she succeeded in doing. Though her economic legacy is highly controversial, no government has attempted to undo it. The Thatcherite mix of privatized utilities, low taxes for the highly paid and restrictive trade union legislation survived even thirteen years of Labour government. The end of ideology changed the language. Words like 'Marxism' and 'capitalism' went out of everyday use, while 'political correctness' and 'spin doctor' entered the language, as people stopped thinking about where politics might go and turned their thoughts to personal behaviour and the political process.

More change and more conflict were crammed into the 1980s, particularly the first half of the decade, than any other decade in the second half of the twentieth century. Out of political chaos, Britain arrived at a settlement that lasted, for better or worse. The way we live now follows directly from the tumultuous events of the 1980s.

Chapter 1

A Lady Not for Turning

In the middle of the afternoon of Friday, 4 May 1979, Margaret Thatcher stood outside 10 Downing Street and recited a quotation attributed to St Francis of Assisi:

> *Where there is discord, may we bring harmony.*
> *Where there is error, may we bring truth.*
> *Where there is doubt, may we bring faith.*
> *And where there is despair, may we bring hope.*

The Conservatives had won 339 seats in the House of Commons, with Labour reduced to 269. For the first time in British history, a woman was to hold office as prime minister. It was this, more than the change in the government's political colour, which was the day's main talking point; people did not realize that they were at a milestone in British political history, as significant as the Labour victory in 1945. That inveterate diarist Kenneth Williams, too busy during the day of the election to check that Thatcher had won, was pleased and impressed by what he saw on the evening news. He noted: 'Maggie has seen the Queen and is now the first woman PM in Europe and it's the first time since Macmillan that we've had a leader with style and dignity.'[1] The playwright Lee Hall witnessed a contrasting reaction in Newcastle upon Tyne: 'My abiding memory of my first year in secondary school in 1979 was the teachers' long faces the day after Margaret Thatcher was elected prime minister. There was a real sense of despondency which I did not understand.'[2]

But even the despondent teachers in north-east England could take comfort in the thought that a lot of prime ministers had come and gone during their lives. Mrs Thatcher was the fifth in sixteen years – the sixth, if Harold Wilson was counted twice. Politics had been like a swing door since the Labour victory of 1964, with one party governing for four to six years then the other taking over. There was no reason to think this government would last beyond 1984, or make much impact on society. Its manifesto was no more right wing than the one on which the Conservatives had won the 1970 election, which was abandoned when it collided with reality, as was that 'irreversible shift in wealth and power towards working people' that Labour had promised in 1974. As Mrs Thatcher stood waving on the Downing Street steps, the men in the picture – her husband Denis and two uniformed police officers – towered over her; and with her rigid hairdo, short jacket, pleated skirt, her high heels that threatened to topple her forwards, her drooping handbag, high-pitched voice and earnest, humourless, hectoring manner, the woman did not look as if she was built to last. Tony Benn, then an ex-cabinet minister, was brimming with optimism. After surrendering his Whitehall pass and seals of office, he recorded: 'This is probably the beginning of the most creative period of my life. I am one of the few ex-ministers who enjoy opposition and I intend to take full advantage of it.'[3] Within a couple of years, Thatcher and her government were so unpopular that it would have taken a very bold punter to bet on their survival.

The Bennite Left and the Conservative Party agreed on one thing: there was a serious crisis that required drastic action. Margaret Thatcher's and Tony Benn's generation was brought up in a world in which the United Kingdom was one of the superpowers, with an empire on which the sun never set. In their lifetime, that empire had been reduced to scattered fragments and the British economy had slipped remorselessly down the international league table. Between 1954 and 1977, Germany's gross domestic product (GDP) had grown by 310 per cent, France's by 297 per cent and the UK's by just 75 per cent. In 1954, the British workers were substantially better paid than their equivalents in France or Germany. By 1977, average wages in Germany were nearly double those in the UK. 'We are not only no longer a world power, but we are not in the first rank even as a European one. You have only to move about western Europe nowadays to realize how poor and unproud the British have become in relation to their neighbours,' is the lament of Sir Nicholas Henderson, the British ambassador to France, in a 'valedictory' written for the eyes of his superiors at the Foreign Office as he approached retirement.[4]

Sir Nicholas, who was known also as 'Nicko', was a seasoned diplomat whose 'professionalism, cultivated tastes, rumpled charm and attractive if studied eccentricity won him trust and affection wherever he was posted'.[5] He was there when Winston Churchill and Clement Attlee joined Harry Truman and Josef Stalin at the Potsdam Conference to discuss the shape of post-war Europe. His valedictory was not meant to be published but was leaked a month after the Conservatives came to power. Mrs Thatcher praised it as a 'very, very interesting dispatch'; the new foreign secretary, Lord Carrington, told Nicko privately that it was 'identical' to the Conservative election manifesto,[6] and instead of being made to retire, as expected, Nicko was promoted to the most prestigious job in the diplomatic service, as ambassador in Washington, so we can take his words as an accurate reflection of the Conservative state of mind in 1979.

A variety of reasons have been given for Britain's relative decline after the Second World War, including a very high military budget. Sir Nicholas singled out three reasons that should be addressed, and it can be assumed that the new government agreed with his choices. They were a weak foreign policy, poor industrial management and, particularly, the power of the British trade unions. When French or German workers went on strike it got them nowhere, he claimed, whereas 'nearly always in Britain in recent years a strike has led to a very favourable settlement for the employees'.

A few months before Nicko wrote his valedictory, Britain had been through the now infamous 'winter of discontent', which began in autumn 1978 and lasted until the following February, when there was a rash of strikes that did severe damage to the reputation of the Labour government. This period acquired an almost mythical status throughout the 1980s, as Conservatives referred to it again and again as a dreadful warning of what might happen if the Labour Party, funded by the trade unions, was to return to power. The strikes, however, were a symptom of a more invasive malaise that had been affecting everyone's lives continually for years – the continual shrinkage of the value of money. The pound sterling had not been doing well even before the oil-producing nations hiked up the price of oil in 1973; since then, it had been in intensive care. In summer 1975, the annual rate of inflation reached a peak of almost 27 per cent. It had dropped by the end of the 1970s, but was still alarmingly high. This made it difficult for people to keep a basic idea of what a unit of currency was actually worth. Most food and drink had quadrupled in price in the ten-year period from 1970 to 1980, as this table of a few basic prices shows:

	1970	1980
Loaf of white bread	1*s*/9*d*. (8.8p)	37p
Pint of milk	11½*d*. (4.7p)	17p
Eggs, one dozen	4*s*/8*d*. (23.2p)	72p
Rump steak, 1kg	£1.5*s*. (125p)	£5.077

For most people, these rising prices were offset by equally fast rising incomes, which year by year changed people's idea of how much money you needed to be earning to call yourself rich. In 1970, someone on a salary of £3,400 a year was at the prosperous end of the middle class and could afford a house, foreign holidays and private-school education for the children. As 1980 dawned, the lowest paid employees of ICI were on £66 a week (£3,432 a year), and that was before that year's pay round.[8] The minimum pay for a nurse was set in July 1980 at £80.71 a week, a 13 per cent increase[9] compared with £15.0/6*d*. (£15.02) ten years before.[10] A graduate with an engineering degree could realistically aim for a starting salary just under £100 a week.[11] An MP's salary rose from £3,250 in 1970 to £11,750 in June 1980. MPs' expenses were not a political issue, so the annual office allowance could rise in the same period from £500 to £8,000[12] without anyone remarking on it. Edward Heath's salary, when he became prime minister in 1970, was £17,250. In July 1980, Margaret Thatcher's went up to £46,400.[13]

These escalating figures were bewildering enough for people who could protect their living standards either by switching jobs, or by joining a union, but for those on fixed incomes they were terrifying. People living off a lifetime's savings watched helplessly as the nest egg shrank, month by month. As an example, Lady Isobel Barnett was one of the very first celebrities created by the television age. She was a quick-witted, engaging doctor who was a regular panellist on a TV quiz show called *What's My Line*?, which was so popular that when she published her autobiography, in 1956, one reviewer commented that a visitor to Britain from another planet would soon be asking 'What is "*What's My Line*?" and who is Lady Barnett?', and calculated that any Briton between the ages of seven and seventy would know the answer.[14] In 1980, Dr Barnett, by then an arthritic widow, was arrested for shoplifting. Although the evidence was conclusive, she insisted on pleading not guilty and exercising her right to trial by jury, thereby maximizing the publicity that her trivial offence and small fine attracted. After seeing the case plastered all over the Sunday newspapers, Kenneth Williams wrote in his diary: 'It's all so footling and unnecessary. She's an elderly lady who wants psychological help not humiliation. No good will come of it and I don't envy the shopkeeper who reported her to the police.'[15] On Monday morning, 20 October, Lady Barnett committed suicide. The shopkeeper, Roger Fowkes, reacted as Kenneth Williams had foretold: 'It is a terrible, terrible tragedy. I feel deeply sad and deeply shocked,' he said.[16] Since she left no suicide note, we cannot know what combination of stress, illness and depression drove her to her death, but there is a clue to her situation in the stated value of what she stole. It was a carton of cream and a tin of tuna fish, priced 87p. That was 17*s*./5*d*. in the pre-decimal money in which Lady Barnett probably still made mental calculations, an outrageous price for goods that she could have bought not so long before for less than five shillings.

Throughout the 1970s, Labour and Conservative had tried to tackle this problem by using the levers of the state to hold down prices, where possible, and to persuade people not to demand wage increases that kept pace with inflation, arguing that each wage increase added fuel to inflation, which then required another wage increase. The Labour government's prices and incomes policy went through three phases. The first two had some effect, as the unions generally agreed to cooperate. For phase three, in 1978, the government wanted an agreement that there should be no wage rises above 5 per cent. The TUC refused to endorse the policy, and the strikes began.

It is easy to exaggerate the impact that strikes had on everyday life. In the late 1970s and early 1980s, many people went about their daily lives without realizing that somewhere there was an industrial dispute under way (if they had not heard about it on the news). Some groups of employees, such as the Longbridge car-workers or the Fleet Street printers, had a reputation for downing tools on the smallest provocation, but most went on strike rather less often or never at all. Of all the disputes that broke out during the 'winter of discontent' of 1978–9, the one that caused the most comment and has stuck in the collective memory was called by the National Union of Public Employees (NUPE), which represented low-paid council employees. It was shocking in a way that a strike by better paid Ford car-workers was not, because it had never happened before and because the people most affected by refuse collectors and dinner ladies stopping work were, inevitably, vulnerable members of the public. There were instances of gravediggers also going on strike for a few days, with the result that corpses stayed longer than intended in the mortuaries. Those unburied bodies became a stock image of the 'winter of discontent', as if they had been left lying in the street. A greater number of people were affected by the uncollected refuse, which made back alleys behind shops unpleasant. One tabloid journalist old enough to remember reckoned that Britain was 'one big, open-air skip, carpeted in chicken carcasses, rotting vegetables and assorted household detritus'.[17] In reality, most people found out about the strikes on radio, television or read about them in the newspapers. They may have been irritated by them, but did not have their daily routine disrupted.

With a few exceptions, the shop stewards running the NUPE strike were not hardened militants. An internal report compiled by NUPE officials directly afterwards noted that 'a number of stewards had only recently been elected and were not totally immersed in the work of the union. For them, it was literally a baptism of fire, having to take decisions they would never normally have to concern themselves with.'[18] They went on strike because, in the perverse conditions of runaway inflation, it was irrational not to strike. One group of workers after another had discovered that their living standards fell, year by year, if all they did was passively accept the below-inflation wage rises they were offered.

The first strike of the new decade, which started on 2 January 1980, was called by the Iron and Steel Trades Confederation (ISTC). It was one of the most conservative unions in the TUC and had not called a national strike for more than fifty years. What provoked it was that, in a year when inflation was in double figures, when council workers had been awarded a 25 per cent pay rise, and the miners were being praised for their moderation in accepting 20 per cent, the ISTC was told that its members should accept 6 per cent. The steelworkers stayed on strike for thirteen weeks, causing real hardship in steel towns such as Corby, in Northamptonshire, where 8,000 inhabitants out of an overall population of 52,000 worked for British Steel, and of those 6,000 were on strike. After three months, the union settled for 16 per cent.

Had that been the end of the story, it would have been another example of why it made sense to go on strike. But in an early sign that this Conservative government was different from its predecessors, the chairman of British Steel was promptly sacked for giving in to the unions and, without consulting the board, Sir Keith Joseph, the industry secretary, imported a new chairman from the USA, a Scottish-born partner in the New York merchant bank Lazard Frères, named Ian MacGregor, who would live up to the reputation he had established in America as a hard man in his dealings with unions.[19]

The steelworks in Consett, in an unemployment-ridden part of County Durham, had broken even in the last quarter of 1979, yet it was shut down completely in September 1980. The immediate loss of 4,700 jobs and the knock-on effect on local businesses pushed the unemployment rate in parts of the town above 50 per cent during 1981, and it became the first place in

England to qualify for aid from the EEC.[20] The union was too exhausted to resist. The loss-making steelworks in Shotton, North Wales, was also closed at the immediate cost of 6,000 jobs, driving male unemployment in the nearby town of Flint up to 32 per cent.[21] Corby in Northamptonshire fared only marginally better, losing 7,000 jobs by 1981, pushing the unemployment rate above 21 per cent. More jobs went later. By 1987, the town's population had fallen from 54,000 to 50,000.

Against this background, it is not difficult to see why some Conservative radicals were drawn to the new ideology called 'monetarism'. Milton Friedman and other members of the 'Chicago School' argued that governments should not have prices or incomes policies, which only interfered with the free market. A government's first and almost its only economic duty was to make sure that the currency was sound: stabilize the pound, and leave prices and incomes to the market. In 1974, there had been no monetarists in the leadership of the Conservative Party. If the old guard had handled the circumstances of Edward Heath's resignation with more skill, Margaret Thatcher would never have been prime minister and there would never have been monetarists operating out of Downing Street.

The new ideology first took hold in the UK through an organization called the Institute of Economic Affairs, a long established think tank with offices near Parliament, which boasted of being 'the UK's original free market think tank' and which propounded the philosophy that for people to be free it was necessary for most of society's problems to be dealt with by companies, with minimal interference from government. After 1974, an anguished politician became a regular visitor to the institute's office in Lord North Street. This was Sir Keith Joseph, a man whose intense, almost tortured demeanour earned him the nickname 'the Mad Monk'. He had served in Conservative cabinets since Harold Macmillan's time and was now renouncing his past as a high-spending secretary of state for social security in a Damascene conversion to monetarism.

Not many Tory MPs were ready to follow Sir Keith all the way along his pilgrimage of self-renunciation and political rebirth, but aspects of what the monetarists had to say resonated around the parliamentary Conservative Party, particularly the thought that there should be no more wearying and humiliating attempts to agree an incomes policy with the trade unions. More than anything else, the Conservatives were tired of losing elections. Edward Heath had led them to defeat three times and was stubbornly insisting on trying again. Joseph was encouraged to stand for the leadership against him, but self-destructed during a speech in Edgbaston, in which he blundered into the issue of why so many children were growing up in poverty. He blamed young working-class women who did not use contraceptives. He warned: 'The balance of our human stock is threatened. A high and rising proportion of children are being born to mothers least fitted to bring children into the world … They are producing problem children, the future unmarried mothers, delinquents, denizens of our borstals.'[22] From that day on, Sir Keith was known to readers of *Private Eye* as Sir Sheath.

As Joseph's leadership aspirations collapsed under a heap of ridicule, the insurgents transferred their hopes to Margaret Thatcher, though she had given no sign yet that she was a convert to monetarism. To the public, she was 'Thatcher the milk snatcher', because it had been her task, in the only cabinet post she had ever held, as education secretary from 1970 to 1974, to announce the end of free milk for schoolchildren. She had hated doing it. The job was forced on her by the Treasury, and she was so upset by the response that she nearly quit politics. She took pride in being at the head of the second highest-spending government department, outspent only by Joseph.[23] Though she did not have an easy relationship with Edward Heath, she had no personal reason to complain about him. He had promoted her to the position of shadow chancellor, the second most important in the party. And no one in their right mind would put a bet on a woman of relatively limited cabinet experience taking on the leadership of a male-dominated and reactionary political party, especially when she was up against someone of Heath's stature and experience. It says a lot for Mrs Thatcher's nerve and ambition that she even put her name forward. On the eve of the ballot, in February 1975, the Conservative-supporting *Daily Express* reported that 83 per cent of Tory voters wanted Heath to stay, whereas only 8 per cent wanted Mrs Thatcher – fewer than those who would have liked to see Heath replaced by William Whitelaw.[24]

However, she was vastly assisted by Heath's behaviour. He could not see that while his policies were more or less acceptable to most Tory MPs, he was so unpopular that many were prepared to vote for anyone else just to be rid of him. It is assumed that if he had stood aside immediately, his preferred successor William Whitelaw would easily have defeated Thatcher, but since he insisted on staying, loyalty compelled Whitelaw to support him. Thatcher also had a very shrewd campaign manager in Airey Neave, a maverick MP (famous for having escaped from Colditz in 1942), who reassured doubting MPs that voting for Thatcher was a device for prising Heath out of office; it did not mean that they would be landing themselves with a woman leader with a voice which, in the opinion of the editor of the *Daily Mail*, David

English, sounded like breaking glass.[25] Her other advantage was that Sir Keith Joseph fell in faithfully behind her. 'Keith was – and remains – my closest political friend,' she declared, years later.[26] To everyone's surprise, she beat Heath by 130 votes to 119, thereby securing the support of every MP who did not really care who won but just wanted to be on the winning side. In the second round she faced three formidable opponents – Whitelaw, Sir Geoffrey Howe and James Prior – but won decisively.

Heath was not gracious in defeat; nor was Thatcher magnanimous in victory. She went through the motions of offering him a shadow cabinet role, which he turned down, then she refused to allow him any role in the 1979 election campaign. Afterwards, he let it be known that he might accept the post of foreign secretary; what he received was a handwritten note telling him that she had appointed Lord Carrington instead, coupled with an offer to appoint Heath as ambassador to the USA. He turned it down,[27] preferring to remain a glowering presence on the Conservative Party backbenches. They did not speak to one another from about January 1976 until 8 October 1998, when they were persuaded to sit together on stage at the Conservative annual conference.[28]

The new opposition leader had fought her campaign on a 'monetarist' platform, but she did not come equipped with a pre-prepared ideology. She had little more than a gut instinct that she had to break away from the consensus than the two main parties had shared since the Second World War, especially the part of it that treated the trade unions as partners in the running of the economy. Consulting with trade unions over wages, retaining a large section of the productive economy in state ownership, expanding the welfare state – this was not what the Conservative Party had stood for when Mrs Thatcher was growing up. It rather shocked her to hear the self-flagellating Sir Keith Joseph declare 'I have only recently become a Conservative', but she could see his point. 'I both recognized the truth of Keith's remark and also that my own case was subtly different: I had always been an instinctive Conservative, but I had failed to develop these instincts either into a coherent framework of ideas or into a set of practical policies,'[29] she wrote later.

Her self description as 'instinctive' is illuminating. In the long run, she will probably prove to be the only twentieth-century prime minister to give a name to a set of political beliefs. Yet she was not a consistent political thinker on a par with Nigel Lawson or the late Iain Macleod. She never put together a definitive summary of what 'Thatcherism' might be, preferring to deal with each situation as it arose by trusting her instincts. It was left to Nigel Lawson to attempt an authoritative definition of Thatcherism: 'The wrong definition is "whatever Margaret Thatcher herself at any time did or said". The right definition involves a mixture of free markets, financial discipline, firm control over public expenditure, tax cuts, nationalism, "Victorian values", privatization, and a dash of populism.'[30] It is difficult to see anything on this shopping list of political virtues with which William Gladstone would have disagreed. No less an authority than Milton Friedman once declared that Mrs Thatcher was 'not in terms of belief a Tory. She is a nineteenth-century liberal.'[31] However, Victorian liberals lived in a world of rigid social divisions, and vastly unequal and unchallenged divisions of wealth and income, whereas for thirty-four years before Margaret Thatcher came to power, British society had been levelling up, narrowing the gap between rich and poor. What is missing from Nigel Lawson's handy definition of Thatcherism is her assumption that inequalities in wealth and income were not just inevitable, but welcome. She believed in using the levers of government to redistribute wealth, but not to take money from the rich to give to the poor. She endeavoured to devise a system that would encourage and reward those who looked after themselves, and penalize those who expected the state to look after them when they were capable of looking after themselves. Her idea of freedom included the freedom not to pay excessive tax because other people relied excessively on the welfare state. The Cambridge historian Maurice Cowling, who had a profound influence on some Thatcherites, including Michael Portillo (though he did not impress Thatcher herself), put the case: 'It is not freedom that Conservatives want; what they want is the sort of freedom that will maintain existing inequalities or restore lost ones.'[32]

Margaret Thatcher would never have said that quite so baldly, but she did believe in inequality as a spur to achievement. People who worked harder and relied on their own efforts deserved to be better off than those who relied on others. She believed, instinctively, that it was oppressive if hard-working people were heavily taxed to subsidize those who were lazy. These instincts originated in Grantham, Lincolnshire, where her father, Alfred Roberts, a shoemaker's son, raised himself by hard work to be a prosperous and prominent member of the local community. Though he owned two grocery shops and employed five assistants, there was no hot running water or inside lavatory in the Roberts' family flat. Alfred Roberts, an alderman, was the role model for Margaret Hilda, the younger of their two daughters, born on 13 October 1925. In her *Who's Who* entry, Mrs Thatcher identified herself only as his daughter – there was no mention there, or in her memoirs, of her mother, Beatrice, or her older sister. From what we know of Beatrice Roberts, she seems to have been a passive woman, unlike her clever and compulsively active younger daughter. It was from her father that Margaret learnt 'the basis for my economic philosophy [who] liked to connect the progress of our corner shop with the great complex romance of international trade which recruited people all over the world to ensure that a family in Grantham could have on its table rice from India, coffee from Kenya, sugar from the West Indies and spices from five continents'.[33] From watching the alderman's daily schedule of hard work, public service and self-denial, she deduced that employees in routine jobs owed a debt of gratitude to those who created their jobs by running the businesses that employed them.

It must have jolted Alderman Roberts when Margaret returned to Grantham with her husband to be, who was neither a Methodist nor teetotal, had been married before and was ten years older than her. She had met Denis Thatcher at a meeting of a Conservative association; when she married in 1951, she said goodbye to Methodism, teetotalism and Grantham. Denis retired from the board of Burmah Oil in the year that Margaret became leader of the Conservative Party and he spent the next fifteen years walking one step behind her, an ever-present source of like-minded support.

Ever mindful of the importance of not wasting time, Thatcher had both her children, one son and one daughter, on the same day. Her daughter, Carol, was the stronger character who, with a degree of panache, handled the extraordinary pressures of living in their mother's shadow, but it was her son Mark – 'an "international" businessman possessed of no visible abilities, qualifications or social conscience, pursued from Britain to Texas to South Africa by lawsuits, tax investigations and a persistently unsavoury reputation'[34] – on whom she poured her maternal affection. For him, uniquely, she would put her reputation for personal integrity at risk. In April 1981, when she could ill-afford any bad publicity, Mark joined her during an official visit to Oman. A £300m contract was up for grabs to build a new university there. Mrs Thatcher exhorted the Omanis to award it to a British firm. Mark, aged twenty-seven, was working for a marketing company, promoting the construction firm Cementation International. He brought no qualifications to this task other than his family connections. The contract was awarded to Cementation and Mark Thatcher's firm received a commission, reportedly in six figures. Two years later, when the *Observer* uncovered the story[35] and alleged that the commission paid to Thatcher's firm was at least £350,000, the prime minister faced such a flurry of written questions in the Commons, she feared she might be forced to make a lengthy statement to the House. A thirteen-page draft was drawn up, in which, among other things, she was going to say of Mark: 'He is under no obligation to reveal to me details of his business or personal affairs. Like most parents, I only know what I am told.'[36] In the event, the statement was never delivered, but in answers to written questions she stoutly insisted that she had never said anything about Cementation to anyone in Oman while she was there, batting for British industry,[37] and therefore questions about whether or not she knew that Mark was representing the firm were 'irrelevant'.[38] But it is quite possible that the Omanis thought they were being encouraged to put business in the way of the British prime minister's son. Four years later, Mrs Thatcher secured what is reputed to be the biggest arms deal in history: the Al-Yamamah contract with Saudi Arabia. Again, rumours surfaced that Mark Thatcher had made millions from the deal in some unspecified way. In his biography of Mrs Thatcher, John Campbell asks his readers to imagine what her upright father Alfred Roberts would have made of his grandson's mysterious ways of making millions.

When she was in full flight, Mrs Thatcher sounded like a bossy matron with a closed mind and a startling inability to measure the impact of her words. Her mind was often too literal to grasp a simple joke. One Tory MP who was helping her draft a light-hearted speech in praise of a colleague suggested that she could say he was clever but never let his brains go to his head, to which she exclaimed: 'I can't say that! If his brains aren't in his head, where will people think they are?'[39] She had no ear for sexual innuendo, thus her famous comment in praise of her deputy, William Whitelaw – 'every prime minister needs a Willie'. Another, possibly apocryphal story, is that on a visit to the Falklands she posed for a photo opportunity on the gun of a battleship, which vibrated alarmingly and she turned to a naval officer to ask: 'Can this thing jerk you off?'

Yet despite idiosyncrasies that sometimes veered into self-parody, Thatcher was formidably intelligent and quick on her feet, as she demonstrated twice a week during Prime Minister's Question Time. She was relentlessly hard-working. Though she called herself an instinctive Conservative and a 'conviction' politician, she did not rely on either quality to win an argument, but would bludgeon an opponent with her command of detail. She also developed a commanding body language. She would remain very still when movement was unnecessary, as for instance when she was listening to someone speak in the Commons; when she moved, it was with an economy of movement that gave an impression of immense self-belief.[40]

She took endless care over her appearance and complexion. Soon after her arrival in Downing Street, her voice became less rasping and her hairstyle less severe – on professional advice, no doubt. At close quarters, the skin on her neck looked a decade or so older than her face. She kept her sexuality under tight control, as was expected of women of her generation, but could suddenly become almost flirtatious in private when it seemed appropriate.[41] She liked to be surrounded by men who appreciated her femininity, and she could be forgiving of their private peccadilloes. She did her very best to protect her court favourite, Cecil Parkinson, when he was embroiled in a sex scandal, and after he had been forced to resign she brought him back into her cabinet as soon as she decently could.

By contrast, her behaviour towards other ministers could be shockingly rude and aggressive. The worst example was the way she treated Sir Geoffrey Howe, who was chancellor during the first four tumultuous years of her premiership. She owed him more than she owed any other colleague. Had she not been working alongside a stubbornly consistent chancellor with a first-class forensic mind, her first couple of years could have been a disastrous failure. But Sir Geoffrey was a man of no charisma. The most famous remark ever made about him came from Denis Healey, the previous Labour chancellor, who, having sat through Sir Geoffrey's plodding critique of government policy, remarked that 'part of his speech was rather like being savaged by a dead sheep'.[42] It would never have crossed Howe's legal mind to flatter or flirt with the prime minister. As the years went by, he increasingly got on her nerves. She could not resist humiliating him in front of others, until the worm turned. His spectacular resignation destroyed her premiership.

Others, who were old enough and sufficiently right-wing, found her combination of cold self-control and latent sexual chemistry irresistible: 'But goodness, she is so beautiful … quite bewitching, as Eva Peron must have been,' Alan Clark reckoned.[43] After Kingsley Amis had been introduced to Thatcher, he had recurrent dreams about her, saying she was: 'One of the most beautiful women I have ever met.'[44] Calling to congratulate her on her speech at a Conservative Party conference, Woodrow Wyatt, the *News of the World* columnist, told her: 'You looked beautiful, so beautiful that I fell in love with you all over again.'[45] She was 'delighted' by this compliment, he noted. The French president, Francois Mitterand, when briefing his minister for Europe, Roland Dumas, reputedly told him: 'Cette femme Thatcher! Elle a les yeux de Caligule, mais elle a la bouche de Marilyn Monroe.'[46] The Conservative MP Sir Nicholas Fairbairn – not a wholly reliable source, it should be said – told the story of a man who drank too much at a reception hosted by the lord high commissioner of the Church of Scotland, and who approached the prime minister to say that he fancied her, to which she retorted: 'Quite right. You have very good taste but I just do not think you would make it at the moment.'[47]

It did not take long for her reputation as a hard-line Conservative to seep into public consciousness. The Soviet authorities did her a great favour by denouncing her as the 'Iron Lady', which she naturally took as a great compliment. Yet even as the Conservatives sailed ahead of Labour in the opinion polls prior to the 1979 election, Mrs Thatcher's personal rating lagged well behind that of the avuncular prime minister, James Callaghan. She was also less trusted by the public than Edward Heath; one NOP poll in November 1978 suggested that whilst the Conservatives had a 3 per cent lead under Thatcher, it would have been 14 per cent if Heath were still leader.[48]

However, she did not need the public's affection to win the upcoming general election. The Labour government had been through five dismal years struggling with inflation and industrial decline, hitting its nadir in September 1976 when Chancellor Denis Healey admitted defeat in his six-month struggle to prevent a run on sterling, and applied to the International Monetary Fund for a £2.3 billion loan. It came with a condition that public spending had to be cut. After the experience of the 1930s, all the main British political parties and virtually every government in the capitalist world had accepted the Keynesian view that when unemployment was rising, governments borrowed more to spend their way out of recession. Now a Labour government was being required to do the opposite, with dire consequences for the very people the Labour Party was formed to protect. On his return from Washington, Healey was allotted five minutes on the rostrum at the Labour Party annual conference to explain his decision to the delegates. Tony Benn recorded: 'There were hisses and boos when he came forward to speak. He then went on to shout and bully and rule out alternative policies … I couldn't even clap him, his speech was so vulgar and abusive.'[49]

On that same day, Callaghan delivered the main address to the conference. He warned:

> The cosy world which we were told would go on forever, where full employment would be guaranteed by a stroke of the Chancellor's pen, cutting taxes and deficit spending is gone. We used to think we could spend our way out of recession and increase employment by cutting taxes and increasing government spending. I tell you in all candour that that option no longer exists.[50]

With those words, a Labour prime minister ushered in the policies now known as Thatcherism.

Government spending peaked in the year 1975–6, when it consumed 49.9 per cent of the nation's total output, or GDP. That figure fell very quickly as Healey's IMF-imposed economies took effect, reaching a trough in 1979–80 at 44.8 per cent of GDP. Healey had cut government expenditure by 1 per cent of GDP per year for five years, a feat no other chancellor came near to repeating. This austerity tore apart an already fractious Labour Party.

Worst hit by the cuts were public employees, particularly low-paid council employees, most of whom were members of the National Union of Public Employees (NUPE), a fast expanding, well-organized union whose leaders were driven leftwards by the crisis. It was this which set off the winter of discontent, which Labour sought to defuse by appointing the Clegg Commission to report on public sector wages. It came out with an eye-wateringly generous proposal: council workers' wages were to be increased by 25 per cent in one year, without any requirement that there should be efficiency savings. This would knock a huge hole in Healey's efforts to reduce public spending, but Mrs Thatcher and her team were mindful that there was an election looming and that public employees had votes, so they promised to implement Clegg's recommendations in full. It would be a while before council workers felt the need to go on strike again. Labour's parliamentary majority had long since been whittled away in by-election defeats and it could not survive without the support of the Liberals, the Scottish Nationalists and a few Ulster MPs. It was defeated by a majority of one when the Scottish National Party perversely tabled a vote of no confidence, forcing a general election that delayed Scottish devolution by eighteen years.

In short, Mrs Thatcher could not claim the 1979 election as a personal victory in the way that she was able to do after the one that followed four years later, and she did not emerge from it in the commanding position that she would later achieve. She had to work with a cabinet dominated by strong-willed men who did not share her new ideology. She would have liked to have appointed the wayward Sir Keith Joseph as her chancellor, but felt that she had to offer him a less sensitive post, as industry secretary, while allocating the two major offices of chancellor and home secretary to Howe and Whitelaw, who had run against her. Both served her well. Whitelaw was a stickler for loyalty and a source of sensible, restraining advice, while Howe had become a fervid convert to monetarism. John Biffen, whom Thatcher trusted as an old opponent of Heath, and Nigel Lawson, were Howe's deputies, thereby ensuring that the Treasury was in Thatcherite hands. So was the Department of Trade, run by John Nott and Norman Tebbit.

The only economic department not under Thatcherite control was the Department of Employment, headed by Jim Prior. This meant that the gelding of the trade unions came about more slowly than Thatcherite outriders such as Norman Tebbit would have liked. During the steel strike, the steelworkers picketed dockyards and privately owned steelworks, whose owners protested to the government that their businesses were being hit by a dispute in which they had no role. The reaction from the Tory right was to demand all secondary picketing should be made illegal immediately, whereas Jim Prior wanted to move one step at a time. When the call was taken up in the House of Lords, the venerable Lord Hailsham, the oldest and most experienced member of cabinet and the only one possibly better known to the country than Margaret Thatcher, was shocked: 'If I thought the Conservative Party in its manifesto had taken the line that it was going to stop all secondary action, I should certainly not have supported the manifesto myself, and I certainly should not have accepted office in the present government.'[51]

The most pressing issue was not the trade unions, however, it was the constant decline in the value of money. Inflation had been coming down since 1976, but was still too high and was likely to get worse because the 1979–80 revolution in Iran that brought Ayatollah Khomeini to power had almost tripled the price of oil. Thatcher and Howe set about applying the monetarist remedy with an enthusiasm that was almost masochistic. Howe's first Budget looked like a wilful application of fuel on the fire. It contained a lavish gift to the rich – a cut in the top rate of income tax from 83 to 60 per cent. To make this giveaway more palatable to those on middle incomes, the standard rate of income tax was also cut, from 33 per cent to 30 per cent. Then, to stop middle-income taxpayers from stoking inflation by spending their tax rebate, interest rates went up by a full 2 percentage points, and when that did not work, they went up another 3 points in November, by which time the basic rate had gone from 12 to 17 per cent in six months. Though the consequences for anyone with a mortgage were dire, the pound was now very attractive to foreign investors. In October 1976, when Denis Healey was forced to go to the IMF for a loan, the pound was worth $1.62; by October 1980, it had risen to $2.42 – that is to say, it had regained half its value against the US dollar. It had risen by similar proportions in relation to other currencies, which was excellent news for Britons who took holidays abroad, but created a vast problem for any firm making British goods for foreign markets.

Meanwhile, at the Department of Trade, John Nott and Norman Tebbit simply abolished the Price Commission because monetarist theory laid that there was no need for governments to attempt to control prices in the private sector. That decision was a shock even to cabinet ministers, not least to Francis Pym, who had pronounced only a few weeks earlier that they were not going to abolish the Commission. Those prices that remained under direct government control were hoisted upwards. The state-owned British Gas Corporation raised its prices by 10 per cent more than the rate of inflation for three consecutive years. Rates, school buses and National Health Service prescriptions all became more expensive. At an election press conference, a week before polling day, Mrs Thatcher accused Labour of running a 'scare campaign' that the Conservatives might put 10p on the price of a school meal. As children went back to school after the Christmas break, they discovered that the price of a school meal had indeed gone up by 10p.

When wages in the public sector went up by 25 per cent, as recommended by the Clegg Commission, the private sector unions naturally demanded matching pay rises. The overall effect was to flood the economy with money whilst making everything more expensive. Inflation had been slowly falling in the last years of the Labour government, but started rising within two months of the Tory election victory, going above 17 per cent by the end of 1979. An item that cost £1 when Margaret Thatcher came to power would cost, on average, £1.22 one year on. In the words of Sir Ian Gilmour, a member of the 1979 cabinet: 'A government whose chief objective was to defeat inflation had in its first year succeeded in doubling it.'[52]

When the future chancellor Nigel Lawson set out his definition of 'Thatcherism' years later, two prominent items on his list were 'firm control over public expenditure' and 'tax cuts'. The new government delivered immediate cuts in income tax, but only in order to switch to a system where people were taxed when they spent money rather than when they earned it. A week before polling day on 3 May 1979, the *Daily Mail* had filled its entire front page with a story headed 'Labour's Dirty Dozen – 12 big lies they hope will save them',[53] exposing the black propaganda allegedly emanating from Transport House, the headquarters of the TGWU. One 'lie' was that the Conservatives would double VAT, when Thatcher had promised that very week that they had 'no intention' of doing so.[54] In fact, they put up VAT from 8 to 15 per cent, so they just avoided doubling it. Public spending as a proportion of GDP, which the Labour government had reduced at such huge political cost, jumped from 44.8 to 47.3 per cent during 1980–1, and continued rising until it reached 48.5 per cent. It took a full seven years to get back down to the 1979 level. In short, the Conservatives had not decreased the tax burden; they had increased it and redistributed it, with the very rich as the main beneficiaries.

One reason that government spending was so high was the cost of keeping people out of work. The most famous political poster of the 1979 election, and one of the most famous in British political history, was produced for the Conservatives by the Saatchi brothers; it showed a snaking dole queue and bore the devastating caption 'Labour Isn't Working'. Anyone who saw that poster could be forgiven for believing that it promised lower unemployment under the Conservatives, particularly if they had heard Margaret Thatcher telling an audience in the unemployment-ridden north-east of England during the election campaign: 'We Conservatives believe in policies that will create real jobs'.[55] In May 1979, the official unemployment figure was 1.1m, a shocking number to anyone who remembered the economic stability of the 1960s, but it would never be that low again in the eleven years that Margaret Thatcher was prime minister. Despite the government's repeated adjustments to the way the figures were compiled, each one designed to nudge them downwards, the lowest unemployment recorded during Thatcher's reign was 1,596,000, in April 1990. In 1980 alone, the figure rose by 836,000, the highest recorded annual rise since 1930. The January 1986 figure of 3,070,621 represented 12.5 per cent of the working population, but that was only an overall average, brought down by the high level of employment in the south of England. In Northern Ireland, unemployment was 20 per cent, while in some areas dominated by declining industries it was much higher.

As ordinary Britons grappled with the high taxes, high prices and job insecurity, they were given a revealing glimpse of how one rich family had been getting along through these difficult times. The Vestey family had made a vast fortune shipping refrigerated meat from Argentina to the UK, and had become specialists in avoiding tax. Their 7,200 shop assistants started on wages of £2,860 a year, which was above the legal minimum laid down by the wages council, but below average for the retail trade. The *Sunday Times* employed some fine investigative journalists, including Phillip Knightley, who revealed that for the previous year the firm had reported profits of £4.1m, on which it had paid just £10 in tax. Edmund Vestey said: 'We paid exactly what we were obliged to pay. We have certainly kept to the letter of the law.' He was also quoted as saying: 'Let's face it, nobody pays more tax than they have to. We're all tax dodgers, aren't we?'[56] Lord Thorneycroft, a former chancellor whom Margaret Thatcher had brought out of retirement to be chairman of the Conservative Party, agreed and was quoted as saying: 'Good luck to anyone who can make a success of a business.'[57]

So, in its first year in office, the new government had brought higher unemployment, higher prices, higher public spending and a lavish transfer of wealth to the highest paid. To quote Sir Ian Gilmour's summary of the two years, 1979–81, when he was in cabinet:

> Many of the better off did well even out of the earliest Thatcher period. But monetarist dogma was so cruelly discredited by its results, and Thatcherite economic policy in its opening years so patently disastrous that the survival of either of them, let alone their continuing relentless implementation, provides cause for surprise.[58]

It hardly needs saying that Gilmour and other cabinet ministers who were not part of the Thatcherite project, the ones she contemptuously nicknamed the 'wets', were not asked their opinions ahead of the most sensitive economic decisions. Jim Prior, the leading 'wet', first learnt that VAT was to be increased when he was tipped off by the director general of the CBI, John Methven, but did not believe it.[59]

By the summer of 1980, several cabinet ministers, including Prior, Lord Carrington, Gilmour and the agriculture minister Peter Walker, were in almost open revolt, and in November the defence secretary, Francis Pym, threatened to resign rather than accept the cuts in the defence budget demanded by the Treasury. But, in public at least, Thatcher was unflinching. The acronym Tina – for 'There is No Alternative' – was already in circulation. Her speech to the annual Conservative Party conference that year contained one of her most memorable lines, crafted by her speechwriter Ronald Miller: 'To those waiting with bated breath for that favourite media catchphrase, the "u turn", I have only one thing to say: "You turn if you want to. The lady's not for turning".'[60]

Then, in January 1981, Howe came to her with devastating news. It was a monetarist axiom that governments must restrict how much they borrow, as measured by the Public Sector Borrowing Requirement (PSBR). This was the first statistic that the IMF examined when a government applied for a loan and it was the main measure of the amount of money in circulation. In 1976, the Labour government had set about reducing the figure, but by 1978–9, with unemployment rising and tax receipts falling, it had slipped back up to £9.25 billion. Howe's target was to bring it down to £8.25 billion in 1979–80, but all he had done was put it up, despite the money now coming from North Sea oil. The news that Howe brought to an incredulous prime minister was that it was now on course to reach £14.5 billion in the coming year.

This was the most testing moment Thatcher ever faced in her capacity as an economic manager. If there are three incidents that defined her as prime minister, they are the miners' strike, the Falklands War and the economic crisis of 1981. The country was deep in recession, with unemployment rampant, much of it as a direct result of government policy. In the circumstances, any Keynesian economist would have advised Thatcher to let the PSBR keep rising; indeed 364 economists did, in a signed letter to *The Times* in March 1981. But Mrs Thatcher had a new economic adviser, Alan Walters, professor of economics at the London School of Economics, who urged her to cut the deficit by £4 billion by raising taxes, which ran counter to nearly fifty years of accepted practice and would do nothing for the Conservatives' claims to be the tax-cutting party. But she and Howe agreed. In March, a shocked House of Commons heard Howe announce a grim package of indirect taxation and cuts in personal tax allowances, including an increase of 17p on the price of a packet of twenty cigarettes. 'They may get rid of me for this,' Mrs Thatcher told Walters, adding: 'At least I shall have gone knowing I did the right thing.'[61] The only good news was that having put this Budget through, Howe felt able to cut interest rates, but this led to a run on the pound. Having done so well in 1976–80, sterling lost a third of its value during 1981 and was worth just $1.81 by October, 25 cents less than it had been when the Conservatives took office. Howe then had to put interest rates up to prevent it falling further.

In July 1981, as Toxteth in Liverpool was being torn apart by riots, Mrs Thatcher faced the most serious cabinet revolt of her premiership, led by Michael Heseltine, the environment secretary, with at least five other cabinet ministers joining in, but she did not buckle. She let the summer pass and then sacked three cabinet ministers, including Christopher Soames, the lord privy seal, son-in-law of Winston Churchill, who was so outraged that he shouted at her for twenty minutes, declaring that he had never been spoken to by a woman in so abusive a manner. Jim Prior was shunted off to Northern Ireland, and into an enlarged cabinet she brought a praetorian guard of Thatcherites: Nigel Lawson, Norman Tebbit and Cecil Parkinson. She had increased her hold over the cabinet, but had not made herself loved by the country, where she was – to quote a headline in *The Times* – 'The Most Unpopular Prime Minister Since Polls Began'.[62]

By the beginning of 1982, there were signs that the worst was over and that the unpalatable medicine dispensed by the Conservatives was beginning to work. Inflation had peaked at 21.9 per cent in May 1980 and now fell to 16.9 when the VAT increase dropped out of the annual comparison. In April 1982, it was 12 per cent and by the end of 1982 it was 5 per cent. Rampant price increases, which had so disrupted everyone's lives for so long, had at last been exorcized, making Howe's tax-raising Budget look more like a far-sighted act of courage than the destructive folly that it had first seemed to be. The future chancellor Kenneth Clarke, who was no Thatcherite, believed that it was 'the finest Budget of the 1980s'[63] – though there were others, even in the Conservative Party, who vehemently disagreed. After more than twenty-seven years had passed, Clarke mentioned the subject in passing in a speech in the Commons, only to be interrupted by another Tory veteran, Sir Peter Tapsell, who told him that what Thatcher and Howe did back then was 'intellectually and economically illiterate – the West Midlands has never recovered. The 1981 Budget is the reason why now, with the collapse of our financial industry, we do not have a proper industrial base.'[64]

What mattered at the time was what the Budget did for Thatcher's reputation and self-belief. According to Nigel Lawson, 'she saw as her Government's finest hour, her equivalent of the Battle of Britain, to which her mind was always harking back, as having been the 1981 Budget'.[65] Tina was alive and well and would serve as a political mantra for the remainder of the decade. She had proved that she was 'not for turning'.

Chapter 2

Sisters Are Doin' It for Themselves

There was a murder in 1980 that had more impact on public opinion than even the assassination of John Lennon. The victim was Jacqueline Hill, a third-year student at Leeds University, whose discarded handbag was discovered near the hall of residence on the evening of 17 November 1980. The student who discovered it did nothing at first, but when he took a second look, he noticed bloodstains and rang the police. Two officers arrived, but did not see any cause for alarm. People were nervous everywhere in the north of England because there was an infamous killer known as the 'Yorkshire Ripper' at large. One of the officers made a semi-jocular remark about him, but the police went on their way without instigating a search for the missing woman. There were too many demands on their time. Burglar alarms were every shopkeeper's new must-have accessory, but they were notoriously unreliable; on the evening that the missing handbag was found, ninety alarms went off in the Headingley area, of which eighty-seven were faulty. As the police scurried from false alarm to false alarm, Jacqueline Hill lay dying from hideous injuries. She may have been alive at the moment when an officer made that off-colour remark about the Yorkshire Ripper,[1] but she was dead when her mutilated body was found the next morning – the thirteenth woman killed by a criminal so vicious and elusive that, like the original 'Jack the Ripper', he became a catalyst for social change.

There had been a lively, growing women's movement in the 1970s, but its impact was felt principally in the universities and on the libertarian left, where it asserted the right of women to be independent of men, to have the right to control their own bodies, dress as they please and challenge sexist language; in other words, more than anything else, feminism asserted its right to exist. By 1980, attitudes that might have counted as vanguard feminism ten years earlier were seeping into the mainstream. Women's independence and sexuality were celebrated in drama and in music, such as in the comic song 'It's Raining Men', recorded in 1982 by the Weather Girls, or the 1985 Eurythmics song, sung by Annie Lennox and Aretha Franklin, 'Sisters Are Doin' It for Themselves', or by the riskily named theatre group, Cunning Stunts. Victoria Wood's gentle television comedies might also have been thought risky in a previous decade. In one, she cast herself as a nervous working-class girl setting out to lose her virginity, only to find that when the opportunity had been created, the man she had solicited did not want sex without love.

There was tension in the women's movement between those who wanted to stay inside the protective isolation of exclusive women's groups and those who wanted to turn outwards. Sheila Rowbotham, a well-known feminist writer, warned in the late 1970s that 'feminist politics can become preoccupied with living a liberated life rather than becoming a movement for the liberation of women. Our lack of structure can make it difficult for women outside particular social networks to join. It can lead to cliquishness.'[2] A few years later, another writer noted, with reference to meetings of women's groups, 'The last one I consciously avoided concentrated on peaceful and painless methods of male extermination.'[3]

As feminists turned outwards, their presence was felt in the Labour Party. The annual Labour Women's Conference, which had the reputation of being a preserve of people who were good at making tea, was suddenly invaded by women in dungarees, demanding radical change, whose most visible long-term achievement was the election of more than a hundred women Labour MPs in 1997. The introduction by Labour of a national minimum wage was also a sign of feminist influence. It had been opposed by some of the stronger, male-dominated trade unions on the grounds that it would erode pay differentials. It was the unions with large numbers of women members, such as the public employees' union, NUPE, and the shopworkers' union, USDAW, who successfully put the case that the employees least likely to be protected by collective wage agreements were low-paid women workers.

Law enforcement was not traditionally the home turf of the left, and given that the revived women's movement was a product of 1960s permissiveness, it might seem an unlikely turn of events that feminists would be on the streets demanding that police put more effort into a criminal investigation such as the Jacqueline Hill case, or demanding that films and printed material should be subject to tighter censorship, or that certain offenders should be sent to prison rather than fined. In 1979, a government-appointed Committee on Obscenity and Film Censorship had produced an anti-censorship report, just in time to be ignored by the incoming Conservative administration. Chaired by the philosopher Bernard Williams, former husband of the Labour cabinet minister Shirley Williams, it recommended that there be no censorship of the written word and light censorship only of pictorial images that might be seen by people who did not wish to see them. 'We unhesitatingly reject the suggestion that the available statistical information for England and Wales lends any support at all to the argument that pornography acts as a stimulus to the commission of sexual violence,'[4] it concluded. It was like a last call for 1960s liberalism, which looked indulgently on pornography as a harmless outlet for men's sexual frustrations, as if a man who finds relief in masturbation or prostitution is thereby less likely to commit a sexual assault. One notable submission to the committee disagreed, arguing that pornography encouraged men to think that they had proprietorial rights over women's bodies and so encouraged sexual violence. It came not from some right-wing campaigner for censorship in the Mary Whitehouse mould, but from the feminist collective who produced the magazine *Spare Rib*.

Of all the writers in world literature, the one most revered by the left around the beginning of the 1980s was Bertolt Brecht who, while generally sound on what were classed as women's issues, had written the lyrics of a popular song, 'Mack the Knife', the opening number of *The Threepenny Opera*, mythologizing a fictional serial killer similar to 'Jack the Ripper'. The accompanying novel by Brecht explained:

> The people in the great stone tenements of Whitechapel were excellent judges of the difference between the accomplishments of a fancy General and those of their own heroes. To them it was plain that the 'Knife' carried out his crimes at a far greater personal risk than the official picture-book heroes did theirs.[5]

That was fiction, but in the Yorkshire and Manchester regions, in 1980, women were becoming seriously frightened by a real-life murderer, who killed randomly and whom the police seemed to be incapable of finding. He behaved differently from most serial killers who escape detection for a long time, concealing the bodies of their victims so that the police do not know that there is a killer at large. This was the case with Dennis Nilsen, the notorious 1980s multiple murderer, arrested at his home in Muswell Hill, London, on 9 February 1983, after plumbers investigating a blocked toilet discovered human remains in the drainage system; most of Nilsen's fifteen victims, young homosexuals all, had not been reported missing, and the investigation went 'backwards towards detection, rather than forwards towards arrest', as the police began with 'a suspected murderer, and as yet no idea who had been murdered'.[6] The horror was over before the public knew about it. By contrast, the 'Ripper' left his handiwork in the open, and from the moment that the second body turned up the police knew they were hunting for a man who killed at random and would continue killing. The *Sun* reported in January 1976 that the Yorkshire police were hunting a serial killer. The publicity expanded with each new murder and there was – as Brecht could be said to have forecast – a strand of public opinion that admired this anonymous loner who was eluding the largest manhunt in British criminal history. He was a constant topic of pub talk, particularly in the north of England. Police at football matches were occasionally taunted by chants of 'Ripper – 13, police – nil'. Men, after all, had no reason to be afraid, but women across Yorkshire and Merseyside found themselves almost under curfew, because no woman out on her own after dark could be sure that she would live to see the morning. So when feminists raised a clamour against male callousness and the incompetence of the police, they reached a wider and more receptive audience than all the debates about gender-specific language and patriarchal structures ever had.

It was alleged that because senior police officers were male, they didn't take the case as seriously as they should. This does not really stand up to the known facts. The head of Leeds Criminal Investigation Department (CID), Chief Superintendent Dennis Hoban, knew at once that he was pursuing a very dangerous man; when he died in 1978, aged fifty-two, friends and colleagues suspected that the stress of the Ripper hunt had hastened his death.[7] He deployed 137 officers, and within a year of the second murder the police had invested 64,000 hours, filled 6,400 index cards, made 3,700 house-to-house inquiries, checked up on 3,500 vehicles and taken 830 statements.[8] By the end of 1980, there were 289 police officers working full time on the case, 188 in West Yorkshire alone. The problem was not lack of effort, but disorganization. Computers existed, but the police would not use them. The government offered the West Yorkshire police access to the computer at the Atomic Research Establishment, in Harwell, for a fee of £25,000, plus an annual rent of £156,000, but the police decided that it would not be worth the money,[9] so every report of every investigation or interrogation was recorded on paper. The inquiry drowned in paper. Police officers would head off to interrogate Peter Sutcliffe, a Bradford lorry driver, unaware that he was being questioned over and over again by different officers, and that no one had noticed the evidence piling up against this one name.

Another problem was that the UK has no national police force, and the killer was no respecter of police boundaries. When he killed in the Manchester area, the inquiries were handled by the Manchester police, who held by the far the strongest clue to his identity. A woman murdered in Chorlton-cum-Hardy, in the Manchester area, in October 1977, had a freshly minted £5 note in her handbag. Her body had lain undiscovered for days, and it was evident that the killer had come back to the scene, looking for the incriminating note. It had been issued only days before the murder to one of 34 firms, employing a total of about 6,000 people, including T. & W.H. Clark (Holdings) Ltd, of Hilliam Road, Bradford, where Sutcliffe worked. Chief Superintendent Hoban had deduced back in 1975 that the killer drove a lorry. Yet the Manchester police could not question anyone in Bradford without cooperation from West Yorkshire, who were not that interested in a clue held by a rival force. Nevertheless, two detectives, one from each force, visited Sutcliffe. They thought he was odd, but his wife provided him with an alibi, and there the matter rested.

The man leading the hunt in West Yorkshire, Assistant Chief Constable George Oldfield, had a lead in which he invested much greater faith. In March 1978, he and the *Daily Mirror* received letters from someone claiming to be the Ripper, which they did not take seriously until a year later, when a second letter came from the same source, accompanied by a tape made by a man with a Wearside accent. Oldfield's instinct told him, beyond the possibility of doubt, that it came from the killer. The tape was played at a press conference in June 1979. By the end of the day, millions of people had heard it. For years, they had been reading about this elusive killer; now, people imagined they were hearing his voice. For the next eighteen months, hundreds of officers from Northumbria were deployed, interviewing men with Wearside accents to see if they could account for their movements on the days the murders had been committed. In West Yorkshire, any man with a Yorkshire accent was assumed to be innocent.

After Jacqueline Hill's murder in November 1980, and a broadcast by her stricken parents, the ineptness of the investigation became a public scandal. Anger was directed not only at the police, but at anyone who seemed to think that there was entertainment value in sadistic murders. In Leeds, several hundred women stormed cinemas showing horror films called *The Beast* and

Dressed to Kill. They pummelled men in the audience and threw red paint at the screen. In south London, 200 women invaded the cinema where *Emanuelle: Queen Bitch* was on show. In Margate, women picketed the cinema where *Dressed to Kill* was to have been shown, until the manager agreed to remove it from the programme. The following month, eight London cinemas were invaded in a synchronized operation by Women Against Violence Against Women. This invasion led to fights with male onlookers. Eight women were arrested, whereupon the feminists picketed Bow Street police station in solidarity. Another nine were arrested after throwing eggs and paint at a cinema screen in Kilburn, north London. In Cambridge, feminists invaded a sex shop, a cinema and a news-stand selling pornography. A sex shop in Leeds was also damaged. On 12 December, it was the turn of the *Sun* offices, off London's Fleet Street, to be invaded by women protesting about the 'Page 3' girls. Ten days later, there was an eruption when it was reported that MGM was planning a film on the 'Ripper'. Lawyers for Jacqueline Hill's parents lodged a protest in Los Angeles and the very next day MGM cancelled the project. Feminists also protested against the advice given from the police that women should stay indoors after dark. A group of women lecturers from Bradford University suggested that: 'If there are to be curfews, it would be more rational to require men to stay off the streets as women seem more able to go about their business and their pleasure without attacking people.'[10]

In the midst of this outcry, Leeds Crown Court heard a very different case involving a violent death. Two sisters, Annette and Charlene Maw, aged twenty-one and eighteen, admitted stabbing their drunken, abusive father, who had repeatedly beaten his wife and daughters. After one beating, Charlene picked up a bread knife, which she passed to her older sister, who sank it into their father's neck. They pleaded guilty to manslaughter and, on 17 November 1980, were sentenced to three years in prison. The case roused an already angry feminist movement. In December, as it went to appeal in the high court in London, where Charlene's sentence was reduced to six months, a hundred women demonstrated outside the court. 'We are horrified by this decision. It means there is no justice at all for women in the courts of this country. Only this week a man convicted of raping a seven-year-old girl was given a suspended sentence,' [11] one of them told journalists.

Margaret Thatcher was not a feminist. On the rare occasions that she mentioned feminists, it was to ridicule them. Speaking to the Conservative Women's Conference, she said: 'We don't seek to advance women's rights by insisting that you, Madam Chairman, be addressed as Madam Chairperson,

Madam Chair, or, worse still, just plain "Chair". With feminists like that, who needs male chauvinists?'[12] And yet, there is an intriguing story in one of the first biographies of Thatcher, by Hugo Young, which suggests that her reaction to Jacqueline Hill's murder was not so different from that of the sisters. Reputedly she announced, in that imperious way of hers, that she was going to Yorkshire to take over the investigation in person, because 'nobody but her, she thought, really cared about the fate of these wretched women'.[13] Home Secretary William Whitelaw had to talk her out of this madness. This story is not repeated either in Thatcher's memoirs, or Whitelaw's, or in Hugo Young's diary, and might seem to be one of the many myths that have grown up around Mrs Thatcher, were it not that unpublished documents in the Home Office archives prove that she did personally intervene in the 'Ripper' enquiry, and to good effect.

A week after the Hill murder, on 25 November, Mrs Thatcher summoned Whitelaw, Cabinet Secretary Sir Robert Armstrong, and Head of the Home Office Sir Brian Cubbon to tell them that 'the local police had so far failed totally in their enquiries into a series of murders that constituted the most appalling kind of violence against women' and that 'it was now a matter of public confidence'.[14] Whitelaw had evidently been forewarned, and had his answer ready. The previous day, he had summoned Chief Inspector of Constabulary Sir James Crane to the Home Office, and that same day, Regional Inspector Lawrence Byford was dispatched to Leeds. Byford must have been familiar with the scene of the Jacqueline Hill murder because his son Mark, a future deputy director-general of the BBC, was a recent graduate of Leeds University. On 26 November, he informed the Home Office that Oldfield was off the case and that a team from outside, headed by Leslie Emment, the deputy chief constable of the Thames Valley police, had been called in. Emment's team, which included Stuart Kind, director of the Home Office Central Research Establishment at Aldermaston, took no time at all to conclude that the messages from Wearside could be treated as 'an elaborate hoax'.[15]

Three days after Mrs Thatcher's intervention, and nine days after the discovery of Jacqueline Hill's body, the pointless hunt for a man with a Wearside accent could be called off, at last. Soon afterwards, Stuart Kind gave the police written advice that they should look for a man living in or near Bradford.[16] On 2 January 1981, two police officers in a patrol car in Sheffield's red-light district spotted a couple in a parked car that had false number plates. They arrested the man, who identified himself as Peter Sutcliffe, from the Heaton area of Bradford, and who confessed that he was the 'Yorkshire Ripper', kitted up for his fourteenth kill.

Most, but not all, of the women Sutcliffe attacked were prostitutes, giving rise to a myth that he was on a maniacal mission to clean the streets of these women, though the evidence suggests that he simply enjoyed killing women and selected prostitutes because they were easily available. A generation later, when young prostitutes were being picked off by a serial killer in Ipswich, relatives of the dead women went on television to talk about their sense of loss, but public attitudes in 1981 did not allow anyone to speak for the prostitutes killed by Peter Sutcliffe. The public was not even told that one victim, Wilma McCann, had a seven-year-old daughter, Sonia, and a son, Richard, aged five, who wondered why their mother had not come home and ventured out across the fields at 5.30 a.m. in search of her, passing close by her mutilated body. Sonia never recovered from that night, and committed suicide.[17] Richard wrote a vivid, bestselling autobiography,[18] though he was moved to remark that 'the way these women were being portrayed did nothing for my self-esteem'.[19] There was a general separation of victims into the innocent, such as Jacqueline Hill, and those who, some believed, deserved what they got, like Wilma McCann. During Sutcliffe's trial, Attorney General Michael Havers described Sutcliffe's victims to the jury: 'Some were prostitutes, but perhaps the saddest part of this case is that some were not. The last six attacks were on totally respectable women.'

These remarks invoked a furious reaction from feminists outside the courtroom, who handed out a statement saying: 'This distinction between prostitutes and "respectable" and "innocent" victims has been made all along by the police and the media – the murder of prostitute women seems irrelevant and unimportant. This attitude towards prostitutes, much the same as the Ripper's, allowed him to carry on murdering women for five years.'[20] Pat Barker's novel, *Blow Your House Down*, published in 1984 and loosely based on the Ripper murders, was a reaction to this mindset; it focused on the humanity of the victims and treated the murderer as an incidental character in their story. It was such a bleak read, however, that it was never likely to break into the popular market.

If the Sutcliffe murders can be said to have had any positive social impact, apart from the improvements that they inspired in police methods, it was through the attention they drew to the terrain on which they were perpetrated: those desolate bits of waste ground inside decaying cities, which seemed to have reverted to pre-civilization, where women desperate for money offered their bodies for sale. It also caused people to question if women on the receiving end of male violence were properly treated by the police. The Thames Valley police, perhaps unwisely, allowed a BBC crew to do a fly-on-the-wall documentary series, broadcast in January 1982, which included film of male officers interrogating a woman with learning difficulties who complained that she had been raped. One of the police officers told her that her story was 'the biggest bollocks I have ever heard'.[21] In the next day's *Daily Mail,* the columnist Lynda Lee-Potter described the reaction she heard from one young woman who had been watching: 'Did you watch that programme? God, I'd never go to the police after that.'[22]

This coincided with a scandal that erupted in Scotland when the *Daily Record* published information about a case that had been thrown out by the courts. In 1980, a twenty-nine-year-old woman walking home from a pub after quarrelling with her boyfriend was dragged off a Glasgow street into a derelict hut by three teenagers, who raped her and slashed her with a razor, noughts and crosses style. She needed 168 stitches. The police had forensic evidence against the three, a confession and a statement from an eye-witness that placed them at the scene, but when the case came to court, in June 1981, the defence lawyers gave notice that they were going to claim that the woman consented to sex. She appeared to be too distressed to give evidence, so the court ordered a psychiatric report. Three months later, just as the BBC documentary had focused attention on rape, the *Daily Record* revealed that the case had been dropped. By inflicting sufficient injuries on the woman to reduce her to suicidal despair without actually killing her, the men had ensured they would never be prosecuted. Or, as the Labour MP Jo Richardson put it: 'What has happened in Scotland gives licence to rapists to rape and then cut up their victims knowing they will get off scot-free.'[23] Sir Nicholas Fairbairn, the Scottish attorney general, was quoted in newspapers as having rubbished the story, saying 'this unfortunate woman's mental stability was irrelevant', but he said something very different when he faced an angry House of Commons. He then claimed that the case had been dropped for the sake of the woman's health, an argument weakened somewhat by a public statement issued by the woman herself, saying that she had been prepared to give evidence, that she first learnt that the case had been dropped by reading it in the newspaper and that she was considering a private prosecution. Sir Nicholas also floundered as he tried to explain why, even if the rape charge was to be dropped, they had not gone ahead and prosecuted the men for the razor attack. He pleaded: 'The question of the victim's consent is critical to the proof of the crime. I can see no way in which, out of fairness to those who are accused, one could conduct the trial in her absence.'[24] Fairbairn was a devoted Thatcherite, and Margaret Thatcher had stood by him the previous month when the *Daily Star* revealed that a Commons secretary had attempted suicide outside his flat when he ended their affair, but after this performance he resigned rather than be sacked.

In the same week, there was another case that caused as big an outcry as the Glasgow rape. Hitch-hiking was then such a popular means of travel that a kind of subculture had grown around it. There was a manual, first published in 1979, by the travel writer Simon Calder that offered advice on the best sites to hitch a lift out of 200 towns and cities, 'with hitching ratings for every junction, plus techniques and gimmicks, the art of signwriting, legal problems, what to wear, hazards and how to avoid them and route planning'.[25] Predating that, there was a similar guide to Europe, which inspired Douglas Adams to write the radio series, *The Hitchhikers' Guide to the Galaxy*, which was made into a TV series in 1981. While the young loved to hitch, others thought it disgraceful that they should be entitled to travel without paying. One seventeen-year-old girl who had been at a party at the US air force base at Lakenheath hitched a ride home from a businessman who spotted her by the roadside, and was raped. At Ipswich Crown Court, Judge Bertrand Richards let the attacker off with a £2,000 fine, because 'I am not saying that a girl hitching home late at night should not be protected by the law, but she was guilty of a great deal of contributory negligence.'[26] Less than three weeks later, a seventeen-year-old American who lived on the Lakenheath air base tried to hitch home, and was also raped.

The judge's remarks in this case were contradicted by Lord Hailsham, the lord chancellor, and Lord Lane, the lord chief justice. However, in December 1982 Cambridge Crown Court heard the case of a woman who had been taken down into a basement, where she pleaded in vain to her assailant not to rape her. Judge David Wild was not impressed. Pleading not to be raped might be a woman's way of saying 'stop it, I like it', he told the jury. If she had genuinely resisted, she would have bruises to show for it. He continued:

> Women who say no do not always mean no. It is not just a question of saying no, it is a question of how she says it, how she shows and makes it clear. If she does not want it, she has only to keep her legs shut and she would not get it without force.

After the accused had been acquitted, it transpired that he had already served a long prison sentence for rape.[27]

Four years later, there was a rape case so clear cut that not even a judge as obtuse as David Wild could imagine that the victim had asked for it. In March 1986, three burglars broke into a vicarage in Ealing, west London, and came upon the vicar, his daughter and her boyfriend. They coshed the two men, leaving them with fractured skulls, and one burglar took the young woman upstairs to subject her to a revolting attack, that lasted a full hour, with another burglar looking on.

The first controversy this case threw up was over privacy. It was illegal to name the victim in rape trials or pre-hearings, but the law did not extend this protection in a case where the rapists were still at large. Within a week, different newspapers had told their readers that this victim was a vicar's daughter, that she was twenty-one years old, that the attack had happened at a vicarage in Ealing, close to the home of Neil Kinnock, the Labour leader, and that the vicar, whose name was Michael Saward, had described the victim as 'a jewel in my crown'.[28] The *Sun* also published her photograph, partly blacked out. The Labour MP Robin Corbett demanded that the *Sun* be prosecuted, but the attorney general's reply was that, since no one had been charged with rape, no law had been broken – though the law was changed in 1987 as a result of the case. That was too late for the Ealing rape victim. Anyone who knew the family, including the entire congregation at Rev. Saward's church, knew that she was the vicar's daughter, Jill Saward. Fortified by her religion, she came through the ordeal well. When she was aged thirty-nine and the mother of three boys, she made a BBC programme in which she said:

> Ealing Vicarage Rape Victim – that's been my tag for the past eighteen years, because at the age of twenty-one as a virgin I was raped, buggered and indecently assaulted whilst my father and boyfriend were beaten up by burglars who came to our home. I make no complaint about this tag as it has enabled me to challenge politicians and work for change.[29]

There was a second part to the story that was almost as shocking as the crime itself. The three burglars went before a judge in February 1987. Martin McCall, Jill Saward's attacker, was sentenced to five years for rape and five years for aggravated burglary. Another man was sentenced to three years for rape and five years for burglary. The next day, the judge dealt with a third defendant, Robert Horscroft, who had instigated the raid on the vicarage and was implicated in the violent attack on the vicar and his daughter's boyfriend, but had been repelled by the rape and had tried to persuade McCall to leave Jill Saward alone. His sentence was fourteen years. As he left the court, he shouted: 'What about the fucking rape, you prick?',[30] which, though crudely put, was pretty close to the reaction outside when news of the sentences reached the public. People simply could not comprehend how a judge could think that burglary was more serious than rape. It was made no more comprehensible by the judge's remark that the effect of the assault on Jill Saward was 'not so great', as if her resilience mitigated McCall's crime.

In all these cases it was the women's movement and politicians from the Left – Women Against Rape, the Glasgow Rape Crisis Centre, the Labour MPs Jo Richardson, Jack Ashley and Robin Corbett – who led the charge for more severe penalties for rape and better protection for the victims. After the hitch-hiker case, Jack Ashley campaigned for the attorney general to have the right to appeal against sentences that were too light, something for which there was then no precedent in British law. That reform was passed in 1987, in the wake of the Ealing case. And it was left to Clare Short, on the left wing of the Labour Party, to raise the tattered banner of the anti-pornography crusaders in Parliament. One Friday morning in January 1986, a half-empty House of Commons was discussing a private member's bill to curb obscene publications, which did not have a chance of becoming law, when Short was provoked by a flippant comment from a male MP to say, on impulse, that she might introduce a bill 'to outlaw showing pictures of partially naked or naked women in mass circulation newspapers'.[31] At first, there was little reaction, except that her remarks were picked up by the wire service and published in local newspapers, and she was surprised to receive letters from women around the country, urging her on.[32] Thus encouraged, she introduced her Indecent Displays (Newspapers) Bill to the Commons, on a Friday in March 1986, and by and large divided the Commons on party lines, with the Conservatives rallying to the defence of soft pornography while Labour MPs, including Tony Blair, voted for censorship. There were exceptions. When Robert Adley accused Short of wanting to take away 'one of the few pleasures left to us today',[33] a fellow Tory, Tony Marlow, rebuked him for being flippant.

Outside the Commons, the *Sun* of course came boldly out in favour of its version of press freedom. Its campaign was fronted by Samantha Fox, famous for having posed for Page 3 days after her sixteenth birthday, thus becoming the nation's youngest professional topless model.[34] 'Save Our Sizzlers' (SOS) was the slogan of this campaign. Short was denounced time and again as 'killjoy Clare', 'crazy Clare', and the 'crackpot MP'. Undeterred, she brought her bill back to the Commons in March 1988 and picked up support from 165 MPs, including three of the more impressive women on the Conservative side: Emma Nicholson, Gillian Shephard and Ann Widdecombe. In

November 1989, she led a squad of thirty women in a raid on WH Smith to sweep the offending publications off the top shelf. The following year, the *News of the World* took revenge by running a story across two pages, accusing her of having once been involved with a man who was later shot and killed in what appears to have been a gangland assassination.[35]

After so much activity and so much publicity, it would be pleasing to record that attitudes to sexually related violence had been transformed by the end of the 1980s. They had changed certainly, but not in every courtroom. In February 1989, a woman named Sara Thornton was charged with murdering her alcoholic husband, a former police officer. The police had been called to her home several times after reports that he had assaulted her; a neighbour testified that he 'beat her black and blue'; yet she was sentenced to life imprisonment. The case would become one of the major feminist causes of the 1990s, until in 1996 the charge was reduced to manslaughter.[36] It was linked to the case of Kiranjit Ahluwalia, also sentenced to life imprisonment in 1989 for killing her husband, at whose hands she had suffered ten years of rape and abuse. After he threatened to burn her with a hot iron, she threw petrol over his duvet while he was sleeping and set it alight. He died ten days later. Her case was taken up by the pressure group Southall Black Sisters and, after a retrial in 1992, the charge was reduced to manslaughter and she was released. Her appeal set the precedent that women who kill as a result of severe domestic violence should not be treated as cold-blooded murderers.

Even after the Ealing case, the idea that in every male there is a natural supply of sexual aggression that requires expression lingered on in the minds of some judges. In 1988, Sir Harold Cassel refused to pass a prison sentence on a former policeman who had sexually assaulted his twelve-year-old daughter because his wife was pregnant and consequently unavailable to him at night, causing 'considerable problems for a healthy young husband'.[37] In April 1990, Judge Raymond Dean, aged sixty-seven, congratulated an Old Bailey jury who had cleared a Chelsea property dealer of rape, saying: 'As the gentlemen on the jury will understand, when a woman says "no" she doesn't always mean it. Men can't turn their emotions on and off like a tap like some women can.'[38]

Chapter 3

Protest and Survive

Away from the small islands ruled by Margaret Thatcher, the continent of Europe was split between the vast military alliances, NATO and the Warsaw Pact, who eyed each across a physical and ideological border that sliced Germany into two and kept Poland, Hungary, Czechoslovakia, Bulgaria and Romania sealed off from their neighbours to the west and south. NATO's strategists feared that a 'missile gap' was developing that might threaten the principle of mutually assured destruction that supposedly deterred the hostile alliances from going to war. The nuclear weapons that NATO held in Europe were carried by ageing British Vulcan bombers and American F1-11s. If these aircraft were scrapped and not replaced, NATO would be unable to launch a nuclear strike against the Warsaw Pact other than with long-range missiles held in silos in the USA. But would the Americans want to fire those missiles and risk retaliatory strikes on their cities, if the Red Army rolled into West Germany? NATO feared that their Warsaw Pact counterparts might calculate that Washington would not risk millions of American lives for Western Europe's sake, and that, without the means of launching a nuclear strike from European soil, NATO's nuclear deterrent would lose its credibility.

When James Callaghan was prime minister, in 1976–9, he did not seem to think that the problem was urgent, but Margaret Thatcher emphatically did. She had been in office for only a week when she was telling Helmut Schmidt, the German chancellor, that Germany needed more missiles. Schmidt did not think German public opinion would warm to the idea, so in September 1979 she decided that 144 American-owned ground-launched cruise missiles should come to the UK instead. Another sixteen were to have been deployed in Germany, but Schmidt rang Downing Street on the off-chance that she might be persuaded to take them off his hands. She agreed and, in June 1980, 160 cruise missiles were delivered to Greenham Common in Berkshire and to the RAF base at Molesworth in Cambridgeshire.

It also worried Mrs Thatcher that Britain's own nuclear deterrent, Polaris, introduced in secret by a Labour government in the 1960s, was out of date. In December 1979, a small group of ministers agreed that they should buy the more modern and potentially destructive Trident missiles from the USA. President Jimmy Carter was at first reluctant to sell, having staked his reputation on disarmament talks, but changed his mind after the Soviet invasion of Afghanistan at the end of 1979. A deal was announced in the Commons on 15 July 1980. Four months later, Carter was defeated by his Republican challenger, Ronald Reagan. Reagan and Thatcher were soulmates. In time, their relationship would be the closest there had ever been between an American president and a British prime minister. But in the short term, Reagan's arrival complicated her plans because he wanted to scrap the old Tridents and replace them with updated versions. Since the technology was undeveloped, it was impossible to say what it might cost. Despite the ghastly state of her government's finances, Mrs Thatcher agreed to buy at whatever price.[1]

To her, it was all a matter of retaining a credible nuclear deterrent to protect Western Europe from invasion, but others took the view that, at best, she was indulging in useless expense, and, at worst, she could be preparing the country for collective suicide. The average age of the Soviet Politburo was over seventy and there were fears, which proved misplaced, that when younger leaders took over they might be more aggressive in pursuing the goal of destroying capitalism. If nuclear war broke out, the Warsaw Pact's first target was obviously going to be Britain, where so much nuclear hardware was stored. Philip Noel-Baker, a Nobel Peace Prize laureate, warned that 'nuclear warfare will destroy civilization, and perhaps exterminate mankind'.[2]

Some of the experts on the other side of the argument accepted that there was a real risk of nuclear war, but did not think that it would destroy the human race. They did speculate, though, on how the population might react if a nuclear bomb hit a British city. They hoped that, if proper preparations were made, they could count on people to rally, as they did during the Blitz; but as the eminent historian, Professor Michael Howard, argued in an influential letter to *The Times* in January 1980, it would necessitate investing much more money and care in civil defence to ensure that the country could recover quickly from a 'limited' nuclear strike – which, he avowed, might kill 20m people. Otherwise, he warned, the UK's 'independent deterrent' would be shown up as an 'expensive bluff'.[3]

In February 1980, *The Times* revealed that the government had updated a booklet called *Protect and Survive*, a civil defence manual originally published as a series of six pamphlets in 1949–50. The revelation provoked considerable public interest, but anyone who applied to Her Majesty's Stationery Office for a copy of the pamphlet, including the French embassy, was told that none was available.[4] An organization called Civil Aid, a voluntary group set up to prepare the population for a nuclear attack, stepped into the breach by publishing a pamphlet along similar lines, full of practical suggestions for staying alive after the bomb had dropped. 'If you saw a frog running about, you would have to wash it down to get rid of active dust, cook it and eat it,' the vice-chairman, Robin Meads, told a press conference.[5] An opinion poll in April 1980 suggested that 40 per cent of the public thought that nuclear war was likely to break out within ten years. It was also reported that about 300 firms were marketing fallout radiation suits, etc.[6] A month later, the government gave in to public demand and published the official version of *Protect and Survive*, which included what became a famous illustration of an idyllic nuclear family – Dad, Mum and two small kids – who had sensibly built a shelter out of bags filled with earth, sand and so on, so that they could crawl into it armed with supplies to survive the nuclear strike together. Wisely, the booklet refrained from recommending a diet of radioactive frog.

The Campaign for Nuclear Disarmament (CND) had existed since 1957, when it was founded on a wave of popular support after the Suez crisis and the Soviet invasion of Hungary had made the threat of nuclear war seem real. President Kennedy's success in handling the 1962 Cuban missile crisis and the disarmament talks that followed took the urgency out of the problem, and for the best part of two decades CND limped along, half-forgotten but still there, run by volunteers from a cramped Georgian building in Bloomsbury. Suddenly, in February 1980, it was attracting so many recruits that it could afford a full-time general secretary, a Catholic priest named Bruce Kent. By April, he and two other paid staff were having to cope with forty to fifty letters a day from people wanting to join. New CND groups sprung up everywhere. In June, a new group came into being in Newbury, the nearest town to Greenham Common, where the cruise missiles were stationed. They were led by Joan Ruddock, who worked at the local Citizen's Advice Bureau. Nationally, membership more than doubled in 1980, to around 9,000. In 1981, it more than doubled again, to 20,000. By 1984, it had reached 100,000.

The man who emerged as the public face of a revived CND was the historian E.P. Thompson, author of *The Making of the English Working Class* and other works of popular history. In 1980, he produced a pamphlet, later expanded into a book, whose title *Protest and Survive* was a parody of the government pamphlet; its sounding-off point was Professor Howard's letter to *The Times*. Thompson argued that:

> once 'theatre' nuclear war commences, immense passions, indeed hysterias, will be aroused. After even the first strikes of such a war, communications and command posts will be so much snarled up that any notion of rational planning will give way to panic. Ideology will at once take over from self-interest. Above all, it will be manifest that the only one of the great powers likely to come out of the contest as 'victor' must be the one which hurls its ballistic weapons first, furthest and fastest …[7]

On 5 September 1981, a group of footsore women arrived uninvited at the perimeter of the Greenham Common base. They had walked from Cardiff to deliver a letter and, they hoped, to receive a verbal reply. The letter, handed to the base commander, said: 'We fear for the future of all our children and for the future of the living world which is the basis of all life.' Their request for a debate was ignored, so the women set up camp. That temporary arrangement would be there in one form or another for the next nineteen years as Britain's most lasting and visible protest against nuclear weapons. This hardy band was known simply as the Greenham Women, for the good reason that their camp was women only. Men were permitted to visit during the day, but at night there was a curfew. Some of the women there were veteran feminists who had lived independently of men for years; others paid a personal price for being there at all. One had been told by her husband, 'You either stay at home and be a proper wife and mother, or you go to Greenham, but not both.'[8] Though the peace camp failed to chase away the missiles, it was a phenomenal demonstration of female self-confidence. Thousands of women took part, blocking the gates, cutting the fence, dancing on the silos. On 12 December 1982, about 30,000 women linked arms in a human chain around the entire perimeter, which they decorated with children's toys and pictures. Early in 1983, forty-four women were up in front of the magistrates. When sentencing was about to begin, a line of policemen marched into court to separate the defendants from the spectators, who included dozens more Greenham women, whereupon the defendants and spectators all stood on their chairs and began to sing. That Easter, they formed a fourteen-mile human chain from Greenham to the atomic research facility at Aldermaston, via the Royal Ordnance Factory at Burghfield.

The fear that there was something sinister about the nuclear industry inspired one of the decade's best drama series, *The Edge of Darkness* (1985), created by the writer Troy Kennedy Martin of *Z Cars* fame and produced by Michael Wearing, and spread over six episodes on Monday evenings on BBC2. It was the story of a detective, played by Bob Peck, looking for his daughter's killers and learning that she had been involved in left-wing politics, making powerful enemies in the nuclear industry. 'Monday is suddenly the best night of the television week,' one critic enthused.[9] Kennedy had wanted to call the drama 'Magnox', but was advised by BBC lawyers that the name was the property of British Nuclear Fuels.[10]

CND's leaders were always careful to emphasize that they opposed all nuclear weapons, not least those that the Warsaw Pact were pointing at Britain. It was always likely that the movement would be infiltrated by Soviet fellow travellers, or even paid agents. The KGB appears not to have been interested, but the East German intelligence service, Stasi, retained a regular informant. This was the historian Vic Allen, a professor at Leeds University, who for a time was on CND's national committee and came fifth in a field of five when he ran for the CND presidency in 1985. When he was exposed as a Stasi informant in 1999, he defended himself on the grounds that everyone who knew him also knew where his sympathies lay.[11]

Coincidentally, he was not the only agent operating in CND's Yorkshire region: there was a well-known figure in left-wing circles called Harry Newton, who had been a trade union activist since the late 1950s and was a long-standing member of CND. He died in 1983. At about that time, an MI5 officer named Cathy Massiter became disturbed by the freedom with which her fellow officers were finding reasons to snoop on CND. For instance, they decided that an interview that Joan Ruddock gave to a Soviet newspaper in 1981 constituted contact with a hostile intelligence agency, and set to work. Ms Ruddock said:

> Between 1981 and 1986, I was frequently subjected, as a direct consequence of my involvement in CND, to frightening and intimidating behaviour. I shall never know whether those events related to MI5, but I feel certain that my privacy, and that of my

> family, was systematically invaded, and my character, impugned, with absolutely no justification.[12]

Cathy Massiter thought this was wrong, but in the secretive world of spies there was no complaints procedure through which she could voice her objections, so she resigned and wrote a brief letter to a magazine explaining why. She disappeared from public sight for nearly two years until an alert BBC producer contacted her and persuaded her to take part in a programme about MI5. She made a series of allegations, which she backed up in a sworn affidavit, including that MI5 was not only watching the miners' leader, Arthur Scargill, and listening in to his telephone conversations, but had been doing the same to Patricia Hewitt and Harriet Harman, who until 1982 were leading officers of the National Council of Civil Liberties. Harman was by then a Labour MP, and Hewitt was press secretary to the Labour leader Neil Kinnock. Massiter also revealed that Harry Newton had been an MI5 informer for so long that he was almost an *agent provocateur*.

She had come out of the cold just as MI5 was struggling to recover from the Michael Bettaney affair, which suggested that they were so busy investigating innocent people that they missed what was happening under their noses. Bettaney was an officer in counter-intelligence who, hoping the Soviets would pay him to be a spy, pushed an envelope full of secrets through the letter box of Arkadi Gouk, senior KGB officer in London. Suspecting a trap, Gouk consulted his deputy, Oleg Gordievsky, who was secretly a British agent. Bettaney was arrested and sentenced to twenty-three years in prison, of which he served fourteen. The resulting commission of inquiry heard that a woman colleague had seen Bettaney drink two bottles of neat whisky at a party and set fire to himself, after telling anyone who was prepared to listen that he would rather be working for the Russians than the British. She had not felt able to pass on this information, because there was no one in MI5 whose job was to listen to the concerns of middle-ranking staff.[13] As a result of these two scandals, MI5 appointed its first staff counsellor in 1987, and ever since there has been someone, usually a retired permanent secretary, in whom employees could confide any doubts they had about their colleagues or their work. This seems to have worked, because it was ten years until the next scandal, when an MI5 officer, David Shayler, was arrested for passing documents to a journalist.

It might be thought that the radical Left would have been grateful to Cathy Massiter, but she actually received a very mixed reaction. Pat Arrowsmith, one of the best known of the first wave of CND activists, had known Harry

Newton for twenty-five years – or thought she had. She refused to believe Massiter's story,[14] even though Massiter gained nothing personally from actions that cost her a career and the universal condemnation of her old colleagues. 'It is difficult to convey now, from the standpoint of the twenty-first century, how amazing and shocking this event seemed to us then,' said Stella Rimington, who was then Massiter's section head and was on her way to becoming the first female director-general of MI5:

> We had been brought up to accept that not only did you not talk in public about the work that you did, but more than that, you did not even tell anyone that you worked for MI5. Yet here was this erstwhile colleague, someone we all knew well, talking about her work on nationwide TV and what's more giving an interpretation of it which to us seemed distorted and unrecognisable. It was breathtaking.[15]

It could hardly have been 'breathtaking' if what she said had not been essentially true.

What made CND formidable was not just the large numbers it could draw into the streets or around Greenham Common's perimeter, but more significantly the support it picked up within the Labour Party. Some party activists who had taken part in Aldermaston marches in their adolescence, twenty years earlier, now held positions of influence, giving rise to the prospect that a Labour government might abandon nuclear weapons.

The convulsion in the Conservative Party that had brought Margaret Thatcher to the fore was as nothing compared with the agonies that the Labour Party went through after the fall of the Callaghan government. The membership of the party was undergoing a change, accelerated by defeat. There are no accurate figures for Labour Party membership at the time, because of a quaint convention that every constituency Labour Party was deemed to have 1,000 members for the purpose of casting a vote at annual conference; but the best available evidence suggests that membership went up from around 284,000 to around 300,000 between 1978 and 1981.[16] During that time, as many as 20,000 party members may have left to join the breakaway SDP. So it is possible that by 1981, 10 per cent of the party had joined since the fall of the Callaghan government.

There is no doubt about who most of the recent recruits were. They were the students who had packed protest marches in the late 1960s, who in their early twenties had considered themselves far too radical to join the stuffy Labour Party but, ten years on, were thinking that it was time to be involved in mainstream politics. Wards that had been run for years by long-serving Labour councillors, never discussing anything more contentious than street lighting, were suddenly having to cope with university-educated radicals who wanted to talk about nuclear weapons, or Nicaragua, or why Jim Callaghan was a class traitor. The most famous of the Vietnam demonstrators, Tariq Ali, announced in the *Guardian* in 1979 that he was joining the Hornsey Labour Party, setting off a chain reaction that nearly led to the Hornsey party being disbanded, and which ended with Tariq being formally expelled in October 1983. Feminists who had made a point of organizing themselves separately from men during the 1970s were also joining up, having decided that they did not need to keep their feminism to themselves. John Silkin, a former cabinet member who ran for the deputy leadership in 1981, remembered it as a strange time when 'it was a disadvantage to have been in the Labour Party for more than two years'.[17]

In earlier times, the Labour Party could have absorbed this influx without difficulty because the party was consciously structured to make sure that the membership was excluded from any decision that mattered. Votes at party conferences were rigidly controlled by the block votes of the big unions. The general secretaries of the four biggest, the TGWU, NUPE, Amalgamated Union of Engineering Workers (AUEW) and General Municipal Boilermakers and Allied Trades Union (GMBATU), held more than 50 per cent of the total voting strength; more than 600 constituency party delegates had barely 10 per cent. The big unions traditionally used their strength to support the party leader. The election manifesto was written in the leader's office. The party leader was elected by MPs. The choice of who became Labour MPs was also effectively controlled by the regional secretaries of the big unions, through the paid delegates that they placed on constituency party committees.

However, this particular generation of rebels did not content themselves with exhorting their leaders to be more left wing, as previous rebels had. Even before the 1979 election, there was a well-organized campaign under way to overhaul the entire party structure and to increase the influence of the active party membership, which rapidly gained strength after the defeat. The campaign was aided by two political assets. The first was that, instead of being treated as intruders, the incoming student leftists quickly discovered common ground with many of the trade union shop stewards they encountered. The Labour government's efforts to grapple with recession had hit their own natural supporters so heavily that several unions, including the TGWU and NUPE, had been driven leftwards. The AUEW also had a powerful left-wing presence, leaving Callaghan with only one of the big four, the GMBATU, which he knew to be reliable.

Historically, the union block had acted like a vast battery of powerful guns at the disposal of the party leader. Now some of those big guns were turning around to fire in the opposite direction.

The Left's other great asset was a credible leader around whom they could unite. Tony Benn was the only British politician of the 1980s, apart from Thatcher, to give his name to a political ideology; the words 'Bennites', 'Bennism' and even 'Bennery' were part of the political language of the time. His had been an unusual political trajectory. Originally, he had been a liberal technocrat rather than a socialist, who played a role in the 1959 general election similar to the one that Peter Mandelson would perform in 1987, exploring ways to use television as a medium for campaigning. Soon afterwards, he made constitutional history by being the first hereditary peer to renounce his seat in the House of Lords and fight successfully to stay in the Commons. It was only after Labour's defeat in 1970, when Benn was forty-five, that he started on a political journey that mirrored that of Keith Joseph. Whereas Joseph believed that the government had intervened too much in the free market, Benn proposed a huge increase in nationalization and state intervention.

Benn was unlike other tribunes of the Left, who had a habit of resigning from office to enjoy the freedom to speak out. Michael Foot held no government office until he was approaching the age of sixty. Neil Kinnock never held a ministerial office. Dennis Skinner would not even accept the chairmanship of a party committee. Others, including Eric Heffer, held office for a short time before resigning in a blaze of principle. But Benn was not a resigner. He stayed in the cabinet until the government fell, and was supported by Michael Meacher, Margaret Beckett and others who stayed on to the end. In opposition, he refused to run for a place in the shadow cabinet, but that was because his sights were set on securing the party leadership, which he could do only if the party rulebook was overhauled. His visible ambition made him a highly controversial figure who attracted quite extraordinary vitriolic abuse. 'Some say Tony Benn is raving bonkers. But what really goes on in the mind of the country's most notorious left winger?', the *Sun* inquired, on one occasion. They fed some facts about Benn to a 'top American psychiatrist', who was reported to have reached a diagnosis without knowing the identity of the patient; though the psychiatrist subsequently complained that he had been 'lied to, misquoted'.[18] Actually, as David Owen observed, Benn 'was not mad, nor was he a simple militant purist. He was a deeply ambitious politician.'[19]

The economic crisis of 1976, and the Labour government's sudden change of policy, brought home to the average party member how little influence they had over their leaders. Organizations such as the 'Campaign for Labour Democracy' came into existence, and quickly learnt how to use an archaic party rule book to get the rules changed, achieving rapid success directly after the 1979 general elections. They wanted three major reforms, each of which would shift power towards those middle-ranking activists who were the foot soldiers of the Bennite Left. It was proposed that election manifestoes should be controlled by the party's National Executive Committee (NEC); that all sitting MPs should be subjected every Parliament to a selection procedure in which they would fight to keep their jobs against other aspirants; and that instead of having the party leader elected exclusively by Labour MPs, the franchise should be widened to involve the party at large and its trade union affiliates.

These three proposals went before the annual party conference in Brighton in October 1979. Given that the TGWU and NUPE were going to vote with the Left, and the GMBATU were for the status quo, the future of the Labour Party was in the hands of the engineers. As it happened, seventeen of the thirty-four AUEW delegates solidly supported the Bennite Left and sixteen were reliable supporters of Jim Callaghan. In the event of a tie, the union's general secretary, Terry Duffy, another loyal ally of Callaghan, had a casting vote. Therefore, everything came down to how the sole independent delegate chose to vote. This was Jim Murray, chief shop steward from the Vickers arms factory in Elswick, Newcastle upon Tyne.[20] He voted with the Left and, to audible groans from the MPs, the proposal that they should undergo a contested reselection in each Parliament was passed by 4.008m votes to 3.039m. The next day, Murray again voted with the Left and control of the manifesto passed from the leader's office to the NEC. But the most pressing issue of the moment was how to elect a party leader. This would decide whether or not Tony Benn had any chance of succeeding Callaghan, which he certainly could not do until the franchise was widened. Murray, however, thought that the best people to judge a potential leader's qualities were the MPs, and he voted with the right, leaving the AUEW delegation split 17–17. Duffy deployed his casting vote, and the proposal to change the voting system was defeated by 3.033m to 4.009m.

The Left did not give up yet. At the next annual conference, in October 1980, they pushed through a decision that there would be a unique conference in January 1981 solely to agree a new system for electing the leader. In the three-month gap, while the old rules still applied, Callaghan resigned. In this way, he niftily and ruthlessly made sure that his immediate successor would not be Tony Benn. He anticipated handing over to Denis Healey, the most experienced, strong-willed and best-known member of his old cabinet. However, Healey was also a controversial figure – the man who had scythed through public expenditure – a powerful intellectual with a sharp tongue, and though he led on the first ballot, the MPs settled on Michael Foot.

Already sixty-seven years old, Foot would serve for three years as the best-loved and least successful of all the post-war Labour leaders. Though very well known within the Labour Party as a writer, anti-fascist campaigner, CND marcher and left-wing rebel turned cabinet minister, he was not a household name (like Denis Healey or Tony Benn). He was possibly not even the best-known member of the Foot family, given the eminence of his journalist nephew, Paul Foot. *Private Eye* certainly thought not; in November it ran a spoof report that Labour's new leader was 'Michael Spart, the hitherto little-known uncle of revolutionary leader Dave Spart.' His public image was of a slightly dishevelled old gentleman, who used a walking stick and was unfairly accused of wearing a donkey jacket at the Cenotaph on Remembrance Day. Throughout his three years, Foot was buffeted by enemies and critics on the left and light. David Owen, on the right, and Tony Benn, on the left, declined to serve in his shadow cabinet. David Owen recalled: 'Why could we not behave as he had done in the past, was his unspoken rebuke. We allowed you to govern when the Right was in control of the party, you are not letting us govern now that we, the Left, are in control.'[21]

Another person absent from Michael Foot's team was Roy Jenkins, the former home secretary, who had once had a greater following in the country than any other Labour politician. He had never been as popular inside the Labour Party, though, and had left Britain in 1977 to be president of the European Commission, but his term of office was ending and he was thinking of a re-entry to British politics. He laid down a marker in November 1979 when he delivered the annual Dimbleby Lecture, which guaranteed him a primetime television audience and which he used to make an elegant case for proportional representation and coalition government. As Labour moved to the Left, Jenkins and Owen, independently, were increasingly attracted to the idea of a new party of the centre left, free from union control.

Unfortunately, they did not get on personally. Jenkins considered himself to be the new party's natural leader, the only person with the political and intellectual stature to make it credible. Owen, who had been foreign secretary at the age of thirty-seven, had the ability and limitless self-belief to lead, but did not have the necessary following either in Parliament or among the voters. He did, however, have an ally in the shadow cabinet in Bill Rodgers, who although virtually unknown in the country, had good contacts in

Labour's northern heartland, whereas Owen and Jenkins were obvious southerners. None of these three, however, could match the popularity, inside Parliament and out, of Shirley Williams, who was judged to be essential to the enterprise but was very reluctant to cut her ties with the Labour Party. Nevertheless, Owen and Rodgers plotted to draw her in, hoping that she would be leader of the new party, in name, while they actually ran the show. Jenkins and his friends, meanwhile, schemed to bring Williams, Owen and Rodgers into a new party led by him.

On 18 January 1981, Jenkins invited the other three to his house in the picture-postcard village of East Hendred in Oxfordshire, but when Shirley Williams read an account of the upcoming meeting in that morning's *Observer*, written as if the leader, back from exile, was summoning his generals to his side, it made her so angry that she refused to go. After an exchange of telephone calls, the meeting was transferred to Bill Rodgers' London home. Williams turned up late and was highly displeased to discover that the press had got there before her. Despite a frosty start, the four politicians and their advisers managed to knock out a draft statement, which was no more than a call to Labour to reform itself.

The statement was very rapidly overtaken by events: this was the week of the special one-day Labour conference in Wembley to discuss the changes to the leadership election procedure, which came to a result that no one expected. The next leader of the Labour Party was to be chosen by a complex electoral college, in which trade unions held 40 per cent of the voting strength, with the rest divided equally between Labour MPs and constituency parties.

This was too much even for Shirley Williams. It raised the possibility that there could be a Labour government facing another 'winter of discontent', with the additional hazard that the striking unions would use their voting power to remove the prime minister from office. The 'gang of four', as they were now called (with reference to the power struggle in China that followed the death of Chairman Mao), met again on 25 January, in David Owen's home in Limehouse, east London. They finalized a document that became known as the Limehouse Declaration, which ended with the portentous words: 'We recognise that for those people who have given much of their lives to the Labour Party, the choice that lies ahead will be deeply painful. But we believe that the need for a realignment of British politics must now be faced.'[22]

From there, the four were propelled forwards by the expectations and latent public support generated by the publicity given to the Limehouse Declaration. An advertisement in the *Guardian* produced 8,000 replies, two-thirds of which contained donations, giving them a cash reserve of £25,000. A steering committee was formed, dominated originally by Labour MPs, though its membership was widened later to include David Sainsbury (from the family that owned the grocery chain), who would be a major source of funding; the journalist Polly Toynbee; Roger Liddle, who would later work for many years as a political adviser to Tony Blair; and a lone Tory, Christopher Brocklebank-Fowler.

On 2 March, twelve Labour MPs resigned the Labour whip and declared that they now sat as Social Democrats. The new party, called the Social Democratic Party (SDP), with a logo in red, white and blue, was formally launched on 26 March. The launch event was an unqualified success because of the huge and generally sympathetic media interest. The reception in Parliament at Prime Minister's Questions that afternoon was not so comfortable. Replying to Mike Thomas, one of the new SDP MPs, Mrs Thatcher said:

> I recall hearing a comment on the radio this morning about the new Social Democratic Party being a new Centre party. I heard someone say that such a Centre party would be a party with no roots, no principles, no philosophy and no values. That sounded about right, and it was Shirley Williams who said it.[23]

Her remarks did not stop more MPs from defecting. In all, twenty-eight Labour MPs and one Conservative MP switched to the new party. Each defection generated another flurry of publicity that was good for the SDP and bad for Labour. In September, the support for the two Centre parties – the Liberals and the SDP – was so high that David Steel told the Liberal Assembly: 'Go back to your constituencies and prepare for government.'[24] By October 1981, the SDP had more MPs than the Liberals and membership was approaching 78,000, which may have exceeded the number of Liberal Party members. Meanwhile, belying his reputation as a man averse to taking risks, Jenkins showed himself determined to get back in the Commons at the first opportunity. That arose when the Labour MP for Warrington resigned. This was a solid Labour seat, where even in 1979 the party took more than 60 per cent of the vote, and Labour's candidate was an experienced campaigner, a former MP named Doug Hoyle. Even so, an opinion poll by the *Sun* suggested that if Shirley Williams, who had been out of Parliament since the 1979 election, were to stand as an SDP candidate, she would win, whereas Roy Jenkins would lose; but she was not confident of winning and announced that she was not interested. Jenkins leapt boldly in and cut Labour's majority from 10,274 to 1,759 in an astonishing 23 per cent swing to the SDP. He lost, but he proved that the SDP could tear huge chunks off the Labour vote and take from the Tories too. David Owen ruefully concluded that Jenkins' boldness, and Williams' hesitancy, cost her the party leadership.[25]

The next by-election on British soil was in the Conservative-held seat of Croydon North West. This time, the Liberals insisted on running and the SDP had to stay away. The Liberal candidate quadrupled his share of the vote and took the seat. Next, there was Crosby, in November 1981, where the Conservatives took 57 per cent of the vote in 1979. Shirley Williams insisted that it was her turn. She almost wiped out the Labour vote and took nearly a third of the Conservatives' to win convincingly. Jenkins had to wait until the following March, when he seized a chance to take Glasgow Hillhead from Labour, just in time to put himself forward in the first election to the leadership of the SDP, which he comfortably won against David Owen. Jenkins was already thinking in terms of an eventual merger with the Liberals, which Owen adamantly opposed. For the time being, Jenkins and Steel reached a pact under which – had it worked perfectly – there would have been either a Liberal or an SDP candidate in every constituency in the 1983 election, but not both. It broke down only in one seat, in Liverpool Broadgreen, handing victory to the Labour candidate, Terry Fields. Roy Jenkins was put forward as the Liberal-SDP Alliance's prospective prime minister.

Though it was not obvious at the time, the SDP had already peaked before Jenkins assumed the leadership. The MPs who joined it were repeatedly taunted for not resigning their seats and calling by-elections to allow their constituents to decide whether or not they wanted to be represented by the SDP. Owen and some of the others would have been willing to do so, but Bill Rodgers talked them out of it. Rodgers was vindicated when one defector, Bruce Douglas-Mann, insisted on calling a by-election, which was held in the heat of the Falklands War in June 1982. It produced a huge shift of votes from Labour to the SDP, which let in the Conservative candidate, Angela Rumbold, who held the seat for fifteen years. After that, there were no more defectors. For all the excitement it generated at the time, the SDP turned into one of the great non-stories of the 1980s.

Tony Benn did not accept the validity of the 1980 Labour leadership election and wanted to make use of the new electoral college. He could not produce a clear political case for challenging Michael Foot, but there was plain daylight between party policy, as determined principally by Tony Benn, and the known view of Denis Healey, whom the MPs had elected as Foot's deputy to compensate for denying him the leadership. As Benn went around collecting the necessary nominations to challenge Healey for the deputy leadership, word reached Neil Kinnock, Robin Cook and others of the Left whose loyalty was now to Foot, and who thought that a bitterly fought deputy leadership contest would be like an oxygen tent for the SDP. They planned to get fellow left-wing MPs to call upon Benn to back off, but he forestalled them by arriving in the parliamentary press gallery at 3 a.m. on 2 April to give a press release, announcing his candidature to the astonished gallery reporters working the night shift.

For seven months, the Labour Party was convulsed by a frenetic campaign, fought out before the television cameras with little restraint or mutual respect. The main casualty was Michael Foot, caught between two powerful figures backed by large well-organized factions. A small number of MPs, including Neil Kinnock, tried to carve out an independent position for him by putting up a third candidate, John Silkin, who gathered almost no support outside Parliament. The widened franchise did not give every party member a vote. Very few constituency committees asked their members' opinions, but simply decided to back Benn, who garnered 80 per cent of the vote in the constituency section. With a substantial majority of MPs backing Healey, the union votes proved decisive. NUPE was almost the only union to ballot its members. Though its leaders backed Benn, the membership backed Healey. Until almost the last minute, no one knew which way the huge TGWU vote would go; eventually, its general secretary, Moss Evans, placed his weighty cross, equal to the votes of seventy-two MPs, or the combined votes of all the constituency parties in Scotland and the north of England, against Tony Benn's name. This made the result so close that Healey won by a margin of less than 1 per cent. If Neil Kinnock and a few others had voted for Benn, instead of abstaining, the history of the Labour Party would have been very different indeed. As it was, Tony Benn's fortunes never recovered.

However, for another twelve months Benn was still a major player as chairman of the Home Policy Committee of the National Executive Committee (NEC), which meant that he, rather than Michael Foot, had the last word on what was included in Labour's general manifesto. 'New Hope for Britain', as the document was called, was assured its place in political folklore when Gerald Kaufman pithily described it as 'the longest suicide note in history'.[26] It was certainly long – about 25,000 words. It proposed to bring unemployment down from 3.2m to 1m within five years, through rapid, planned growth guided by a new Department of Economic and Industrial Planning and a National Planning Council, financed by a new

National Investment Bank. Another new body, the Foreign Investment Unit, would keep watch over foreign-owned multinational companies. All major companies were to negotiate development plans with the government. This was to be paid for by government borrowing, rather than raising taxes, and by cancelling all new nuclear power stations and nuclear weapons.

The manifesto also stated that all the restrictive trade union laws introduced by the Thatcher government were to be repealed, and the unions given greater influence than ever before. Exchange controls were to be brought back, along with new restrictions on imports. Interest rates were to be cut to bring down the value of the pound. Enterprises privatized by the Conservatives were to be renationalized and the government would also buy into industries in which it had not intervened before, including computers, pharmaceuticals and construction. There was to be government aid for workers' cooperatives, through a new Co-operative Investment Bank. Much of this would have been barred under European Union law, but Labour proposed to forestall that problem by overriding the referendum held only a few years earlier, and by pulling out of the Common Market.

And still there was more. Spending on the NHS and on personal social services was to go up by at least 3 per cent a year above inflation. Child benefit and pensions would also be substantially increased. Unnecessary car journeys were to be discouraged by abolishing the tax disc and making up the lost tax through higher petrol duty. The number of prisoners was to be reduced through lower sentences for non-violent offences. There was to be a huge programme of council-house building and repairs. Local authorities were to be given more powers than ever before, including in some cases the power to convert private schools into state schools. The charitable status enjoyed by Eton and other public schools was to be abolished, along with everything that the upper classes seemed to enjoy most, including corporal punishment (then still practised in schools), the House of Lords and fox-hunting. However, angling, which was popular with Labour voters, was to be encouraged, by giving anglers better access to common land.[27] When challenged during a televised press conference to explain the apparent inconsistency between fox-hunting and angling policies, the former sports minister, Denis Howell, declared that 'fish feel no pain'. This statement – how Mr Howell feels qualified to say such things – is one of the many enduring mysteries of that disastrous election campaign.

Curiously, this document remained unchanged, although the NEC passed out of Bennite control in 1982 after a well-organized coup run by right-wing union fixers. One of them, John Golding, head of the Post Office Engineer's

Union, replaced Benn as chairman of the Home Policy Committee, but did not use this position to change the manifesto because, he said: 'I was determined that the left would get the blame for the certain defeat in the coming general election, as we on the right had been blamed in 1979. And defeat was certain . . . it was no use thinking that things could be changed in the short term'.[28]

He was right about the certainty of defeat. The Conservatives held 42.4 per cent of the vote, down 685,000 votes on 1979, which was an achievement considering the government's unpopularity in 1981. However, what was truly remarkable about the 1983 result was how the other votes divided – a little under 8.5m for Labour, and nearly 7.8m for the Liberal-SDP Alliance. A line could be drawn across the map of England, through the Midlands, below which there were entire counties where no Labour candidate had even come second and there were only three Labour seats outside central London. There were 119 Labour candidates who had not even collected the necessary one-eighth of the votes to save their deposits. The Liberal-SDP Alliance had lost just 11 deposits, was runner up in two-thirds of the seats that the Conservatives held and had 25.4 per cent of the popular vote. In England, the gap between Labour and the Alliance was only half a per cent. Analysts who tracked the polls taken during the campaign reckoned that if the campaign had lasted one more week, Labour would have dropped to third place. 'While the Alliance did not break the Conservative monopoly control of government, it did break Labour's monopoly claim as the opposition party,' was the conclusion of one expert analysis. 'The Labour Party has contributed to the decline of class politics in Britain by becoming a failed ghetto party. It is no longer the party of the working class.'[29]

Labour was saved, to some extent, by the unfairness of the electoral system. The Conservatives returned 397 MPs, including more than 100 who were entering Parliament for the first time, who were generally more hard-line Thatcherite than those already there. Labour had 209 MPs, 60 fewer than before, while the Alliance, with over a quarter of the vote, had just 23 MPs. This meant that the Conservatives had one MP for every 32,777 votes for their party, but it took 338,286 to elect an Alliance MP.

Michael Foot immediately announced his resignation, with the words: 'I am ashamed.' Two trade unions, the TGWU and Association of Scientific, Technical and Managerial Staffs (ASTMS), kick-started the ensuing leadership campaign by declaring for Neil Kinnock. Since Tony Benn was among the many ex-MPs now looking for alternative employment, the election became a contest between Kinnock and Roy Hattersley, the former secretary of state for prices and consumer protection. On paper, Hattersley was by far the better qualified candidate and had the support of the old Labour establishment, including Callaghan and Healey. As a young MP, he had been seen as Roy Jenkins' right-hand man, and the founders of the SDP had hoped he would join them. But these old right-wing connections were a handicap in a party that had shifted to the left, and it was not certain that Hattersley had the stomach for the gruelling and unrewarding task of leading the Labour Party. Kinnock campaigned with more vigour and won easily, and Hattersley settled for the job of deputy. The Labour Party quickly forgave the amiable old gentleman who had led them to defeat; at that autumn's annual conference, Foot was warmly applauded by delegates, and watched as his protégé became his successor.

The Labour Party now began a long and difficult process of self-examination, which would occupy the party for the rest of the decade. Labour's defeat would be cited over and over again as a salutary warning about the perils of disunity and disorganization, a lesson taken to heart by several of the Labour candidates who fought their first general election that year, including Cherie Booth, who was not elected, along with her husband Tony Blair and Gordon Brown, who were.

There were many reasons for Labour's humiliation, but what appears to have been the single most damaging political issue was not the ambitious recipe for economic revival, but the same emotive issue that had swelled the membership of CND. Michael Foot sincerely believed in nuclear disarmament and believed the country could be won over to this. For the first part of the election campaign, it was estimated that 30 per cent of the content of the speeches he delivered were on the subject of peace. He was persuaded by party researchers to switch to talking about unemployment only after Labour had the worst moment in its whole, dismal election campaign. Jim Callaghan delivered a speech in Cardiff, on 25 May, in which he said: 'Britain and the West should not dismantle (their nuclear) weapons for nothing in return . . . We should not give them up unilaterally.'[30] That, of course, was exactly what Labour's manifesto promised to do, though it was well known that most of the shadow cabinet, including Denis Healey, privately agreed with Callaghan. Even the Labour-supporting tabloids, the *Daily Mirror* and *Daily Star*, did not play down the enormity of this challenge to Foot's authority. Their headlines were, respectively: 'Callaghan in Arms Revolt', and 'Callaghan's Bomb Shock for Labour'. David Owen reckoned: 'If the Labour Party had ever had a chance – which it did not – this was a blow from which it could not recover.'[31]

Michael Foot's authority had hit such a low that Jim Mortimer, the loyal general secretary of the Labour Party, told the following morning's televised press conference: 'At the Campaign Committee this morning we were all insistent that Michael Foot as the Leader of the Labour Party speaks for the party, and we support the manifesto.'[32] It was two weeks to polling day, and it apparently required a discussion by the Campaign Committee to remind the Labour Party as to who was their leader.

What made this issue so sensitive, pushing the defence of the British Isles to the forefront of the minds of people who might not normally have thought it important, was that the previous year a group of islands thousands of miles away had been occupied by the soldiers of a distant country, because of an obscure dispute about sovereignty.

CHAPTER 4

DIANA AND THE NEW ROMANTICS

On 24 February 1981, Britain and the world were electrified by the news that Charles Philip Arthur George, HRH the Prince of Wales, Earl of Chester, Duke of Cornwall, Duke of Rothesay, Earl of Carrick, Baron Renfrew, Lord of the Isles, Prince and Great Steward of Scotland and heir to the throne of the United Kingdom, was engaged to be married. His coy, virgin fiancée, the first bride of a Prince of Wales since 1863 and the first English bride of a future king since 1659, was a sweet-looking nineteen-year-old kindergarten nurse. Together they were embarking on what would be the most highly publicized event of 1981, although until a few weeks earlier Diana Spencer was barely recognized even within that smart set of wealthy, well-connected young Londoners called the 'Sloane Rangers', whose icon she would become.

A year of disturbing events, 1981 saw recession, violence in Northern Ireland, and political turmoil, but Diana was a counterpoint to all that. She was the princess of all that was bland. It was entirely fitting that her engagement should be announced in the same week as the launch of the SDP, and that her name should be linked to the Sloane Rangers and to the New Romantics, who – with occasional exceptions – set blandness to the sound of synthesizers. None of these escapist phenomena survived the 1980s, least of all the royal romance between Prince Charles and Lady Diana.

The ever-vigilant royal watchers from the tabloid press had been having fun for years, looking out for the next queen. They had put a series of young women through a cruel process that involved naming them as Charles's suspected girlfriends, then trawling through their past and present lives until it became obvious they either could not or did not want to withstand the attention. Diana Spencer was first noticed in September 1980, when three royal correspondents were staking out a spot on the River Dee, near Balmoral, where they knew Charles liked to go fishing. Behind him, on the bank, they noticed a tall blonde in fishing gear, but before they could snap a picture of her, she had ducked behind a tree. From there, she used a compact to take a second look at the hunters. James Whitaker, royal correspondent for the *Daily Star*, thought: 'A cunning lady. You had to be a real professional to think of using a mirror to watch us watching her.'[1]

He and his rival from the *Sun* independently established the mystery girl's identity. 'He's in love again,' ran the headline in the *Sun* on 8 September, 'Lady Di is the new girlfriend for Charles.' For the rest of the year, the teenager was under siege in her London flat, an ordeal that she handled with a shrewdness and self-restraint that earned her the respect of her future in-laws. For weeks, the public was treated to countless images of Diana walking demurely past the frenzied press pack, looking silently out from under her blonde fringe. She was nicknamed 'Shy Di', though in reality 'Shrewd Di' would have been more accurate. She had learnt from a mistake made by her older sister, Sarah, who ruined her moment in the spotlight as one of Charles's girlfriends by blurting out her life's story to James Whitaker and another tabloid journalist, Nigel Nelson, for which she was frozen out of the royal entourage. Diana enjoyed the attention and saw the royal correspondents as friends. Unlike the royals, she read the tabloids for pleasure.

She had another great advantage to go with her reticence – a spotless past. Contraception was safe and cheap in the early 1980s, the AIDS scare had not yet begun and not many girls held back to give their future husbands the pleasure of deflowering them, but Diana was such a rarity. One of her first appearances in print was in an article in *Tatler* about two eminent Sloanes: 'There are still a few girls left in Britain who haven't been to bed with Jasper Guinness or Prince Stash Klossowski and all of them are friends of Lady Diana Spencer.'[2] In her unhappy childhood she had devoured the novels of Barbara Cartland, and it seems that she really believed in the romantic template of the pure, undervalued young woman whose life is transformed by the arrival of the strong, knowing male. Moreover, she believed that the gawky and self-centred Prince Charles was an ideal male, and had dutifully saved her virginity for no one but him. 'I knew I had to keep myself tidy for what lay ahead,' [3] she explained.

It may well have been true, as the *Sun* proclaimed, that Prince Charles was in love. Whether or not he was in love with Diana Spencer was another matter. He liked older women who knew how to provide a service. The trauma he had suffered the previous August, when his favourite uncle, Earl Mountbatten, had been assassinated by the IRA, had driven him back into the arms of an old girlfriend, Camilla Shand, who was now married to an officer in the Household Cavalry named Andrew Parker Bowles. He was so well-connected that by 1987 he was Commanding Officer of the Household Cavalry and Silver Stick in Waiting, and did not object to his wife's infidelity because he had extra-marital interests of his own. Nor did Camilla oppose the idea that Charles should marry Diana; it apparently suited her that someone else would carry out the public duties of Charles's wife while she privately saw to his sexual needs.

At the age of thirty-two, Charles had the habits of a confirmed bachelor, and in an agony of indecision he set off on a long visit to India, during which he did not make any contact with the young woman with whom he was supposed to be besotted. When he returned, he received an angry note from his father, who thought that the press speculation about Diana had gone on long enough. Charles interpreted this as an instruction to marry, and dutifully proposed. At last, Diana was permitted to end months of silence, to speak publicly, and to pose for photographs in the garden of Buckingham Palace, dressed in air-hostess blue. She said, sweetly, 'I am absolutely delighted, thrilled, blissfully happy. With Prince Charles beside me I cannot go wrong.'[4]

'I am positively delighted and frankly amazed that Diana is prepared to take me on,' said Charles.

'And in love?' a BBC interviewer asked.

'Of course,' Diana answered at once.

But Charles, in that self-deprecating manner that shied away from any expression of strong emotion, remarked: 'Whatever "in love" means.'[5] He had apparently used the same words to her in private when he proposed marriage, in a conversation that involved no physical contact.[6]

The royal family had co-opted a new superstar, a fashion-setter, who was on her way to being the most photographed woman in the world. The cult of Diana has lasted to this day because she was a more interesting and complex figure than she first appeared. On the one hand, she was pedigree aristocracy. One Spencer had married the Duke of Marlborough's daughter, creating the line of Spencer Churchills that included a prime minister. Another, Diana's great-aunt Margaret, married Henry Douglas-Home, and so became the sister-in-law of Alec, another Conservative prime minister. Diana's maternal grandmother, Baroness Fermoy, was a lady-in-waiting to the queen. When Diana was thirteen, her father, the 8th Earl Spencer, inherited Althorp House and 14,000 acres of countryside in Norfolk, Northamptonshire and Warwickshire. As a young child, Diana romped in the nursery with Charles's brother Prince Andrew. No one could accuse Lady Diana of being a social interloper.

On the other hand, she had none of the haughty self-confidence of an aristocrat, but seemed very shy and normal, a 'tabloid girl in a tiara'.[7] She suffered a sense of inferiority and worthlessness, which can be attributed to having been the third daughter of an unloving couple desperate for a male heir, who was abandoned by her mother when she was six. Frances Shand Kydd had left Diana's father for another man and lost the battle for custody of the children; she reappeared in Diana's life long enough to try in vain to persuade her not to marry Charles, but thereafter stayed away, explaining to the *Daily Mail* that she was 'a firm believer in maternal redundancy'.[8] Diana missed her mother and loathed her father's second wife, Raine Legge, the strong-willed daughter of her childhood idol, Barbara Cartland. 'I hate you so much, if only you knew how much we all hated you for what you've done: you've ruined the house, you spend Daddy's money and what for?'[9] she once told her stepmother. Having no educational qualifications, Diana believed that she was stupid, though events would demonstrate that she was blessed with more emotional intelligence, and more skill in the art of handling the mass media, than any member of the family into which she was marrying.

In those first few months after the announcement of her engagement, she was deeply unhappy and vulnerable. She had to be whisked from her home like a dangerous prisoner and incarcerated alone in a suite of rooms in Clarence House, the queen mother's residence, and then in Buckingham Palace. She was given professional help to prepare for her role. The queen's lady-in-waiting, Lady Susan Hussey, spent hours teaching her how to wave and how to hold her handbag. Journalists who rang the palace press office to ask about the princess did not know that the nervous girl answering their questions was likely to be Diana herself, doing shift as a trainee press officer. Even with this preparation, it all threatened to be too much. Crossing Vauxhall Bridge in an official car with the queen's press secretary, Michael Shea, she saw a newspaper hoarding with the headline 'Diana – the True Story' and 'collapsed on the seat, crying that she could not take it – and that was before her marriage'.[10]

What she lacked was not professional advice but emotional support. At the age of nineteen, she had been torn away from everything that was familiar, and abandoned in the corridors of Buckingham Palace, where emotional contact was unknown. She later complained, 'I couldn't believe how cold everyone was. I was told one thing but actually another thing was going on. The lies and the deceit.'[11] The visible symptom of her distress was that she lost weight so rapidly that her dress designers worried about how to design a wedding dress to fit. This was the first sign of bulimia, a disease that had afflicted her mother and her sister. Until July, she at least had the distraction of the upcoming wedding to raise her spirits, which ducked and soared between depression and elation. She chose a sapphire ring costing £28,500, which had a catastrophic effect on the market for diamond engagement rings – that year, every fiancée wanted sapphire. On the night before the wedding, she went downstairs to chat with the staff – something the queen's children would never have done – and seeing a bicycle belonging to an equerry she leapt aboard and cycled round and round, ringing the bell and chanting 'I'm going to marry the Prince of Wales tomorrow.'[12]

But the honeymoon was not a happy one; sexual relations were not helped by Diana's inexperience and Charles's indifference, by the presence aboard the honeymoon yacht of 21 naval officers, a 256-man crew, a valet, dresser, private secretary and an equerry, or by her throwing up regularly because of her bulimia. The second part of the honeymoon, in Balmoral, was worse. Afterwards, life in the emptiness of royal palaces drove the young woman almost to self-destruction.

The first incident was in January 1982, when the newlyweds were at Sandringham. Diana was suffering from morning sickness, desperate for sympathy and attention, and threatening self-harm; Charles wanted to go out riding. Never in his thirty-three years on earth had Charles been expected to interrupt his day's schedule for someone else's emotional needs, so what she got was 'just dismissal, total dismissal. He just carried on out of the door.'[13] She threw herself to the bottom of a flight of stairs, where the Queen saw her. Luckily, a medical examination showed that her unborn child, the heir it was her function to produce, was unharmed. On other occasions, she reputedly threw herself against a glass display cabinet in Kensington Palace, slashed her wrists with a razor blade, cut herself with the serrated edge of a lemon slicer and stabbed herself with a penknife.[14] By 1986, the marriage had broken down; Charles had certainly resumed his affair with Mrs Parker Bowles, and may have done so two or three years earlier, while Diana took revenge by starting an affair with James Hewitt, a Guards officer.

Yet all these problems were kept out of the public eye for the whole of the 1980s, during which Diana was, after the Queen, the greatest public-relations asset the royal family had known for generations. The phoney love story fulfilled a public yearning for good news to compensate for stories of inflation, unemployment, political and industrial strife, terrorism and crime. In the few weeks that the couple were engaged, shop windows filled up with an estimated £400m worth of 'wedding souvenirs' – commemorative plates, tea towels and other hastily manufactured tat. The wedding itself, on 29 July 1981, was a public holiday in Britain and was watched by an estimated 750m people worldwide. In London, around 1m people lined the route on which the couple rode in an open carriage, with the crowd waving and shouting 'I love you'. From 8 a.m., the crowds in the Mall and Trafalgar Square were 'so thick that it was almost impossible to move'.[15] Throughout the country, pubs stayed open all day so customers could crowd in to watch the proceedings on widescreen televisions. Even the weather favoured the newlyweds with brilliant sunshine.

After the event, there was a voracious appetite from the public for more, but nothing much to tell. The couple were married and were going about the dull routine of life in the royal family. Their first joint public appearance, in October 1981, brought camera crews from as far afield as Japan and the USA, which descended on Welsh villages for a shot of the young princess, who was terrified and feeling sick, as she was in the first stage of pregnancy. 'I cried a lot in the car, saying I couldn't get out, couldn't cope,'[16] she later told her biographer, Andrew Morton. When the couple paid a visit to the White House, the press corps stationed outside was twice as large as it had been for the Pope a week earlier, though Diana was not yet so famous that Ronald Reagan had remembered her name – he raised a toast to 'Prince Charles and Princess Andrew.'

Early in her first pregnancy, Diana slipped out of the palace to buy wine gums; the photographers spotted her, and the news was all over the tabloids. This worried the palace to such an extent that the editors of twenty-one national newspapers, plus the BBC and ITN (but not including Kelvin MacKenzie of the *Sun*) were called to the palace to hear a plea from Michael Shea, backed up by the Queen, for the Princess to be allowed privacy. Only Barry Askew, of the *News of the World* ventured to argue in front of the monarch. 'If Lady Di wants to buy some wine gums without being photographed, why doesn't she send a servant?', he demanded. According to another participant, 'the semicircle of editors froze, and then collapsed in laughter as the Queen, with a smile, replied: "What an extremely pompous man you are!"'[17]

An eager public was not kept waiting long for news of a birth. Prince William Arthur Philip Louis arrived on 21 June 1982, followed by his brother, Henry Charles Albert David, usually known as Harry, on 15

September 1984. Diana overcame her terror of crowds and cameras, and taught herself to dress fashionably and look confident, hiding her insecurity and low self-esteem. She continued to be the most photographed woman on the planet.

Fittingly, Diana's favourite group was Duran Duran, who also existed to be photographed. And just as the royal family badly needed Diana to revive support for the monarchy, so the music industry was in desperate need of a band like Duran Duran. An industry that had taken the world by storm in the era of The Beatles was in a sorry state by 1980. EMI, the biggest of the British labels, the ones who had signed up The Beatles, showed a trading loss of £4.7m in 1980–1.[18] It was around that time that it lost its dominant position in the British market to CBS, an American multinational.

The industry was also beset by scandals. In August 1980, a Granada TV *World in Action* programme exposed the practice of chart-rigging. The teenagers who were the voracious buyers of new singles generally only wanted records that made the charts – to own a hit was to be cool, to own a record that missed was to open yourself to ridicule – so nothing sold a record so well as evidence that it was already selling. Gallup, who compiled the charts, took returns from 275 shops out of roughly 5,000 in the UK. Everybody seemed to manage to get hold of the lists of those shops, whose managers were besieged either by mystery punters coming in to buy large numbers of a single that no one else wanted, or by promoters offering free-gift T-shirts to go with their records, or just offering outright bribes. In July 1983, members of The Nolan Sisters' fan club each received letters telling them that if they bought the latest single 'Dressed to Kill' at any one of 100 shops listed on the letter, they would be given a free poster. Gallup saw the list, and removed the single from the charts. Heavy fines were handed out to others caught attempting to rig the charts; EMI was fined £10,000 in March 1984. Eventually, Gallup brought in what was then very new computer technology so that they could police the sales returns sent by shops and spot any suspicious figures, which meant that if you wanted to rig the charts, you had to do it simultaneously in every shop Gallup was monitoring in order to avoid suspicion – but the potential gain was not worth the effort.

Alongside the chart-rigging scandal, there were the court battles between artists and record companies. Sting, lead singer of The Police, and the Virgin Group, headed by Richard Branson, met in court in July 1982. According to Miles Copeland, formerly of The Police, Virgin had risked just £200 on launching Sting, and had got back £5m. Branson claimed in the *New Musical*

Express that it had actually risked £2,000, and the return had been £1.5m. The 1970s star Gilbert O'Sullivan went to court in the same year with a similar story: his albums had generated a gross income of £14.5m; he had received £500,000. Elton John issued a writ against his record company in the hope of recovering the copyright for his early songs. Hazel O'Connor also embarked on a gruelling legal battle with her record company, making a familiar complaint that it had induced her to sign a contract when she was alone and desperate to break into business, which meant that she was now seeing a derisive portion of the money she generated. In 1983, the new duo Wham! came to court with a very similar story about their record company, Innervision, run by a hard-nosed twenty-three-year-old named Mark Dean, who had discovered the duo. Wham! had sold millions of records worldwide, but the two performers, George Michael and Andrew Ridgeley, were receiving something like £40 a week. They settled out of court, were signed by CBS, and were multi-millionaires by the time Wham! split in 1986.

None of this unseemly litigation would have stopped teenagers from buying records, if the music had been there to draw them. Punk rock, which exploded on to the British scene in 1976, had not caught on abroad, and by 1980 had degenerated into 'a movement dominated by blank-eyed, gobbing, safety-pinned droids'.[19] The big sensation of 1980, if it can be called that, was Bucks Fizz, a two-boy, two-girl singing group cobbled together by a promoter named Nichola Martin to perform a song written by her husband Andy Hill, which had been accepted as an entry to the 'Song for Europe' competition to find Britain's entry for the Eurovision Song Contest. The band had a huge run of success churning out one catchy, forgettable song after another, until about 1984, when they were injured in a serious road accident. One of the women Martin recruited, Cheryl Baker, moved on into a solo career, but success brought no happiness for Jay Aston, the band's youngest member. After that near fatal accident, she had a brief affair with Andy Hill, and then attempted suicide when Nichola Martin found out. She fought a court battle to escape from her contract, which left her almost bankrupt. It took almost ten years for her life to pick up. She married, launched a solo career, and founded the Jay Aston Theatre Arts School in Chelsea.

Meanwhile, tribes of spiky-haired teenagers were awaiting a new fashion to fill the void left by the collapse of punk. It was ingeniously filled by a figure who called himself Adam Ant, whose trademarks included eye make-up, a white band across the cheekbones and bridge of the nose, copied from the Apache Indians, a nineteenth-century military tunic, previously worn by David Hemmings in the film *The Charge of the Light Brigade*, earrings and other androgynous items of self-adornment. In sharp contrast to Bucks Fizz, everything about Adam – his songs, his image, his style of dress, his band, his name and his persona – were his own invention. He started life as Stuart Goddard, from Marylebone, London, the grandson of a Romany gypsy. He was a bright child, whose teachers at St Marylebone Grammar School thought he should try for Oxford University, but he insisted on going to the Hornsey School of Art. There, he had a breakdown and emerged from psychiatric treatment insisting that everyone call him Adam. It is arguable that his true vocation was as an actor; he certainly immersed himself in playing the character he had invented, refusing to be guided or controlled by others. The one exception to this self-imposed rule was when he fell briefly under the influence of Malcolm McLaren, the man who had launched the Sex Pistols after going into business with Vivienne Westwood, running a boutique called SEX on the King's Road in Chelsea. McLaren was looking for a group that would help promote the Westwood look and even had in mind a name, Bow Wow Wow. Unable to manipulate Adam, he persuaded his three backing musicians, the Ants, to walk out on him. McLaren then added a fourteen-year-old singer, an Anglo-Burmese girl from Liverpool called Myint Myint Aye, who changed her name to Annabella Lwin. He had her pose in the nude with the three ex-Ants for a record sleeve that parodied Eduard Manet's *Le Déjeuner sur l'Herbe*, and launched Bow Wow Wow into the Top Ten with a single called 'Go Wild in the Country'. One of their subsequent singles was about masturbation.

After the McLaren episode, Adam's fortunes were so low that, according to his official biographer, 'the only music label that was interested in signing him was EMI [who] only took him on because they were unaware of what had happened, which was the funniest thing in the whole affair. Anybody who was in touch with the street was saying, "Adam is finished, he's a joke ... " It was only EMI that was sufficiently out of touch.'[20] However, the abandoned singer had two valuable assets – his dogged determination and his 'Ant people', the corps of dedicated fans who turned up in whichever town he was performing. In 1980, with his reformed band, he made a single called 'Dog Eat Dog', a title borrowed from a newspaper article about the kind of society that Margaret Thatcher was creating. It climbed high enough in the charts to earn the band a slot on BBC's *Top of the Pops*, helping the record to reach no. 4. The follow-up, 'Antmusic', would have reached No. 1 had it not been for the success of 'Imagine', reissued after John Lennon's murder. At the relatively advanced age of twenty-six, Adam Ant was an international star, the biggest live name in British music. Curiously, having battled so hard to break into the big time, he gave up singing in 1985 to become an actor.

The post-punk generation had no collective name until an article in the *Evening Standard* used the term 'New Romantic' to describe the strangely dressed young clientele of a new club in Covent Garden, called the Blitz. It was run by a man who called himself Steve Strange, and who later enjoyed transient fame as the front man for Visage. The club drew a mix of fashion-conscious 'straight' men (such as the handsome young Martin Kemp), cross-dressers and 'out' gays, who, according to Peter York, created 'a powerful mix of magpie retro, fastidious taste (it was hard to wear the look if you were a true-born slob) and market exploitation, tailor made for what they were calling the art form of the eighties'.[21] The club was deliberately exclusive; Strange stood at the door turning away anyone who looked out of place, including Mick Jagger, who arrived in sneakers and a baseball jacket. David Bowie was an honoured guest who featured the clientele of the Blitz in the video that accompanied his No. 1 hit 'Ashes to Ashes'. 'Inside the Blitz there was only one God and his name was David Bowie. It wasn't just the music, it was his chameleon dress sense,' according to Midge Ure, who also noted: 'It was never an overtly gay scene, more a little limp around the edges, like an old lettuce leaf.'[22] George O'Dowd, soon to be known as Boy George, worked in the cloakroom until Steve Strange sacked him on suspicion of theft. O'Dowd did not think much of the club or the 'New Romantic' scene. He reckoned: 'There really was no scene. It wasn't a national phenomenon like punk.'[23] But it did throw out one successful new group, Spandau Ballet, with Gary Kemp as singer/songwriter, and his older brother Martin as bass player. Their first single, 'To Cut a Long Story Short', reached No. 5 in the charts in 1980.

The origin of Spandau Ballet's name speaks volumes about the attitudes of the New Romantics. It arose after a group of youths from London, including Robert Elms, an aspiring young music journalist, paid a visit to Berlin. The city was divided by the notorious wall, patrolled by East German guards with orders to kill anyone attempting to cross without permission. The group came upon Spandau prison, where Rudolf Hess, the eighty-five-year-old former deputy leader of the Nazi Party, was the sole prisoner. This did not cause these young men to reflect at all on recent European history; they were interested in how the locals might react to their outfits – which in Robert Elms' case was 'bondage trousers (there was a minor punk revival thing going on), with white socks and loafers and a skin-tight satin top with a Lenin badge on it'. Elms spotted a piece of graffiti, saying 'Spandau Ballet', which he thought 'nicely nonsensical'.[24] Martin Kemp liked the name because it was 'trendy enough for the designers and hairdressers not to be frightened away, but heavy enough in case we ever made it to Wembley'.[25] Such indifference to anything as serious as international politics was not born of ignorance or stupidity; it was a deliberate, conscious attitude of mind, a reaction to the economic decay and seemingly unsolvable political problems besetting Britain. Elms claimed, 'Even my travels had revealed to me that my country was odd, perhaps ill, but that its sickness – some kind of national autism perhaps – gave us a contemporary brilliance at just one thing: youth culture.'[26]

It was from a similar source that Duran Duran found their name. One of the worst films that Jane Fonda ever starred in was *Barbarella*, a failed attempt to transfer a popular cartoon strip, which featured a villain named Durand Durand, to celluloid. In 1979, it was shown on BBC television. A lot of young people in Birmingham watched because Barbarella was also the name of one of the city's main punk venues. Among them were John Taylor, Nick Rhodes and Stephen Duffy, art students who dreamt of being rock stars, who went on to perform their first gig as Duran Duran at Birmingham Polytechnic shortly afterwards, four weeks before Margaret Thatcher became prime minister. Duffy, probably the most gifted of the trio, later reckoned that 'by far the best thing about the band' was its name.[27] He left soon afterwards, which, since the other two could neither play instruments with any skill nor write songs, might have been the end of Duran Duran, but their ambition to be rock stars remained. They had a stroke of luck when, in May 1979, Gary Numan had a sudden and unexpected hit with 'Are Friends Electric?', featuring heavy use of synthesizers. The sudden popularity of electronically generated sounds relieved Taylor and Rhodes of the need to play instruments well. They found a drummer, Roger Taylor, from Castle Bromwich, and acquired a management team, the brothers Michael and Paul Berrow, who ran a successful club in Birmingham. An advertisement in *NME* brought in a guitarist, Andy Taylor, from Newcastle upon Tyne, who had been a professional performer since his teens (the only alternative to an apprenticeship in the shipyards). None of the three Taylors were related. Finally, they recruited a singer, Simon Le Bon, from Bushey in Hertfordshire.

In July 1981, the band released their third single, 'Girls on Film', which reached No. 5 even before it was complemented by a raunchy video made by Godley and Creme, which was banned by the BBC but did wonders for the band's reputation in bars and clubs across the USA. Their album, *Rio*, released in May 1982, went to No. 2 in the UK. Four of its tracks went into the Top 20 singles chart. Though the sophisticated crowd at the Blitz might look down on Duran Duran as naff provincials, they had a mass appeal unmatched by any other New Romantic band. After the release of *Rio*, they went on tour to

Australia, Japan and the USA. Their first foray into the American market faltered, because the term 'New Romantic' meant nothing on that side of the Atlantic, but in November 1982 *Rio* was re-released as a dance album, went into the charts and opened the way to the first significant British invasion of the American rock scene since the rise of the Beatles, more than twenty years earlier. British newspapers even referred to Duran Duran as the 'Fab Five', just as The Beatles had been known as the 'Fab Four'.

By now, the band was living in the extravagant rock-star style, with Le Bon and John Taylor, each of whom considered himself the leader of Duran Duran, competing to see who could bed the greater number of female fans. Boy George, whose turn as a pop phenomenon had not yet begun, thought that 'the champagne-swilling, yacht-sailing Duran Duran touted "playboyeurism" and a new pop superficiality. Suddenly it was OK to be rich, famous and feel no shame. Some saw it as the natural consequence of Thatcherism.'[28]

What made Duran Duran popular was that they were all very handsome and had good dress sense. They belonged exclusively to children entering their teens. The future novelist Andrea Ashworth was age thirteen when she had pictures of the group on the walls around her bunk bed; and enjoyed a 'once in a lifetime' experience when her friend's parents gave her a ticket to a Duran Duran concert in Manchester in 1982. The ticket cost 'almost £10' – way beyond anything her mother and stepfather could afford:

> Duran Duran gave Hayley and me a new moon on Monday and an ocean of emotional freedom. They poured out music we could dive into and flounder extravagantly about in, gesturing at great depths, raving, not drowning. The lyrics were polished, arty crosswords, blessedly obscure, so you could ponder them as long – or as little – as you liked. The music was turbulent but buoyant, urging elation and anger, frustration, insouciance, conquest, sometimes all in the same song. It let you write words such as 'chiaroscuro' and 'euphoria', 'epiphany' and 'solar plexus' in your diary; it inspired you to slam that diary shut and dervish about, twanging air guitar, making your hair fly as if there were no tomorrow.[29]

What was much more important, from the point of view of the managers and shareholders of the companies that ran the record labels, was that the success of acts such as Adam and the Ants and Duran Duran started the tills ringing again. In 1984, the UK public spent £141.2m on albums, £78.8m on singles, and £104m on cassettes. More importantly, a growing number of people were thinking that vinyl might be on the way out and were buying the new and very expensive compact discs; that year they bought £5m worth. That came to a total of £329m, which was 27 per cent less in real terms than people had spent on records in 1974, but it was a 14 per cent increase on 1983.[30] The long decline of the UK music industry had at last been turned around.

Duran Duran's place as Diana's favourite group was sanctified in July 1983. By now, though none of the band had yet reached the age of twenty-five, they were tax exiles, living on the Caribbean island of Montserrat to be out of the reach of Inland Revenue. However, they flew home to perform at a Prince's Trust concert in front of Charles and Diana. They were mobbed at the airport, posed for photographs at the Grosvenor House Hotel on Park Lane, and filled pages of the tabloid press. The *Daily Mirror* was so intent on recruiting readers from Duran Duran's army of fans that the next day's front page was dominated by a large photograph of Diana meeting members of the band, with the headline in huge type, 'Diana's delight'. At least, that was the first-edition headline, prepared early in the evening before the band stepped on stage. Sadly, life beyond the reach of Inland Revenue had been so demanding there had been no time to rehearse, and their stage performance was so dire that in the later editions of the *Mirror* 'Diana's delight' became instead 'Diana's let-down'.[31]

In the middle of the decade, just as Duran Duran were breaking up, losing their drummer and guitarist in rapid succession, the British public was treated to yet another royal wedding. On 23 July 1986, the Queen's second son, Andrew, married Sarah Ferguson, whom he had known since childhood. The event did not quite match the Diana wedding for worldwide popularity. An estimated 500m watched on television, two-thirds of the numbers who had tuned in for Charles and Diana, but a substantial audience all the same. Minutes before the groom arrived at Westminster Abbey, his mother conferred on him the title of Duke of York. Unlike Diana, the new Duchess of York vowed to 'obey' her husband – though like Diana, she didn't.

Before this happy event, there was a taster for something that would become a regular event in the next decade – a royal scandal. In 1978, Prince Michael of Kent, grandson of George V and fifteenth in line to the throne, had married a lively German divorcée named Marie Christine Agnes Hedwig Ida von Reibnitz (who became known as Princess Michael) in a civil ceremony in Austria. Because she was Roman Catholic, he surrendered his place in the line of succession, although their two children were twentieth and twenty-first in line. In 1985, however, Princess Michael was hit by an unwelcome press revelation: the *Daily Mirror* discovered that her father, Baron von Reibnitz, who had died in Mozambique two years earlier, had joined the SS in 1933 and risen to the rank of major.[32] The Princess went on television to say that the news had come as a 'total shock' and caused her 'a deep shame'.[33] Within a few days, opinion had swung decisively behind her after her mother, who lived in Australia, admitted concealing this family skeleton from her daughter and produced the verdict of a de-nazification court, sitting in 1948, which accepted that the baron had been only a nominal member of the SS.

However, the tabloids did not give up on Princess Michael. She was a lady of spirit, known in royal circles as 'Princess Pushy', who did not allow public exposure to interfere with her pursuit of pleasure. In July 1985, the *News of the World* came out with a yet tastier story, and this time the princess could not plead innocence. She was having an affair with John Ward Hunt, the thirty-eight-year-old heir to a vast oil fortune. When she turned up at his London apartment, disguised in a red wig, a press photographer was laying in wait, evidently tipped off by someone close to the princess. True to the aristocratic tradition that tolerated infidelity within marriage provided outward appearances were maintained, Prince Michael and his wife used the final of the Wimbledon tennis tournament to appear together in the royal box, during which she showered her husband with public shows of affection. This royal performance attracted almost as much interest as the match taking place on the centre court, in which the seventeen-year-old German, Boris Becker, became the youngest men's singles champion in the history of the tournament.

The bemused Princess Michael wondered what the tabloids thought she had done wrong. 'Why do they attack me?', she asked the newspaper columnist Woodrow Wyatt, a man to whom it was never a good idea to entrust with a confidence. 'Princess Anne has had at least five affairs. Prince Philip has had lots of affairs. The Duchess of Kent has had a lot too.' Wyatt advised her that the press did not attack royalty in the centre, so went for someone 'on the fringe' instead.[34]

Had he reflected a bit more, he might also have made the observation that the popularity of Britain's monarchy tends to rise and fall according to the political weather. In times of crisis, royalty plays a role as a soothing symbol of continuity amid the chaos; when things settle down, people are more likely to complain that it is an expensive pageant. The public was unimpressed by the pomp that surrounded the investiture of Prince Charles as Prince of Wales in 1969, but loved the silver jubilee in 1977. Prince Andrew's marriage, when the political situation had stabilized a year after the miners' strike, did almost nothing for the popularity of the monarchy, but Diana's wedding, against the background of urban riots, was royalty's biggest hit since the coronation. Her arrival in the story of the royals was perfectly timed. She continued to be a star because she was glamorous and photogenic, and because her neurotic search for happiness made her a dramatic character with whom people could identify. Her exit from official royalty, through her separation and divorce in the early 1990s, was also well-timed because, in those settled times, the public did not feel that they needed the comfort of an unchanging monarchy, as they had in the troubled summer of 1981.

Chapter 5

Inglan is a Bitch

Throughout the 1960s and 1970s white Britons quarrelled fiercely with other whites over British attitudes to race, against a background of near silence from those most directly affected. It was not until the 1980s that Britain's ethnic minorities found a voice that the white majority could hear. In 1980, immigration from what was termed the 'New Commonwealth' – India, Pakistan and the Caribbean islands – was still sufficiently recent that anyone over the age of twenty from any of those backgrounds was more likely to be an immigrant than a native-born Briton.

A substantial section of white opinion did not want these immigrants to think that Britain was their permanent home. Enoch Powell made a household name of himself with a speech delivered one Saturday afternoon in 1968 in which he claimed to foresee a river 'flowing with much blood' because of the presence of too many people of a different skin colour. By 1979, Powell was no longer a Conservative MP, but was still an influential presence in the Commons, as an Ulster Unionist, and within the Conservative Party were influential people who heartily shared Powell's view on immigration. They were organized in a pressure group called the Monday Club. No government minister belonged to the Monday Club, but it had a strong presence in the party and on the Conservative backbenches, and whatever measures the government took to restrict immigration, the Monday Club was there to demand more.

If there had been a complete ban on anyone Asian or Afro-Caribbean entering the country, the stalwarts of the Monday Club would not have been satisfied. Like Powell, they wanted those already in the country to think about leaving. Neo-fascist organizations such as the National Front were demanding that people of the wrong skin colour should be forcibly removed from the UK, but the official Conservative line did not go that far. The Conservative manifesto of 1979 promised: 'We will help those immigrants who genuinely wish to leave this country – but there can be no question of compulsory repatriation.' During the 1980 Conservative Party annual conference, the MP for Beaconsfield, Sir Ronald Bell, reminded a fringe meeting of the right-wing Monday Club of this promise and pointed out, petulantly, that it was not happening;[1] immigrants were not queuing up to be paid to leave the country in which they had put down roots. In 1983, minutes of the Monday Club's Immigration and Repatriation Committee were leaked to *Private Eye.* They restated that the club's policy was: 'An end to New Commonwealth and Pakistani immigration, a properly financed scheme of voluntary repatriation, the repeal of the Race Relations Act, and the abolition of the Commission for Racial Equality; particular emphasis on repatriation.'[2] The committee chairman was the Conservative MP for Billericay, Harvey Proctor, and the committee secretary in 1981–3 was a student activist from north London, John Bercow, who many years later became Speaker of the House of Commons. (Sir Ronald Bell, that articulate voice of white middle-class rectitude, was no longer there to speak for the Monday Club, having died suddenly in 1982, in his Commons office, while having sex with a woman who was not his wife.) Bercow cut his ties with the Monday Club in February 1983, when he concluded that some of its members were racist.

The 'immigration' issue was not actually about immigration but about race. Although people would complain that the British Isles were overcrowded and could not take in any more arrivals, it was not a genuine problem. More people emigrated during the 1970s and 1980s than were permitted to enter, so that even with a rising birth rate, the population was almost static. It was 55.9m in 1971, 56.4m in 1981 and 57.8m in 1991.

That it was entirely a matter of race is shown up in unpublished documents about the first major humanitarian crisis on which the incoming Conservative government had to take a stand. Hundreds of thousands of refugees were fleeing Vietnam by boat and arriving, destitute, in whatever port would take them. The UN appealed to the developed world to help, and asked Britain to take in 10,000 of the 'boat people' in 1979. Politically, there was no reason for a Conservative government to object. These were mostly ethnic Chinese families who had formed Vietnam's entrepreneurial class, which was why a communist regime was driving them out. Once settled, they could be expected to look after themselves, contribute to the economy and be staunchly anti-communist. Foreign Secretary Lord Carrington was keen to comply, partly for the sake of the UK's international reputation, but principally because refugees were pouring into Hong Kong, which was then a British colony, and whose government was pleading for help. Home Secretary William Whitelaw was conscious that public opinion had been aroused by the television pictures of desperate families in overcrowded boats. The Home Office had a fat postbag of letters from the public who believed that the government should offer help. None of this impressed Mrs Thatcher. 'All those who wrote letters in this sense should be invited to accept (a refugee) in their homes,' she said, when she discussed the matter privately with Carrington and Whitelaw in July 1979. If Britain was going to take refugees from Vietnam, she argued, they should compensate by refusing entry visas to a corresponding number of children and other dependant relatives from other parts of Asia. Nor was she impressed that the Conservative-led Greater London Council had offered 400 homes for Vietnamese families. It was 'quite wrong that immigrants should be given council housing whereas white citizens were not,' she said. On the other hand, she added, she had 'less objections to refugees such as Rhodesians, Poles and Hungarians since they could more easily be assimilated into British society.'[3]

Many of the people who argued like this would have been offended to have been called racist. What was at stake, in some people's minds, was national identity, which they believed to be under threat from the arrival of hundreds of thousands of black and Asian immigrants. A few months before Margaret Thatcher came to power, she made a much quoted remark that white people were being 'rather swamped by people with a different culture'.[4]

In this atmosphere, the opportunities for people from ethnic minorities to find work and get on in the world were limited. A few children of the Caribbean islands had achieved national prominence, including the young comic Lenny Henry, the ITN journalists Trevor McDonald and Moira Stewart, and Viv Anderson, the first black footballer to play for England. A few were taking their first step into local politics. There were a number of Asians who were prospering in business, but they kept out of the public eye. No matter how wealthy they had become, almost all supported the Labour Party, because they saw the Conservatives as the party of Enoch Powell, although Powell had left it years earlier. But generally, to be black meant to be consigned to a low-paid job or no job at all, to live in substandard housing in an inner-city ghetto and to have your children go to one of the worst of the state schools. In a recession, the ethnic minorities were hit first. In the year to February 1981 unemployment among the population as a whole rose by two-thirds, while among black people, whose chances of finding work were already low, it went up 82 per cent.[5] To be young, black and out on the streets meant risking arrest and, old or young, there was the insulting and sometimes frightening spectre of white racism. In 1981, a Home Office study concluded that Afro-Caribbeans were thirty-six times more likely to suffer racially motivated attacks than whites, Asians were fifty times more likely and that 'the police failed to pursue the aggression with energy'.[6] Yet the ethnic minorities seemed to bear all these disadvantages in resigned silence.

By 1980, change was due. In the opening words of Hanif Kureishi's novel, *The Buddha of Suburbia* (1990), its fictional protagonist declares: 'My name is Karim Amir, and I am an Englishman born and bred, almost. I am considered to be a funny kind of Englishman, a new breed as it were, having emerged from two histories. But I don't care – Englishman I am (though not proud of it).' For the first time, there were many thousands of teenagers and young adults of Asian or Afro-Caribbean descent who were either born in Britain or had arrived in the country so young that it was the only homeland they knew. The idea that there was a country to which they could be 'repatriated' was an insult. They had nowhere else to go, and no choice but to do what they could to make life tolerable in a white-dominated society.

The first sign of changing times was a campaign called 'Scrap Sus', which took off in the late 1970s, mainly in inner London. The Metropolitan Police had been making free use of the 1834 Vagrancy Act, which gave them the power to stop and search passers-by on the mere suspicion that they might be planning a crime. In 1978, 3,800 people were arrested on 'sus', the vast majority of them young blacks. The campaign against arbitrary arrest was so successful that one of the first pieces of legislation introduced by the incoming Conservative government was to repeal the Vagrancy Act. That success introduced young blacks to the idea that they did not have to accept unfair treatment from the police without resisting.

Anyone taking a walk through Brixton in south London in 1980 would have been struck by the noise and vibrancy of the neighbourhood. Inner cities can be silent and empty at night, but not Brixton. The average age of its inhabitants was several years below the norm, because the middle-aged property owners had decamped to quieter suburbs. Yet, despite a falling population in Brixton, there were far too many people packed into an inadequate supply of decent housing. About a third of the housing stock was substandard. Empty houses were used by the locals as gambling clubs, dope centres or venues for all-night blues parties. The triangle formed by Railton Road, Frontline and Mayall Road was a favoured location for left-wing squatters. Jobs were acutely short. These problems bore down particularly on the children of immigrants; half of the nineteen to twenty-one-years-olds in Brixton and 40 per cent of children of school age were Afro-Caribbean. Rather than hang around bored in their overcrowded homes, these teenagers lived out on the streets, built their own culture around dope and reggae music, and spoke their own patois.

To the police, all this noise and street activity looked suspiciously like a threat to law and order. In 1981, the Metropolitan Police was probably the most racially mixed force in Britain, yet the chance of seeing a black or Asian policeman on the streets of London was about 200 to 1. In a force of 24,000 officers there were 110 who were not white. The men, and the small number of women, patrolling London were the children of skilled workers, self-employed traders or shopkeepers, the same class of people who had moved out of places such as Brixton as immigrants moved in.

Police statistics recorded 10,626 serious crimes in the Brixton division in 1980, compared with 9,423 four years earlier, and including a disproportionate number of cases of robbery or violent theft. 'Concern', a local charity, disputed the objectivity of these numbers, claiming that they were exaggerated by the prejudices of those who compiled them.[7] What is certain is that the commander of 'L' Division of the Metropolitan Police, which had its headquarters in Brixton, believed that there was an issue to be resolved about who controlled the surrounding streets. On six occasions in less than five years up to September 1980, officers of the Special Patrol Group (SPG) poured into Brixton, setting up road blocks and making early morning raids and random street checks. The local commander did not think it necessary to consult local liaison groups or elected representatives, or even tip off the local beat coppers, before sending the officers in. Lambeth Council, which under the leadership of Ted Knight was then arguably the most left-wing council in Britain, set up a working party to examine these tactics, the tenor of whose report can be deduced from the chapter headings and subheadings: 'Army of Occupation', 'Intimidation', 'Misuse of Laws', 'Continual harassment', etc. 'Whilst us whiteys only get the occasional incident, West Indian people have it all the time,'[8] one woman told them.

Sooner or later, some confrontation between the police and young blacks was almost inevitable. On 2 April 1980, a riot broke out in the St Paul's district of Bristol with such ferocity that the police withdrew for four hours, leaving hundreds of exuberant black youths to an unrestrained display of reckless anger. Thirty-one people were reported injured. In London, the first overt trouble had its origins several miles from Brixton, in New Cross, south-east

London. At about 5.50 a.m. on Sunday, 18 January 1981, fire broke out in a Victorian-built council house at 439 New Cross Road, where an all-night party – the joint sixteenth birthday celebration for Yvonne Ruddock and Angela Jackson – had been in progress. Fifty teenagers were still in the house. Within minutes, they were trapped in the flames or jumping from upstairs windows to escape. Walton Williams, aged nineteen, clambered out, clung to a drainpipe and tried to drag a friend to safety through the window, 'but the drainpipe collapsed and the next thing I remember is lying on the pavement,' he said in a BBC interview later that day. In hospital, he learned that his friend was one of eleven teenagers who had died in the flames. More than twenty others were injured. Yvonne Ruddock was pulled out with horrible burns, and died in hospital less than a week later. Her brother, Paul, brought the death toll to thirteen when he died from his burns early in February. One of the survivors suffered a trauma from which he never properly recovered; two-and-a-half years later he died after falling, or throwing himself, from a balcony.

After a tragedy of this magnitude, civic and political leaders normally send messages of condolence to the afflicted families. Five weeks after the New Cross fire, when a terrible fire in a discotheque in the Irish Republic left forty-eight dead, there were messages from the Queen and Margaret Thatcher, among many others. The Irish teenagers who had died so horribly were white. There were no such messages for the families of the victims of the New Cross fire, who were black. 'Not one word of sympathy was offered to us,' Nerissa Campbell, who lost a seventeen-year-old son in the fire, complained years later.[9] She also repeated the frequently heard complaint that when the police investigated the fire they interrogated the traumatized young survivors 'as though they were criminals'. A teenage girl told the police that she had seen a white man throw someone through the window of No. 439, but the police attached very little weight to her evidence. One survivor, Robert McKenzie, complained: 'They gave me no respect and I felt like I had been arrested – not asked to share information. They didn't want to listen to the truth.'[10]

A quarter of a century and two inquests later, it is now generally agreed that the police were right; the dead were not victims of a racially motivated attack, and the only way to find out why the fire broke out so suddenly and spread so swiftly was to question the survivors. Over time, a rift developed between the unfortunate woman whose house was No. 439 (she lost two children), and other bereaved parents, as the suspicion spread that sexual jealousy and a family quarrel had given rise to the catastrophe. At the second inquest, twenty-three years on, in May 2004, one witness seemed uncomfortable on the stand

and, as she stepped down, a woman in the audience hissed at her 'you murdering bitch!'[11]

Back in 1981 as the families struggled to come to terms with their losses, their initial response was to unite against a world that did not seem to care. Meetings were called and the New Cross Massacre Action Committee formed. The slogan 'Thirteen dead and nothing said' gained currency. On Monday, 2 March, up to 10,000 demonstrators from London, Bristol, Manchester and Birmingham assembled outside the burnt-out house, laid flowers in remembrance and marched for seven hours through some of London's busiest streets, across Blackfriars Bridge and along Fleet Street, Regent Street and Oxford Street to a rally in Hyde Park, causing havoc for the traffic on their way. At the rally, they stood in pouring rain as speakers, including the television presenter Darcus Howe, addressed them from the back of a lorry. A small number of those taking part objected to the heavy police presence and there were skirmishes. While the BBC and ITN reported the reasons for the march, paying little attention to the disturbances, the newspaper coverage was all about the 'Rampage of a Mob' (*Daily Express*); the 'Day the Blacks Ran Riot in London' (*Sun*).[12] To others, the march was the first sign that one of the country's ethnic minorities was gaining the confidence to organize itself and demand to be heard. A historian of London's black communities has written that 'the most important spur to the development and reception of black London history was the New Cross Fire'.[13]

Five weeks later, on Monday, 6 April 1981, the police launched another campaign to bring order and control to Brixton's streets in an operation codenamed 'Swamp 81'. This time, the SPG (Special Patrol Group) was not used as a concession to local feeling, but ten squads, each made up of between five and eleven police officers, flooded Brixton's streets between 2 p.m. and 11 p.m. every day for a week. They stopped and questioned 943 people, more than half of whom were young blacks, and made 118 arrests.[14] On the Friday evening, just after 6 p.m., a constable tried to stop a black youth who was running through the streets, but he broke free and ran on. The constable then noticed bloodstains on his uniform. Evidently, the youth had been injured, presumably in a fight. Two police officers gave chase, but he escaped. A message was circulated to all officers in the area to look out for an injured man on the run. A few minutes later, other officers saw him being helped into a taxi cab. They stopped the cab, bandaged his wounds and demanded to know how he had come by his injuries. Soon, a crowd of thirty to forty young blacks gathered. They did not believe the officers' protestations that the injured youth was being given first aid, and that an ambulance had been summoned; they thought that the police were preventing an injured man from getting to hospital. They pushed the police aside to let him escape. More police were called in. Soon a running battle had developed along Railton Road, which lasted about half an hour, at the end of which six people had been arrested, six officers had been injured and four police vehicles had been damaged by flying bricks.

In the morning, the police were out in force, determined not to allow the rioters to rule the streets. 'The cops usually patrol the Frontline, but on that Saturday they parked up and down the Frontline every fifty yards, just sitting in their vans waiting for something to happen,'[15] one resident claimed. A rumour had gone round firstly that the injured youth had been injured by the police, and secondly that he had died. Both assertions were false, but they added to an incendiary atmosphere. Early in the afternoon, two young constables spotted the black driver of a parked minicab putting something into his sock. They suspected he was drug-dealing and challenged him. He laughed, and said that in Brixton, it was best to keep your money hidden. He agreed that they could see for themselves. The police searched him, but found nothing incriminating, just the folded notes in his sock. The officers evidently did not like being made to look silly. The older of the two, who was twenty-four, wanted to search the cab. The driver at first invited them to go ahead, but then did not like the officer's demeanour and accused him of planting evidence. By now, a crowd had assembled. Words were exchanged, a youth was arrested, reinforcements called. When more senior officers arrived, irate residents told them that one of the officers involved in the confrontation had an iron bar hidden in a plastic bag he was carrying, and that two plainclothes officers on patrol were wearing National Front badges. The two NF sympathizers were identified and sent back to Brixton police station; the allegation about the iron bar was apparently not investigated.

The time for negotiations between police and residents had now passed, as Brixton went up in flames again. This time, it was not only bricks, stones and other debris being hurled at police; for the first time on the British mainland, the rioters threw petrol bombs. It appears that someone set up a makeshift bomb factory. As the police retreated down Mayall Road, the delighted rioters set fire to the vehicles they had left behind. 'Up goes a cop's van – wild cheers, laughter, dances of joy,'[16] one participant recalled. In Railton Road, a local clergyman saw a group of 'grimly determined' black youths invade the George public house and then the newsagent next door, wrecking both. When the vicar tried to intervene, they explained their reasons: the landlord of the George, they alleged, had discriminated against black customers and the newsagent had refused to serve gays. On that day, 279 police officers reported receiving injuries, at least 45 members of the public were injured, 61 private cars and 56 police vehicles were damaged, with most set on fire, 82 people were arrested and 145 buildings were damaged, including 28 that had been torched.[17]

Sunday morning was quiet. In the afternoon, Home Secretary William Whitelaw arrived to tour the scene with the Metropolitan Police Commissioner Sir David McNee. Seeing the damaged buildings, Whitelaw said it felt like he was: 'back in the war during the London blitz'.[18] Their visit was perhaps not a good idea. Whitelaw and his party were jeered by residents, and within half an hour another riot had started as police clashed with a crowd outside a burnt-out pub in Railton Road. No buildings were set on fire that night, but there was some organized looting; it was thought that white criminal gangs had moved in to profit from the disturbances. By the end of the evening, another 165 people had been arrested, it was reported that another 122 police officers and 3 members of the public had been injured, and 61 police vehicles and 26 private cars were damaged.[19]

The Brixton riots were given a vast amount of publicity, making it an obvious risk that copycat riots would break out somewhere. In fact, there were six quiet weeks before riots suddenly broke out in almost every city centre in England. On Friday, 3 July, a group of white skinheads from London's East End turned up for a concert at a pub called the Broadway, in Southall, West London, an area with a large Asian population. Some of them decided to engage in the sick sport of 'Paki-bashing', but this time, unexpectedly, the victims retaliated. When the police arrived, they were confronted by a large crowd of young Asians who wanted to mete out rough justice to the skinheads. The police tried to disperse them, and in no time the Southall riot was under way.

On that same Friday, in Toxteth, Liverpool, a youth named Leroy Alphonse Cooper fell off his cycle as the police were chasing him. A crowd of about forty black youths saw him being arrested and came to his rescue, pulling him away from the police. There was then a fight that went on for two hours, in which three officers were injured. The next day Merseyside police mobilized a large force with riot equipment, but the trouble they anticipated did not start until the evening, when three officers who were looking for a stolen car around Upper Parliament Street were attacked. Black and white youths rioted together, burning cars and buildings, and looting shops. A BBC television crew was attacked and a £12,000 camera stolen. The riot lasted through the night. At 7 a.m., the police baton-charged the crowd. On Sunday, it started again, and by about 2 a.m. it was clear that the police had been driven out of parts of Toxteth. 'Scenes like this can never have been seen in a British city under the rule of law this century,' the local Liberal MP, David Alton, declared.[20] In the middle of the night, William Whitelaw was woken by a telephone call from Merseyside's chief constable, Ken Oxford, asking permission to turn CS gas on the crowd, something the police had never done before on the British mainland. The imperturbable Mr Whitelaw gave his consent and went straight back to sleep.[21]

Even with CS gas in use, the rioting continued for a total of nine days, during which 468 police officers were injured, 500 people were arrested and at least 70 buildings were demolished.[22] There was sporadic trouble for the rest of the month, including a notorious hit-and-run accident, in which a police vehicle pursuing stone-throwing youths knocked down and killed a twenty-two-year-old disabled man, and just drove on.

The argument about the cause of the rioting was more political in the case of Toxteth than any of the other riots that year. Liverpool was where a left-wing group called the Militant Tendency was strongest. This was a Marxist group inspired by the writings of Leon Trotsky, which by the mid-1980s had several thousand members. Unlike other Trotskyite organizations, it claimed not to be a political party, but an informal group of like minded members of the Labour Party, united only in that they all read the weekly newspaper, *Militant*. This was a fiction that they maintained in the hope of avoiding being expelled en masse from the Labour Party. Militant controlled the Labour Party Young Socialists (LPYS) members, the official youth wing of the party. The LPYS put out a leaflet in Liverpool blaming the riot on 'brutal harassment' by the police, but despite allegations made at the time by David Alton and others, no evidence was ever found that the riots were politically organized. As in Brixton, there was a toxic mix of high unemployment, bad housing, racial tension and hostility to the police that underlay the violence. The Labour Party tended to blame unemployment. For several years, the number of registered jobless at the Toxteth dole office had been consistently around 18,000 or below; by June 1981, it was suddenly up to 21,000, though the figure was actually higher in neighbouring Croxteth, with its almost exclusively white population, where there was no riot. Toxteth's MP, Richard Crawshaw, who had defected from Labour to the SDP, was adamant that the cause was neither unemployment nor bad housing, but 'a genuine belief' among black and white youths alike that the police were 'not even-handed'.[23]

On 8–9 July, there was another major riot, in Moss Side, Manchester. There were others in Birmingham, Blackburn, Bradford, Derby, Hull, Leeds,

Leicester, Preston and Wolverhampton, all in early July. While the Brixton, Southall and Toxteth disturbances merit the description 'race riots', others did not. It was as if everybody who was young in an inner city wanted to join in. But after a few tumultuous days, it all seemed to fizzle out, in the quiet euphoria of the royal wedding, leaving the authorities to argue over what, if anything, the riots said about British politics. On 13 July, Margaret Thatcher visited Toxteth, saw the wreckage, but did not see anyone driven to desperation by joblessness and urban decay. She saw a pleasant enough city centre ruined by its feckless inhabitants. She recalled:

> The housing there was by no means the worst in the city. I had been told that some of the young people got into trouble through boredom and not having enough to do. But you had only to look at the grounds around those houses with the grass untended, some of it waist high, and the litter, to see that this was a false analysis. They had plenty of constructive things to do if they wanted. Instead, I asked myself how people could live in such circumstances without trying to clear up the mess.[24]

A more famous reaction came from Norman Tebbit, the recently promoted employment secretary, in reply to a speaker at the Conservative annual conference who suggested that the riots might be linked to rising unemployment. Tebbit's much-misquoted riposte was that his father had been unemployed in the 1930s, but 'he didn't riot, he got on his bike to look for work'. During the same session, Tebbit conceded that the figure of 3m unemployed was high, but 'of course some of these three million are less keen to find work than others'.[25]

This was not the unanimous view of the cabinet. Michael Heseltine, the environment secretary, eight years younger than Thatcher, and her most formidable rival, feared that 'there was a political menace in the relatively small scale disturbances which no responsible government could ignore'.[26] He persuaded Thatcher to allow him to leave the running of his department to his junior while he spent two-and-a-half weeks in Liverpool, being the 'Minister for Merseyside', by night ensconced in the Port of Liverpool suite on the sixteenth floor of the Atlantic Tower Hotel, and by day in the offices of the Merseyside Urban Development Corporation. His visit included a tense two-hour meeting with the Liverpool 8 Defence Committee and other black leaders from Toxteth, and a bus tour with local business leaders. For the remainder of his time as the environment secretary, Heseltine aimed to visit the region once a week. His influence and restless energy helped push through several major construction projects in Liverpool and in Knowsley, including the building that now houses Granada Television and the 1980s housing in Stockbridge Village.

Lord Scarman, who was asked by the government to report on the causes of the Brixton riot, took the Heseltine view and made several recommendations to improve relations with the police, including positive discrimination. All this was ignored, but the government enshrined in legislation his more punitive recommendations, including the creation of a new offence of 'disorderly conduct', introduced in the 1986 Public Order Act, which was widely seen as an attempt to bring back the notorious 'sus' law under a new name. Under pressure, the government conceded that the law would be written in such a way that the police could arrest someone for 'disorderly conduct' only if they could identify a victim who was harassed or intimidated by the offender's behaviour.[27]

There was one more outbreak of rioting, in 1985, which was also primarily about race. In August, police accidentally shot and killed a five-year-old boy in Birmingham. For two weeks, there was little local reaction until suddenly, in mid-September, as if for no reason, a riot flared in the Handsworth area where local youths fought the police and temporarily drove them out. In London, there was a forewarning of trouble in September when the police raided a house in Brixton, looking for an armed man, Michael Groce. They burst into an upstairs bedroom and shot his mother, Cherry Groce, paralysing her from the waist down. Youths surrounded Brixton police station and went on the rampage for several hours. Michael Groce helped calm them by saying: 'Rioting is not going to get us anywhere. It is just going to make things go on longer. Just let it cool down now and leave it to the legal people.'[28]

Exactly a week after Mrs Groce was shot, the police stopped an unemployed twenty-four-year-old named Floyd Jarrett in a car in Tottenham, north London. They wrongly believed that the car was stolen and went to his parents' home on the Broadwater Farm estate looking for stolen property. His mother, Cynthia, who weighed 20st, was prepared to cooperate, but an argument broke out after another of her sons arrived. An officer pushed Mrs Jarrett, who fell and died of a heart attack. On Sunday afternoon, 6 October 1985, her relatives led a peaceful protest march to Tottenham police station. That evening, there was a public meeting on Broadwater Farm, where Bernie Grant, who had taken office as leader of Haringey Council in April, pleaded for calm but was told, ominously, by someone in the audience that it was 'too late for words'.[29] By 9 p.m. Broadwater Farm was a dangerous place for any outsider, including journalists, two of whom were injured by shotgun pellets. It was especially dangerous for the police: one was shot and seriously injured and, twenty-five minutes later, at around 10.15 p.m., PC Keith Blakelock was surrounded and stabbed to death. While Tory MPs reacted by calling for the restoration of the death penalty, Bernie Grant, who had a notoriously quick temper, told a cheering crowd outside Tottenham town hall on the Tuesday morning: 'The police were to blame for what happened on Sunday night and what they got was a bloody good hiding. There is no way I am going to condemn the actions of the youth on Sunday night.'[30] That outburst immediately turned Grant into Britain's most famous and most reviled black politician, though nothing in his later record suggested that he condoned violence. He empathised with Tottenham's disaffected youth and must have been caught in the emotion of the moment.

Fifteen months after the Tottenham riot, six young men went on trial charged with Blakelock's murder. The leader of the gang was alleged to be Winston Silcott, the child of Seventh Day Adventists from Montserrat, who was on bail at the time, charged with killing a boxer and reputed gangster named Tony Smith. The prosecution presented an atavistic story of rampaging hooligans attempting to cut off the police officer's head to parade it on a pole. Three of the defendants were convicted, but their convictions were subsequently quashed when forensic evidence demonstrated that the police had tampered with the handwritten record of their interrogations, inserting the sections that condemned them.[31] While the others were released, Silcott spent eighteen years in prison for the Smith killing, which he claimed was in self defence.

None of these riots weakened the Conservative government, and those who wanted to improve the circumstances of Britain's ethnic minorities turned to more constructive methods than trashing the places where they lived. The Labour Party suddenly felt the presence of very determined young black activists, especially in London. Patricia Hewitt, the former general secretary of the National Council for Civil Liberties, who had become Neil Kinnock's press secretary in 1983, was lobbied by a group of recently enlisted party members, including Sharon Atkin, a Lambeth councillor, and Diane Abbott. They persuaded her that the way to get around the reluctance of people of black and Asian descent to participate in meetings dominated by whites was for them to form separate black sections, which would be recognized as affiliated organizations entitled to be represented at every level of the party. Hewitt came close to persuading Neil Kinnock of the case, but the whole idea came up against a wall of opposition, not least from established leaders of the Asian communities who had already developed their own ways of operating, almost invisibly, within the party. Labour's deputy leader, Roy Hattersley, became an outspoken opponent of black sections after being lobbied by Asians in his Birmingham constituency. Within a faction-ridden party, it was extremely difficult for anyone to broker a sensible compromise as the argument became more and more heated and polarized.

In June 1985, a way through presented itself when the local party in the safe Labour seat of Brent South drew up a shortlist of potential parliamentary candidates, all of whom were from ethnic minorities. This opened the possibility that there would be a non-white MP in the next Parliament, for the first time in decades. But Brent South also had a black section, which the local party recognized as legitimate, but the national party did not. They were told by party officials that they could select from the shortlist they had drawn up, provided that no delegates from black sections took part in the selection meeting. This set off a furious argument within the black sections. A GLC councillor, Paul Boateng, the son of immigrants from Guyana, became the first black person selected for a safe Labour seat – and would go from there to become Britain's first black cabinet minister – to the sound of a noisy protest meeting outside by Sharon Atkin and comrades from the black sections.[32]

After that breakthrough, Diane Abbott and Bernie Grant were also selected for safe Labour London seats, and Keith Vaz was selected for a winnable seat in Leicester. Even Sharon Atkin found a winnable seat in Nottingham East. In local government, some of those involved in black sections became council leaders in charge of multimillion pound budgets, including Grant in Haringey, and a twenty-seven-year-old woman, Merle Amory, who was briefly leader of Brent Council. When the leader of Lambeth Council, Ted Knight, and other councillors including Atkin, were barred from public office, the new council leader to emerge was Linda Bellos, an articulate convert from Poale Zion (Marxist Zionists) to the black sections, whom Knight and Atkin duly denounced for selling out to the 'white Right'. In April 1987, as a general election loomed, black-section activists held a meeting in Birmingham, at which Atkin rashly accepted an invitation to speak. Under pressure from young blacks who accused her of selling out, she declared: 'I don't give a damn about Neil Kinnock and a racist Labour Party.'[33] The comment was caught on camera. By that evening, Atkin was national news; within days, she was disqualified as a Labour candidate. The person loudest in her defence was Linda Bellos, who went on national news to say: 'The Labour Party is racist . . . It does have within it practices and procedures and even individuals who adhere to and practice racism.'[34] None of this improved

Labour's prospects in the 1987 election. There were two seats, in Lewisham and Nottingham, where the arithmetic suggested Labour would win but the black candidates lost, perhaps because of the Atkin affair. However, the bigger news was that for the first time since the 1920s, blacks and asians – Abbott, Boateng, Grant and Vaz – had made it to the House of Commons.

After the Brixton riots, a lawyer named Rudy Narayan was chosen to head a new Brixton Defence Committee, until the local youths decided that he was too much of an establishment figure and replaced him with the beat poet Linton Kwesi Johnson, who had arrived in Britain from Jamaica in 1963 as an eleven-year-old boy. The poetry that Johnson began publishing early in the 1970s was highly political and drew a bleak picture of the lives of immigrants. Previously, he was known only to those who followed the London reggae scene or read the magazine *Race Today*, but the album he produced in 1981, of poems set to music, reached a bigger audience than before. Its title track was 'Inglan is a Bitch', about the experience of a fifty-five-year-old Jamaican turned on to the dole, who concludes: 'Inglan is a bitch, dere's no escapin' it'. Another poem included in the collection was 'New Crass Fire' which alleged 'di police dem plat an scheme canfuse an canceal'. His main poetry rival was Benjamin Zephaniah, who was brought up in Handsworth and first reached a white audience by persuading Alexei Sayle and other comedians to let him perform his poetry as part of their set. A poem called 'Dis Policemen Keep on Kicking Me to Death' always went down well.

Hanif Kureishi was the first major British-born writer to emerge from any of the ethnic communities. He was born in Bromley, south London, in 1954 to an English mother and a Pakistani immigrant. As the only Asian pupil at David Bowie's old school, he was expected to show a sense of humour when he was called 'Pakistani Pete' or when his contemporaries talked about going Paki-bashing. Yet his works were joyously scandalous and bawdy. In 1985, he posted a film script to Stephen Frears, an established director who had never heard of Kureishi. Scripts sent in by post on spec are normally either ignored or rejected, but Frears read this one and loved it because it portrayed British Asians not as victims but as successful, corrupt and glamorous. He sold the idea to Channel 4 and made the film on a budget of just £600,000, intended just for television. However, it created such a sensation at the Edinburgh Film Festival in August 1985 that it went on release in cinemas around the world.

This was *My Beautiful Laundrette*, the story of an unlikely pair – one a Pakistani, the other a skinhead – who are also old lovers. They run a laundrette together, with Johnny's thick-skulled old skinhead chums and Omar's rich but not virtuous relatives hovering in the background. The critics, who had begun to despair of the British industry's ability to produce a decent full-length film, were bowled over. 'This marvellous comedy of interracial manners . . . has a richness of wit and conception one had despaired of seeing in British movies.'[35]

Whereas Linton Kwesi Johnson saw only social barriers that kept the black man down, Kureishi saw opportunities for adventure and self-advancement in the gaps between communities. The protagonist of his first novel, *The Buddha of Suburbia*, is subjected to gratuitous racist abuse by the father of a white girl, Helen, on whom he is paying a call. However, he manages to continue seeing her on the sly, even enlisting her help when he goes to meet a new arrival from India at the airport, in a borrowed car:

> This was a delicious moment of revenge for me because the Rover belonged to Helen's Dad, Hairy Back. Had he known that four Pakis were resting their black arses on his deep leather seats, ready to be driven by his daughter, who had only recently been fucked by one of them, he wouldn't have been a contented man.[36]

Of all the ethnic and religious minorities, the one that was possibly the most inward-looking and least 'visible' in the early 1980s was Britain's million or so Muslims. During the decade, there were three violent incidents involving terrorists who were Muslim, but they were not British Muslims. One of the strangest episodes opened on 30 April 1980, when a group of gunmen burst into the Iranian embassy in London and seized twenty-six hostages, including PC Trevor Lock and two BBC employees. The gunmen were Arabs from Iran (where Arabs were a subdued minority), who opposed Ayatollah Khomeini's revolutionary government. The Home Office went into its standard, slow procedure for negotiating with hostage-takers. Four hostages were released over the first three days, including a BBC employee, but by Monday, 5 May, which was a bank holiday, the gunmen were exhibiting symptoms of hysteria. They killed the Iranian press attaché, threw his body out of a window and threatened to blow up the building. By now, millions were watching the live television coverage, and less than half an hour later they saw thirty masked SAS men move into action. They heard the screams, the explosions and gun shots, and learnt that nineteen hostages had been rescued, although one had been killed and two injured in the shooting. Five of the six terrorists were killed, but one, Fowzi Nejad, cheated death by posing as a hostage. Nejad then spent twenty-eight years in British prisons; he was spared deportation to Iran, where he was likely to have been put to death.

Within four years, London was to witness another embassy under siege. On 17 April 1984, opponents of Colonel Gaddafi's regime held a demonstration outside the Libyan People's Bureau, watched by a couple of police officers (who happened to be informally engaged). PC Yvonne Fletcher's original application to join the police had been rejected because she was below regulation height, but somehow she had talked her way in, and at five foot four inches she was probably the shortest officer in the country.[37] When someone decided to open fire on the demonstrators from inside the building, one of the bullets found Fletcher and killed her, before her fiancé's eyes. Eleven demonstrators were injured. Armed police then surrounded the embassy, preventing anyone from leaving, while the Libyan government threatened retaliation on Britons all around the world if the building was stormed. For several tense days, the blue tarpaulin that sealed off Charles II Street was London's oddest tourist attraction. The UK broke off diplomatic relations with Libya; the entire staff of the Libyan People's Bureau – including Yvonne Fletcher's unidentified murderer – left the country on 29–30 April, at the same time as the staff of the British embassy left Tripoli.

The worst terrorist incident on British soil occurred on 21 December 1988, when Pan Am Flight 103 was brought down by a bomb, scattering debris across 850 square miles of southern Scotland, most of it on Lockerbie village. All 243 passengers, 16 crew members and 11 people on the ground were killed, a combined death toll of 270. The names of the dead are inscribed on memorial in Dryfesdale cemetery in Lockerbie. The atrocity, inevitably, had political consequences that would last for decades. It helped finish the political career of the then transport secretary, Paul Channon, who made the mistake of flying off on holiday to Mustique for a Christmas break, leaving his deputy, Michael Portillo, to face biting questions in the Commons from Labour's transport spokesman, John Prescott. After Christmas, the Scottish Labour MP Tam Dalyell was alarmed by what a police officer told him about American investigators crowding over the site of the accident. Dalyell became convinced that the crime had been committed by drug-runners from Lebanon or Syria, at the behest of the Iranian government, seeking revenge for the shooting down of an Iranian airliner by a US gunboat, which cost 350 lives. He also believed that the US authorities had known enough to tell senior personnel not to take Pan Am Flight 103, freeing up seats at the last minute for students wanting to get home for Christmas, including twenty-four-year-old Flora Swire, from Bromsgrove, who wanted to be with her American boyfriend.[38]

The US and British governments, however, concluded that the atrocity was committed by Libyans. More than ten years after the bombing, when Libya was seeking to break out of diplomatic isolation, its government handed over two men for trial at an international court in the Netherlands. One was acquitted; the other, a former officer named Abdelbaset Ali Mohmed Al Megrahi, was convicted in January 2001 of 270 murders and sentenced to life imprisonment. He was held in Greenock Prison. The numerous people who believe he was the victim of a miscarriage of justice include Jim Swire, Flora's father, the best-known campaigner on behalf of the bereaved families. The official position of the British government is that Megrahi was properly convicted, but the devolved Scottish administration released him on compassionate grounds on 20 August 2009, after he was diagnosed with terminal cancer and doctors warned that he might have only three months to live.

None of these incidents arose from the religion-driven fanaticism that would soon make its mark in the West, and none involved British citizens as perpetrators. What roused Britain's Muslims to take to the streets for the first time as a religious community was, in fact, a work of fiction.

Salman Rushdie, whose parents were Indian Muslims, moved in circles far removed from Brixton or Handsworth. He was brought to England at the age of thirteen, in 1961, to be put through one of the country's more expensive public schools, Rugby, where he learnt that boys from privileged backgrounds can be incredibly racist. He left Cambridge University hoping to be an actor, gave that up and went into advertising, and is alleged to have been responsible for telling the public that Aero bars were 'irresistabubble' and cream cakes 'naughty but nice'. His second magical realist novel, *Midnight's Children*, published in 1981, won several awards, including the Booker Prize, and on the twenty-fifth anniversary of that prize, in 1993, it was judged to have been the best of all the Bookers.

His fourth novel, *The Satanic Verses*, was published in September 1988. Trouble began when the first copies reached India, the land of Rushdie's birth. It sold out immediately, to the disgust of Syed Shahabuddin, an MP from the opposition Janata Party and a vociferous advocate of Muslim religious rights. He had not read the novel, but had heard about the chapter that retold in fictional form an episode from the life of Mohammed, which he denounced as 'indecent vilification of the Holy Prophet'.[39] As a precaution against the possibility of riots, the Indian government banned the book. Several countries with large Muslim populations followed India's example. Ironically, one of the first countries to ban *The Satanic Verses*, months before the Ayatollah's fatwa, was South Africa, the land of apartheid. In January 1989, after 1,000 Muslims had taken to Bradford's streets and burnt copies of the book, WH Smith withdrew it from the shelves. The next month, after a peaceful demonstration by 3,000 people in Birmingham, a violent one outside the American Cultural Centre in Islamabad and a riot in Kashmir, Ayatollah Khomeini, who had now ruled Iran for ten years, issued his infamous fatwa to Muslims worldwide to kill Rushdie and everyone involved in publishing the novel. The death sentence forced Rushdie to go into hiding for almost ten years, with armed bodyguards watching over him each time he ventured out. He was not harmed, but others were. In July 1991, Ettore Capriolo, the book's sixty-one-year-old Italian translator, was stabbed in his apartment in Milan. He survived, with superficial wounds, but a little over a week later, Hitoshi Igarashi, aged forty-four, an assistant professor of comparative culture who had translated the novel into Japanese, was found stabbed to death in a hallway in Tsukuba University in Ibaraki, Japan.[40]

In Britain, Salman Rushdie stirred up a mixed pot of reactions. As a well-established member of the country's liberal, literary elite, he drew hostility from people who would normally be expected to be militantly supporting anyone who was under attack from radical Muslims. One of the most vitriolic pieces written about the author, when he was in hiding in fear of his life, was by Norman Tebbit, former chairman of the Conservative Party, who called him 'an outstanding villain', whose 'public life has been a record of despicable acts of betrayal of his upbringing, religion, adopted home and nationality'.[41] And yet, it was the Conservative government that unhesitatingly broke off diplomatic relations with Iran and provided Rushdie with round-the-clock protection, while one of the biggest anti-Rushdie demonstrations, by thousands of Muslims who marched through Leicester in March 1989, was led by the recently elected Labour MP, Keith Vaz, who called for the novel to be banned.

The Rushdie case was the first example of a dilemma that the British Left has still not satisfactorily resolved, twenty years later. Late in 1989, the Commission for Racial Equality and the Policy Studies Institute, a liberal think tank, organized a series of seminars to discuss the Rushdie affair. They did not invite the feminist writer Fay Weldon, whose publicly declared view was that burning and banning books was intolerable, whoever was doing it; but they did invite Shabir Akhtar, a Cambridge graduate in philosophy, who called for a 'negotiated compromise' that would 'protect Muslim sensibilities against gratuitous provocation'. The correspondent from the *Independent* wrote: 'We are witnessing, I fear, the birth of a new and dangerously illiberal "liberal" orthodoxy designed to accommodate Dr Akhtar and his fundamentalist friends.'[42] Rushdie's friend, the journalist Christopher Hitchens, later remarked:

> Most bizarre of all, though, was the noise by a number of eminent writers and authors. John le Carré, John Berger, Roald Dahl, Hugh Trevor-Roper, and others began a sort of auction of defamation in which they accused Rushdie variously of insulting Islam, practising Western-style cultural colonialism and condescension, and damaging race relations.[43]

At the start of the 1980s, it was common to hear speakers within the left-dominated sections of the Labour Party, and other left-wing elements, group together women, blacks and gays as common victims of discrimination by a society controlled by white heterosexual males. If there was, for instance, a Jamaican male at the meeting, he might object, but his objection would be politely overruled. The same people who campaigned against discrimination were also keen defenders of free speech until, in the anti-Rushdie demonstrations, the Left was faced by a movement that was anti-western, anti-capitalist, self-organized, rooted in the ethnic minorities, and yet illiberal, intolerant and male-dominated. The 'rainbow coalition' of downtrodden minorities that politicians such as Ken Livingstone hoped to assemble as a force for change became a chimera. The Left was left not knowing whether to defend free speech and cultural differences.

At the end of the 1980s, voices from left and right could be heard implying that race relations were no better than they had been ten years earlier. 'It is a common fallacy among Americans to believe Europeans are nicer than Americans and more liberal than Americans,' Diane Abbott told a conference of the National Council for Black Studies in Philadelphia in April 1989. 'Far from Britain being a nicer and more liberal society, the British invented racism. They built an empire on which racism was the organizing principle. I believe Britain is one of the most fundamentally racist nations on earth.'

At the opposite end of the political spectrum, Christopher Gill, newly elected Conservative MP for Ludlow, complained in July 1988 that whites 'resent the fact that they are almost exiles in their own country because of the way in which the characters of our towns and cities have been altered by successive government policies on immigration'.[44] As Norman Tebbit surveyed the mixed crowds at cricket matches, cheering England, India, Pakistan or the West Indies according to choice, he formulated his famous cricket test. 'Which side do they cheer for?', he asked the *Los Angeles Times* in April 1990. 'It's an interesting test. Are you still harking back to where you came from, or where you are? And I think we've got real problems in that regard.'[45]

However, immigration was not the issue it had once been, even on the right wing of the Conservative Party, where they were now more concerned about the threat they believed that the EU posed to British sovereignty. The Monday Club had not changed, but its influence was now minimal. During the Conservative annual conference in October 1989, the Monday Club put round a leaflet with a drawing showing immigrants pouring out of a dustbin, only to be denounced by the local government minister, David Hunt, for spreading 'poisonous passions'.[46] The political classes had turned against such overt expressions of hostility towards the ethnic minorities. Within weeks of John Major becoming prime minister, the new party chairman, Chris Patten, set his sights on ensuring that at least one black Tory MP would be elected next time. When the apparently safe Tory seat of Cheltenham became vacant in December 1990, the local association was presented with a shortlist containing only one name, that of John Taylor, a black lawyer from Birmingham. Sadly, Patten had misjudged the temper of the local party. There was a public revolt by association members who objected to having an outsider imposed on them. One of them, Bill Galbraith, a well-known figure in Cheltenham, was expelled from the Conservative Party for calling the new candidate 'a bloody nigger'.[47] The damage caused the Tories to lose the seat to a Liberal Democrat.

John Taylor was by no means the only black or Asian to break into a white-dominated profession only to find that he was not universally welcome there. The Metropolitan Police spent over £1m in the 1980s advertising for black and Asian recruits, with the result their number rose from 110 in 1980 to 467, or fewer than 2 per cent of the total, in 1990. In November 1990, noting that the speed at which black recruits dropped out was three times higher than whites, Scotland Yard sent out a memo to all its officers warning them that racist jokes and other 'insensitive' behaviour was making these rare black officers feel isolated and demotivated.[48] There was a similar problem in the armed forces, highlighted in a report published in January 1990 by the consultancy Peat Marwick McLintock, which stated that 'racially offensive views and language exist in all ranks of the services'.[49] In 1989, the Commission for Racial Equality issued a similar warning about the rarity of non-white teachers in state schools. They feared that young blacks were put off teaching as a profession while still at school, by hearing fellow pupils directing racist taunts at black teachers. One of the most visible advances made by Afro-Caribbeans during the 1980s was in professional football. In 1975, twelve out of fourteen managers of First Division clubs responded to a survey by saying they would never sign up a black player; by 1990, there were 175 blacks among the top 2,000 professional footballers.[50] However, they routinely endured racist abuse from the supporters of opposing clubs, symbolized by a famous photograph of John Barnes in full Liverpool kit back-heeling a banana that had been thrown at him by an Everton fan.

Yet, for all these problems, the glass ceilings were beginning to crack. There were signs that positions previously occupied only by whites were starting to come within reach. The first Asian judge, Mota Singh, was appointed in 1982. In 1988, John Roberts, from Sierra Leone, became Britain's first Afro-Caribbean QC. He had been a part-time Crown Court judge since 1983. In 1989, Gurbux Singh, from Wolverhampton, became chief executive of Haringey Council. As the decade drew to a close, officialdom agonized over whether or not to risk including a question on ethnic background in the census they were preparing, which would be held in 1991. The Home Office tried some focus group tests and discovered that only 1 per cent of those from ethnic minorities refused to fill in a questionnaire that asked them their racial background. The vast majority wanted accurate statistics about Britain's racial mix made available because, far from fearing that it would be used by racists, they believed it would be a tool for combating discrimination. It was a sign, according to specialists in the field, that 'the minority groups are better integrated and more prepared to fight for the elimination of discrimination'.[51]

Chapter 6

Islands in the Fog

Amid the mountainous waves and freezing fogs of the South Atlantic, 8,000 miles from Great Britain, is a cluster of about 100 small islands known to European sailors since the sixteenth century, but avoided because of their treacherous shallows and jutting rocks. 'The islands are empty, bleak, desolate, inhospitable. I never saw a single tree,'[1] a visiting soldier recalled. It was no-man's-land until 1833, when English settlers made their permanent home on the main island, which they called East Falkland.

In 1980, the total human population of all the islands was 1,813, more than half of whom lived in Port Stanley on the eastern tip of East Falkland. The other 800 or so lived on scattered farms where they raised about half a million sheep. Sheep-rearing was the only profitable activity on the islands, and the only market for Falklands wool and hides was Britain. In 1980, exports came to £2.8m; the budget of the Falkland Islands government that year was just under £2.3m.[2] Most of the inhabitants had been born on the islands, with little prospect that they would ever leave, even for a holiday. A boat left Port Stanley for Tilbury Docks in London once every three months, and there were occasional flights by light aircraft to Buenos Aires. Otherwise, contact with the outside world was by radio, which worked when the weather was good. Girls born on the islands looked to the small British garrison for husbands who could take them away, although the islands could not afford to lose anyone. The population fell by at least a hundred in 1980 alone.[3] At that rate, the islands would have been emptied of their human inhabitants before the end of the century. Almost every adult on the islands was employed either by the Falklands administration or by the Falkland Islands Company (FIC), which owned most of the arable land. The FIC was itself an asset on the books of one multinational company after another. In 1982, it was a subsidiary of the coal company, Charringtons. The farms that were not owned by FIC belonged to nine other absentee landlords, all residing in Britain. This left no scope for enterprise or self-advancement for the islanders, with predictable effect on their morale. In 1978, Major Ewen Southby-Taylor, the officer commanding the small marine detachment on the islands, thought that the majority of the islanders were 'a drunken, decadent, immoral and indolent collection of dropouts'.[4]

Indolent they may have been, but they were defiantly British. Unlike the English and Welsh settlers on mainland Argentina, the Falkland islanders acknowledged no affinity with the South American continent. They wanted only to speak English and to be ruled by a governor appointed from London. However, the British claim to the islands, which were classed as a 'dependency', had never been sanctioned in any international agreement. The Treaty of Utrecht, of 1713, assigned them to Spain. When Argentina obtained independence from Spain, its government considered that they had also inherited 'Las Malvinas'. They appointed a governor, but he became embroiled in a violent conflict with American seal hunters. The Argentine government sent a warship to restore order, but it was intercepted by two warships from London. Having arrived in January 1833, the British never left, while the Argentinians never ceased to claim that the islands were theirs.

The Foreign Office maintained a sneaking suspicion that the Argentine claim was, to quote an internal memo written in 1910, 'not altogether unjustified' and that the British occupation in 1833 had been, to quote another memo dated 1946, an 'act of unjustified aggression'.[5] In the 1930s, thought was given to recognizing Argentine's sovereignty in return for a 'lease-back' deal that would keep the islanders under British rule. Negotiations began when Argentina raised the issue with the United Nations in 1965, and dragged on inconclusively. In 1977, when it appeared that Argentina had lost patience and might resort to force, the Labour government quietly dispatched a nuclear submarine and two frigates to deter them.

Negotiations resumed, but had got nowhere when, in 1979, responsibility passed to a newly appointed minister of state at the Foreign Office, Nicholas Ridley. He was not interested in foreign affairs. Mrs Thatcher had placed him there as a counterweight to Lord Carrington, the foreign secretary, and his deputy, Ian Gilmour, who were both in the aristocratic One Nation Tory tradition she so distrusted. Ridley, too, was an old Etonian and the brother of an earl, but unusually for someone of that background, he was also a Thatcherite, whose loyalty to her never wavered. He was also the last British minister to attempt to resolve the Falklands issue. He twice made the 16,000-mile round trip to Port Stanley, hoping to persuade the islanders of the merits of a lease-back deal. They were not persuaded, and neither was Margaret Thatcher, who had already had enough grief from the Tory right over allowing Rhodesia to become Zimbabwe, but Ridley bravely insisted on putting the idea to the Commons in December 1980. The result was a display of the Commons at its self-righteous worst. MPs from the Labour Party, the Liberals and the Tory right, fired up by an efficient lobbying campaign paid for by the Falkland Islands Company, combined to give Ridley the kind of parliamentary roasting that could have destroyed a minister's career. To one Tory MP, Sir Bernard Braine, the very idea of conceding sovereignty was 'an insult to the Falkland islanders'; another, Julian Amery, called it 'profoundly disturbing'; and it caused 'grave disquiet' in the breast of the aristocratic Viscount Cranborne. Another Tory, John Farr, experienced such 'intense dissatisfaction' that he announced that he was going to force a second debate a few days later. Opposition MPs were every bit as indignant. 'Why can't you leave the matter alone?', the former Labour cabinet member Douglas Jay demanded, instead of concocting what a Liberal, Russell Johnson, described as 'shameful schemes for getting rid of these islands'.[6]

South America at that time was a playground for military dictators, and of all the murderous and unstable regimes in the continent, Argentina's was one of the worst. The country had been under direct military rule since March 1976, when President Isabel Perón, third wife and widow of Juan Perón, was bundled off to exile in Spain. Even before that coup, Marxist revolutionaries, union organizers and other left-wing activists had begun 'disappearing' without trace. In 1979, Amnesty International calculated that the number of '*desaparecidos*' abducted, tortured and possibly killed by government agents in four years could be as high as 15,000. This grisly operation seems to have begun with the tacit approval of Washington, where the Republican administration certainly believed that a military takeover was preferable to a Marxist revolution; but Democrat President Jimmy Carter, who took office in 1977, was more particular about human rights. By 1979, the junta felt the need to try to improve its international image by releasing some prisoners and reducing the rate at which new victims disappeared. It also supplied bookshops across Europe with complimentary copies of a book called *The Strategists of Fear*, by a well-known French historian and anti-communist, Pierre de Villemarest, which attributed Argentina's bad reputation to poison being spread by rich Jews living in Buenos Aires, aided by their co-religionists in Europe and their contacts in the White House.[7]

In 1981, this much criticized regime suddenly found itself back in the sunlight because Ronald Reagan had taken office in Washington. His foreign policy adviser during the election had been Jeane Kirkpatrick, author of a theory that differentiated between 'totalitarian' and 'authoritarian' dictatorships according to whether they interfered with or permitted free enterprise. Whereas the Nicaraguan government was totalitarian, the Argentina junta was merely authoritarian. Relations between Buenos Aires and Washington were suddenly so good that there was talk of Argentina being the first South American government to supply troops to fight insurgents in El Salvador.

Also in 1981, the British made two announcements the significance of which was over-interpreted in Buenos Aires. Going against advice from the Foreign Office, John Nott, the defence secretary, decided as an economic measure to scrap the only naval ship patrolling the South Atlantic. At about the same time Home Secretary William Whitelaw introduced an immigration bill to prevent the residents of Hong Kong from flooding into Britain as the colony prepared to be returned to Chinese rule, which also incidentally deprived 800 Falkland islanders of their British citizenship. Each minister had his reasons independent of the Argentine claim over the Falklands, but in Buenos Aires it seemed that Britain had lost interest in its South Atlantic dependency, especially when British MPs who visited Argentina showed less interest in the islands than in helping to re-equip the Argentine navy, which of all the branches of the Argentine military was the one pushing hardest for the recovery of Las Malvinas. Back in England, the Tory MP Neville Trotter indicated to his local newspaper that there might be work for the Tyne shipyards building warships for Argentina. He declared, 'The Navy are very pro-British. They have a British atmosphere.'[8]

On December 1981, Argentina swapped one military junta for another, headed by General Leopoldo Galtieri. The head of the navy, Admiral Jorge Anaya, gave his support on condition that the junta reclaim the Falklands, by diplomacy or by force, before the 150th anniversary of the British occupation. Talks between British and Argentinian diplomats resumed in New York. In March 1982, a group of Argentinian scrap-metal dealers landed on South Georgia, an island 800 miles southeast of the Falklands, which Argentina also considered to be part of its sovereign territory. The dealers had a contract from a Scottish firm to clear away scrap whaling material littering the island. They raised the Argentine flag, refused to observe the normal courtesy of contacting the island's chief magistrate, and generally behaved as if they were on home soil. The British government decided that military intervention was required. HMS *Endurance*, which was supposedly on its last voyage, was dispatched from Port Stanley, with thirteen Royal Marines and nine men from the Falklands garrison, and reached South Georgia's main settlement, Grytviken, on 24 March. A week later, having seen off the scrap-metal dealers, the ship headed back towards Port Stanley, and so was in neither one place nor the other, but uselessly at sea, when Argentinian troops landed on the Falklands. The junta had not intended to launch its attack yet, but fearing that the precipitous action of the scrap-metal dealers would have alerted the British, they brought forward the date.

On Wednesday evening, 31 March, John Nott was disturbed in his Commons office by the breathless arrival of intelligence officers bearing intercepted messages that showed that the Argentine navy was at sea, heading for the Falklands. Nott went straight along the corridor to Margaret Thatcher's room, where a meeting was convened with civil servants and two junior foreign ministers. After what had happened to Ridley, Thatcher knew that she could expect a very rough reception from the Commons if, as feared, the Argentinian troops were disembarked on East Falkland, but no one in the room had a sensible suggestion as to what she could do next, other than ring Ronald Reagan.

That might have been all that resulted from the indecisive meeting in Mrs Thatcher's Commons office had a messenger not looked in to announce that there was an admiral in full dress-uniform in the corridor. It was First Sea Lord and Chief of Naval Staff, Sir Henry Leach, or 'First' as he was known, who had scuttled over to Parliament hoping to speak to the prime minister. He had been held up by a policeman in the central lobby and might have got no further had a government whip not passed by and stopped to ask why he was sitting alone on a bench in the corner. 'First' was on a mission. His life had been devoted to the Royal Navy, and now that he was senior enough to have to deal with politicians, he judged them solely by their commitment to the senior service. Francis Pym, Thatcher's first defence secretary, had ruined his relationship with her by opposing all cuts in the defence budget, but had still not been nearly zealous enough to satisfy Sir Henry. When Sir Henry's secretary informed him that Pym had been shifted sideways and replaced by John Nott, in January 1981, Sir Henry's response, recorded in his memoirs, was: '"Well," I replied, "at present we have a charming man but one for whom decision making does not seem to come easily. I know nothing about Nott, but it must be a change for the better." How wrong I was.'[9]

Sir Henry was not the only senior naval officer who had learnt to despise Nott. The Second Sea Lord Admiral Cassidi, would not speak to him but 'just scowled'; the Vice-Chief of Naval Staff Admiral Staveley talked to him often enough, but Nott thought he was stupid.[10] Rear Admiral Sandy Woodward, who would command the Falklands battle group, thought that 'John Nott possessed the cold heart of the career banker.'[11] Right-wing Tory MPs agreed. Alan Clark spluttered in his diary about 'that fucking idiot Nott, and his spastic "Command Paper" which is effectively running down the entire Royal Navy to keep the soldiers in Rhine Army happy'.[12]

The admirals, obviously, loved their impressive, expensive ships that patrolled the surface of the sea, whereas Nott, like Ridley, was an unsentimental Thatcherite, and a banker, looking for the most cost-effective way to defend the UK. The only war in which he could envisage the Royal Navy being involved was against the Soviet Union. Surface ships were vulnerable to Soviet submarines and, in Nott's estimation, they were the least cost-effective weaponry the services possessed. There was also the book-keeping question of how to account for Trident. Nott reckoned that since Trident was carried in submarines the entire cost should come out of the navy's budget. The navy called him the 'hatchet man' and briefed against him to any journalist who would listen, including Hugo Young of the *Sunday Times,* who wrote: 'In more reflective moments, First would muse, "I don't think I actually hate John Nott – but then perhaps I am not a hater."'[13]

Now Sir Henry had a chance to get his own back. A war in the Falklands would have to be fought with surface ships; it was exactly the sort of operation that would be rendered impossible when Nott's economies came into effect. Once admitted to Mrs Thatcher's room, Sir Henry told her that in forty-eight hours he could assemble a task force large enough to take on the Argentinian navy. He also exceeded his authority by telling her that they not only could retake the islands but, in his view, they should. It was the sort of talk she wanted to hear. 'Margaret, very much an impressionable lady, was always impressed by men in uniform,' Nott claimed, in his account of the meeting.[14] First was given the go-ahead.

Before dawn on Friday, 2 April, the Falkland islanders had a noisy awakening. One recalled:

> From the front window we could see an awe-inspiring stream of tracer shells arcing from somewhere in the harbour. Shouting, screaming and the sound of machine gun fire permeated the crisp air. The Royal Marines were having a hell of a battle at Government House. The radio

> once again crackled into life. Argentines had manned the studio and waved their guns. Suddenly, edicts were being read by the Argentines: 'We want no bloodshed' etc. Too late . . . The time flew by. As suddenly as it began it was all over. The marines and Falklands Islands Defence Force volunteers had been rounded up. The governor had surrendered and later was deported with his family. Huge Argentine navy vessels anchored triumphantly in the harbour, busy unloading men and seemingly endless supplies of dust-coloured Mercedes Benz military vehicles . . . The roads hadn't seen so much traffic.[15]

In London, the Foreign Office waited anxiously for news, but heard nothing. At 11 a.m., a minister assured the House of Commons that the invasion had not begun, when in fact it had, but bad weather had prevented the radio message from Port Stanley from getting through until the captain of a vessel carrying out a survey in the Antarctic picked up a ham radio broadcast from one of the islanders, and passed the message to the Foreign Office. The diplomats' first reaction was to downplay the crisis. They were concerned that if the British government overreacted someone might be killed, that there might be repercussions for British expatriates in Argentina or that there would be damage to Britain's position internationally. This was consistent with the fears felt by some of the islanders, such as Jim Burgess, a carpenter from Port Stanley, who told *The Times*: 'There will be a bloodbath here if the navy tries to recapture Stanley. If they try to take Stanley, they will destroy Stanley. Everything is made of wood here. Half a dozen fires and a good wind and the town will be gone for ever.'[16] But such words of caution were to be ignored. The tone was not set by the people who understood the problem but by the House of Commons, which met for a three-hour emergency session the following morning.

For MPs to be called back from their constituencies on a Saturday morning is rare indeed. The last time had been on 3 November 1956, during the Suez crisis. The very fact of being back in Parliament on this unusual day created a sense of momentous crisis reminiscent of the national humiliation Britain had suffered during Suez. The competition among the tabloids to out-jingo one another had already begun, with the Labour-voting *Daily Star* taking an early lead. 'Britain must go into the Falkland Islands now and throw the invading Argentinians into the sea' was the opening paragraph of its editorial.[17] The *Sun* was the first to raise the possibility of a nuclear strike on Argentina – in a report stating that there had been a spontaneous demonstration outside the Argentine embassy in London by youths singing 'Don't Cry for Me Argentina, We're going to Nuke You'.

For Margaret Thatcher, that Saturday Commons debate was 'the most difficult [she] ever had to face'.[18] For Michael Foot and other opposition politicians, it was an opportunity. After eighteen miserable months leading a divided, fractious Labour Party, Foot at last had an opening to reprise the role he had played when he was young: excoriating the Tories for appeasing fascist dictators. He declared:

> The people of the Falkland Islands have the absolute right to look at us at this moment of their desperate plight, just as they have looked to us over the past 150 years. They are faced with an act of naked, unqualified aggression, carried out in the most shameful and disreputable circumstances. Any guarantee from this invading force is utterly worthless.

The islanders had been betrayed, he said, and words were insufficient to absolve the government of the charge of betrayal; it required deeds.[19]

With hindsight, this was one of the most foolish speeches Foot ever made, but at the moment of delivery, it seemed to be his finest hour, perhaps the one occasion when he looked like a leader who could truly lead the nation. The next speaker, Edward du Cann, an eminent Tory MP who chaired the highly powerful 1922 Committee, thanked Foot for the way 'he spoke for us all'. Alan Clark thought that Foot was 'excellent', in contrast to 'poor old Notters', who 'stammered and stuttered and gabbled, faltered and fluttered and fumbled . . . against a constant roaring of disapproval and contempt'.[20] At the end of the three-hour debate, Labour's defence spokesman, John Silkin, in a slip of the tongue, referred to Michael Foot as 'the leader of the nation'; when barracked, he remarked with utter confidence, 'he soon will be'.[21]

The 'debate' was almost over before the Speaker called anyone who dissented from the general belligerence. The first note of caution came from a Conservative MP named Raymond Whitney, a former diplomat and chairman of the backbench committee on foreign affairs, who suggested that being led by the attitudes of tabloid writers and 'the people in the pubs' was not always the highest form of courage, an inference that outraged his fellow Conservatives. He was interrupted no fewer than six times in a ten-minute speech, each time by a right-wing Tory. When he refused to give way to any more, John Biggs-Davison, the MP for Epping Forest, rose to demand of the Speaker: 'If defeatism of this kind is to be spoken, should it not be done in secret session?' Struggling to be heard above the commotion, Whitney replied: 'It's not a question of defeatism – it is a question of realism.'[22] Whitney, incidentally, was also on the right of the Tory party; he thought that CND was run by Communists and believed in good relations with anti-Communist regimes.

After that lead from the Commons, it was no surprise that the first opinion poll, broadcast by ITV on the Monday night, 5 April, showed that 70 per cent of the public thought the distant islands worth fighting for, even if that meant sinking Argentine ships and putting British lives at risk. Only 5 per cent thought they were no concern of Britain.[23] A quarter thought that Margaret Thatcher should have resigned, but that was hardly surprising, given her general unpopularity. For the present, her position was secure, which was more than could be said for either Minster of Defence John Nott or Foreign Secretary Lord Carrington, who were identified by the *Daily Express* as the 'guilty men'. Carrington and the department he headed came in for particularly ferocious attack. 'If he has not the grace to resign, she should sack him,' said the *Daily Mail.* Both ministers offered Thatcher their resignations. She prevailed upon Nott to stay, but Carrington did not need the job; he was the sixth baron in his line and a landowner, Humphrey Lyttleton had been his fag at Eton; and he was fed up with being traduced for something that was not his fault. 'I have been responsible for the conduct of the policy; I think it is right that I resign,' he informed Thatcher, by letter. Two junior foreign ministers who could less afford to lose their positions went with him. The *Sun* celebrated their departure with an editorial that took up a whole page attacking the Foreign Office as a 'nest of appeasers', but James Reston, of the *New York Times,* observed, with more wit: 'The British are not very good at holding their empire together, but at least their officials know what to do when they let the side down; they resign in style and retire to their houses in the country.'[24]

Carrington's departure took some of the political pressure off Thatcher and seemed to sober up the Labour Party front bench. Having goaded Thatcher into going to war, they now woke up to the possibility that she might do just that – and that people would die. The *Daily Mirror* argued consistently, from the day the task force set sail, that the islands were not worth fighting for and that the islanders could be paid to settle somewhere else. The Labour Left took the same line, with Tony Benn, in particular, arguing forcefully for the recall of the task force. When the Commons debated the Falklands again on the Monday, Denis Healey argued so insistently for a negotiated solution that the right-wing Labour MP Bob Mellish wanted to know what he was proposing the task force should do if it reached the Falklands before a settlement had been agreed – should it turn around and go home? He did not get a straight answer.[25]

As the task force made its slow way to the South Atlantic, the US administration made strenuous efforts to resolve the conflict between its two allies. The US Secretary of State Al Haig flew thousands of miles in every direction trying to find a means to prevent war. If American diplomacy had taken its normal course, it would have tilted in favour of the Argentinians. Successful US governments from Franklin Roosevelt onwards had treated the former British Empire as an anachronism that was not worth defending. The Reagan administration would demonstrate this the following year by sending US marines to overthrow the Marxist government of Grenada, in October 1983, without troubling to consult the British government, although Grenada was a former British colony and a member of the Commonwealth. The first priority of US foreign policy during the Reagan era was to eradicate or contain any left-wing movements in Central or South America, and in this struggle the Argentine junta was a valuable ally. As Argentinian troop-ships were heading towards the Falklands, Jeane Kilpatrick, now the US Ambassador to the United Nations, had dinner with her opposite number from Argentina, and did not mention the Falklands. From this the junta naturally deduced that the Americans were not interested in a quarrel over some sparsely inhabited South Atlantic islands. They were shocked to discover that they were wrong when Ronald Reagan, having been spoken to by Margaret Thatcher, phoned Galtieri, but by then it was too late to call off the invasion without a serious loss of face.

On 24 April, the day that the task force reached South Georgia, Haig found a peace formula acceptable to the new British foreign secretary, Francis Pym, who went back to London to put the Haig formula to Mrs Thatcher. Pym had been placed in this sensitive position because he was the only available cabinet minister with adequate experience of foreign affairs, and not because Mrs Thatcher trusted him. Only the previous year, she had demoted him from the post of defence secretary for arguing with her over the defence budget. When she heard what Pym and Haig had agreed, she refused to countenance it because the agreement would have given Argentine citizens the right to settle and acquire property on the islands, making it inevitable that they would eventually outnumber the Britons. Pym and Thatcher took their differences to the war cabinet. She did not say so then, but she had decided that if the decision went against her she would resign.[26] That was never likely. The other war cabinet members were Nott, Whitelaw and Thatcher's new protégé Cecil Parkinson, none of whom was going to cross her on a matter of such importance. Parkinson's inclusion was a significant pointer. He was the chairman of the Conservative Party, in charge of planning how to win the next election. The chancellor, Sir Geoffrey Howe, a far more senior figure, was excluded. In this crisis, no attention would be paid to expense, but minute care would be taken over the interests of the Tory party.

On 25 April, South Georgia was retaken without a shot being fired, a small success that produced one of the most memorable images of the war, when Thatcher and Nott stepped out of Downing Street to announce the good news. Irritated by the reaction of journalists, who were more interested in whether a war was about to begin than in the recapture of a barely inhabited island, Thatcher told them: 'Just rejoice at that news and congratulate our forces and the marines.'[27] For the rest of the war, the nation still seemed to hear that voice ringing in their ears, ordering them to rejoice.

At the end of April, Ronald Reagan called a halt to Haig's shuttle diplomacy and declared the USA's support for Britain. He introduced sanctions against Argentina, while Britain unilaterally imposed a Total Exclusion Zone (TEZ) for 200 miles around the Falklands, warning that any Argentine vessel or aircraft inside the zone would be attacked. On Saturday, 1 May, Port Stanley was given a deafening awakening, when twenty 1,000 lb bombs fell out of the sky, from an altitude of 10,000 feet, smashing the runway to pieces. They were dropped by a Vulcan bomber that had made a 7,860-mile round trip from Ascension, a journey that required repeated refuelling in flight. On the same day, a dozen Sea Harriers took off from a nearby aircraft carrier to attack Argentinian planes. An unknown number of Argentinian pilots and ground staff died that day, including Captain García Cuerva, who skilfully flew his damaged aircraft back to Port Stanley, only to be shot down and killed by Argentinian ground troops who thought his plane was a Harrier.

Out at sea, Admiral Woodward was nervously aware that the Argentinians were on both sides of him: the land forces on the islands and, out at sea, a battleship and two destroyers. It was an old US battleship that had come out of Pearl Harbour undamaged, and had been bought by the Argentine navy in 1951 and renamed the *General Belgrano*. The *Belgrano* was outside the TEZ, but Woodward sent an urgent message to London, requesting that the orders be amended so that the HMS *Conqueror*, a submarine that was tracking the ship, could sink it. The war cabinet, meeting at Chequers at 10 a.m. on 2 May, agreed. That evening, HMS *Conqueror* fired three torpedoes at its quarry, at close range, and escaped before the accompanying destroyers could retaliate.

News of the *Belgrano*'s destruction inspired the most infamous newspaper headline of the campaign, when the *Sun*, frantically competing to be 'the paper that supports our boys', ran a single word in huge type: 'GOTCHA!'[28] At that time, the newspaper was being brought out by a small number of executives, during a journalists' strike. As they saw the enormity of the possible death toll, which could have been as high as 1,200 (it was in fact 323, after hundreds of survivors had been rescued by Argentine ships), the newspaper's editor, Kelvin MacKenzie, had second thoughts and wanted to pull the headline, but Rupert Murdoch liked it and it stayed.[29]

The sinking of the *Belgrano* became the single most controversial incident of the war. It transpired that not only were the *Belgrano* and its accompanying destroyers outside the exclusion zone, they were sailing west, back to Argentina, having been withdrawn from action. The ship's commander, Captain Hector Bonza, clearly had no idea that his ship was under any threat. Even some of the task force officers wondered if the action was justified. The commander of HMS *Coventry*, Captain David Hart-Dyke said: 'I feared that our action had been politically damaging. By sinking it, we had risked losing much of the international support which London had been working so hard to win on the diplomatic front.'[30]

The previous day, Fernando Belaúnde Terry, the president of Peru, had suggested to Haig a possible compromise that involved the Argentinians withdrawing from the islands so that negotiations could begin over their long-term status, but that initiative sank with the *Belgrano*. The Labour MP Tam Dalyell suspected that Thatcher gave the order to fire precisely because she wanted a war; he would spend years pursuing the issue remorselessly. Mrs Thatcher's most uncomfortable moment during the next general election came when she faced questions about the *Belgrano* from Diana Gould, a grey-haired geography teacher from Cirencester, during a live televised phone-in programme. Thatcher was asked why she had given the order to sink the ship when it was sailing away from the Falklands. Her immediate reaction was to deny that it was sailing away, but Mrs Gould had the precise coordinates to hand and refused to let her get away with it. Sue Lawley, who was moderating the programme, said that afterwards Thatcher was 'white with fury'.

Argentine retaliation came quickly. On 4 May, three destroyers named after British cities – *Coventry*, *Glasgow* and *Sheffield* – were on picket duty in the dangerous waters between the task force and the Argentine air force when the seaman who was watching the radar screen aboard HMS *Glasgow* sounded a warning that he had picked up two blips that appeared to be enemy aircraft. The *Glasgow* sent up chaff – a huge cloud of radar-reflective metal bric-à-brac that fills an area larger than the ship, in the hope of fooling either the pilot or his missile. It was unnecessary; after a few anxious minutes they knew that the missile fired from the aircraft was not aimed at them.

Aboard HMS *Sheffield* Captain Sam Salt was in his cabin, not the operations room. The *Sheffield* did not see the blips on the radar and did not send up chaff. Two lieutenants up on the bridge saw a trail of smoke six feet above the water, about a mile away, heading in their direction at 700 miles per hour. Five seconds later, the *Sheffield* became the first British ship torpedoed by an enemy since the Second World War, as an Exocet ripped a hole measuring four feet by fifteen feet in its starboard side, just above the waterline; twenty-one men were killed and twenty-four injured.

By the end of that day, the BBC had picked up rumours in London that a British ship had been hit, but could not get confirmation before the start of the *Nine O'Clock News*. Suddenly, in the middle of that bulletin, they cut live to the Ministry of Defence press room, where Ian McDonald, the acting head of public relations, was sitting at a desk like a newscaster. The war had turned McDonald into a familiar figure through the televised briefings that he read out. He had no training in dealing with cameras, but someone had advised him to speak slowly, and he did – very, very slowly. It was said that he was the first person ever to speak in Braille. Viewers found his lumbering amateurishness reassuring. On this occasion, live in front of 12m viewers, McDonald was so nervous that it was touch and go whether or not he would get through the announcement, but with a struggle he revealed that the crew of HMS *Sheffield* had been forced to abandon ship. It was not known how many casualties there were. The author Robert Harris recalled:

> It was a dramatic piece of television – the sombre, dark-suited McDonald with his funereal parody of an announcer's voice . . . The news was heard simultaneously all over the country: by the wives and families of men who had been on board the *Sheffield*, by fellow naval officers in the wardroom at Davenport, where McDonald's statement was greeted by a stunned silence followed by swearwords, and by MPs at the Palace of Westminster.[31]

In the Cavalry Club in London, Admiral Woodward's wife was dining with relatives when she noticed a waiter moving quietly from table to table, spreading the news. Charlotte Woodward declared, 'As from that moment, I rather stopped regarding the Argentinian navy as something out of Gilbert and Sullivan.'[32]

The whole affair had seemed more like a comic opera than a war, particularly in the first three weeks, when the task force was on its way south but nothing appeared to be happening. The mood was captured by a cover of

Private Eye in which Nott was depicted giving Admiral Lewin his battle orders: 'We launch a surprise attack, in three weeks' time.'[33] The *Sun*, which had a correspondent aboard the HMS *Invincible*, offered its readers invincible knickers. They sold so well that the paper was soon reporting: 'We've already said knickers to the Argies. Now its Garters to those Tartars.'[34] As the death toll began, the joviality ended and opinion polarized. On the home front, a hunt began for traitors. Very soon, the BBC was in the firing line. As the first reports of casualties came through, a BBC defence correspondent, Peter Snow, reported on *Newsnight* that the British and Argentinian governments were giving conflicting figures, and added that 'until the British are demonstrated either to be deceiving us or to be concealing losses' their version should be believed. John Page, a Tory MP and former artillery officer, heard this comment and denounced it as 'almost treasonable'.[35] A few days later, on 6 May, he intervened at Prime Minister's Questions in the Commons to invite Mrs Thatcher to join him in his condemnation of the BBC. She replied: 'I understand that there are occasions when some commentators will say that the Argentines did something and then "the British" did something. I can only say that if this is so it gives offence and causes great emotion'.[36]

Early the following week, the BBC ran a short film on *Panorama* by the journalist Michael Cockerell, who had interviewed two Labour and two Conservative MPs opposed to the war. The switchboard was overwhelmed by calls from angry viewers. Tory MPs tabled a Commons motion accusing the BBC of 'anti-British bias'. Mrs Thatcher accused the BBC of failing to put Britain's case 'with sufficient vigour', and George Howard, the BBC's chairman, and Alasdair Milne, managing director of programmes, appeared at a crowded meeting of the Tory Media Committee, which turned into a shouting match. *Panorama*'s presenter, Robert Kee, wrote to *The Times* disowning the broadcast, for which he was dropped from the programme. He resigned from the BBC later in the month.

Taking its cue from the prime minister, the *Sun* ran an editorial headed 'Dare Call It Treason', levelling the charge of treason at Peter Snow, the *Guardian* and the *Daily Mirror* on the basis that 'a British citizen is either on his country's side – or he is its enemy'.[37] The *Mirror* retaliated with an editorial headed 'The Harlot of Fleet Street', accusing the *Sun* of sinking 'from the gutter to the sewer'.[38] Overtaken in the jingo stakes, the *Daily Star* tried to recover ground with a broadside against 'this evil enemy at home . . . the odious group of Labour MPs who, in effect, voted for Galtieri . . . led by power-mad Tony Benn'.[39]

The mood on the streets was also volatile. For most of the British public, it had become a straightforward story of British servicemen risking their lives for the cause of freedom. At a funeral in County Durham for a young sailor killed in action in late May, the local Labour MP, Giles Radice, was deeply impressed by the 'strong vein of working-class patriotism' displayed by the huge congregation.[40] In Newcastle upon Tyne, on match days, you would hear the crowds on their way to St James' football ground singing 'if you hate the fucking Argies, clap your hands'. Margaret Thatcher was thoroughly in tune with the mood of the mob. Called back on 17 May to discuss the final negotiating position that Britain was going to present to the UN, it was noted how 'the PM veered the whole time towards being uncompromising, so that the rest of us, and in particular the Foreign Office participants, constantly found themselves under attack from her for being wet, ready to sell out, unsupportive of British interests etc.'[41] The belligerence on the street was not necessarily born out of any accurate knowledge of the geography of the conflict. A woman cheerfully distributing anti-war leaflets in Gosforth, a middle-class suburb of Newcastle, was told by a police officer that she would stop laughing when 'the Argentinians are here, raping and looting'.[42] Even Denis Thatcher needed to reach for his atlas at the start of the crisis to find out where the Falklands were.[43]

For the government, there was always a danger that they would take the blame when British servicemen were killed, but during May, any Tory fears on that score were put to rest by two tests of popular opinion. Two days after the sinking of the *Sheffield* most of the country voted in local council elections; instead of the anticipated swing against the government, the Tories picked up seats and took control of Birmingham council. On 25 May, the navy had its worst day since the loss of the *Sheffield*, when HMS *Coventry* was hit by two 1,000 lb bombs. Captain Hart-Dyke recalled:

> In the operations room there was a vicious shock wave, a blinding flash and searing heat. I felt as though I had been caught in a doorway and a heavy door had been slammed against me: the force and the impact shook my whole body to the core. I was stunned into unconsciousness.[44]

When he came to, he saw men on fire. The ship went down with nineteen of its crew killed. On the same day, the container ship, *Atlantic Conveyor*, which was being used to transport aircraft, had to be abandoned after being hit by an Exocet, with twelve dead. Two days later, there was a parliamentary by-election in Beaconsfield, near Slough, which, remarkably, was the only by-election in the entire eighteen years of Conservative government in which their share of the vote was higher than in the preceding general election.[45] This had nothing to do with the quality of the candidates: the victorious Conservative, Tim Smith, had an undistinguished career that ended in scandal when it was revealed he had accepted thousands of pounds in cash in return for asking parliamentary questions; the defeated Labour candidate was Tony Blair. Blair absorbed his lesson; in his ten years as prime minister, he never let himself be out-jingoed by the Conservatives or the tabloid press.

On 3 June, the task force landed at Fitzroy at the southern end of East Falkland. To strengthen the beachhead, HMSs *Sir Tristram* and *Sir Galahad* were sent with equipment, ammunition and troops. Five days later, the sight of these two ships sitting unprotected in broad daylight, crammed full of troops, horrified Major Southby-Taylor, the same officer who held so low an opinion of the islanders on whose behalf he was fighting. He demanded that the troops be disembarked, but regulations did not allow troops and ammunition to be shipped ashore in the same craft. The major went angrily to staff headquarters, where they refused at first to believe that there were still troops on board ship, but then agreed to send more landing craft. Before that order had any effect, an Argentine Skyhawk had hit *Sir Galahad*, setting it on fire. Captain Hilarian Roberts of the Welsh Guards was on deck:

> I experienced an extraordinary slow-motion feeling of being burnt, and watched my hands become the colour of those rather sticky white-grey washing-up gloves. Under the intense heat my hands enlarged and the skin peeled off like talons of wax. And then I found my hair on fire and with these useless hands I was trying to put my hair out![46]

Simon Weston, a twenty-year-old guardsman, was trapped below, also staring at his hands. 'I watched, transfixed by horror, as they fried and melted, the skin bubbling and flaking away from the bone like the leaves of a paperback burning on a bonfire.'[47] To escape he had to run through a wall of fire, leaving behind other young soldiers too badly injured to move. As he ran, he heard the sound of guns going off, suggesting that some may have killed themselves to escape the hideous pain of burning to death. The death toll was forty-eight, with many more injured. Weston survived 46 per cent burns, but reached Britain so hideously injured that his mother did not recognize him. His scarred, mask-like face would become a familiar memento of the war.

However, once the British troops were on land, there could be no serious doubt of the outcome of a firefight between professional soldiers from one of the world's best-equipped armies and conscripts with inferior weapons. The first land battle, at Goose Green, on 28–9 May, saw 12 British and 50 Argentines killed; the last was on the night of 13–14 June, when British troops stormed Mount Tumbledown, the high ground above Port Stanley. The death toll was 10 Britons and 30 Argentines, with more than 150 wounded. Port Stanley was taken on 14 June, at which point Argentina admitted defeat. The crisis had lasted two-and-a-half months. The serious fighting had been concentrated into six weeks. The total death toll was 255 Britons and 649 Argentinians.

There was no material gain for the United Kingdom. It is sometimes suggested that Britain's real motive for going to war was to secure mineral rights in the South Atlantic. The UK had a disputed claim for a triangular wedge of the Antarctic measuring about 600,000 square miles, which was first staked out in 1908 and was based on the possession of the Falklands and South Georgia. That claim did not include the right to explore for minerals, for which the technology did not exist. In October 2007, the Foreign Office indicated for the first time that the UK was going to claim sovereign rights over the seabed, in anticipation of a time when oil and gas exploration became technically feasible.[48] Drilling started in October 2009, setting off a new diplomatic feud. The fact that Argentina had become a democracy did not alter its claim to sovereignty over the islands, and the arrival of an oil rig that had been towed from Scotland to the South Atlantic provoked a complaint to the United Nations and a threat to boycott British firms. But there is no evidence that oil exploration was on Thatcher's mind, or anyone else's at the time in 1982, when it would have saved the British taxpayer considerable sums if the government had abandoned the islands.

In 1982, no community under British rule was more welfare-dependent than the Falkland Islands. The cost of supporting it was a running sore for the Department of Overseas Aid, who were obliged to pay annually £850 per capita to the islanders. Even the Treasury does not know how much it cost to retake the islands and hold on to them in the years that followed, because the information is scattered between forty and seventy separate paper files,[49] but it would include £624m added to the defence budget in 1983–4 to replace equipment lost or destroyed in the fighting and to maintain a garrison on the islands, plus £684m the following year, and £552m in 1985–6, making £1,860m in just the first three years.[50] There was also a one-off bill of £500,000 in 1982 – nearly £3,000 per islander – to add to the already generous overseas aid they received.[51] The smashed-up runway at the Port Stanley airstrip was repaired and extended. In place of the garrison of about twenty, they were granted a permanent air base at Mount Pleasant, employing up to 2,000 military and civilian personnel. So much cash went into developing fishing and tourism that by 1992 the islands had achieved self-sufficiency in everything but the huge cost of maintaining the garrison, which in 2008 worked out at about £150,000 per islander, per year. GDP had reached £75m or £25,000 per head by 2008. The 2006 census gave the population of the islands as 2,478, not counting the personnel on Mount Pleasant. More than 2,000 of them lived in Port Stanley, now a much enlarged village with 930 houses. Yet while Port Stanley has survived, the drift of the population out of the rest of the islands has not abated. In 2006, there were 363 people living in the outlying islands, all but 42 of them on the two main islands.

Another gainer was the Royal Navy, whose precious surface ships were saved from the scrapyard; HMS *Endurance* was given an extra ten years of active service. However, the greatest beneficiaries of all were Mrs Thatcher and the Conservative Party, who had secured a poll lead that would see no fewer than 100 new Conservative MPs elected the following year, giving them the biggest parliamentary majority any party had enjoyed since the Second World War. The Falklands made an international celebrity out of Mrs Thatcher. She, of course, fully intended to put her new status to use. Speaking to a rally of Conservative Party activists in Cheltenham, less than three weeks after the Argentine surrender, she used the 'Falklands Factor' to warn the railway workers' union to abandon industrial action and the NHS employers to drop their demand for better pay:

> There is a new mood of realism in Britain. That too is part of the Falklands Factor. The battle of the South Atlantic was not won by ignoring the dangers or denying the risks. It was achieved by men and women who had no illusions about the difficulties. We faced them squarely and we were determined to overcome. That is increasingly the mood of Britain. And that's why the rail strike won't do.[52]

In January 1983, as the islanders marked 150 years of British rule, Mrs Thatcher descended for a three-day visit to 'shabby shell-shocked Stanley' – as the governor, Rex Hunt, termed it. 'You were all marvellous,' she told the surprised, delighted islanders. One of them, Mike Bleaney, standing nearby with his son on his shoulders, replied: 'You didn't do so badly yourself, M'am.'[53] Her visit was no doubt a great morale booster on the islands; it also furnished great pictures for the voters back home.

The impending general election was perhaps already won by then. Certainly, once those happy images had been seen back home, the Labour Party did not stand a chance, though during the campaign they tried to knock the shine off her image as a war leader. Neil Kinnock called for an inquiry into the sinking of the *Belgrano* and Denis Healey accused Thatcher of 'glorying in slaughter', but given that the Labour Party had called for and supported military action, their protestations sounded feeble. A more effective attack, because it was so unexpected, came from Robert Runcie, Archbishop of Canterbury, who during the war had defended the principle that sometimes military force was necessary and justified. When he presided over the official thanksgiving service in St Paul's Cathedral, instead of the victory celebration that the Conservatives demanded Runcie and other clerics insisted that the service should be on the theme of peace. 'War is a sign of human failure, and everything we say and do in this service must be in that context,'[54] Runcie said in his sermon. Mrs Thatcher attended, but reputedly left fuming. That afternoon, Denis Thatcher was escorting some paratroopers on the terrace at the House of Commons: 'The Boss was livid,' he told them. So was the Tory MP Julian Amery, who said: 'I was very shocked. There were no martial hymns like Fight the Good Fight and Onward Christian Soldiers, and there were none of the great prayers. I thought it was a deliberate counter-attack against the mass of opinion of this country on the part of the pacifist, liberal wet establishment.' Fellow Tory Sir John Biggs-Davison thought: 'it was revolting for cringing clergy to misuse St Paul's to throw doubt upon the sacrifices of our fighting men'.[55]

Mrs Thatcher's government allowed no bad news stories from the Falklands to spoil the sweet taste of victory. It was essential, for instance, that no one should know that four of the British dead had been killed by 'friendly fire'. On 6 June, as troops were landing on East Falkland, a Gazelle helicopter was dispatched to Goose Green to collect two passengers. Seven minutes later, it was shot down, killing everyone on board. An inquest held in Southampton in December was told that it had been hit by an Argentine missile. This was not true, as the Ministry of Defence well knew; fragments found at the scene showed that the fatal missile was a Sea Dart fired from HMS *Cardiff*. The truth was quietly slipped out in answer to a written question in the Commons four years later.[56] When the navy eventually held an inquiry in November 1986, it established that the helicopter did not have its identification system switched on, so the navy assumed, without checking, that it must be Argentinian. The findings were kept secret until the Ministry of Defence released them in July 2008.[57]

Another incident quietly passed over was the killing of an unarmed Argentinian PoW, Suboficial Primero Felix Artuso, the first fatal casualty of the war. He was killed almost a week before the sinking of the *Belgrano*, when it still seemed possible that the crisis might be resolved without further bloodshed. When the task force retook South Georgia on 25 April, they captured a damaged submarine, the *Santa Fe*, and ordered its Argentinian crew to move the vessel the next day, under the eyes of armed British guards. The Argentinians were so pleased that no one had been hurt in this first encounter with the British that they were friendly and chatty, but the man guarding Artuso, in the lower control room, could not understand a word his prisoner was saying. He used sign language to tell Artuso not to touch a lever that the guard believed controlled the submarine's torpedoes. His gesticulations must have bemused Artuso, because he was actually pointing at a lever that controlled the ship's buoyancy. Artuso was given an order by telephone to switch on the air system, and made straight for the very lever that he had been banned from touching. The guard shot him five times. The navy held an immediate inquiry and exonerated the man who fired the shots, while mildly criticizing his commanding officer. Their findings were also held back for 25 years.[58]

Another shocking internal report that was withheld from the public for a quarter of a century was into the seaworthiness of the SS *Atlantic Conveyor*. This ship was laid up in Liverpool when the Falklands were invaded and was rapidly converted into a ferry ship and aircraft carrier. On 25 May, it was hit by two Exocets. Three crew members died in the fire and nine drowned. The Board of Inquiry discovered that its firefighting equipment was inadequate and that its internal communication system was so 'rudimentary' that 'at least six people were below decks when the missile struck, completely unaware that the ship was at emergency stations'.[59] Evidently, there was also a scramble for the life-rafts, which might explain why more men died in the sea than in the fire, but even when the report was declassified in 2007 the description of what happened as the men struggled to safety in the chilly water was blanked out.

Perhaps the most serious question of all was whether or not the sinking of the *Sheffield* could have been avoided. The lengthy report by a Board of Inquiry was peppered with comments such as 'at this point, matters started going severely wrong'; 'Sheffield, perhaps lulled into a sense of security by the false alarms and subsequent inactivity still did not carry out acknowledged and practised procedures'; and 'if all the right reactions had been taken very quickly indeed and particularly if chaff had been fired . . . it might have been possible to frustrate this determined and very professional Super Exocet attack'.[60] The clear implication is that the *Sheffield*'s crew underestimated the Argentines and carelessly allowed their ship to be destroyed. Sandy Woodward's memoirs suggest that he would have had some of the crew court-martialled, but was overruled because there was to be no 'souring the general euphoria'.[61]

There was also the strange, sad tale of an eighteen-year-old private, Philip Williams of the Scots Guards, for whom the war did not end until seven weeks after the Argentinian surrender. He was a stretcher-bearer during the battle for Mount Tumbledown and was either knocked out or got lost. He wandered about in atrocious weather, sleeping in a shepherd's hut, and saw no one other than dead Argentinians, until he stumbled into a remote farmhouse on 1 August. His family had been told that he was dead. His return was reported worldwide, first as a good-news story, until it became apparent that he was not in a fit mental state to act out the role of a returning hero. A whispering campaign then began. Somebody tipped off the *Daily Mirror* that the teenager would face a regimental inquiry 'that could lead to a court-martial'.[62] That did not happen, but he returned to Chelsea Barracks isolated, vulnerable and a target for bullies. He went AWOL, had a breakdown and was discharged.[63]

Another young Scots Guard, Alexander Findlay, also acted as a stretcher-bearer on Tumbledown. He saw one friend shot in the throat, and a fellow stretcher-bearer cut in half by a mortar. He stayed in the army, though he was so traumatized that his wife found him one day hiding in a fox hole that he had dug in the garden. In 1990, when he was serving in Northern Ireland, he had had too much to drink, pulled a gun, threatened to kill two fellow soldiers, threatened suicide, fired into a television set and surrendered. Instead of sending him for treatment, a court-martial sentenced him to two years in prison.[64]

In November 1988, after some hesitation, the BBC broadcast the play *Tumbledown,* the story of Lieutenant Robert Lawrence, a Scots Guard who had half his brain blown away by a bullet in the final battle of the war. The film, which combined fact and fiction, was based on Lawrence's account of the treatment he received back in Britain. Paralysed on one side of his body and confined to a wheelchair, he was an ugly sight that the government, he believed, wanted to hide away. 'The government seemed to do their best to massage and manipulate the images of the war to ensure they did not show the real costs of it and the real harm it had done,' he said, in one interview.[65] Other wounded survivors backed his account, but the army and the Ministry of Defence were offended by it. The film was dropped from the schedules in 1987, in case it impacted on the general election. One twelve-second sequence was cut on the army's insistence and the rest went out in May 1988 to a storm of controversy. The fire was inadvertently given fuel by the film's director, Richard Eyre, who admitted in a question and answer session that it was 'deeply political', which gave a Home Office minister, Lord Renton, occasion to denounce the film in the House of Lords as 'the product of a pacifist who has declared that all his work is subversive'.[66] John Stokes, a Tory MP said:

> I cannot think why it was written and why the BBC put it out. I can only think that the underlying point is to undermine the sacrifices and heroism which enabled us to repossess the Falkland Islands. It is, in my view, another example of the BBC stabbing the nation in the back.[67]

One claim made for the Falklands is that it brought democracy to Argentina by bringing down the junta – not that Margaret Thatcher had any general objection to Latin American military dictators, as she demonstrated through her enduring friendship with Chile's murderous ruler, General Augusto Pinochet.[68] Actually, the age of military dictators in South America was coming to an end, anyway. Ecuador reverted to civilian rule in 1979; Argentina in 1983; Uruguay in 1984; Brazil in 1985; Chile in 1988; and Paraguay in 1989. The most that could be said about the Falklands War is that it may have nudged Argentina a little further up the queue. While a democratically governed Argentina is unlikely to launch a sudden attack on the islands, it has not surrendered its claim to them, and the billions that the UK government has sunk into the islands has not shortened the 8,000-mile journey from London to Port Stanley. The problem has been suppressed but it has not been solved.

CHAPTER 7

DARLING, WE'RE THE YOUNG ONES

In the second half of 1980, a few specialist cinemas in big cities were showing an unusual film called *The Secret Policeman's Ball,* which was no more than a stage show recorded on celluloid, made cheaper by the fact that none of the performers was paid. John Cleese performed with Peter Cook, who had once been his mentor. Three of the Monty Python team reprised a famous sketch in which four Yorkshiremen competitively boast about their deprived childhoods, repeating the catchphrase 'you were lucky'. The fourth role was filled by a twenty-four-year-old graduate with a degree in electrical engineering, who later took to the bare stage alone to perform a simple but very funny routine: pretending to be a schoolmaster reading the roll call. He had a rubbery face, flawless timing and a strange way of emphasizing the letter 'B' – which, it would emerge years later, was the result of having to battle against a stutter. He also had a mock bored, bad-tempered air that made his audience scream with laughter at lines such as 'Nibble, leave Orifice alone!' Most of the live audience cannot have known who he was, but by the time the film was on release most of those whose who saw it would have recognized the face, if not the name. It was Rowan Atkinson.

The 1980s was the best decade that British television comedy has ever had. One sharp new comedy series followed another in an explosion of inventiveness that raised young comedians to the status of rock stars. Their trade was no longer dominated by old troopers such as Morecombe and Wise or Spike Milligan, who had spent years perfecting a live act before they were exposed to a mass audience. The new comedians were on radio and television when they were barely out of university, operating in a liberated regime that allowed them to act like adolescents and make jokes about subjects that their parents found either embarrassing or too serious to be laughed at. Anything from the lavatory, to race, sex and Margaret Thatcher were suitable sources for humour. This meant that the 'alternative' comedians, as they were known, did not need scriptwriters who could devise the kind of elaborate wordplay of *The Two Ronnies*, or the professionalism that went into Morecombe and Wise's dance routines. Alternative comedy assumed a high level of education in its audience, and relied on sharp social observation and energetic delivery. There had been no very notable additions to the nation's comedians since the Monty Python team of ten years earlier, until suddenly Rowan Atkinson, Rik Mayall, Dawn French, Jennifer Saunders, Nigel Planer, Ade Edmondson, Hugh Laurie, Stephen Fry, Ben Elton, Harry Enfield and many more tumbled into the public eye, becoming the idols of a generation.

To begin with, there was *Not the Nine O'Clock News*, the show that made stars out of Atkinson and three other unknowns. It was the brainchild of John Lloyd, a Cambridge graduate with a law degree, who had gone into radio hoping to be a performer or a scriptwriter, but ended up as a producer and discovered a valuable talent for manoeuvring his way through the internal politics of the BBC. Since most producers were much older than Lloyd, he was the one that young comics wanted to work with. He had produced more than 100 radio shows, including *The News Quiz* and *Quote Unquote*, and helped Douglas Adams with the original radio version of *Hitchhiker's Guide to the Galaxy*, when in 1979, still aged only twenty-eight, he asked for an opportunity to move to television. The BBC was then good at turning out tame satire for a mass audience that offended no one, such as *Open All Hours* or *The Good Life*; *Monty Python's Flying Circus* was anarchic, but never hurtful. When the Python team decided to risk causing offence by poking fun at the New Testament, they did it on film. Television viewers were permitted to watch studio debates about whether *Life of Brian* (1979) was funny or merely offensive, but there was no suggestion that the film itself was suitable to be beamed into the home. Mike Yarwood, the leading mimic of the 1970s, was so gentle in his impersonations that Harold Wilson willingly appeared on a chat show with him, while Denis Healey used to impersonate Yarwood's impersonation of him.

As Yarwood's career collapsed, into the breach came the situation comedy *Yes Minister*, launched in 1980 with Paul Eddington as Jim Hacker, an incompetent, cowardly cabinet minister, terrified of decisions and obsessively trying to find out whether people thought he was doing well or badly. He was manipulated at every turn by Sir Humphrey, his permanent secretary, played by Nigel Hawthorne. The writers, Anthony Jay and Jonathan Lynn, mined the diaries of Richard Crossman, a former Labour cabinet minister, for comic inspiration. 'There was nothing in it that you couldn't have found if you read the Crossman Diaries from cover to cover,' Lynn confessed. He added: 'We made politics comprehensible in human terms and we also made people realize that politicians cannot do what they want to do. It had a traditional comedy formula, too, of the servant who is more able than his master – the same formula as Jeeves and Bertie Wooster.'[1] The show won awards, year after year. Mass audiences loved it, but its most avid fans, generally, were civil servants and career politicians because it was accurate enough to be recognizable while not cruel enough to be upsetting. Lord Allen of Abbeydale, former permanent secretary at the Home Office, praised the spoof diaries of Jim Hacker as 'rather more accurate than Dick Crossman's'.[2] Margaret Thatcher particularly liked the way that, without ever mentioning her even obliquely, it played to her self image as a lone fighter up against a hidebound establishment and spineless ministers.

The show even received a token of approval from Mary Whitehouse, a former teacher and Christian revivalist from the West Midlands, who had been campaigning since 1963 against what she saw as the spread of corruption and filth in television. Though now more than seventy years old, Mrs Whitehouse had lost none of the fire that made her a household name. In 1982, she launched a private prosecution of the National Theatre over a scene in Howard Brenton's play *The Romans in Britain* in which an actor simulated anal rape. She also campaigned against video nasties and some of Channel 4's more esoteric programmes, and seemed to hope that she could get mainstream television back to where it was in the 1950s. As a way of demonstrating that crusading Christians also enjoyed a good joke, in January 1984 the National Viewers and Listeners Association, which she ran almost single-handedly, gave *Yes Minister* an award for making the nation laugh without resorting to blasphemy or smut. Margaret Thatcher came to the presentation ceremony, and performed in a specially written sketch, as herself, telling a startled Hacker and a horrified Sir Humphrey that she had decided to abolish economists. Eddington commented ruefully: 'This occasion represents something of a low point. We had lots of conferences when the show was being produced, and we thought it was designed to annoy everybody. We must have failed.'[3]

The creators of *Not the Nine O'Clock News* were never in danger of receiving an award from Mrs Whitehouse. They did not attempt to compete with *Yes Minister*; their benchmark was *Monty Python's Flying Circus*. The show was not a situation comedy but a series of short sketches, aimed at the same audience as *Python*. The pilot even featured John Cleese. However, to avoid too close comparison, they eschewed surreal silliness and concentrated on mimicry and observation. The first series of six shows, featuring Atkinson, Chris Langham, Mel Smith and Pamela Stephenson – all of them unknown to TV audiences – bombed. The producers blamed Langham, who was allegedly not a team player, and sacked him via the cruel device of not telling him that a second series was being prepared. Griff Rhys Jones was brought in to complete the quartet, and the second series took off. The critics loved the tightness of the writing, the quality of the performances, and the way that the show made fun of anybody and anything. In one sketch, a post-punk youth dressed in leather, with zips and safety pins everywhere, is seen in a urinal, unable to remember which zip he needs to undo. They also parodied the new craze for expensive videos that promoted each new record release in a song called 'Nice Video, Shame About the Song', which as one critic put it, 'had the quality of all true satire: it showed that those poking fun were as good and better at producing the parodied material than those being ridiculed'.[4] There was a nicely observed studio discussion about why fat people should be proud of their weight, and call themselves 'stout', though an obese vicar was not prepared to go so far as to run down the street naked crying 'Look at me, I'm enormous'. The clergy were a favourite target; in one sketch on whether or not the Church of England should reach out to devil worshippers, a trendy London vicar advocates 'a bit less of the "Get thee behind me, Satan!", and a bit more of the "Come on in, old mate, have a cup of tea".'[5]

Though the show did not directly ridicule Thatcher or her ministers, with whom the BBC had to negotiate the annual licence fee, it did hit more distant or indirect political targets, including Ronald Reagan and the Youth Training Scheme. The Ayatollah song, which poked fun at Iran's supreme leader, now looks more daring than it did then. The show also caused waves of offence among older viewers when, after the death of Sir Oswald Mosley, the former fascist leader, the cast dressed up as skinhead Nazis to sing a mock tribute, interspersed by the genuine tributes culled from upmarket newspapers. But the most extraordinary aspect of the show was the way it went for the police. The Brixton riots had given the Special Patrol Group (SPG) in particular an unenviable reputation, though *Not* ...'s best known creation, Constable Savage, was a uniformed beat copper. He is called in for a dressing down over the 117 occasions on which he has arrested a Mr Winston Cudoogo on such charges as 'possession of curly black hair and thick lips'. 'You're a bigot. Your whole time on duty is dominated by racial hatred and personal vendetta.

There is no room for men like you in my force, Savage,' says his furious superior. 'I'm transferring you to the SPG.'

John Lloyd fell out with the BBC when the books he put together as spin-offs from *Not the Nine O'Clock News* became bestsellers, and he decided to go freelance. In May 1982, Tony Hendra, from whom he had borrowed the idea of a title beginning with 'Not', joined him in a pub off the Brompton Road in Knightsbridge, to introduce him to two artists named Peter Fluck and Roger Law, who had been well-known in the early 1970s as the makers of hideous puppet caricatures of politicians, which would be photographed for publication in the *Sunday Times* colour magazine. They lost their market when the Sunday supplements moved into lifestyle journalism, but had set up a workshop in London, with money from Clive Sinclair, inventor of the home computer. Hendra had brought them along to push the idea of a satirical puppet show for television. The upshot was *Spitting Image*, a unique melding of puppetry and satire. It was perhaps just as well that the quartet in the pub in west London could not see the mountain of problems before them. Whereas putting together a show like *Monty Python's Flying Circus* was a comparatively straightforward business of getting the gags written, the performers rehearsed, and then telling the technicians to do their stuff, a small army of puppeteers, costumiers, voice impressionists, mould-makers, electricians, cameramen, foam experts, set-builders, model-makers and funny writers was needed to get the puppets saying their lines in front of a camera. Lewis Chester, *Spitting Image*'s first historian, observed:

> Most innovatory comedy shows began with a core of like-minded enthusiasts. *Spitting Image*, however, was essentially based on the recruitment of skills to put something very complicated together. Since the skills were highly refined, the people involved tended to be individualistic and highly protective of their own value. In consequence, the kind of mutual support exhibited in the origins of their comic predecessors was conspicuous by its absence.[6]

The show gave a great deal more pleasure to those who watched it than to those who produced it.

When they began, the technology did not exist for creating puppets with moveable eyes and mouths. The nearest equivalent to *Spitting Image* was *The Muppets*, but creating animal puppets was technologically far less challenging than creating humans. Fluck and Law wasted a lot of time trying to learn from Hollywood's special effects, before they realized that a puppet created for film was built to last only as long as it took to shoot the relevant scenes; whereas they needed puppets hardy enough for a series of programmes. This created immense financial problems, because it was impossible to draw up an accurate budget for creating the puppets until they knew how the programme was going to be done. Sinclair's financial advisers were quick to panic and withdrew support.

Compared with all this, the job of selling the idea to a television company was almost straightforward. Thames Television turned it down; John Birt, at LWT, thought it would cost too much; Jeremy Isaacs, at Channel Four, liked the idea but did not come forward with the money. However, in September 1982 Central Television was persuaded to put up £60,000 for a short pilot. This was nowhere near enough money. The team had been working on Nancy the Parrot, who talked like Nancy Reagan and sat on Ronald Reagan's shoulder. She alone cost £6,000 to construct, but her metal head turned out to be prohibitively heavy and she was never used. But having persuaded a Yorkshire businessman to put up yet more money, the team produced a pilot that Central liked so much that they announced they wanted twenty-six continuous weekly shows. Foreseeing the crippling demands of such a commitment, John Lloyd had to beg for less. They settled for thirteen shows.

Fluck and Law made their puppets in a studio in London, which was also where most of the other technicians and creative people were based and where it would have been easiest to record the show. However, union rules would not permit that, so each week the puppets had to be carefully packed in a van and driven to Birmingham. On arrival, the problems of operating in a cramped studio were compounded by rivalries between the different agencies, by a never-ending dispute between John Lloyd and Tony Hendra about the sort of show they wanted to create, and by the occasional clash with Central Television's management. An early battle over censorship almost led to resignations that could have sunk the show. Fluck and Law were very proud of their puppet queen, and wanted the first show, transmitted in February 1984, to include a sketch in which she was in her kitchen, frying sausages, when Margaret Thatcher paid a call. The queen would have invited the prime minister to sit down, stand up, sit down, stand up until an exasperated Mrs Thatcher asked whether or not this was protocol, to which the queen replied: 'No, no. It's just fun being Queen.'[7] However, Central was opening a new £21m complex in Nottingham the following week, with the Duke of Edinburgh as guest of honour, and they ruled that it would be discourteous to broadcast a hideous puppet caricature of his wife so close to the ceremony.

Lloyd wanted short, topical sketches and as floor manager he wanted the freedom to make last-minute changes to keep up with the day's news; but Hendra, the initial winner in this struggle, envisaged a series of running sitcoms, including scenes from a retirement home for ex-prime ministers, where Macmillan, Home, Wilson, Heath and Callaghan hung out. It did not work because the fun of watching the puppets was in the initial shock of recognition; their range of facial expression was too limited to sustain the joke for more than a few minutes at a time, and the critics panned the first show. Lloyd then won his fight with Hendra, and the long gags were dropped in favour of quick-fire sketches. Fluck and Law had wanted the whole show to be political satire, but that ambition was a casualty of the need for a large number of gags. Though the writing team included Ben Elton and Ian Hislop, there were not enough writers who understood politics and could be funny, so show-business and sports personalities were included in the show's list of targets. Even so, the main business of *Spitting Image* was ridiculing and insulting the nation's political leaders with a venom that had never been seen before on television. The most famous sketch showed Thatcher – whose voice curiously, was supplied by a male impressionist, Steve Nallon – at a restaurant with her cabinet, who were portrayed as a group of grunting morons. Thatcher ordered her meat raw and when asked 'What about the vegetables?', she replied, 'They'll have the same.'

Sometimes the show's attacks hurt their targets. David Steel was sure that his puppet, which was small enough to fit in David Owen's pocket, went a long way towards undermining his standing as co-leader of the Alliance. A few celebrities, including Paul Daniels, Andrew Lloyd Webber and Claire Rayner, were satisfyingly offended, but others, to Fluck and Law's great disappointment, were flattered by the recognition. 'We were reliably informed that junior members of the Cabinet, and Shadow Cabinet, were absolutely delighted when their puppets appeared. It showed they were on their way up,'[8] Law admitted ruefully. A tape of the show was delivered by Central Television each Monday morning to the House of Commons for the benefit of MPs who had missed it. The tabloid press soon switched from hostility to raving enthusiasm, and by the latter part of 1985 the quality press had caught on. One critic observed: 'It seems like years since anybody really got down to the vital national tasks of corrupting the young, hurling mindless abuse and libelling politicians. For two decades, nobody seemed to do anything really gratuitously disgraceful – until *Spitting Image*.'[9]

The one sensitive area continued to be the royal family. For a year, they left the Queen Mother out of it, until her absence looked like a loss of nerve. Then in February 1985 an executive from Central TV let slip in an interview with the *Birmingham Daily News* that he personally had long resisted having her puppet included, but the battle had been lost. This set off a firestorm of tabloid outrage, with the *Daily Express* urging its readers to switch off their televisions. The team had a sketch prepared in which the Queen Mother was to have been seen, Assisi like, talking to animals, except that she was asking the horses for racing tips – but it now seemed tame after such hype. Lloyd came up with a stylish solution. The show went ahead and, until thirty seconds before the end, it appeared to everyone that they had lost their nerve and cancelled the Queen Mother's appearance. Then up came large letters, filling the screen with a message thanking everyone who had rung in to complain and assuring them that '*Spitting Image* has never made such a puppet and were on holiday when it wasn't made. Thank you.' Then on staggered the Queen Mother, declaring: 'Oh, what a pity. I was so looking forward to it.'[10] That evening, the show that *Express* readers had been exhorted to switch off reached an audience of 11.4m.

Though *Not the Nine O'Clock News* and *Spitting Image* gave a substantial number of previously unknown performers their first break, there were always more aspiring comics than television needed. Others had to make their way by doing stand-up routines in the clubs, pubs and student bars in the hope of being recognized. Anyone living in or near London who wanted to be a comedian beat a path to a club called the Comedy Store, which opened in 1979, the address of which could be found in London listings magazines. Anyone could turn up, make himself or herself known to the compere, and go up on stage to do a turn. If the audience did not rate the performer, which they usually did not, the call went up for the gong to sound and the performance was over. Some determined characters came back week after week for a repeated humiliation.

It was, of course, impossible to impose any quality control, so the better performers shifted to the Boulevard Theatre, and set up Comic Strip, which became a test-bed for comedy that assumed an audience of liberal, anti-racist, anti-sexist, *Guardian*-reading, Thatcher-loathing young professionals, who would not be offended by swearing or sexual explicitness, but would object to racist or sexist humour. The master of ceremonies was – to quote one critic – 'a human volcano called Alexei Sayle . . . possessed of a Michelin body, a very loud voice, and a brain that only works on overdrive', whose idea of pandering to his audience was to announce that the evening was to be a charity event in aid of 'Help a Kid – Kill a Social Worker'. The same critic was impressed by 'two young women called French and Saunders, whose effective humour derives from the accurate observation of some so far underexamined social stereotypes'.[11] When this was written, Dawn French was twenty-three and Jennifer Saunders twenty-two. They were daughters of RAF officers, who had spent part of their childhood on the same RAF base, though they did not know each other until they met on a course for drama teachers. When they graduated, they developed a 'cringeworthy' stage act called 'The Menopause Sisters'.[12]

The driving force behind Comic Strip was Peter Richardson, the leading half of a stand-up comedy duo with Nigel Planer, who was both funny and equipped with a sharp business brain. He seized the opportunity offered by the planned launch of Channel 4 by negotiating a deal for six half-hour films, the first of which was *Five Go Mad in Dorset*, a pastiche of the Enid Blyton novels the comedians had read as children. The cast included Richardson, French, Saunders and Ade Edmondson, another product of the Comic Strip reviews, where he appeared in a double act with Rik Mayall. Another forty Comic Strip films of varying length and quality followed over the next decade, each artistically controlled and starring Peter Richardson. The most memorable was *The Strike* (1988), which retold the story of the miners' strike as a romantic adventure in Hollywood style.

The BBC was also open to the idea of giving airtime to these new 'alternative' comics and commissioned a series – *The Young Ones* – based on some draft scripts co-written by Rik Mayall and his then girlfriend, a young American named Lise Mayer. They used the standard sitcom format, but took it to extremes never seen on television before. The characters were like a dysfunctional family – a father figure whose plans for self-betterment never worked, a put-upon housewife and two uncontrollable egocentric teenagers – except that these were four students from Scumbag College. One of the retarded teenagers, played by Rik Mayall, purported to be an anarchist, but was too cowardly and self-regarding to stand by his beliefs when the going was tough – 'a two-year anarchist whose dad is probably a bank manager and he'll probably end up one too,'[13] as Ben Elton described him. The other was a psychopathic punk played by Ade Edmondson. The mother figure was a depressed hippie named Neil, played by Nigel Planer, forever preparing meals of lentil stew. There was also Mike, the self-appointed leader of the squat, who should have been played by Peter Richardson, but he was accustomed to having artistic control of everything in which he appeared, thus provoking an irresolvable personality clash with the series director, Paul Jackson. The part therefore went to Christopher Ryan. Finally, there was not one landlord, but an entire ghastly landlord family called Balowski, each member of which was played by Alexei Sayle.

The series ran from 1982 until the twelfth episode in 1986, when the whole cast went over a cliff in a stolen bus. There were no recognizable plot lines, nor did the series pay regard to plausibility. There were musical interludes, when the sitting room suddenly metamorphosed into a stage for Madness or Dexy's Midnight Runners, and there were wacky and often tasteless cutaways. In one episode, two rats that infested the student hovel are heard discussing Euripides, until Rik spots them and kills one by smashing it with a guitar. In the next cutaway, the surviving rat is seen eating his former companion. This was crudity of a kind not seen before on mainstream television, and it was not to everyone's taste. The show owed a comic debt to Spike Milligan; he was not flattered, however. He once said: 'Rik Mayall is putrid – absolutely vile. He thinks nose-picking is funny and farting and all that. He is the arsehole of British comedy.'[14] That, of course, was part of his appeal to the young target audience. Mayall rivalled Rowan Atkinson as the most popular comic of his generation.

There were old-boy networks even in this meritocratic world. Ben Elton, who had known Mayall and Edmondson at Manchester University, had his first big break when he was drafted in as a scriptwriter on *The Young Ones*. Afterwards, he teamed up with Richard Curtis, one of the regular writers from *Not the Nine O'Clock News*, to create a new vehicle for Rowan Atkinson, whom Curtis had known at Oxford. The producer, again, was John Lloyd. It was an expensively produced film series shot on location in Northumberland called *The Black Adder*, set in the late fifteenth century in the fictional reign of Richard IV, and broadcast on BBC1 in June and July 1983. The form was the old Jeeves and Wooster joke, with Atkinson playing the cowardly, inept Black Adder, ever reliant on his wise servant, Baldrick, played by Tony Robinson. It did not work. The series was an expensive failure, but somehow, the makers of this turkey persuaded the BBC to let them try again, promising this time that they would produce a more standard sitcom that could be shot in a studio at far less cost. Elton and Curtis also overturned the relationship between the main characters. Now, Blackadder was transported to the Elizabethan era; he was the intelligent one, eternally exasperated by the stupidity of the powerful, while Baldrick was the put-upon little fellow on whom he could vent his frustration. '*Blackadder II* is the only exception to the rules of sycophancy and whimsy which now dominate television comedy,' one hard-to-please critic reckoned:

> *Blackadder II* frequently pillories sycophancy. One of the central jokes is the extent to which everybody (except gormless Nursey) kow-tows

> to the Queen who – contrary to the fond English classroom image, though interestingly in line with modern scholarship – is portrayed as capricious, cruel and deeply insecure. Splendidly played by Miranda Richardson, Elizabeth has about as many good jokes as Blackadder himself.[15]

The formula was used for two more series, though it never worked quite so well without Miranda Richardson. *Blackadder the Third* made a star of Hugh Laurie, playing the idiotic Prince Regent. In *Blackadder Goes Forth,* the role of brainless boss went to Stephen Fry, as General Melchett. Set in the trenches in the First World War, it invited comparisons and contrasts with *'Allo, 'Allo,* one of the most popular comedy series of the late 1980s, which also was unlike anything else that had ever been seen on British television. It supposedly had a historical setting, in Nazi-occupied France, but did not make the least pretence of realism. It was all absurd humour, with characters running across a field disguised as a pantomime cow, or hiding in a piano trying to conceal their presence by singing 'plinky, plinky, plonk, plonk' to the tune of 'Lillee Marleen'. A favourite character was an English spy who supposedly spoke French badly – except that he was actually speaking bad English, greeting people by saying 'good moaning'. The silliest fools in this charade were the Nazis. Meanwhile, on another channel, Edmund Blackadder spent the fourth series devising desperate schemes to avoid being killed, until he and all the other regular characters, except Melchett, were wiped out in a finale that did not pretend to be funny. 'Where the jokes in *'Allo, 'Allo* turn the Nazis into harmless idiots, Curtis and Elton turn the British generals into idiots to show their harmfulness,'[16] the critic Mark Lawson observed. An idea of the success of the series can be gained from the Broadcasters' Audience Research Board's secret weekly report that gave programmes a numerical rating according to how much their audience enjoyed them, rather than the published audience figures. In the week ending 29 October 1989, only two programmes made the Top 20 in both charts; one was the hospital-based soap *Casualty*, the other was *Blackadder Goes Forth.*[17] *Blackadder* had the bigger audience, having been watched that week by 12.34m people.[18]

With that success to his credit, the next obvious step for Ben Elton was to go in front of the camera. He had tested himself on stage at London's Comedy Store, where he developed a polemical style, a staccato delivery, and very pronounced views on what was, and what was not, funny. Bodily functions were funny, sexism not. In 1985, he was writing scripts for a show called *Saturday Live*, for London Weekend Television, when he suggested to its director that he should deliver them himself. The result was another cult comedy show, better known as *Friday Night Live* after it had been moved forward one night. This show launched the careers of yet another wave of comics, including Jo Brand, Julian Clary and Harry Enfield. It was Elton's 120-word-a-minute monologues that held the show together. Funny and serious, they were the beginning of what would be a growing phenomenon – the comic as opinion leader. Andrew Collins, a third-year student in 1986, put it thus:

> Ben Elton is my big favourite at the moment. He's my guiding light. My moral compass. He's mobilised all the instinctive humanitarian, left-wing feelings that have been brewing up in me since leaving home and given voice to the way I feel deep down inside. I've never before been this laid bare with guilt – but good guilt, useful social guilt, practical guilt; not abstract, debilitating girlfriend-induced guilt . . .[19]

The comedy was mainly for a university-educated audience. What was being offered at the other end of the market also, coincidentally, took a giant leap upwards in quality in 1982 with the arrival of *Minder*, which ran from October 1979 to March 1994, and *Auf Wiedersehen, Pet*. A sign of the times was that both these series featured the working-class struggle to make money. The scriptwriters of *Steptoe and Son*, *Till Death Us Do Part* or *The Likely Lads* only occasionally allowed their characters' needs to earn a living to intrude on the humour, if at all, but hardly an episode of *Minder* went by without the hero, Terry McCann, being drawn into some dubious money-making scheme dreamt up by the unscrupulous Arthur Daley, played by George Cole. Though McCann, played by Denis Waterman, was an honest character, he was denied an honest living because he had recently been in prison. And the whole point of *Auf Wiedersehen, Pet*, first broadcast in November 1983, was that its cast of anti-heroes had been driven to find work on a German building site because there was none in their native Tyneside. At the time, the show's biggest star was Jimmy Nail, playing the Germanophobic Oz, though his fellow regulars Kevin Whately and Timothy Spall went on to greater success. Amid the humour, the writers Dick Clement and Ian La Frenais included a few sharp observations on unemployment and on British attitudes to the Germans.

Minder's success meant that the BBC was open to suggestions for a good comedy series about working-class Londoners on the make. John Sullivan, creator of the 1970s sitcom *Citizen Smith*, had unsuccessfully offered them a treatment for a series about a dodgy street-trader who would sell anything to anybody, but dealt only in cash. He then offered a series about the manager of a rundown football club, which was commissioned and allocated television time, but the controller of BBC1, Bill Cotton, suddenly pulled the plug on it because it clashed with a different project. This left Sullivan with no work and the BBC with an empty slot for a new series. Sullivan and his producer, Ray Butt, repaired for an emergency conference in a pub in the North End Road, during which Sullivan mentioned the rejected treatment. Butt, whose father had worked as a street-trader after leaving the RAF at the end of the war, thought the idea worth reviving. A few weeks later, Sullivan turned up at BBC Television Centre with a draft script for a show called *Readies*. Butt and the head of comedy, John Howard Davies, liked it and it was quickly expanded into a series.

The main problems that lay ahead were finding the right actor to play the principal character, Del Trotter, and choosing a new title. Sullivan had an idea that long titles grabbed people's attention, but no one at a senior level at the BBC knew the expression 'only fools and horses work', which beautifully suited the show's joke that the Trotter brothers worked day and night looking for the break to spare them from ever having to work again. Eventually, Sullivan's suggestion passed, for want of a better idea. Meanwhile, the lead role was offered first to a comic actor named Enn Reitel and then to Jim Broadbent, who turned it down. Two weeks before filming was to begin, Butt was watching a repeat of an episode of *Open All Hours*, and saw David Jason play the delivery boy. The idea of giving him a lead role met stiff resistance high up in the BBC, where they feared that it might offend Ronnie Barker, the star of *Open All Hours* and their greatest comedy asset. Sullivan was also doubtful, though one point in Jason's favour was that he did not look remotely like Nicholas Lyndhurst, the twenty-year-old former child star already cast as Del's younger brother, Rodney. One obstacle in Del Trotter's lifelong search for the easy life is the loss of both parents, which left him with a much younger brother to care for; Sullivan thought it would add poignancy if there was an element of doubt as to whether or not they really had the same father. Jason was shown the script and saw at once that landing this part could lift him out of a lifetime of being a supporting actor who played the elderly and the hopeless. He was hired, and work on the first series began in May 1981. There was a near disaster when Ray Butt, who was supposed to be the producer and director, was hospitalized for three weeks with a slipped disc, but even without him the first episode of *Only Fools and Horses*, in which Del endeavoured to sell a batch of suitcases that would not open, went out as scheduled in September 1981.

The series ended in December, having attracted an audience of 7.7m and a pile of letters to the BBC asking what the title meant. With some difficulty, Sullivan persuaded the corporation to commission a second series and allow him to supply a new theme song that explained the title. One episode in the new series had an ending drawn from real life. Sullivan's father was a plumber and had worked in a house where there were two valuable chandeliers that needed to be temporarily removed so that they would not be damaged by the work on the plumbing. Sullivan senior and his mates were on a ladder waiting to catch the chandelier, but the lad in the room above unscrewed the wrong one, which fell to the ground, shattered and earned all of them the sack. 'A Touch of Glass' drew an audience of 10.2m, the highest yet for the show. Even so, the future of the series was looking doubtful even when the second series ended; more people were still watching David Jason in *Open All Hours* than in *Only Fools and Horses.* It was only when the second series was repeated in summer 1983 that it suddenly became one of the most popular sitcoms ever broadcast on British television, running to seven series over twelve years. When the cast was brought together again for a Christmas trilogy in 1996, the final episode was watched by 24.3m people. It added new words to everyday language, as Sullivan collected new slang like 'plonker' and 'wally' and had Delboy popularize them. 'Wally' had been around for about eight years, in memory of a dog of that name who got lost during an open-air rock concert,[20] but the word entered the mainstream only in 1983, with the publication of a handbook explaining how to be a wally, should you want to be one.[21]

It was the accuracy of the observation of working-class life that gave the series its edge. Sullivan said:

> I was sick to death of the kind of comedies I saw on telly which were almost always based in the forties or earlier, with toffs and that sort of tugging-the-forelock, Gor-Bless-You-Guv type of stuff, which didn't exist. Now we had a modern, vibrant, multi-racial, new London where a lot of working-class guys had suits and a bit of dosh in their pockets, and that was a very different thing. That's what I wanted to write about.[22]

This statement could be taken as applying generally to so much 1980s television comedy: it was funny, because people recognized that, in its way, it was true.

Chapter 8

We Work the Black Seam

On Sunday morning, 4 March 1984, every man in the little village of Brampton, near Rotherham, appeared to be heading to the welfare and social club hall, built fifty-nine years earlier, and paid for by 3*d.* a week contributions from coal miners' wages. Anyone born in Brampton would have as the backcloth of their childhood the towers and slagheaps of the coal mines. Seeing Pit Lane teeming with miners walking to work for the 4 a.m. shift or emerging at lunchtime to repair to the miners' club in Knollbeck Road was as fixed in the daily routine as the school bell; the noise of the winding shaft was as familiar as road traffic. Most of the men in the village had known nothing else in their working lives but the furious and occasionally dangerous task of hewing coal hundreds of feet below ground.

The shift began with the descent into the earth in a metal cage. 'Most don't like it,' a Yorkshire miner recalled. That was understandable; it was dangerous work, with a level of fatal casualties 50 per cent higher than even the construction industry. In 1983, thirty British miners were killed underground. The miner continued:

> They go very quiet on the cage. You find people in there like myself, in an animated discussion just prior to, and then actually stepping on the cage; but then as soon as I know everybody is on it – I always go quiet at that time. Other people make light and tell jokes and carry on and it's as well they do, because when the cage lifts up off the keps [iron bars holding the cage in place] and you know it's going to come, at that moment it's a terrible thing.

After that alarming descent, there were hours of heavy labour in the surreal atmosphere hundreds of feet below ground.

> Who could understand, coming on a scene like this? Dense dust, heat, water, men rocking and shovelling, sweat pouring off their faces, throwing stones off their shovels, and like demented moles laughing their daft heads off. The furious pace can make it very difficult, because if you're not keeping up and the stone starts to mount up, when the man in front stops for a minute . . . you're clearing away the backlog.[1]

But it was work, the source of a livelihood, of social cohesion and self-respect. Without Cortonwood Colliery, where 1,000 men were employed, Brampton would lose its economic reason for existing. This was a productive pit, which in 1984 had at least another five years' life, the miners had been told; some of them had only recently been transferred from less promising sites. But Jack Wake, branch secretary of the National Union of Mineworkers (NUM), was summoning the men to pass on a message from George Hayes, South Yorkshire director of the National Coal Board (NCB), that Cortonwood was to close.

Recent research by Francis Beckett and David Hencke has thrown up the intriguing possibility that it was all a mistake. The Coal Board had a closure list, which their chairman Ian MacGregor intended to present to Arthur Scargill, president of the NUM, on 6 March, hoping that the union's reaction would be a strike ballot, which they might lose. Cortonwood was not on the list.[2] George Hayes had misunderstood his instructions and clumsily provoked a strike in an area of the country where the union solidarity was unbroken. Wake was not a militant shop steward in the Scargill mould, but a pragmatic, moderately right-wing local councillor. However, faced with a pit closure, he had no hesitation in admonishing the older miners not to be tempted by the NCB's recently improved redundancy terms of £1,000 for each year of service, which would allow some of them to dream of more than £30,000 in the bank – a king's ransom to anyone on working-class wages – but to put the interests of the younger miners first.[3] That night, at midnight, a small group of volunteers threw together a makeshift shack at the entrance to Cortonwood pit and declared themselves to be a picket line. The greatest strike in post-war Britain had begun.

No event in post-war history has divided public opinion in Britain so fiercely as the miners' strike. For many, it was a moving story of pit villages withstanding great adversity and immense political pressure to defend their communities against cold economic logic and a hostile government. It has inspired more books, documentaries, drama and song than any other industrial dispute in Britain, exceeding even the General Strike of 1926. One example is the very fine track 'We Work the Black Seam' on the 1985 album, *The Dream of Blue Turtles* by Sting, which lamented the 'economic logic' that destroyed the mining families' way of life. There is also Ewan MacColl's 'Daddy, What Did You Do in the Strike?', Pulp's 'Last Day of the Miners' Strike' and Billy Bragg's 'Which Side Are You On?' The strike forms the background to the highly acclaimed film *Billy Elliot,* and an episode of the television drama *Our Friends in the North*, as well as Comic Strip's spoof of a Hollywood movie, *The Strike*, in which Peter Richardson played Al Pacino playing Arthur Scargill. There are many more.

Another version of the story of the miners' strike is that it was an attempt by an almost insanely ambitious and dictatorial union boss to use the tough young men manning picket lines to taunt the police and defy the will of an elected government – parliamentary democracy versus Arthur Scargill's thugs. The most powerful evidence deployed in defence of this argument is that during the entire year of the dispute, Scargill wilfully refused to ask his men, through a national ballot, whether or not they wanted to be out on strike. He used union solidarity to try to picket out the non-strikers.

Elected president of the NUM in 1982 at the age of only forty-three, having won an unprecedented seventy per cent of the votes cast, Scargill was indisputably the most famous and most charismatic union leader of the post-war period. Intelligent, self-educated, strong-willed, a confident television performer and superb platform speaker, he was also intolerant, didactic and difficult to work with or reason with. His friend, Vic Allen, an unreconstructed Stalinist who knew Scargill well, described him as 'essentially a shy person who projects himself as compensation for his shyness'.[4] Scargill socialized, but in contrast to most trade union leaders, he did not drink and did not enjoy trading gossip. He could inspire intense loyalty, but sometimes loyalty turned to bitter enmity, as in the case of Jim Parker, who was constantly at Scargill's side as his driver and minder for years, but turned against him late in the 1980s. He also evoked a particular fear and loathing in people who did not like militant trade unionists. The Tory MP Geoffrey Dickens told the Commons: 'Arthur Scargill is a confessed Marxist, surrounded by communist aides and advisers. Even more serious . . . support for Mr Scargill is coming from the Kremlin'.[5] The word 'communist' was often hurled in those days at people who were nothing of the sort, including Tony Benn and Ken Livingstone, but in Scargill's case it was reasonably accurate. He was a former

Young Communist, who transferred to the Labour Party without abandoning the Leninist view of the class struggle, and he had no problem about accepting Soviet aid for the strike. In old age, he was one of the last people in Britain with words of praise for the late Josef Stalin.[6]

None of this detracted from the admiration he inspired in young miners. On the picket, they chanted 'Arthur Scargill walks on water', and in the miners' clubs they told jokes that were a tribute to his stature. One was that when his predecessor Joe Gormley died, he was offered a place in heaven, but accepted it only after he had been promised that Scargill was to be consigned to hell. Later, Gormley was knocked off his cloud by a fast-driven limousine with the number plate AS 1, and complained to St Peter that he had been deceived. 'Oh don't worry,' said St Peter, 'that's just God. He thinks he's Arthur Scargill.'

The reason that Scargill refused to hold a strike ballot was that he had held three already, and had been thrice bitten. There was a strike ballot in January 1982, during the interregnum after he had been elected NUM president, but before Joe Gormley had left office. The NUM was demanding a 23.7 per cent pay rise, but on the eve of the ballot, Gormley wrote an article in the *Daily Express* urging the men to accept the Coal Board's offer of 9.5 per cent, which they did by a margin of 55 to 45 per cent. It was, as the newspapers reported at the time, a clear 'snub' for Scargill.[7] In October, six months after Scargill had assumed office, another round of pay talks broke down. Scargill toured the coalfields urging the men to vote for a strike, but they voted by 61 per cent to 39 per cent against. In March 1983, the South Wales, Yorkshire and Scottish miners all voted to strike in opposition to pit closures, but the areas with less militant traditions did not react. Scargill summoned the NUM executive to an emergency meeting and told them that he wanted to call a national strike without a ballot, which they had the power to do under a rule change he had recently introduced, but other members of the executive warned that he risked tearing apart the union. Scargill reluctantly agreed to a ballot, and once again, the men voted 61 to 39 per cent against a strike.

By March 1984, as the strike that started in Cortonwood spread across the whole Yorkshire region, and another strike – also over pit closures – began in Scotland, Scargill's mind was made up: no more ballots. He argued that there was a legitimate case for not balloting over pit closures. Unlike a pay offer, which affected every union member equally, redundancies affected some members but not others, and those whose jobs were safe would be in a position not to support those who were under threat. Peter Heathfield, the recently elected general secretary of the NUM, who was expected to be a moderating influence on Scargill, backed him without reservation throughout the momentous events that lay ahead. 'Can you reasonably say to miners working in relatively successful coalfields "you have the right to determine whether people working in less successful coalfields can defend their jobs"?'[8] he asked, rhetorically.

On Tuesday, 6 March, Ian MacGregor called in the leaders of all three mining unions to inform them that he intended to bring the industry to break-even point by 1988 and, to that end, he proposed to shut twenty pits in the coming year alone and make 20,000 miners redundant. As the miners' leaders emerged, the older and rather wiser Mick McGahey, NUM vice-president, and a lifelong Communist, was heard to say: 'I want to make it clear that we are not dealing with niceties here. We shall not be constitutionalised out of a defence of our jobs.'[9] On the same day, the Scottish NUM called its members out on strike over the threat to close the Polmaise Colliery. Two days later, on 8 March, the Yorkshire and Scottish areas went to the NUM National Executive asking for its approval for a strike that had already begun, and the executive decided to make it a nationwide strike. Only three members of the executive, from the East Midlands, voted for a ballot.

Pickets rapidly formed outside the pits where miners were still working. The Yorkshire miners, in particular, were formidably well-organized. Each evening, at about 7.00 p.m., an NUM branch official arrived at the miners' welfare office at Maltby Colliery with a brown envelope containing instructions for the next day's pickets. The miners would then pore over maps looking for back roads where they could avoid police blocks. And off they went. From Monday 12 March onwards, thousands poured out of Yorkshire into Nottinghamshire, Derbyshire or Lancashire, to appear at the gates as their colleagues arrived to begin their shifts. The executive had hoped that even those miners who had not voted to strike would balk at crossing a picket line, but there was a tradition of bad feeling between the Nottinghamshire and Yorkshire miners dating back to the General Strike of 1926, when the men from Nottinghamshire formed a breakaway union and went back to work. Though almost no one involved in that dispute was still alive in 1984, the pit villages knew their history. Pay was better in Nottinghamshire and the long-term future more secure, and the miners objected to being told by men with Yorkshire accents that they should strike without a vote. At the end of the first day, eighty-one pits were on strike, eighty-three were working. Within a couple of days, picketing had reduced the number of working pits to twenty-nine, but that was as far it got. From the very start of the strike, the miners' union was catastrophically split.

The miners' other weakness was that, this time, they had not caught the government unprepared. For eight years the Conservatives had been thinking about a possible miners' strike and making preparations. In 1978, when they were in opposition, a group headed by Nicholas Ridley had produced a strategic report on how a Conservative government might defeat union militancy. They concluded that 'the most likely battleground will be the coal industry', and laid out a series of precautions that needed to be taken against this possibility, including building up coal stocks at the power stations, making plans to import coal and switching to dual coal/oil-firing as fast as possible.[10] At the time, this was all too radical for Margaret Thatcher, who was single-mindedly interested in winning an election. Even afterwards, she recoiled at the thought of taking on the mighty NUM. Three years before the miners' strike, in January 1981, NCB chairman, Sir Derek Ezra, warned that the price of coal was falling and that the twenty-three least productive pits were losing around £85m per year, or nearly £20 per ton of coal. Someone on the management side is thought to have quietly tipped off the union that a pit closure programme that would affect thousands of jobs was on the way. As unofficial strikes broke out in Kent and South Wales, Energy Secretary David Howell and his deputy, John Moore, were prepared to take them on. Unions and the press were briefed that there would no government climb-down, until Margaret Thatcher studied the battlefield. 'I was appalled to find that we had entered into a battle we could not win,'[11] she wrote. No pits were closed, and when a new energy secretary, Nigel Lawson, was appointed later in the year, the first thing Thatcher told him was 'Nigel, we mustn't have a coal strike.'[12]

There was no strike on Lawson's watch, but he was assiduous in following the advice in that old 1978 discussion paper. He sacked Glyn England, the chairman of the Central Electricity Generating Board, because 'he had little stomach for a fight with the NUM' and replaced him with Walter Marshall, an enthusiast for nuclear power who, for that reason, had been sacked by Tony Benn when he was energy secretary and therefore 'had no affection for Benn's friend and ally, Scargill'.[13] Next, he sacked Derek Ezra, who had worked in the coal industry since being demobbed in 1947, and replaced him with the seventy-year-old Ian MacGregor, who had completed his three-year stint running British Steel, where he cut its workforce from 166,000 to 71,000, making it almost profitable and ready for privatization. After much haggling, MacGregor settled for a salary of £58,325, plus a £1.5m fee to Lazard Frères of New York, on top of the £1.8m they had already been paid for their generosity in lending MacGregor to British Steel. 'Ian was widely seen as an overpaid, over-aged, ruthless American whose main achievement at British Steel had been to slash jobs,' Lawson recorded, without a hint of disapproval.[14]

The other task was to move coal from where it was stored at pit heads to the power stations. Glyn England had been reluctant to undertake this, fearing that it might provoke a strike, but once Walter Marshall was in place, part of the railway system was separated off and dedicated twenty-four hours a day, seven days a week, to shifting millions of tonnes of coal for the sole purpose of defeating a strike that had not yet broken out. By 1983, the power stations had more than 58m tonnes in reserve, which allowed them to keep on generating electricity for the entire strike. Four months into the strike, Margaret Thatcher and Norman Tebbit began to fret that time was not on the government's side, and neither of them trusted the wily Peter Walker, who had succeeded Lawson as energy secretary. He was an old ally of Edward Heath, and Thatcher frankly admitted in her memoirs that she kept him in the cabinet only because he would have been more trouble outside. However, Walker brought Thatcher together with Marshall, who produced charts to demonstrate that they could keep the power stations running until November 1985, or longer, if more miners could be induced to break the strike. To win, the miners would have had to stay on strike for a minimum of eighteen months, or possibly two years.

However, Scargill was not anticipating that the NUM would fight alone. The miners had a track record of taking sympathetic action in support of other unions' industrial disputes. This was payback time, and he was counting on the backing of unionized power-workers, lorry drivers and others to bring large parts of the economy to a halt. Other union leaders, particularly the left-wing leadership of the TGWU, were willing in principle to come to the miners' aid, but their members were not. In July, the TGWU called a national dock strike that could have severely disrupted the steel industry, but the dockers showed little enthusiasm for action, and the lorry drivers even less. The strike was called off after ten days. There was a second dock strike in Scotland, in August, over the unloading of imported coal for the Ravenscraig plant, which lasted twenty-six days.

The Ridley Report had also called for a large mobile squad of police to 'uphold the law against violent picketing' and suggested bluntly that the government should 'cut off the money supply to the strikers, and make the union finance them'. Both pieces of advice were quickly enacted. The government announced that families of striking miners were to be deemed to be receiving strike pay from their union. They knew quite well that this was not happening, but the fiction disqualified strikers' families from claiming benefits. In some pit villages, most of the population had no regular income for a year. Lianne Roberts, from a mining family in South Wales, told the BBC: 'During the strike we had to endure no hot water or heating through the winter as we had no coal. We were provided with special school dinner tickets for free meals and received food parcels for the miners' families'. As the months passed, the hardship increased, and the prospect of victory dimmed, but the social cohesion of the mining communities generally held, aided by a massive voluntary effort. There was hardly a street corner in any British city centre without a bucket where people could donate to the miners' families. Some donated rather more than small change: the oil billionaire, John Paul Getty, gave £100,000. Billy Bragg had his first political experience doing benefit gigs for the miners. Kim Howells, the future Labour foreign minister, was then an NUM official in a part of South Wales where not one miner went back to work while the strike was on. He recalled:

> To feed up to 20,000 families each week, as well as paying the huge and myriad costs of picketing, was a problem which was resolved only by creating what amounted to an alternative welfare state. Everyone was mobilised . . . the chapels, churches and political parties both inside and outside the UK. Meetings of over ten thousand were addressed by Welsh miners in Bologna and Milan . . . [M]en and women who in normal times rarely left their villages and valleys were rapidly becoming lay-experts in matters which had never before impinged on their lives. They were travelling vast distances day after day, discovering allies and enemies in the most unlikely places: friendly Hindu communities in Birmingham, hostile steelworkers in Newport; magnificently supportive farmers in the wilds of Dyfed and hostile city councillors in the chambers of Cardiff.[15]

No time was wasted bussing in police officers to protect the strike-breaking miners and make sure that they could get past the picket lines unhindered. The strike formally began on Monday, 5 March. By Wednesday, 3,000 police from seventeen forces were at the pitheads and other locations around the East Midlands. The government was not going to be taken by surprise as it had been in 1972, when 800 police officers assigned to keep the Saltley coke depot open faced the sudden appearance of 25,000 miners, organized by Scargill. MI5 was running a huge intelligence operation, sending in regular reports to the government about Scargill and his immediate colleagues. This fact was later confirmed in the memoirs of Stella Rimington, the MI5 officer who ran the operation, who believed that Scargill, McGahey, Heathfield and, by implication, other NUM officials were subversives intent on destroying democracy, and therefore thought it was the intelligence service's duty to keep watch on them. It was also widely suspected that MI5 was bugging rooms where NUM activists met in order to find out where the pickets were going to appear next, so that the police could be there to stop them. Mrs Rimington denied it:

> The activities of the picket lines and miners' wives support groups were not our concern, even though they were of great concern to the police. But [the NUM] was directed by a triumvirate who had declared they were using the strike to try to bring down the elected government of Mrs Thatcher . . . We in MI5 limited our investigations to the activities of those who were using the strike for subversive purposes.[16]

Their activities included tapping the private and office telephone lines of the NUM leaders and bugging their meeting rooms. Consequently, on certain days there were police blocks on the motorway exits in the East Midlands, and coach or car loads of miners from Yorkshire or Kent were stopped and ordered to go back whence they came. The newly elected MP for Sedgefield, Tony Blair, tried to drive to Nottingham to see what was happening, but was turned back at a police roadblock. He protested in the Commons that 'there was no basis in law' for this interference in the free movement of traffic.[17]

Pickets found their way through none the less, and the sense of adventure in just reaching their destination added to the excitable atmosphere as they confronted lines of officers, whose accents revealed that they had been bussed from far away. Seeing hundreds of miners form a picket line was either enervating or intimidating, depending on which side you were on. These were men accustomed to hard physical labour, fired up and ready for trouble. They liked to ridicule the police by singing or whistling the theme from old Laurel and Hardy films and, if they were sufficient in number, they would literally push the police lines back by chanting 'easy, easy' and heaving in unison. Inevitably, there was violence; in the first six months alone there were 5,897 arrests and 1,039 convictions.

The first fatal casualty occurred before the strike was a fortnight old, when a twenty-four-year-old miner, David Jones, was killed by a brick that hit him in the chest as he walked away from a picket line. He was on foot because the police had made the coach that was bringing the pickets stop some distance away. No great effort seems to have been put into finding the killer; Jones's death merited one sentence in the minutes of the directors of the North Notts

Mining Board.[18] However, his funeral, on 23 March, attracted a procession half a mile long. Two days later, Ian Tarren, a twenty-five-year-old miner who had not joined the strike, hanged himself at home in Peterlee, County Durham, allegedly after being taunted for being a 'scab'.[19] Another strike-breaker, James Clay, committed suicide in June, allegedly after threats to his twelve-year-old daughter. Contrary to what is often claimed, the only miner recorded as having died on a picket line was Joe Green, a sixty-year-old miner who was crushed by an articulated lorry outside the Ferrybridge power station on 15 June, although two South Wales miners died in an accident on their way to a picket line. Other fatalities occurred because desperation drove miners or members of their families to scrabble around on slag heaps collecting lumps of coal, which could be sold for £2 a sack. It was a dangerous way to earn money. In November, two brothers, Paul and Darren Holmes, aged fourteen and fifteen, died when a railway embankment collapsed on them while they coal-picking in the pit village of Goldthorpe, near Doncaster.[20] Another fourteen-year-old from Yorkshire, Paul Womersley, and a Northumberland miner, Frederick Taylor, died in similar circumstances. The NUM put the overall death total at 11, along with 7,000 injured, 11,000 miners arrested and 1,000 miners sacked for their part in the strike.

The best known confrontation between miners and police took place outside the Orgreave coke works, where about 5,000 miners gathered to picket. That they were not stopped on their way suggests that someone in government wanted this to be the battleground where the police and miners faced each other in force. On day one, 29 May, eighty-four people were arrested and sixty-nine injured. The pickets returned the next day, with Scargill at their head. He was arrested, but released on bail. On day three, the pickets surprised the police by dispersing suddenly, as if they had had enough, but the confrontation dragged on, day after day, for three weeks, reaching a climax on 18 June, when an estimated 6,500 pickets, led by Scargill in person, in his trademark baseball cap, faced more than 3,000 police with riot shields or on horseback. A series of running skirmishes followed. After one police charge, which drove the pickets across a railway bridge away from the coke works, Scargill was found sitting on the ground by a burning barricade with his head in his hands. He was taken to hospital with head, leg and arm injuries, one of at least eighty people injured that day. The police claimed that he slipped off the bank and hit his head on a railway sleeper. He said that he was struck on the head by a riot shield.

Scargill was defying the law by being outside Orgreave at all, as he well knew. So was every other miner on the picket line, because the miners' dispute was with the coal board, not British Steel, and this was 'secondary picketing', which had been outlawed in 1981 by Jim Prior, the then employment secretary. This point was not lost on David Owen, the SDP leader, who asked repeatedly during Prime Minister's Questions in the Commons why British Steel did not injunct the NUM. Each time, Thatcher replied grumpily that the steel industry management was at liberty to go to law if they thought that it was in their interests. This was deliberately disingenuous. British Steel would have taken the miners to court if that was what the government had wanted. When Thatcher addressed a private meeting of backbench Conservative MPs on 19 July 1984, she did not pretend that the government was any kind of passive spectator in a dispute between management and a union. This was the occasion when she described the miners' leaders as the 'enemy within'. There is no verbatim record of what she said, but her speech notes have been preserved, on which is written: 'Enemy without – beaten him. Enemy within. Miners' leaders, Liverpool and some local authorities – just as dangerous, in a way more difficult to fight.'[21] But Mrs Thatcher and her ministers were aware of the unpopularity of the law on secondary picketing, which was opposed by every trade union and by the Labour Party. Using it to have Scargill arrested would have played into his hands.

The government was feeling its way towards a much more subtle and destructive way to deploy the law against the NUM. Central to it was a mysterious individual named David Hart, a property dealer, right-wing libertarian and amateur political fixer, who had inherited a fortune from his banker father. Touring the Midlands in a chauffeur-driven Mercedes, using the alias David Lawrence, he built up a network of disaffected miners, while keeping in contact with Thatcher. He introduced himself to Ian MacGregor and opened up to him the possibility that individual miners could be the shock troops who went into legal battle against the NUM. He was, the NCB chairman gratefully recalled, 'the man I had been looking for'.[22] Hart raised money from a number of businessmen, including Sir Hector Laing and Lord Hanson, both major donors to the Conservative Party, and John Paul Getty, who was persuaded to make amends for his generosity to striking miners' families.

With this financial backing, two miners, Ken Foulstone and Bob Taylor, took the NUM to court over the failure to hold a national ballot. In September, a high court obligingly ruled that the strike was unofficial and illegal. Scargill's reaction was predictably defiant. 'There is no High Court judge going to take away the democratic right of our union to deal with its internal affairs,' he pronounced. The next move was to serve a writ on Arthur Scargill for contempt of court. This was not a simple matter because the writ had to be served to Scargill in person, which meant that they had to know where to find him, when he was forever rushing about from picket line to mass meeting. Besides, it would have been a brave or foolish solicitor who handed Scargill a writ when he was surrounded by striking miners. But they knew where to find him on Monday, 1 October, because that was the day the Labour Party annual conference, in Blackpool, would be debating the strike. Hart hired a helicopter to transfer the writ and the man serving it from London to Blackpool. Next, the server had to get into the hall, which he did by producing a photographer's pass issued to the *Daily Express*, to serve the writ in full view of hundreds of party delegates. The moment was captured in a photograph published exclusively in the *Daily Express.* The photographer who took the image later went to the press desk claiming to have lost his pass and asked for another, which he was not given.[23] On 10 October, a court found Scargill and the NUM in contempt of court, and fined them £1,000 and £200,000 respectively.

Scargill's policy on fines such as these was to refuse to pay on the grounds that the Conservatives had no right to pass the legislation under which they were imposed. On this occasion, somewhat to his annoyance, his £1,000 fine was paid by an anonymous well-wisher. However, the union's fine remained unpaid and, on 25 October, a judge ordered the entire assets of the NUM to be seized. Scargill and his colleagues had foreseen this possibility and had squirreled the union's money into a labyrinth of bank accounts where the sequesters could not find it.

As this was going on, coincidentally, the miners were suddenly closer to victory than at any time, because on 28 September the small, half-forgotten National Association of Colliery Overmen Deputies and Shotfirers (NACODS) announced the result of a ballot in which 83 per cent of its members had voted to strike. Its members included all the overseers responsible for safety below ground, without whom it was illegal to operate the pits. The point seemed lost on Ian MacGregor, but Walker and Thatcher understood that a NACODS strike would close the Nottinghamshire pits and possibly force the government to surrender; and since NACODS' leaders had conducted a proper ballot, the legality of their action could not be challenged. 'Apart from the initial few days of the strike in March, this was the time when we felt most concern,'[24] Thatcher admitted. The government's problems were worsened by MacGregor's refusal to treat the threat seriously. Thatcher had to ring him from her room at the Grand Hotel in Brighton, during the Conservative Party conference, just before an IRA bomb almost killed her, to order him to negotiate.[25] Later that same month, when invited by Neil

Kinnock to say that she still had confidence in MacGregor, she changed the subject.[26] Arthur Scargill would say later that he believed that at this point Thatcher knew she was beaten and would have to settle on the NUM's terms. But on 24 October, the NACODS executive decided to accept a 'modified' colliery review offered by the government and to call off their strike, a decision that Scargill thought 'inexplicable'.[27] The miners' last chance of victory had slipped away.

No sooner had that opportunity been lost than Scargill suffered his worst publicity so far when the *Sunday Times* revealed that Roger Windsor, chief executive of the NUM, had been in Libya, apparently soliciting money from Colonel Gaddafi. It was not the only tale of money from dubious foreign sources going to the NUM. In December 1984, Mikhail Gorbachev, who was soon to become head of the Soviet Communist Party, visited Britain and was chided by Thatcher over intelligence reports that the USSR was secretly funding the strike. In fact, some Soviet money was sent to the International Miners' Organisation run from France by Alain Simon, a Communist ally of Scargill. It would be a source of endless recrimination within the NUM in the early 1990s, precisely because the money never reached the British miners. It arrived after the strike was over. But the story of money from Libya was more damaging even than rumours of Moscow gold, because of the shocking incident the previous April when, as discussed in Chapter 5, someone opened fire from inside the Libyan embassy in St James's Square and a stray bullet killed the young police constable Yvonne Fletcher. The *Sunday Times* had also discovered that Scargill had been to Paris earlier in the month, travelling under the alias of 'Mr Smith' to meet foreign trade union leaders, one of whom was Libyan. The inference was that Scargill was accepting money from a regime held responsible for the murder on a London street of a young policewoman. The news finally killed the fragile relationship between Scargill and Neil Kinnock. Without waiting to hear Scargill's explanation, Kinnock pronounced that any offer of Libyan aid would be 'an insult to everything the British Labour movement stands for'. Scargill defiantly insisted that talking to a Libyan trade union leader was not the same as talking to the Libyan government. He also claimed to have 'no idea what happened between Mr Windsor and the leader of Libya'.[28]

This would not be the last occasion that Roger Windsor made front-page news. He was a recent arrival at NUM headquarters, appointed by Scargill, but resigned suddenly in July 1989. It then emerged that he was responsible for an incident several years earlier that had nearly landed the NUM in court, when a letter purportedly written by one of the Nottinghamshire miners' leaders was exposed as a forgery. Windsor had forged it. He had also forged a letter supposedly sent by Peter Heathfield to Sheffield Council, in which the NUM agreed to pay £90,000 for landscaping in return for planning permission to erect steps to the front door of its headquarters. The NUM denied sending the letter, and for five years its head office's main entrance was suspended eight feet above ground.[29] Months after his resignation, Windsor made an explosive reappearance on the front pages after he told the *Daily Mirror* – for a fee of £130,000 – a sensational tale about how he, Scargill and Heathfield had used money donated by Libya during the strike to pay their mortgages. The story came with a picturesque detail of a mountan of cash being brought to Scargill's office, where the NUM president divided it into piles and divvied it out. Until then, whatever else their enemies thought of Scargill and Heathfield, it was assumed that they were incorruptible; now it appeared that they had been exposed as embezzlers. Over time, it was established that there was only one detail in Windsor's story that was demonstrably true: he had indeed used nearly £30,000 of money intended for the miners to pay his own mortgage, for which he was successfully sued in the French courts. Scargill and Heathfield had not. Roy Greenslade, who was editor of the *Daily Mirror* when the story appeared, wrote a 2,000-word apology thirteen years later, saying that he wished he had never published the story.[30] Whether or not any money ever came to the NUM from Libya has not been established.

One explanation for Windsor's behaviour is that he was a fantasist who developed a grudge against Scargill and Heathfield, and needed money. Tam Dalyell, the same Labour MP who relentlessly pursued Thatcher over the sinking of the *Belgrano*, heard another explanation from his contacts in the world of intelligence and alleged, in the House of Commons, that Windsor was an MI5 plant. Windsor denied it, and when he was named as an MI5 agent in the *Sunday Express* by the former Conservative MP Rupert Allason, he sued; the newspaper settled out of court.[31] It is certainly possible that MI5 had an informant at NUM headquarters. Cathy Massiter confirmed that MI5 discussed trying to get Harry Newton employed there, but had to drop the idea because he was too ill. David Shayler, an MI5 officer who went public in 1997, described having seen the organization's forty-volume file on Scargill, which he said confirmed that the MI5 had at least one well-placed source in the NUM. As discussed, Stella Rimington's published memoirs confirm that MI5 was spying on Scargill, McGahey and Heathfield, but she claimed that all the information they forwarded to Margaret Thatcher was 'carefully scrutinized' to make sure that it was 'properly within our remit'.[32] Whether or not that remit included retaining an informant in NUM headquarters, she did not say, though when asked about Windsor, she replied: 'It would be correct to say that he, Roger Windsor, was never an agent in any sense of the word that you can possibly imagine and that MI5 did not run agents in the NUM.'[33]

While the pictures of Roger Windsor consorting with Gaddafi were bad for the miners, something worse – far worse – followed two weeks later. In Wales, a small number of miners had filtered back to work, creating huge resentment among those still on strike. There, as in England, the resources of the state were liberally expended in protecting and encouraging strike-breakers and, allegedly, in acts of provocation. One miner's wife was walking home in the dark in the little town of Abertillery, when a van pulled up ahead of her. 'I could hear the voices of the men shouting "Slut, prostitute!" . . . When I got alongside the van, it was full of policemen,'[34] she claimed. One strike-breaker was David Williams, from Rhymney, who worked at the Merthyr Tydfil coalfield six miles from his home. Each morning, a taxi called at his door and he was driven to work along the A465, accompanied by two police cars and a motorcycle outrider. The procession followed the same route ten days in succession. On the tenth day, 30 November, a 46 lb concrete block was dropped from a bridge over the road. It hit the car, only slightly injuring Williams, but instantly killing David Wilkie, the taxi driver. Wilkie had two children under thirteen by a previous relationship, and a fiancée, by whom he had a two-year-old daughter and who was pregnant with a baby, born six weeks after Wilkie's death. His mother had a heart condition and was taken to hospital after she heard of his death. His funeral was led by the Bishop of Llandaff, and his death created an outcry that the death of the miner, David Jones, never had. The police soon found the culprits, two young miners named Dean Hancock and Russell Shankland, who were convicted of murder and sentenced to life imprisonment in May 1985. The verdict set off a strike by 700 miners in Merthyr Tydfil who had only just gone back to work. When the case went to appeal in October, a high court ruled that the judge had been wrong, and reduced the conviction from murder to manslaughter. The two men spent five years in prison.

By the time of Wilkie's death the mood had changed on the picket lines. Confrontations with the police became rarer; arrests and injuries were fewer. The sense of defeat was pervasive. It was winter, but the power stations were easily coping with demand. The NUM's attempts to hide its money in foreign bank accounts were coming apart. Everything, even the union headquarters, had been seized by the sequestrator. In December, leaders of the TUC approached the government, using Robert Maxwell as an emissary, in the

The dawn of an era: Margaret Thatcher talks to television interviewers as she arrives at No. 10 Downing Street to assume office, 4 May 1979. (PA Photos/TopFoto)

(left) On 24 February 1981, Prince Charles posed for photographs for the first time with his new fiancée, the nineteen-year-old Lady Diana Spencer. (Topham/PA)

(below) Between the engagement and the wedding, Brixton went up in flames. Locals are seen here walking past a burnt-out building on the morning of 13 April 1981. (Getty Images)

(above) Steel helmets left behind by the defeated Argentine conscripts after the battle of Goose Green, 21 May 1982. (PA Photos/TopFoto)

(left) Protest and survive: the leader of the Labour Party, Michael Foot, heads a CND march, October 1983. (Robin Weaver/Alamy)

(above) The shattered remains of the Droppin' Well disco, Ballykelly, Northern Ireland, where British soldiers used to go to meet local girls. An INLA bomb killed sixteen people on 7 December 1982.
(PA Photos /TopFoto)

(left) Some wonder whether the miners' leader, Arthur Scargill, was lured into making the Orgreave coke works the scene of the main confrontation between pickets and police. Typically, he was there in person, until the police took him away.
(Martin Jenkinson/Alamy)

Princess Diana, Prince Charles, Bob Geldof and Paula Yates take their places for the Greatest Gig in the Galaxy, 13 July 1985.
(Pictorial Press Ltd/Alamy Property)

Talking Red Wedge. Tony Benn, Billy Bragg and the author crossing Westminster Bridge in July 1985. As I recall, Tony talked, we listened.
(Paul Slattery)

(above left) Jacqueline Hill, the Leeds student who was the last woman murdered by the criminal known as the 'Yorkshire Ripper'. Her death caused a public outcry against police incompetence. (TopFoto)

(above right) Andreas Whittam Smith, founder and editor of the *Independent*, in his office on launch day, 7 October 1986. (TopFoto /UPP)

(right) Nicholas Pearce, Managing Director of Cellular One, showing off the latest in state-of-the-art technology. He was, he claimed, talking to someone in the USA. (PA Photos/TopFoto)

(above left) Some public figures were flattered to see themselves caricatured on *Spitting Image*. What Diana and her sister-in-law, Fergie, Duchess of York, thought of these hideous creations can only be surmised. (Trinity Mirror/Mirrorpix/Alamy Property)

(above right) George O'Dowd, from south-east London, aka Boy George, performing with Culture Club. (Ullsteinbild/TopFoto)

(below) Day one of the Big Bang in the City of London, 27 October 1986. (John Sturrock/Alamy)

Hillsborough football stadium, Sheffield, 15 April 1989: desperate Liverpool fans struggling to escape the crush that left 96 dead.
(Getty Images)

It's over: a tearful Mrs Thatcher departed from Downing Street on 28 November 1990, unfairly sacked, as she saw it.
(Trinity Mirror/Mirrorpix/Alamy)

hope of mediating a settlement. They believed that Scargill and the NUM were in the mood to settle, though they were not saying so. This was not really what Thatcher wanted, but on 19 February 1985, she met seven TUC leaders, impressed them with her grasp of detail, and left them with some hope that they might be making headway. A proposal was drawn up by Peter Walker and the next day the TUC leaders presented it to the NUM executive, who unanimously rejected it.

The number of NUM members breaking the strike was now rising by 2,500 a week, and by 27 February, the NCB triumphantly reported that more than half the NUM's membership had turned up to work. On Sunday, 3 March, the NUM called another delegate conference to discuss whether or not to continue. It was preceded by a meeting of the executive, which could not decide what to recommend, being split 11–11. Scargill abstained, as if he knew the game was up but was not going to be the one to call time.[35] The delegates voted 98–91 for a return to work. The great strike was over.

One question left open was how much the strike had cost the nation. Arthur Scargill put the figure at £8 billion; the Treasury's figure, at least for public consumption, was £2.75 billion. It was only in 2008 that the Treasury released papers that gave a more accurate and detailed estimate of the cost. Their published figure did not include the costs that lingered after the miners went back to work, which were £1.1 billion in 1985–6 alone. This was disclosed in a written note to Peter Rees, the chief secretary of the Treasury, by one of his civil servants, who admonished him: 'The aggregate figures for 1985–6 have not previously been quoted and should not be volunteered.' Other large costs were simply excluded, such as the value of coal taken from stockpiles to keep the powers stations going, or the wages that the miners lost by being out on strike. 'Real sophisticates may say the cost is the sum of the accounting losses and loss of miners' pay, i.e. a rough measure of GDP foregone. This would cost well over £5 billion,'[36] a Treasury note suggested.

In addition, there was the immeasurable cost in human terms, from the destruction of village communities and from the enduring bitter enmity between those who worked and those who went on strike. The real cost was borne by the mining villages whose lives had been sustained by the industry. At the onset of the strike, the NCB employed a workforce of 208,000, of whom 184,000 were members of the NUM. Once the union was beaten, the government set about cutting their numbers with vindictive haste. Within ten years, more than 90 per cent of the jobs were gone. In July 1984, Roy Lynk, an NUM official from Nottinghamshire who had assumed leadership of the strike-breakers, formally applied to the NCB for negotiating rights free of the NUM, for which the NUM sacked him and took him to court. The NUM won the judgement, ironically, because Lynk had acted on his own authority without a ballot. The victory was only temporary. With much covert encouragement from the NCB and government, the Nottinghamshire and South Derbyshire miners voted to form a breakaway union, the Union of Democratic Mineworkers (UDM), which exists to this day. At the time of writing, the British coal industry employs 5,700 people, about 1,600 of whom are members of the NUM, with just over 1,000 in the UDM.[37]

Where the pits used to be there are now country parks or urban developments such as leisure and retail centres. The thriving miners' welfare club in Brampton village, where it all began, was vandalized but reinvented to become a social club for plumbers, caretakers, shop-fitters and call-centre staff, there being no miners left in the vicinity. In Shirebrook, on the Nottinghamshire-Derbyshire border, former strikers and strike-breakers still drank in separate pubs, twenty years later.[38]

Chapter 9

Feed the World

Bob Geldof had been through the roller-coaster of show-business since moving to London from his native Ireland. His band, The Boomtown Rats, turned down a £1m offer from Virgin Records, signed up with a smaller label, and had a huge hit in 1979 with *I Don't Like Mondays*, but by 1983 they had been pushed into obscurity by the rise of the New Romantics. In 1984, though his wife Paula Yates was earning a good living as a presenter of *The Tube*, an innovative rock-music programme produced in Newcastle upon Tyne by Tyne Tees TV, Geldof was so distraught about the failure of the band's latest single that he decided to invest £1,000 in a bit of illicit hype. He sent friends out on a chart-rigging mission, buying the single in strategically selected shops. One friend crashed his motorbike while travelling from shop to shop in the Midlands and spent months in hospital, all to no avail. Having given up hope that the band's latest album would even be released, 'I went home in a state of blank resignation and switched on the television. I saw something that placed my worries in a ghastly new perspective,'[1] he recalled.

September and October were normally Ethiopia's rainiest months, but in 1984, the rain did not fall. In a country whose economy was based on agriculture and was already suffering the effects of misrule, civil war and international isolation, it was inevitable that mass starvation would follow. As the first reports of the terrible consequence of the drought reached Britain, the Thatcher government came under political pressure to do something about it. If the crisis had been less serious, the government would have happily had nothing to do with Ethiopia at all. The pro-Western Ethiopian emperor, Haile Selassie, whose government had survived an Italian invasion ordered by

Mussolini in the 1930s, had been overthrown in a military coup in the 1970s. His successor was Colonel Mengistu Haile Mariam, who professed to be a Marxist, and relied on Soviet and Cuban military assistance. Haile Selassie had claimed sovereignty over Eritrea, a former Italian colony to the north, though its Muslim population resisted being ruled by the Ethiopians. The United Nations had brokered a deal under which Ethiopia was supposedly a federation, within which Eritrea was entitled to a large degree of self-rule, but the central government had never honoured the agreement and the Eritrean rebels wanted nothing less than full independence. The UK government had been prepared to back Haile Selassie against the rebels, but when the continuing war was fought with increased brutality by his Soviet-backed successor, all British aid to the country was severed. An internal Foreign Office memo, written as starvation was spreading, emphasized that the UK's principle interest in the country was to see it wrested from Soviet interest, implying that it would rather see the Mengistu regime overthrown than supply it with aid. There was no need for the government to be involved, the Foreign Office minister, Malcolm Rifkind, assured the Commons on 22 October 1984, when charities such as Oxfam and Save the Children were on the scene.

Two days later, the BBC broadcast a report from a camera crew fronted by Michael Buerk, who had been to the areas worst hit by famine and had recorded images of bloated, starving children and wailing mothers, in what Buerk graphically described as a famine of 'biblical'[2] proportions. Suddenly, the political atmosphere changed. Sir Geoffrey Howe, the foreign secretary, during a routine report to the Commons, unexpectedly announced that the government had decided to contribute £5m in emergency aid. The government also announced that two RAF Hercules aircraft would be deployed for a month, airlifting supplies to the stricken regions, and that an officer with specialist knowledge of flying over difficult terrain would be sent out immediately to survey the route. However, when an Ethiopian official was invited to the Foreign Office to be told the good news, he retorted that sending aircraft for just a month was derisory, when it was unlikely to rain until March, and that the RAF officers would be refused visas.[3] On 29 October, Mrs Thatcher summoned an informal ministerial meeting and agreed to send in the two aircraft for three months, though it would cost £2m in addition to the £5m already promised, and ordered that when the decision was announced, 'the uncooperative and surly attitude of the Ethiopian government should not be concealed'.[4]

It was Michael Buerk's report, with its pictures of 'people who were so shrunken by starvation that they looked like beings from another planet', which had a life-changing effect on Bob Geldof. In his words: 'The freefall I slipped into upon leaving school in an endless round of useless jobs and self-abuse finally closed.'[5] In the morning, he gave up the soul-destroying task of ringing around trying to find a region where his single was selling well enough to make it worth promoting, and told his PR people that he wanted to make a record to raise money for Ethiopia. But after his recent experiences, he had lost confidence in his ability to write a hit song or that his name would make it sell. He rang his wife in Newcastle. She was in her dressing room talking to Midge Ure, who was due to appear on *The Tube* with his band Ultravox, whose single 'Vienna' had spent four weeks at No. 2 in January 1981. She passed the phone across and Ure agreed to meet Geldof back in London. When they met, Geldof talked incessantly about his plan to write a song similar to John Lennon's 'So This is Christmas', and enlist Sting to perform it. Ure, who paid for the meal because Geldof was broke, suggested that he get on with it. Ure wrote later, 'What I didn't realize was that Bob's confidence was way down. His career was in the sewers and the Rats were broke. It's impossible to imagine now, but he was too embarrassed to call up Sting . . . Of course, I didn't know any of this for years. Artists don't confess weakness.'[6]

Thus encouraged, Geldof started inveigling other stars, including Gary Kemp and Simon Le Bon, to be involved and was pleasantly surprised by the response. He organized a meeting of four senior executives at Phonogram for advice on how to bring out a record in a hurry. They told him that the slowest part of the process was usually the design of the record cover, so he cold-called Peter Blake, who had designed the cover of *Sergeant Pepper's Lonely Hearts Club Band*. Blake returned the call and took the commission, for no fee. Soon Geldof was ringing around hard-nosed managers of major retail outlets, such as Woolworths, WH Smiths and HMV, to persuade them through a mix of bluff and bluster that they should waive their mark up. He also rang Robert Maxwell, the new proprietor of the *Daily Mirror*. Though Maxwell was a notorious capitalist, and would be remembered as one of the worst thieves in history, he liked flamboyant charitable gestures. He agreed that if the *Mirror* was allowed exclusive pictures of the recording session that Geldof was organizing, they would appear on the front page.

A studio was booked for Sunday, 25 November 1984, just twelve days after Michael Buerk's broadcast, by which time Geldof and Ure had written a song to be produced by Ure and performed by whoever turned up on the day. In those few frantic days, Geldof had created such a buzz that performers were tumbling over one another to offer their services for no fee, some travelling huge distances to be there. Boy George had been woken at 5 a.m. in New York by a telephone call from Geldof insisting that he must return to London at once, and he did, arriving at Heathrow 'looking like a battered housewife, with three stuffed poodles under [his] arm,' only to learn that he was expected to do a solo line, unrehearsed. He recalled, 'I didn't dare throw a pop-star tantrum. The Band Aid event was one of the few times I've felt comfortable around other pop stars. It was as if everybody had deflated their egos for the evening.'[7]

Spandau Ballet were on tour in Germany when their manager broke the news to them that they all had to be aboard a jet plane chartered by Duran Duran, leaving at 7.30 a.m. On arrival in London, the band's saxophone player, Steve Norman, was asked by a television crew if he had anything to say to the people of Ethiopia; he solemnly apologized for the band's failure to go on tour there, promising to make good the omission next year. Martin Kemp confessed: 'That was us. I have to be honest, at this point it was more a case of us not wanting to left out of what was obviously going to be a giant record, than about making money for the African famine victims. I for one didn't have a clue where Ethiopia was.'[8] Nigel Planer also turned up, stumbling about in the role of Neil from *The Young Ones,* allowing Midge Ure a few minutes' relief from the tension in the control room:

> It was great for the TV cameras, and for me as well because it meant that I switched off for 15 minutes, laughing as I watched this guy doing stupid silly stuff. That single moment, when an actor turned up pretending to be a hippy musician, was the spark that led towards Comic Relief.[9]

The other unexpected event of the evening was Robert Maxwell coming on the telephone wanting exclusive rights to use the Band Aid photograph as a publicity poster. He finally agreed to split the proceeds fifty–fifty after Geldof had treated him to some choice language and had threatened to a deal with the *Sun* instead.

It was one of the most memorable days in rock history, as a studio bursting with well-known faces echoed to the sound of a frankly average song with the title 'Do They Know It's Christmas?', which jumped straight into the charts at No. 1 and became the biggest-selling single in chart history. (It was outsold, nearly thirteen years later, by the version of 'Candle in the Wind' that Elton John sang at the funeral of Princess Diana.) It left Geldof bemused by what he had started. He mused, 'Maybe things had been shabby and cynical and selfish for too long. Maybe people in bands wanted to do something, become involved and active again.'[10]

Actually, though it had evidently escaped Geldof's attention, many 'people in bands' were already involved. One of the unintended consequences of Thatcherism was that there was more politics in British popular music, and more political activism by performers, in the first half of the 1980s than at any other time before or since. As the 1983 general election came to a crescendo, stars and sporting heroes turned out at the Wembley Conference Centre to fly the flag for the Conservatives. They included the comedians Bob Monkhouse and Jimmy Tarbuck, the world snooker champion Steve Davis, and the former Yorkshire and England bowler Fred Trueman. The songwriter Lynsey de Paul performed a number entitled 'Tory, Tory, Tory', but the artist who stole the show was Kenny Everett, who strode on stage wearing gigantic hands to say 'Let's bomb Russia', and 'Let's kick Michael Foot's stick away'. Not everyone laughed. The *Daily Mirror* commented, 'Mr Everett may be the foolish face of Toryism, but his audience was the ugly one. The kind of mind which enjoys right wing extremist support is the kind of mind that laughs at Mr Everett.'[11]

There were plenty of other performers who did not want to be the entertainment wing of the Conservative Party. There was Paul Weller, lead singer of The Jam, a scaffolder's son from Woking in Surrey, whose ambitious father nurtured his obsession with rock music and was his manager for thirty years. Weller was aged tweenty-one in 1979, when he saw television pictures of Eton schoolboys jeering at 'Right to Work' marchers. He retaliated with the song 'Eton Rifles', which reached No. 3. David Cameron and Boris Johnson, aged twelve and fifteen, were at Eton that year, and long afterwards Cameron appeared on a BBC programme called 'The Jam Generation' to claim that 'Eton Rifles' was his favourite song of all time, provoking a grumpy response from Weller – 'Which part of it didn't he get? It wasn't intended as a fucking jolly drinking song for the cadet corps.'[12]

Another product of the times was the eight-member reggae band from Birmingham who thought it appropriate to call themselves UB40, after the form Unemployment Benefit 40, with which too many of their fans were familiar. Their debut album was *Signing Off*, the success of which enabled them all to do. Recorded in a Birmingham bedsit in September 1980, it went quickly into the charts, reaching No. 2, and stayed for seventy-two weeks. The Beat, also from Birmingham, had a hugely successful debut album in 1980 entitled *I Just Can't Stop It*, including the track 'Mirror in the Bathroom'. Another track, which gained in popularity as the decade proceeded, was entitled 'Whine and Grine/Stand Down Margaret', which included the lines – 'I said I see no joy/I see only sorry/I see no chance of your bright new tomorrow/So stand down Margaret/Stand down please', which is still the only popular song in British music history to call upon the prime minister of the day to resign. At around the time when David Cameron was trying to demonstrate how cool he was by claiming to have been a fan of The Jam, another Conservative MP, Ed Vaizey, who was twelve in 1980, claimed to have combined a worship of Margaret Thatcher, which he assumed was shared by all, with an uncomprehending love of The Beat. 'I couldn't work out what they had against Princess Margaret,'[13] he said.

A song that was misunderstood even by teenagers who were not at public school was 'Sunday, Bloody Sunday', written by Bono, front man for the perennial Irish group U2, and performed for the first time in Belfast in October 1982. Because it referred to the killing of Catholics by British troops, it was widely thought to have a pro-IRA message. Actually, three members of U2 were practising Christians, and Bono, in particular, as the Protestant child of a Catholic father and Protestant mother, loathed any creed that might exacerbate Ireland's religious divide. In March 1982, the group had pulled out of a gig in New York when they learnt that it was in honour of Bobby Sands, a member of the IRA who died on hunger strike while in prison. Gerry Adams' reaction was to call Bono a 'little shit'. Bono reflected: 'It's not helpful when the leader of an armed struggle who has support in every working-class neighbourhood, and a lot of maniacs on his side, calls you a "little shit". It doesn't make your life easier.'[14]

In December 1983, the charts were dominated by an unusual record called 'Only You', which took the coveted Christmas No. 1 slot and remained there for five consecutive weeks. It was unusual because it consisted of six male voices singing in the a cappella style – it was the first record without instrumental accompaniment to reach the charts for more than a decade. Margaret Thatcher was said to have liked it, a report that caused great amusement on the political left because all the performers were veterans of fringe left-wing theatre groups, and the name they had given themselves, 'The Flying Pickets', was a tribute to a form of trade union activity that Thatcherite legislation had made illegal. Just over a year later, there was an equally unusual occupant of the top slot when a songwriter named Paul Hardcastle shot to fame by creating a dance record called '19', in which snippets of information about the Vietnam war, including the fact that the average age of an American soldier was nineteen, were dealt out against a backing track that made extensive use of a synthesizer.

One of the most remarkable and underrated figures in popular music was Jerry Dammers, founder and lead songwriter of The Specials. Born in Tamil Nadu in south India and raised in Coventry, Dammers formed a reggae band while he was at Manchester Polytechnic, which in its eventual line-up included a Barbadian drummer and a Jamaican guitarist. In 1978, they were performing as a warm-up for The Clash in Bracknell when neo-Nazi skinheads started trouble in the hall. In the late 1970s, the far-right National Front declared that part of its mission was to stop white youths from being corrupted by listening to 'negro rhythms' and instead to have them listening to home-grown working-class music, such as Oi! – so named by the *Sun* journalist Garry Bushell in 1980 – which was notoriously popular with the far Right. Dammers was determined to take music in the opposite direction. He developed a style that combined rock with ska and formed his own record label, 2 Tone Records. Soon there was a musical genre known as 2 Tone, associated with bands such as Madness, which combined punk with Caribbean rhythms.

After some early success, life became serious for Dammers and his fellow musicians in The Specials. Their music was so experimental that neither the critics nor the punters really knew what to make of it. Of their second album, *More Specials,* one critic wrote: 'The second side is curious, disorientating and quite unclassifiable . . . brave and perverse'.[15] On tour, arguments erupted between members of the group, fuelled by drug abuse, and their gigs threatened to degenerate into violence because of their rash practice of encouraging fans to storm the stage. In Cambridge, fights broke out between fans and security guards, after which Dammers and the group's vocalist, Terry Hall, were arrested for incitement and fined £400 each. The constant tension, the chaos and the scenes of urban decay that they witnessed on tour evidently put Dammers in a grim frame of mind, and spurred him to produce a song full of desolation and impending doom called 'Ghost Town', which topped the charts in July 1981. Twenty-one years after its release, a writer in the *Guardian* asserted that it 'remains the most remarkable number one in British chart history'.[16]

Jerry Dammers had assumed that success would put an end to the near-homicidal in-fighting among the members of the band, and that the others would acknowledge him for the extraordinary artist that he undoubtedly was. On the contrary, after a triumphant appearance on *Top of the Pops*, three of The Specials abruptly announced that they were leaving to reinvent themselves as Fun Boy Three. The music they made was, indeed, fun, and commercially successful, and tame; their most lasting achievement was to give lift-off to the long career of the girl group Bananarama, by joining with them to make the hit single 'It Ain't What You Do', a song originally recorded in 1939 by Ella Fitzgerald. None of this put Dammers off the idea of rock music with a serious message. In 1982, he assembled a new line-up of five musicians under the name Special AKA. The lead vocalist was a twenty-two-year-old from Brixton named Rhoda Dakar. The band's first single was 'The Boiler', a grim account of a date rape, whose victim attracted no sympathy because she was not pretty. It was considered too strong to be played on BBC daytime radio, but was pushed by John Peel and reached No. 35 in the charts.

Then in September 1982, the television screens were filled with scenes from the Middle East after Israel had invaded Lebanon to attack the Palestine Liberation Organization bases there, and Christian Phalangist gunmen had been on a three-day rampage in the refugee camps of Sabra and Chatila, slaughtering whole families, and even dragging patients and staff out of hospitals to be killed. The death toll may have been as high as 2,000. During a later Israeli Commission of Enquiry, Menachem Begin, the Israeli prime minister, and Ariel Sharon, the defence minister, denied all foreknowledge of the massacre. 'No-one foresaw – nor could have foreseen – the atrocities committed in the neighbourhood of Sabra and Chatila,' said General Sharon.[17] However, a wide seam of western opinion – Jerry Dammers included – thought otherwise. He persuaded Special AKA to bring out a single entitled 'War Crimes (The Crime is Still the Same)', provocatively comparing the slaughter of the Palestinians to the holocaust: 'From the graves of Belsen . . . to the genocide in Beirut, Israel was nothing learned?'

Dammers also devoted three years to putting together another Special AKA album, *In The Studio*, issued in 1984, which was a commercial failure, though one track has enduring fame. This was 'Free Nelson Mandela', a rare example of a popular song that called for the release of a political prisoner. The venture left the record company with heavy debts. Dammers stopped making records and diverted his energies into Artists Against Apartheid. He was the main organizer of a concert held in Wembley Stadium in 1988 to mark Mandela's seventieth birthday. Mandela spent his birthday in prison, with no release date, which *Spitting Image* noted by making a spoof version of the Dammers song in which, instead of singing 'Free Nelson Mandela', latex puppets with Afrikaans accents sang 'still basically locked up Nelson Mandela'.

Elvis Costello, who had produced The Specials' debut album, also had a huge hit in 1979 with an anti-militarist song called 'Oliver's Army', and in 1983 he had a hit under the pseudonym 'The Imposter' with the track 'Pills and Soap', which was aimed at putting voters off re-electing Thatcher. The news that the government, during the Falklands War, suddenly reopened the shipyards that they had been ruthlessly running down – in order to build warships to replace those lost in the South Atlantic – inspired Costello to write a sarcastic number entitled 'Shipbuilding', with the lines: 'It's just a rumour spread around town by the women and children that soon we'll be shipbuilding'. The song was recorded by Robert Wyatt, the former drummer from Soft Machine and a member of the Communist Party, who was confined to a wheelchair after falling, drunk, from a window. It reached No. 36. Alan Hull, former lead singer of Lindisfarne, went a step further, bringing out a single called 'Malvinas Melody', which, as its title implied, supported the Argentine claim to the islands.

Billy Bragg was another deeply serious troubadour hovering on the edge of the big time. He never had a major hit, but his popularity outlasted most of those who did. He wrote the song, 'A New England', before he bought himself out of the army in 1981, aged twenty-one; Kirsty MacColl took it into the Top 10 in January 1985. The lyrics said that ex-Private Bragg wasn't trying 'to change the world . . . just looking for another girl', as if sexual satisfaction were the limit of his ambition; in reality, changing the world became his lifelong preoccupation. Everything about Bragg was a conscious departure from the norm of the commercial rock scene. He performed live – without gimmicks or accompanying videos – songs about everyday experience; he deliberately eschewed the flash, self-indulgent, conspicuously rich lifestyle associated with rock stars to instead live and behave like an ordinary human; he had a small, independent management and an independent record company. 'By side-stepping both the available technology and the fast track corporate infrastructure, Billy Bragg became an instant cause, a pocket revolutionary,'[18] his biographer observed. He was aided by a disguised piece of good luck when, soon after the appearance of his first album *Life's A Riot* in July 1983, its producer Peter Jenner was sacked when the label was taken over by Richard Branson. Jenner was a 1960s hippy who shared Bragg's take on politics and on the music industry. He set up a firm called Sincere Management, with Bragg as his main client, and signed up to an independent label called Go! Records. For a time, Sincere had an unpaid employee in Andy Kershaw, on his way to becoming one of the nation's favourite and most self-destructive DJs.

In February 1985, Billy Bragg, Peter Jenner and Andy Kershaw called in to see Neil Kinnock. The meeting went well, despite Jenner's insistence on putting the case for legalizing cannabis. Labour was embarking on a 'Jobs and

Industry Campaign', fronted by the future leader John Smith, and wanted to publicize youth unemployment. Bragg agreed to front concerts to support the campaign, and once Smith had consulted his teenage daughters to find out who Bragg was, he was duly impressed and paid tribute to him at that autumn's Labour Party conference as the man who 'pioneered concerts from one end of the country to the other'.[19] At that same time, Bragg appeared on *Tops of the Pops* performing what briefly promised to be an unusual entrant into the charts. The front cover of the EP 'Between the Wars' had a subversive message to 'pay no more than one pound twenty-five pence' for it – in an attempt to discourage record shops from bumping up the price, while on the back there was an announcement that 'this record is dedicated to the work of the Miners' Wives Support Groups'.

Bragg's next step was Red Wedge, an artists' organization formed to help Labour win the 1987 general election. It began with a meeting in the boardroom at Labour Party headquarters in Walworth Road, which pulled in a mixed collection of musicians including Bragg, Paul Weller, managers, roadies, rock journalists, party officials and other interested parties. The meeting could easily have collapsed in mutual incomprehension, but out of it came a concert tour, featuring Bragg, Weller and Mick Talbot of The Style Council, Jimmy Somerville and Richard Coles of The Communards (Coles was a future Church of England vicar), Junior Giscombe, Tom Robinson and other regulars. Morrissey made an unscheduled appearance at a Red Wedge gig in Newcastle upon Tyne, a few months after he had offended public taste by expressing regret that the bomb that went off during the Conservative Party conference at Brighton had not killed Thatcher. Suggs, of Madness, appeared at another Red Wedge event, in London, soon after being denounced on the front page of the *Sun*. The tour also drew in a number of comics including Robbie Coltrane, Tony Robinson, Lenny Henry, Billy Connolly, Harry Enfield and Ben Elton, and others from television, film and fashion, such as Katharine Hamnett. There were occasional problems. Red Wedge engaged Lynne Franks, the head of a PR agency, who was to achieve fame as the person on whom Jennifer Saunders modelled her character in *Absolutely Fabulous*, and this produced publicity that sent Peter Mandelson into a fury. The *Daily Express* reported:

> Buddhist mother of two, high priestess of fashion Lynne Franks . . . has a Buddhist altar in the front room and now prays there twice a day. This former kosher cutie is now a member of the Nichiren Shoshu sect . . . Buddha, however, had nothing to do with persuading the Labour

> Party leader to attend the Absolute Beginners opening night showbiz razzle, where he stood out like a Savile Row suit in an Arab bazaar.[20]

If a relatively small movement like Red Wedge attracted people whose first priority was to promote themselves, the problem of self-seeking was inevitably much greater in the vast phenomenon that Geldof had set in motion, which Billy Bragg liked to call 'Egos for Ethiopia'. By Christmas 1984, Band Aid had £5m in a bank account, the proceeds from just one record, and were now confronted with the responsibility of making sure the money was properly spent. Geldof had started out assuming that his involvement would end at Christmas and he would go back to his old life. However, he was besieged by charities who wanted a share of the money or the publicity generated by Band Aid, or both, and from media organizations wanting to keep the story going. In January 1985, he set off on a plane packed with journalists for Ethiopia and the Sudan, on a trip paid for by the *Daily Star*, *Daily Express* and TV-am. He was duly denounced by Sir Nicholas Fairbairn, the former solicitor general for Scotland, who accused him of getting 'glory out of other people's misery'.[21] The impression that this was all a giant ego trip was reinforced when Robert Maxwell also arrived in Ethiopia to persuade its government to allow an RAF Hercules to bring in relief. Given Maxwell's record for self-advertisement, it is no surprise that one correspondent scathingly described him 'distributing loaves and fishes to the starving',[22] though the Mirror Group could claim that its contribution to famine relief was 'greater than the rest of the press combined'.[23]

The first food shipment donated by Band Aid arrived in March 1985, accompanied this time by Midge Ure, who posed for the cameras and fled back to his homeland after just fourteen hours, so horrified by the suffering that he had witnessed that he never returned. He wrote nearly twenty years later: 'I wish I could have had the courage to go there and confront it all again, but I couldn't. I'd rather hide my head in the sand than confront the horror, or my fear of the unknown. I'm very surprised that I ever got involved in Band Aid.'[24]

Band Aid spawned a series of other events, including an American answer to 'Do they Know It's Christmas?' called 'We Are The World', written by Lionel Richie and Michael Jackson after Harry Belafonte had publicly expressed his dismay at seeing 'a bunch of white English kids doing what black Americans ought to have been doing'.[25] The recording session attracted a galaxy of famous names, but did not reproduce the makeshift spirit of Band Aid. Geldof, who was so broke that he had to beg for the plane fare so he cound be at the session, noted that: 'The tables were loaded with smoked salmon, meats and canapés of every description. Drink was stacked in limitless quantities. The room was full of Hollywood fat cats and their wives eating and drinking effortlessly and talking smoothly about how wonderful it all was, this contribution to famine relief.'[26] After USA for Africa, there was Northern Lights for Canada, Austria fur Afrika, Chanteurs Sans Frontières and about twenty more. Back in the UK, Comic Relief was launched on Christmas Day 1985, during Noel Edmonds' *Late Breakfast Show*, from a refugee camp in Sudan. It featured a biannual telethon, every other March, alternating with Red Nose Day. By the end of the century, the charity had dispersed £174m in grants among forty-three African countries and in every county of the UK.

After the triumph of Band Aid, Bob Geldof was talking about following up the record with a live concert, without being entirely sure that it was achievable. The breakthrough came when he received an unsolicited offer to use Wembley Stadium, free of charge. The offer fell through, but by the time it did, the concert was well on the way to being organized, with promises from Paul Young, Paul Weller, Spandau Ballet and, more importantly, from the country's leading rock promoter, Harvey Goldsmith. A second promoter, Maurice Jones, was also enlisted. By the time Geldof met them in April 1985, he had a long list of bands ready to perform and had conceived the wild idea of a simultaneous satellite link-up: a rolling concert would begin at noon in the UK, go on until 5 p.m., then restart in the USA from 10 p.m. British time, with fifty bands performing. He wanted the American concert to be held in New York, but it proved impossible to book a venue in time, so it was held in the JFK Stadium in Philadelphia. He proposed that it be organized in just fourteen weeks so that the concert would coincide with Independence Day weekend in the USA. Later, he put it back a week, to 13 July, because the earlier date did not suit Bruce Springsteen, then the biggest name in American rock. Despite much hassling, Geldof did not manage to persuade Springsteen to participate.

Having overcome a mountain of logistical problems and steered around competing egos, Geldof finally stood up to open the Live Aid concert in front of a crowd of 80,000 people in Wembley, with television link-ups around the world that enabled an estimated 1bn to watch part or all of the day's entertainment. As Geldof entered the royal box alongside Prince Charles, Princess Diana and Paula Yates, a Guards' regiment blared out a few bars of the national anthem, which was soon drowned by the sound of Status Quo playing 'Rocking All Over the World'. Phil Collins managed the unique feat of performing live in Wembley, then taking a helicopter to Heathrow, walking directly from the helicopter on to Concorde and flying to Philadelphia in time for a second live appearance. Once the link-up with Philadelphia was achieved, Jack Nicholson walked on stage there to introduce the next act, U2, who were performing in London. Bob Dylan, Mick Jagger, Tina Turner, David Bowie, Elton John, Dire Straits, Paul Weller, Elvis Costello and many more were on the bill. Paul McCartney performed live for the first time in eight years. His gig, by sheer ill-fortune, was preceded by the day's only rainfall; water seeped into the electrics and his microphone did not work. Freddie Mercury, appearing with Queen, was widely reckoned to have stolen the show.

There was not another phenomenon quite like Live Aid in the whole of the twentieth century. It was remarkable not only for the number of artists involved and the sum it raised, but for the cooperation and goodwill it inspired in the less visible and more hard-nosed sections of the entertainment industry: the producers and promoters, the television companies and corporate sponsors. People gave with amazing generosity. As the concert progressed, hundreds of telephone lines were open for people to make donations, spurred by Geldof's breathless exhortations. Credit cards were still relatively rare, so there was a scheme that allowed people to pledge money by telephone then go into the Post Office on Monday to pay by giro. The Sheikh of Kuwait rang to pledge £1m. In all, around £30m was raised in a day. And it was a phenomenon made in Britain, fuelled by waves of enthusiasm coming from the American concert across the Atlantic. There were a number of incidental factors that helped to make it possible at that particular time, such as the fact that British groups like Duran Duran and Culture Club had broken into the American charts, and that Geldof needed a new career. However, the biggest contributing factor, one that is seldom acknowledged, was the miners' strike, which had so politicized and divided British society, and had given the rock industry, in particular, the feeling that there were great events in which they should get involved. Where the strike was divisive, Band Aid united; everybody, whether they were for or against the miners, or undecided, could be against letting African children starve.

After Live Aid, there was less overtly political rock music, as if the industry had done its bit and could go back to singing about love, sex, despair and the other staples. Many of the best bands to emerge in Britain in the decade were not invited to perform at Live Aid, either because it was before their time or, in the case of the Eurythmics, because they seemed to have passed Geldof by. Annie Lennox and Dave Stewart had used a bank loan to set up a small eight-track studio in Chalk Farm, north London, in 1982. After a few flops, they issued 'Sweet Dreams (Are Made of This)' as a single in May 1983, along with a video that helped to propel it to No. 2 in the UK charts, and then to no.1 in the USA. They repeated this success by re-releasing 'Love is a Stranger', which became a major hit after having bombed the first time around. The Smiths, formed by Steven Morrissey in 1982, released their first major hit 'Heaven Knows I'm Miserable Now' in June 1984. Then, in December 1987, a single of extraordinary originality suddenly smashed its way into the charts. This was 'Fairytale of New York' by Kirsty MacColl and the Pogues, which is routinely though inaccurately voted the greatest Christmas No. 1 of all time. Actually, it was released so late in the year that in most charts it did not make the top slot until after Christmas. The song told a serious story about a woman struggling to maintain a relationship with an attractive drunkard, a role for which The Pogues' lead singer, Shane MacGowan, was singularly well cast. The Pogues also sang about Irish emigration and about living rough in London, and produced one of the finest anti-war songs in the history of British music, 'The Band Played Waltzing Matilda', about the Australian experience in Gallipoli.

A lesson commonly drawn from the experiences of Live Aid and Red Wedge is that rock and politics do not mix, and that if bands want to be effective they should confine themselves to uncontroversial issues such as famine relief. On the face of it, the argument is a no-brainer. Red Wedge's purpose was to secure a Labour victory in the general election of 1987. Before that election, there were 209 Labour MPs and the Conservatives had an overall majority of 144; afterwards, there were 229 Labour MPs, and the Conservative majority was 102. By contrast, Live Aid and its offshoots persist every year in raising millions for charity. However, there are a couple of caveats to be registered here. Firstly, Red Wedge was not the outright failure that the bald figures imply. At the 1983 general election, Labour's support fell to 33 per cent among 18–24 years olds, the only part of the electorate ever likely to be influenced by Red Wedge. In 1987, it moved back up to 40 per cent. Among all voters, Labour's support crept up from 27.6 to 30.8 per cent. Labour would still have lost even if they had achieved the same swing in all age groups as they did with first-time voters, but they would have knocked a far bigger hole in Margaret Thatcher's majority, and might have been able to stop some of her more contentious proposals, such as the poll tax, from reaching the statute books.

A larger point is that Band Aid also set itself too big an ambition, and also failed. Starvation persists, especially in Africa, because it is not a problem that can be solved by charitable donations, even on the scale generated by the Live Aid concert. Bob Geldof realized very early in his campaign that it was never going to be enough. By his figures, the £8m generated by the initial Band Aid record was enough to feed Africa's 22m starving people for eight days.[27] In the coming years, Geldof would spend a great deal of time in the company of politicians, lobbying them about aid budgets, trade rules, writing off Third World debt, and much else – often accompanied by Bono, who was twenty-five when he performed at the Live Aid concert, and who followed it up by making an unpublicized visit to Ethiopia in September, and spent a month working in a feeding station.[28]

This explains Margaret Thatcher's attitude to the phenomenon. Less than two years before Band Aid, the prime minister paid a lyrical tribute to the Victorian ideal of charitable relief work when 'as people prospered themselves so they gave great voluntary things . . . schools . . . hospitals . . . even some of the prisons, the Town Halls',[29] yet she wanted no part in Band Aid or Live Aid. When people bought 'Do They Know It's Christmas?', each penny of the cover price went to Africa, but the VAT went to the government, who refused to waive it despite the pleas of a delegation of MPs, led by Labour's recently appointed shadow trade minister Tony Blair, who went to the Treasury in December 1984. Thatcher was invited to give a video address to the Live Aid concert, but decided not to, though she wrote a supporting letter. When she met Bob Geldof at an awards ceremony a few days later, Thatcher told him: 'We all, you know, have our own charities.'[30]

It says something for Thatcher that she never felt the need to be seen with rock stars or other celebrities, but a less appealing side to her was her utter indifference to world poverty. Under other prime ministers, international development was the responsibility of a government department headed by a cabinet minister, but not under Thatcher. Her lengthy memoirs have nothing to say on Africa, Third World aid, Live Aid or Bob Geldof, subjects that just did not interest her.

Chapter 10

Loadsamoney

The act that defined the second half of the 1980s was Harry Enfield's routine, performed on Channel 4's *Friday Night Live* in 1988, as an anonymous plasterer boasting about his money. He had so much that the cash machine jumped out of the wall and legged it down the pavement in a vain attempt to prevent him drawing any more. This creation was inspired by seeing the behaviour of Tottenham fans near his flat, waving £10 notes at supporters of clubs from the unemployment-stricken north. Enfield's act was so popular that he made a spin-off record that was featured on *Top of the Pops*, and 'loadsamoney' became the catchphrase of the year. Neil Kinnock adopted it. Enfield, a Labour supporter, did not mind that, but he did not like it when the *Sun* took it up as a celebration of Thatcherism, using '£oadsamoney' to plug its Lotto and Bingo games. He instructed his solicitors to try to warn them off, but gave up after the *Sun* counterattacked, telling him to 'buy yourself a sense of humour'.[1]

The phenomenon that Enfield was observing did not originate in Tottenham's White Hart Lane. It came out of the City of London, which in a few dramatic years was transformed from a club run by an old-boy network of public-school alumni to a place where the ambitious sons of working-class families were given free rein to make a great deal of money quickly. This development could be said to have begun when Margaret Thatcher called Cecil Parkinson to her office in June 1983 to reward him for his valiant work as chairman of the Conservative Party, presiding over the party's best election result since the 1930s. She offered to make him foreign secretary, but he had to confess that he could not ask his wife Ann to accompany him to the many functions to which a foreign secretary is invited because he had made another woman pregnant, and she was trying in vain to hold him to a promise to marry her. Thatcher promoted him generously nonetheless, by giving him charge of the merged departments of trade and industry. Not knowing when a scandal might break over his head, Parkinson arrived in a hurry to achieve something. He decided to end a seven-year dispute between the government and the London Stock Exchange.

The Stock Exchange was one of the nation's least loved cartels, with its brokers and jobbers who never crossed one another's demarcation lines under rules introduced after the South Sea Bubble of 1720. Brokers handled accounts for clients outside the Stock Exchange; jobbers did no business with anyone on the outside, but made their money by standing on pitches in the City like racecourse bookies, buying shares off the brokers if they thought the price was right, and selling when the price went up. There were also specialist investment houses to advise companies that wanted to float their shares on the Exchange. The investment houses charged fees, the jobbers made money from speculation, but the brokers' only income was from their commissions. To protect the brokers' livelihoods, Stock Exchange rules banned anyone from undercutting the standard commission and, to keep outsiders from upsetting this time-honoured system, no outside interest was allowed to own more than 10 per cent of a firm operating within the Exchange.

Within the City, there was an ossified class structure that seemed to belong to another century. Stockbrokers were public-school educated; jobbers might be the sons of barrow boys – hard-edged, hard-working gamblers – though the people at the top of the firms that employed them were, for the most part, also from public school. In one stockbroking house, Cazenove, the partners were allowed to give their sons jobs in the firm, as of right. Peter York observed:

> The class divisions were completely staggering. Them and Us were written in letters a mile high, down every street, in every doorway. Posh chaps got panelled boardrooms and beautiful wool suits and proper signet rings and patronized crushingly old-fashioned restaurants that dished up boiling coronary food; yobs (separated by no more than a wall, but at the same time, a thousand miles away) got sweaty chipboard work stations, grimy white socks, horrible shat-upon pubs and winebars where they got arsed out their heads . . . and red Ferraris.[2]

In 1976, the Labour government had passed a law to break up such cartels, and the Office of Fair Trading (OFT) had pronounced that the Stock Exchange's protective demarcation lines were illegal. This led to a seven-year legal stand-off, until Parkinson sent for Sir Nicholas Goodison, the chairman of the London Stock Exchange, and offered a deal: he would instruct the OFT to call off its legal action if the Stock Exchange could come up with a reasonable scheme to set its own house in order. The only catch was that he wanted a reply before July 1983, when the Commons started its long summer break. Sir Nicholas knew a good offer when he saw one. It was very likely that the Stock Exchange would lose the court case that OFT was bringing, which was due to be heard in January, and would have to disentangle its centuries-old customs in one chaotic Big Bang. After consultation, he came back to Parkinson and said that the Stock Exchange would comply with the law, and organize its own Big Bang, but not yet. Instead of doing it almost overnight, as Wall Street had already done, they would have a gentle three-year changeover. Parkinson agreed.

There followed a slow explosion in the City. Size was going to count in a deregulated money market, so firms merged and recruited, and salaries spiralled, sweetened by huge golden hellos, golden handcuffs and other perks. House prices shot up within miles of the City as banks and finance houses encouraged their young employees to take on huge mortgage commitments in the hope of tying them down. This gold rush would not have lasted so long and would probably not have produced such rich rewards if Parkinson had not allowed the City those three years of preparation, which financial commentators did not think he needed to have done. 'The government has caved in to pressure from the City at an odd time,' the *Economist* commented.[3] The financial editor of the *Financial Times* concurred:

> There was not much to be said for the hasty cobbling together of a settlement by Mr Cecil Parkinson and Sir Nicholas Goodison behind closed doors and constrained by a wholly artificial deadline imposed by the holidays of the courts and Parliament . . . The agreement has turned into something of a public relations disaster.[4]

However, by the time Parliament reassembled in the autumn, Cecil Parkinson was in no position to defend his decision, because a paragraph in *Private Eye*, which wrongly named another Tory MP as the father of Sara Keays' baby, had forced him to own up. Thatcher would have overlooked the offence because her favourite minister had done what she regarded as the right thing by staying with his lawful wife, but representatives at the annual Conservative conference in Blackpool were outraged. Reluctantly, she accepted his resignation. It was the number one sex scandal of the year.

Amid all this excitement, the Stock Exchange was presented by an obliging government with the biggest share issue in living memory, when half of British Telecom went on sale in November 1984, with almost half the available shares set aside for individual buyers. More than 2m people joined the bonanza, and everyone made a profit except the short-changed taxpayer. The government had set the share price so low, at 130p, that it rose by 43p on the first day and never fell back to its starting point. Anyone who bought £1,250 worth of shares on the day they were issued had made a £1,000 profit in just two years. The sale was so popular that some applicants fraudulently put in multiple applications, under different names, so that they could buy more shares than the law allowed. One who got caught was Keith Best, the Conservative MP for Ynys Mon, who was fined £4,500 and subsequently lost his seat.

But no shareholder did so well out of the sale as BT's chairman, Sir George Jefferson, whose pay doubled to £172,206 in two years. This set the pattern for all future privatizations. Overnight, mediocre managers of mismanaged public utilities became world-class entrepreneurs on world-class pay, assuming that the salaries they awarded each other were an accurate measure of their worth. By 1990, Sir George's successor at BT, Iain Vallance, was on a salary of £400,000, to which was added a £150,000 bonus, which Mr Vallance donated to charity. The next year his salary rose to £450,000, plus a bonus worth up to £225,000. When British Gas was privatized in 1986, its chief executive, Robert Evans, was on a salary of £50,000. By 1990, Mr Evans, who had taken on the additional role of company chairman, had seen his annual salary rise to £370,000, and had £20,000 worth of free gas appliances fitted at his private home. Less than ten years after privatization, Mr Evans's successor as chief executive, Cedric Brown, was being paid a basic salary of £475,000, plus a £600,000 incentive deal, £1m worth of share options and the promise of a £180,000 annual pension on his retirement. This had little to do with increased competitiveness, because British Gas was still the monopoly supplier to British homes; nor had it anything to do with what Mr Brown could earn anywhere else, because he had never worked for any other company. The executives of the privatized water and electricity companies also did well, so well that the maverick right-wing Tory MP Anthony Beaumont-Dark was moved to remark that, 'All that Mr Vallance and his cohorts in the water and electricity industries are doing is bringing capitalism into disrepute.' Unimpressed by the news that Mr Vallance had given away his bonus, Mr Beaumont-Dark snorted: 'He can afford to sound like Goody Two-Shoes at the same time as acting like the wicked baron.'[5]

If the aforementioned Keith Best felt that his services as an MP were not properly rewarded by an MP's basic salary, he was by no means alone in his grievance. Many years later, a scandal would explode in the faces of British politicians as it emerged that they had been systematically supplementing what they regarded as their inadequate pay through expenses claims that did not stand up to public scrutiny. This was not something new. It originated in the Thatcher years, or possibly even earlier, and went undetected for more than a quarter of a century. In 1982, an MP's salary was £14,510. It had fallen back year by year, in comparison with other professional salaries, because as successive governments took unpopular measures to suppress inflation they were not prepared to attract the kind of public reaction that a generous pay rise for MPs would have invoked. In 1982, an all party committee suggested that MPs should at least get an annual rise in line with the national increase in annual earnings. The government turned that down, but the leader of the House, John Biffen, agreed to have the Top Salaries Review Body report on MPs' salary the following year, 1983. That body compared MPs' pay with that of senior civil servants and recommended that it should shoot up by more than 30 per cent, to £19,000 a year. Their proposal came out just as Mrs Thatcher was ready to hold the post-Falklands general election, so there was no hope of the government implementing it. Instead, as the MPs reassembled after the election, their pay went up a miserly 4 per cent, to £15,308.

However, their finances were eased by a little-publicized arrangement under which they were paid £6,000 a year as an allowance for having to maintain two homes, one in London and one in their constituencies. The allowance was taxable, but they could also claim expenses against tax, including a daily amount for meals on days when they were working in the Commons. It is not clear whether the Fees Office had the authority to ask to see receipts or any other evidence of costs incurred; what is certain is that they never did. One MP routinely claimed £19.40 for meals for every day that Parliament sat during 1981–2, thereby pocketing £3,395. Another claimed £2,693 in 1980–1 for 'renewal of carpets'. The next year, another MP claimed £1,109 for 'dining table and large fronted bookcase and sideboard'. Yet another claimed £7,306.60 for everything from bedroom furniture to spare towels and sheets.[6]

The public knew nothing of this. The Inland Revenue knew, but until 1982 they overlooked it, changing its policy only when a few MPs started putting in expenses that exceeded their £6,000 allowance, so that they were not only paying no tax on that, but were claiming the right not to be fully taxed on their basic salary either. Then the Revenue started sending MPs backdated tax demands, some of which ran to four figures, producing a predictably outraged reaction from the affected MPs. There was then a prolonged exchange of memos, involving Sir Geoffrey Howe and Nigel Lawson (the successive chancellors of the exchequer), the chief whip, the leader of the House, the financial secretary to the Treasury, a young political adviser named Michael Portillo who worked in 10 Downing Street and others, including, finally, Margaret Thatcher herself. 'If details of what was being allowed and disallowed became public knowledge, the House would be brought into ridicule,' Nigel Lawson warned Thatcher, twenty-five years before exactly that happened.[7] She summoned a meeting, at which it was decided that, in future, MPs would be entitled to make expenses claims up to £6,000 tax free, but would be taxed on any claims over that limit, which would mean a drop in net income for about fifty MPs with the highest claims. The next problem was how to change the rules without attracting the public's attention. Nigel Lawson did not want to do it on Budget day, lest it 'cast an undesirable shadow' over his speech,[8] therefore it could not be included in the original draft of the Finance Bill. Instead, an extra clause was slipped into the Bill as it was going through its committee stage in the Commons.[9]

When the Big Bang came, on 27 October 1986, the separate tribes of jobbers and brokers merged and huge multinational finance houses moved in. The City of London regained its competitive edge, at the cost of ending what had been, for many, a cosy way of staying prosperous. On the day of the Big Bang, Sir Nicholas Goodison was sharing a lift with Guy Farage, a well-known character in the city, who accepted that the changes had to happen, but regretted them. Asked for his opinion, he told Sir Nicholas: 'You have destroyed the finest gentleman's club in the world.'[10]

The City became a draw for American investment banks that were going through a stage of aggressive expansion, backed by a US administration as keen on deregulation as Mrs Thatcher. In the three years from December 1985, the number of staff employed in London by the Wall Street investment bank Salomon Brothers rose from 150 to 900, with state-of-the-art new premises near Victoria Station to accommodate them. Michael Lewis, a Salomon Brothers trader seconded to London in December 1985, wrote: 'London became the key link in this drive for world domination. Its time zone, its history, its language, its relative political stability, its large pools of dollar-hungry capital and Harrods (don't underestimate the importance of shopping opportunities in all this) made London central to the plans of all American investment bankers.'[11]

It is often suggested that the 1980s, or at least their second half, were years of rampant greed, let off the leash by a government that encouraged people to grab what they could and enjoy it. Mrs Thatcher had staked out her position when she was first elected leader of the Conservative Party. She declared that 'the pursuit of equality itself is a mirage . . . opportunity means nothing unless it includes the right to be unequal and the freedom to be different'.[12] Her mentor, Keith Joseph, put the case for inequality more bluntly: 'Making the rich poorer does not make the poor richer, but it does make the state stronger . . . The pursuit of income equality will turn this country into a totalitarian slum.'[13]

The audiences for Caryl Churchill's verse play, *Serious Money*, which opened at the Royal Court in spring 1987, were notoriously swollen by the City types that the drama satirized, who all loved it. The crooked American financier Ivan Boesky, who told an audience at Berkeley University that 'greed is healthy', was seen as the voice of the times in the USA. In 1989, Gordon Brown wrote an assessment of Thatcher's record, to which he gave the title 'Where Greed is Good'. Yet, having grown up in reasonable comfort, and having married a rich man when she was young, Mrs Thatcher herself was not greedy; the political historian, Mark Garnett, who is a long way from being a Thatcherite, concluded that 'a verdict of "greedy" could only be brought in by a jury which was biased against her for other reasons'.[14] It would be an exercise in futility to try to measure whether the British were more or less greedy after 1985 than in other periods since the war.

What had changed was that the middle classes could no longer fulminate about the greed of working men who went on strike for higher pay, because the power of the unions had been broken. Now the most visible greed in the land was that of the newly enriched middle classes, particularly the young middle class, who were ostentatiously enjoying the low taxes and rich rewards to be found in the free market. One young woman, interviewed by *Tatler* about her home life, said:

> One passion we don't share is my passion for cars. I *love* speed. I drive a BMW 318i. Ian's got a BMW 323i with every extra you can think of, but he just wants a car to get from A to B. I have an absolute craving for a Porsche 911. I spend a lot of time shopping for clothes. I adore clothes.[15]

Not only were salaries rising for those who were not among the 3m unemployed, but handling and borrowing money had become startlingly easy. When the decade opened, almost all transactions took place face to face. Credit cards were relatively rare, and the technology to buy and sell remotely by entering data into a computer did not exist. A huge proportion of the British economy was cash only. It was a common sight, usually on a Thursday, for someone from the finance department in an office or factory to circulate with a tray of small brown envelopes, each marked with an employee's name, containing that employee's weekly wages. A quarter of the working population had no bank accounts and those who had were cosseted in a world as specialized, and protected by Chinese walls, as the Stock Exchange. To obtain a cheque book, you needed an account in one of the clearing banks, of which there were just five – Barclays, Lloyds, Midland, National Westminster and the Royal Bank of Scotland. Until 1984, all cheques, and other money orders and instructions, were taken each working day to a central hall in London where they were redistributed to the desks of the clearing banks and the Bank of England. If you wanted to save, you moved your money out of your cheque-bearing account and transferred it to a building society, which offered a better rate of interest and the prospect of becoming a home-owner. Banks did not offer mortgages, any more than building societies offered cheque books; and neither banks nor building societies dealt speculatively in the money markets. Banks loaned their clients' money to businesses, again almost always after a face-to-face meeting between the businessman and the bank's representative. Customers normally stayed with the same bank throughout their adult lives, and certainly there was no point in anyone with a mortgage moving from one building society to another, because the societies were a cartel; they all charged identical rates of interest and penalized disloyalty.

Even as it became technologically possible to move money across national borders, from computer to computer, there was a bureaucratic obstacle in the way. There were rules imposed by governments seeking to protect their currencies against speculation, which limited the sums that could legally be transferred overseas. Since 1939, anyone wanting to move sterling across the water had to apply to a Bank of England department that employed 750 full-time staff. But such rules such were becoming increasingly hard to enforce anywhere in the developed world. NASDAQ, a virtual stock exchange founded in the USA in 1971 and consisting of 20,000 miles of telephone wires connecting terminals in dealers' offices around the world, would soon overtake the London Stock Exchange in the volume of business it handled. Reuters responded to this challenge in 1980 by introducing a system that allowed dealers to trade by telex. Thus, huge sums were being transferred across international borders electronically, making a nonsense of exchange controls. Some of the world's finance ministers were criticized for being slow to wake up to that reality, but that was not a charge that anyone could level at Sir Geoffrey Howe. In October 1979, exchange controls came to a sudden end, those 750 Bank of England officials were out of work and the only memento of their department was a celebratory tie that Howe wore for years.[16]

Gradually, other changes came into view. By 1984, the blackboards were gone from the walls of the Stock Exchange, replaced by video screens supplied by two fast expanding and highly competitive financial news services, Telerate and Reuters. The cash dispensers that had appeared in the walls of banks in the main cities were rapidly replaced, at considerable cost, by the more efficient ATMs. Between 1982 and 1985, their number doubled,[17] making it possible to deposit or withdraw money, order a cheque book or print off a bank statement at any time of the day or night, without the need to speak to a bank teller. Once home computers had gone on sale, another thought occurred to the more innovative members of the banking profession – customers did not need to visit a bank at all. If they were connected up properly, they could manage their own accounts on their home computer. In 1983, the Nottingham Building Society teamed up with the Royal Bank of Scotland and Prestel in an ambitious scheme, copied from Germany, under which free consoles were offered to customers with £10,000 or more in their accounts, so that they could look at their accounts, make transfers and pay bills through their televisions. 'Tired of watching re-runs of *Dad's Army* on the television on Friday nights? Why not settle down to sorting out your personal finances instead?' the *Financial Times* suggested – though the same writer forecast, presciently:

> Few people will spend money on home computery simply to gaze at the size of their overdraft. They will want to do a lot more than that. So home banking is likely to change the very nature of the banking institutions. They will have to offer other services – home shopping, information, news services and so on – in addition to their banking functions.[18]

And, he added: 'They won't need many staff a few years from now because their customers will do all the work.'

The prediction that improved technology would create a demand for new services was as true for professionals working full-time in the money markets as it was for the customer with a console. With the computers in place, it became possible to develop complicated financial products such as options, which allowed the investor to take out an option to buy or sell a share, bond or commodity at a future date; swaps, under which for instance fixed-rate debt raised in one country could be exchanged for floating-rate debt somewhere else; collateralized mortgage obligations; financial futures; hybrids; revolving debt; and other complicated 'products'. Michael Lewis, of Salomon Brothers, recalled:

> To attract new investors and to dodge new regulations, the market became ever more arcane and complex. There was always something new to know . . . therefore the trading risks were managed by mere tykes, a few months out of a training programme . . . That a newcomer should all of a sudden be an expert wasn't particularly surprising, since the bonds in question might have been invented only a month before.[19]

By the end of 1985, the central bankers were afraid that the system was changing so quickly that it might be out of control. In September, the governor of the Bank of England, Robin Leigh-Pemberton, sent an open letter to the British Bankers' Association about the losses they could incur as they ventured into fashionable new 'off balance sheet' transactions, which could involve building up liabilities without the necessary capital. 'Managements of banks undertaking such business should ensure they possess the necessary skills and understanding to manage the often complex operations involved, to assess the risks and to establish appropriate internal control and reporting arrangements,' he warned. On the same day, in what was obviously a coordinated operation, his deputy Kit McMahon delivered a speech in Switzerland, not only about the 'rush to take advantage of new freedoms' but about the way banks were poaching one another's staff for ever higher salaries:

> If key staff – and even on occasion whole teams – can be offered inducements to move suddenly from one institution to another, it becomes very difficult for any bank to rely on the commitment individuals will give to implementing its plans, and adds a further dimension of risk to any bank which is building its strategy largely around a few individuals' skills.[20]

With house prices rising, there was a scramble to get on to the property-owning ladder. To own a house was not only a status symbol, it was also a sensible investment. Unlike those who paid rent, homeowners received tax relief on the mortgage up to a value of £30,000 per head, so, if a high-earning couple took a £60,000 mortgage, they could offset the entire cost of their repayments against tax. This generous transfer of wealth from those who paid rent to those who owned property was known as MIRAS. In 1979 it cost around £1,450m,[21] and increased every year until 1988, when Nigel Lawson changed the rules so that couples sharing the property could only make one claim against tax, instead of two. With so many former council properties coming on to the market, there were enough properties to buy, but the building societies were having a struggle meeting the demand for mortgages. The societies had never borrowed on the money markets, lending only what they had on deposit from savers or were receiving in interest and repayments from previous loans. If the money was not available, applicants had to join the mortgage queue. The societies were also notoriously cautious; they liked to lend to married couples with a regular income, who had saved up 5 or 10 per cent of the value of their prospective home. They were averse to customers from the decaying, crime-ridden areas, and they therefore discriminated against ethnic minorities, who were concentrated in the inner cities, and against those who were unmarried, particularly single women.

Those who could not get mortgages from building societies therefore tried their luck with the banks, where they were used to dealing face to face with friendly managers. Helen Thomas was a young nurse working in inner London in 1983, when a godparent left her enough money for a deposit on a flat. She had the income to support a small mortgage, but she was single. She said:

> I was turned down by all of the building societies, so I thought I would try the bank. This was just at the time when banks were starting to give mortgages. Somebody said 'Wear your nurse's uniform, Helen' – so I went in, in full uniform, and met the bank manager. He looked up my account, and said to me: 'You have a lovely little bank account.' He gave me a £17,000 mortgage, which bought me a flat in Camberwell. I can't remember the exact figures, but it certainly was not a 100 percent mortgage. I suppose it was two and a half times my annual salary. But the funniest thing was that after we had finished, he said 'Well, I think this calls for a sherry', and he produced a bottle of sherry, and we drank a toast to my first mortgage![22]

But if the banks dipped their toes in the mortgage business, sooner or later the building societies were going to want a share of the banks' business. The largest and most innovative was Abbey National, headed in the early 1980s by an unusual businessman named Clive Thornton. He came from a working-class family from the north-east of England, and retained some of the socialist beliefs of his youth. (He also had only one leg, which is why at the *Daily Mirror*, where he was chairman in 1983–4 and fought a losing battle to prevent Robert Maxwell taking over, it was said by hard-drinking journalists that 'in the country of the legless the one-legged man is king'.) Thornton's social conscience gelled neatly with Abbey National's need to expand. 'It was said when I was at the Abbey that you could not go and invest in the inner cities because you could not get the security for the money you advanced. I proved it was better to be there,' he said, when interviewed in the unlikely forum of *Marxism Today*.[23] Under Thornton, the Abbey became the first building society to issue cheque books and cheque guarantee cards. The Treasury had been considering whether or not to break up the building societies' cartel. Thornton saved them the trouble by announcing in 1983 that the Abbey was leaving to be free to set its interest rates without reference to other societies, whereupon the cartel collapsed.

In 1986 came the Building Societies Act, which allowed building societies to diversify further, or convert themselves into public companies, and to operate in the same way as banks, borrowing money on the markets if they chose. In the short term, this had the look of another Thatcherite success story. Abbey National, which was still expanding and competing with banks, found the few remaining restrictions on building societies irksome and in 1988 announced that it was going public. This was an immensely complicated process, involving vast legal fees and provoking organized opposition from a pressure group, Abbey Members Against Flotation. However, the society's depositors and borrowers had each been promised 100 free shares in the new company, inducement enough to produce a nine to one majority in favour of flotation. As flotation day dawned, thousands of letters and share certificates were sent to incorrect addresses, refund cheques failed to be sent at all, countless people received the wrong number of shares, and in one unexplained incident share certificates were discovered burning in a skip outside one of the mailing houses. But for all these glitches, flotation enabled the Abbey to grow and grow, faster than the demand for mortgages, and consequently inspired nine other building societies to follow suit.

It was not until nearly twenty years later that people seriously asked whether or not demutualization had been such a good idea. If the building societies had restricted themselves to the service they had always provided, without borrowing on the money markets or becoming institutionally linked to investment banks, none would have been caught up in the crash of 2008. As it was, not one of the ten building societies that had converted to banks had survived on its own. Most had been bought up – Abbey by Santander in 2004, the Halifax by the Bank of Scotland, and so on. Northern Rock converted in 1997, and bankrupted itself by borrowing with a freedom that a building society could not have exercised. The last to demutualize was Bradford & Bingley, which had survived through every recession for 150 years, but in its new incarnation as a bank it went bust in just 8 years.

The Trustee Savings Bank (TSB) was one of the biggest and most popular banking institutions in Scotland. It reached into every Scottish town, employing some 40,000 people in 1,100 branches. Its speciality was serving the 'unbanked', who dealt in sums of money so trifling that the mainstream banks could not be bothered with them. In 1986, TSB caught the bug and decided to convert into a quoted company. The chairman, Sir John Read, and the board gave earnest undertakings that the historic links with the Trustee Savings Bank movement and the company's Scottish identity would both be preserved. Having converted, TSB bought another bank, Hill Samuel, just before the stock market crashed in 1987. Three desperate years later, despite all the promises made before the flotation, it closed the separate Scottish operation. In 1995, TSB was taken over by Lloyds.

But these problems lay in the future. At the time, the flotation of Abbey National was one more development in the spread of share-ownership that began with the sale of British Telecom. The Thatcher government stumbled on this, its flagship policy, rather late. Before 1983, it sold off bits and pieces of state-owned enterprises, including 51 per cent of British Aerospace, Cable and Wireless and Britoil, a company created by the Labour government to produce and sell oil from the North Sea. The last of these was the biggest sale by far and bombed badly when the price of oil dropped abruptly – about 70 per cent of the available shares went unsold. British Telecom was split off from the Post Office, of which it was anomalously a part in 1980, and a bill to privatize it was introduced before the 1983 election, but did not get through the Commons in time. It was revived with enthusiasm when Norman Tebbit replaced the disgraced Cecil Parkinson as secretary of state for trade and industry.

The BT sale was not just a success for those who shared the spoils. The customers also liked it. Before privatization, a telephone was an instrument attached by a cord to a socket in the wall, and if you wanted one installed in your home, you joined a queue. It could take three months or so for the engineer to turn up. In January 1981, the new rock phenomenon, Midge Ure of Ultravox, had two singles in the Top 10, but no telephone. He had to walk to Chiswick, to a red telephone box that stank of urine, to ring his management and be told news such as that his album had sold 150,000 copies in two months.[24] But when BT was no longer a state monopoly, and had to compete with other telephone providers free from government restrictions on public borrowing, investment in the telephone network doubled almost instantly, prices fell, new telephones were available on demand and the number of telephone boxes that actually worked shot up.

Very soon, the first mobile telephones appeared. They were as heavy as bricks and were used only by those who absolutely needed them, or were determined to show off, including Nicholas Pierce, managing director of Cellular One, who arranged to be photographed on 22 November 1984 in a suit and bowler hat, cycling through London on a woman's bicycle, talking on a mobile phone to someone in the USA. The network that made them possible to use was not immediately available nationwide, but spread outwards from London, region by region. Newcastle upon Tyne was scheduled to be linked up on 1 November 1985. However, the death of a local MP in October meant that Vincent Hanna, a BBC journalist with a talent for getting his own way, was due up north to cover the by-election, equipped with one of the new phones. The now customer-conscious BT obligingly extended the network several days early for his benefit.[25]

The success of the BT sale awoke Margaret Thatcher's enthusiasm for something she now called 'popular capitalism'. She declared in October 1986: 'The great political reform of the last century was to enable more and more people to have a vote. Now the great Tory reform of this century is to enable more and more people to own property.'[26] In that spirit, privatizations came thick and fast, and everyone was invited to join the great share sale. The biggest was the sell-off of British Gas, which brought in £5,434m. It would have been more in keeping with the government's free-market principles to have broken it up into several companies, but Thatcher accepted the advice of Peter Walker, the energy secretary who was anxious to see the sale completed quickly. It went ahead in December 1986, preceded by two advertising campaigns cleverly crafted to attract small investors – 'Don't Tell, Sid' and subsequently 'Tell Sid'. Thereafter, small investors were known as Sids. British Airways was next to be sold, in February 1987, followed by Rolls-Royce, the British Airports Authority, the ten regional water companies, sold in November 1989 for £5,110m, and finally in December 1990 the electricity companies, which were sold for just over £5 billion. In all, the number of share-owners increased from 2m in 1979 to 12m in 1989. The share of the nation's capital stock in public ownership fell from 44 to 31 per cent, while the proportion of homes that were owner-occupied increased from 55 to 67 per cent.

There was an unprecedented amount of money passing through customers' pockets in these boom years, but the question was always how to lay hands on more of it, as soon as possible. In the rush to lend, banks and building societies gave 100 per cent mortgages to people who had not saved up at all; they lent three times the main wage-earner's annual salary, or more. Up to the mid-1980s, no one could increase their mortgage unless they demonstrated that they were using the extra borrowed money to increase the value of their home. A building society would lend to someone who wanted a new kitchen, but someone who wanted a new car had to take a short-term loan from a finance company, at a higher rate of interest. Suddenly, that discipline evaporated, and people happily added to their mortgage debt to pay for consumer spending. And why not? In 1988 alone, according to the Nationwide House Price Index, the price of the average property went up by a third. So if you bought a £60,000 house in January 1988, by the following January, you were in a property worth £80,000. Why leave that £20,000 of extra equity doing nothing when it could be improving your standard of living?

All this ready money had its cultural spin-offs. First, there was the arrival of the word 'yuppie', which was new to the language. *The Official Sloane Ranger Diary*, published in 1983, contains multiple references to 'noovos' (nouveau rich), but no yuppies. By the end of 1984, the word 'noovo' had disappeared, elbowed out by an American import, which was originally short for 'young urban professionals' and used to describe those who backed Senator Gary Hart against the more conservative Walter Mondale in the contest for the Democrat nomination in the 1984 presidential election. The Americans had a separate acronym 'yumpie', meaning young and upwardly mobile, but only 'yuppie' crossed the Atlantic, taking on both meanings. It was so popular that it spawned other new acronyms, such as 'dinkies', meaning 'double income, no kids', and 'nimbies', short for 'not in my backyard', which applied to homeowners who accepted in principle the need to build roads, houses, shopping centres, but not near their properties. The sociologist Laurie Taylor noted in 1985:

> The pressure to categorize yourself has become obsessive. No sooner have you decided whether you are a Mayfair Mercenary or a Sloane Ranger than you have to check your NAFF or WALLY tendencies and consider whether you have what it takes to be a YUPPIE, a Yap or a Young Fogey. If you want a grand theory for this phenomenon, you could, I suppose, suggest that it is linked to a firm belief that our

> present status is unlikely to change in these difficult economic times and that, therefore, we should hang on tightly to what we have got.[27]

The rise of yuppies followed hot on the heels of another fashion, which seems to have arisen as an indirect result of the 1981 riots. While Brixton and Toxteth reverberated to the sound of bulldozers clearing away the debris from the riots, the new fashion was to sound streetwise. Well-educated young people from comfortable families struggled to shed the middle-class accents that gave away their backgrounds, and talked like their working-class contemporaries. The expression 'street cred', an abbreviation of 'street credibility', entered the language around 1982, alongside 'ace', used as an adjective, and its synonym 'brill', an abbreviation of 'brilliant'. 'Street cred', like 'yuppie', was an American import. In November 1980, the *Washington Post* paid tribute to the 'street credibility' of the new rock superstar, Bruce Springsteen. Ten months later, a *Guardian* journalist reported hearing 'street cred' used in conversation in Britain for the first time. 'It seems to be used most frequently as a term of approbation among students and others who are anxious not to seem to be exploiting their privileged positions,' he observed.[28] I first heard the expression 'street credibility' used by the future cabinet minister, Mo Mowlam, at a CND meeting in Newcastle in 1982. Soon, the expression had reached advertising copywriters, giving rise to one of the wittiest advertisements ever produced for British television. It was created in 1985 by the Lowe Howard-Spink agency for Heineken lager, whose long-standing boast was that it 'refreshed the parts that other lagers cannot reach'. It was a pastiche of Bernard Shaw's *Pygmalion*, set in a School of Street Credibility, where a cockney tutor is struggling to teach a young woman with perfect diction and a cut-glass accent how to say 'the wa'er in Maj'jorca don't taste like what it ough'a' – which she achieves, at last, after a youth called Del arrives with a six-pack of Heineken.

Manufacturers of beer and lager needed to advertise, because they were losing trade. The overall level of alcohol consumption in the UK fell during the recession at the beginning of the decade from 9.7 litres per adult per year in 1979 to 8.9 in 1981, and did not return to the 1979 level until well into the 1990s. Part of the explanation was that people were switching from beer to wine and spirits as a mark of upward mobility. Wine consumption fell only slightly at the beginning of the decade, and then increased every year from 1982 for the rest of the decade.[29] Consumer habits were also on the move among those who took illegal drugs. Drug-taking had increased substantially since the 1960s, and whereas the use of cannabis had been associated with the rejection of material values, with 'dropping out', by the 1980s drug-taking had become a way of declaring that you were rich, self-indulgent and proud of it. *The Official Sloane Ranger Diary* observed: 'If a Sloane will take a drug, it will be one that is expensive, e.g. cocaine or heroin, the so-called champagne drugs. Lavatories in some stockbroking firms are full of cocaine-sniffers and senior partners wondering where all the cloakroom mirrors have disappeared to.'[30]

One item that distinguished a 'yuppie' was that he or she carried a Filofax, which served as a diary, address book and whatever else. 'Loadsamoney' did not possess one, which put him a step behind Del Trotter, of *Only Fools and Horses*, who had both a mobile phone and a Filofax. Mobile phones were obvious status symbols because they were new, rare, and expensive, but the rise of the Filofax is no more than a parable about the power of marketing. Portable filing systems that looked like fat, oversized wallets were not a new invention. A little firm called Norman and Hill started importing them from the USA in the 1920s. A typist at that firm, named Grace Schurr, who rose to be company chairman (until she retired in 1955), had the idea that they could manufacture their own organizers under the name 'Filofax', which was registered as a trademark in 1930. She did not see them as an item for the mass market and never employed a sales force, but built up a healthy niche market, particularly among army officers. Filofaxes were sold across the counter in only the best shops – Harrods, Fortnum and Mason and John Lewis – and never for less than £20.

In 1980, the company was bought by a thirty-three-year-old businessman named David Collischon, who hired a designer to change the product's image, widened the range to include plastic versions costing as little as £5, and set out to persuade the arriving generations of Sloanes and yuppies that their lives were so busy, and their friends and contacts so numerous, that they could not get by without Filofaxes. The world's first shop dedicated to selling nothing but Filofaxes opened in Camden, north London, in 1983, though even then a consumer journalist observed that the Filofax:

> seems to sell almost entirely by word of mouth. I have never seen it advertised or promoted but there are those who become so enthusiastic about it, who are prone to talk in rather evangelical terms about how it has changed their lives, that its circle of fans seems to widen all the time.[31]

Actually, it was being subtly promoted as a useful fashion accessory for busy, over-committed young professionals at the very time when political fashion made it acceptable to let people know if you were in a well-paid job that kept you busy. From about 1983, sales grew and grew. Paul Smith, a celebrity fashion designer who had a shop in Covent Garden where he sold an eclectic range of clothes, and soon-to-be fashionable luxuries for men, put a Filofax on display. Company turnover multiplied from £100,000 in 1980 to £5m in 1985. The company even took what had been an American invention back to the USA, posing as a British discovery at a time when all things British were fashionable again, and sold them for about five times what they cost to manufacture. About $0.5m worth sold in the USA during Christmas 1985 alone. Woody Allen was said to own twenty. His former co-star Diane Keaton had a Filofax insert named after her.

Filofax was one of the characteristic 1980s toys and gadgets that advertised that their owners were busy, go-ahead people. Peter York wrote: 'From 1985 onwards, we began to get more and more obsessed with the toys of the age – mobile phones, in-car faxes, Sony Walkmen and tiny TVs, lap-top computers – because they said that we were well-heeled *busy* people, people whose time was in short supply.'[32] These toys included the Amstrad computer, which advertised that its owner was busy and upwardly mobile. Soon, Britain was welcoming the American expression 'quality time', which is what exceptionally busy parents reputedly set aside for their children. This phrase, seized upon by working mothers or two-income couples who felt vulnerable to the charge that they were allowing their children to grow up as strangers, had been in use among upper middle-class Americans since the late 1970s. However, even in 1986 it was heard rarely enough in the UK for the *Guardian* to report that the 'latest in tooth-gritting New York terminology is the phrase Quality Time, as in "I'm spending with my kids at the weekend" – that is, as opposed to Quantity Time, which is what stay-at-home housewives give their children'.[33] By 1987, it was no longer necessary to go to New York to hear the phrase; it had infiltrated the English language, at least in the metropolis.

It was socially acceptable now for the young to aspire to a different lifestyle to that of their parents, to own property, to be too busy working to have 'quality time' to spend with children. In some parts of society, it was even fashionable, for the first time since before the Second World War, to behave like the rich young wastrels in the novels of Evelyn Waugh. In 1981, an aspiring young photographer named Dafydd Jones won second prize in a competition organized by the *Sunday Times*, with a portfolio of portraits of Oxford undergraduates from rich families entitled 'The Return of the Bright Young Things'. They included the Hon Pandora Mond, with nipple exposed, and Nigella Lawson. The pictures captured the attention of Tina Brown, editor of *Tatler*, and inspired waves of students to ape this behaviour. Jones said in a recent interview: 'I had access to what felt like a secret world. There was a change going on. Someone described it as a "last hurrah" of the upper classes.'[34]

One of the stars of this new firmament was Darius Guppy, an old Etonian who helped revive the Bullingdon Club, whose antics had been recounted in Waugh's novels. Guppy later went to jail for fraud. Another was Count Gottfried von Bismarck, a descendant of Prussia's Iron Chancellor, who liked to dress up in lederhosen or in women's clothes, lipstick and fishnet stockings. An Oxford contemporary, Toby Young, recalled:

> It was as though Oxford – and no doubt the same was true of Cambridge – was a stage and people like Gottfried von Bismarck and Darius Guppy were the theatrical stars we had all come to see. The reason they paraded around in tailcoats, empty champagne bottles strewn in their wake, was not because they didn't care what ordinary people thought of them. On the contrary, they were playing up to people's prejudices about what people from privileged backgrounds were like – and revelling in the attention it brought them.[35]

Guppy, Bismarck and their contemporaries sat their finals in July 1986, which coincidentally, was the month that the 1986 Wages Act became law. This legislation removed all employees under the age of twenty-one from the protection of the wages council. It had no impact on university students, unless they took part-time jobs in the vacation. Its intention was to depress the wages of hundreds of thousands of school leavers who had gone straight from school into menial jobs, in the hope that lower wages would mean more jobs. The average wage for a sixteen-year-old working a forty-hour week was then £45; the minimum wage for a hairdresser was £34 a week. Without the protection of the wages council, the chairman of the British Youth Council, Malcolm Ryan, forecast that a teenager's average wage could fall below £1 an hour.[36]

None of this needed to worry the bright young things who threw wild parties in Christ Church College, Oxford, when their finals were over. On one occasion, drink and drugs were imbibed in such quantities that several of the revellers didn't leave until after dawn. One youth woke up in a bed in Count Bismarck's rooms to discover that he was lying alongside a woman's dead body. She had overdosed on heroin. Bismarck burst into tears when he learnt what had happened. He flew back to Germany as soon as the inquest was over and sent a servant back to Oxford with a cheque book to pay his debts. He returned to Britain after three months and was fined £80 for possession of amphetamines. A woman undergraduate was also jailed for nine months on drugs charges. The most sensational aspect of the case was the identity of the dead undergraduate. She was Olivia Channon, aged twenty-two, a member of the dynasty that owned the Guinness breweries. Her grandfather, Henry 'Chips' Channon, her grandmother Honor Guinness and her father had each in turn been Tory MP for Southend West; Paul Channon had been promoted into Margaret Thatcher's cabinet as secretary of state for trade and industry just two months before losing his daughter.

Years later, two journalists researching the life of David Cameron came upon a photograph of the members of the Bullingdon Club, which Cameron had joined, for the academic year 1986–7. The photograph showed ten supremely confident young men posing in their navy-blue tailcoats, with white silk facings and gold buttons, and mustard waistcoats. Sitting on a step at the front was twenty-two-year-old Boris Johnson and standing languidly at the back, like the prince of all he surveyed, was David Cameron, aged nineteen or twenty.[37] These 'Buller' lads needed funds way beyond the reach of most people of their age. Their tailcoats alone cost £1,000 at 1984 prices, and their alcohol-fuelled dinners at Oxford's finest restaurants cost about £400 a time.[38] Dinner often ended with high jinks, in which these privileged kids displayed their indifference to law and order. Cameron went to bed early on the night that the police were called after members of the Bullingdon Club had thrown a pot plant through the plate-glass window of a restaurant, so was not involved. Johnson ran from the scene fast enough to avoid arrest.[39] After the old Bullingdon Club photograph was uncovered, the local firm that owned the copyright withdrew permission for it to be used again, which did not stop it being pirated across the internet and in leaflets distributed during the 2010 election. It was an image that Cameron, for one, wished would be forgotten.

CHAPTER 11

FLEET STREET IS UNWELL

Fleet Street in 1980 was more than the highway from the Aldwych to Ludgate Circus; it was a way of life. Every national newspaper and all the major news agencies had head offices on or near this celebrated London street. Its pubs and wine bars were meeting places for heavy-drinking journalists living off their nerves in the manner immortalized in the stage play *Jeffrey Bernard is Unwell*, a celebration of the unexemplary life of one well-known Fleet Street habitué written by another, Keith Waterhouse. Bernard was played in the original version, which opened at the Apollo Theatre in 1989, by Peter O'Toole, who also was no stranger to insobriety. Fleet Street's only rivals in the news business were the evening bulletins from the BBC at 1 p.m., 6 p.m. and 9 p.m., and from ITN at 1 p.m., 6 p.m. and 10 p.m. Anyone who was not in front of a television at one of those times, or one of the small number of people who owned one of the VCR recorders that had recently come on the market, had to rely on Fleet Street for the day's news.

By the end of the decade, Fleet Street as a cultural institution was no more. The national newspapers had all gone elsewhere. Their domination of the news market was under threat. Satellite television had arrived, offering all-day news for its small number of subscribers, and there were more terrestrial channels. In 1980, there had been just three: BBC1, BBC2 and ITV. The first new arrival was Channel 4, which began broadcasting on 2 November 1982 and was rubbished by almost everyone who commented on it. Lord Nugent of Guildford, a seventy-five-year-old former Tory minister, informed the House of Lords in the month the new channel was born:

> I have not personally seen Channel 4 [but] the reports I have show that a whole new perspective of obscenity and bad language has been introduced. I had a reliable report that in a recent programme, *A Star is Born*, there were no fewer than 36 occasions when a four-letter word beginning with 'f' was used. Really, my Lords, can you beat it! How can any responsible person put out such programmes which are going into the homes of our people?[1]

Ominously, on Channel 4's first night there were no advertisements in Scotland, Northern Ireland, or the north-west of England, because of a union dispute. The new channel's brief was 'to cater for tastes and interests not catered for by ITV; to encourage innovation in the form and content of programmes [and] to provide overall a service of a distinctive character'. However, its first programme on its first night was a quiz show, *Countdown*, presented by Richard Whiteley (and until his death twenty-three years later). The critic from the *Financial Times* also remarked on the presence of 'a blonde hostess with big breasts and a slit skirt',[2] whom he did not name, but his attention had probably been caught by the twenty-one-year-old Carol Vorderman, who stayed with the show for twenty-six years. Other offerings from the opening night were not well received either. The new soap *Brookside* was seen as too much of an imitation of *Coronation Street*, while *Five Go Mad in Dorset* was likewise seen as an imitation of Michael Palin's *Ripping Yarns*. In time, the channel would establish itself, and *Countdown* and *Brookside* became long-running favourites with large audiences. *Five Go Mad* is remembered as the first television vehicle for Dawn French, Jennifer Saunders and others.

Another service that the new channel gave to the nation's cultural life was to put up the money that drove a short-lived revival of the British film industry. Channel 4 funded the highly acclaimed 1983 film *The Ploughman's Lunch*, written by Ian McEwan and directed by Richard Eyre. Its lead, played by Jonathan Pryce, was a soulless, opportunistic newspaper journalist, described by the *New York Times* as 'a fascinating variation on all of the angry, low-born young men who populated British novels and plays in the late 1950s and 60s . . . Jimmy Porter of *Look Back in Anger* updated to the 1980s.'[3] But by the end of the year, Channel 4 was picking up just 4 per cent of the total television audience, compared with 46 per cent for ITV, 41 per cent for BBC1 and 9 per cent for BBC2.[4]

The next newcomer to the airwaves was TV-am, launched on 1 February 1983. Other independent television companies were defined by the regions they served; TV-am, uniquely, covered the whole country but was defined by its hours. The franchise was bought by a consortium headed by Peter Jay and David Frost. Frost was a well-known broadcaster and Jay was an erudite economist and journalist who had served as ambassador to Washington when his father-in-law, Jim Callaghan, was prime minister. On the first morning, no fewer than five presenters filled the *Good Morning Britain* sofa – Frost, Anna Ford, Robert Kee, Michael Parkinson and Angela Rippon. Viewers were not impressed. Audience figures started at 800,000, far behind the BBC, and fell within four weeks to 300,000. With the company losing thousands of pounds a week, the board decided that they could not afford all five highly paid presenters, and sacked Peter Jay when he refused to carry out the required surgery. The new chief executive was Jonathan Aitken, a Tory MP and great-nephew of Lord Beaverbrook, owner of the *Daily Express*. He invited the five to take a pay cut, which the three men agreed to do, but Ford and Rippon refused and were sacked. Anna Ford's parting gesture was to pour a full glass of wine over Aitken's head.[5] He handed over the role of chief executive to his cousin, Timothy Aitken, but remained a major shareholder until 1988, when both Aitkens resigned after it emerged that shares they claimed to own were actually owned by Saudi princes.

Brutal though these changes were, they saved the station, mainly because of the inspired appointment of Greg Dyke as programmes editor. He realized that the average viewer did not want to listen to the intelligent thoughts of renowned journalists first thing in the morning. Frost was given a Sunday morning slot to conduct in-depth interviews with politicians, while the job of presenting the programme during the week was turned over to two unknowns, Nick Owen and Anne Diamond, who brought a lighter touch. The other character Dyke promoted as the public voice of TV-am was a puppet, Roland Rat. Driven thus downmarket, the station saw its audience surpass 1m by October – the first known case, it was said in television circles, of a rat saving a sinking ship.

In the mid-1980s, two very rich men bought out national newspapers. In May 1985, Conrad Black, a Canadian millionaire, acquired a minority share in the *Daily Telegraph* and *Sunday Telegraph*, which he used to squeeze out the old owners. Ten months earlier, in July 1984, Robert Maxwell acquired the entire Mirror group – the *Daily Mirror*, *Sunday Mirror* and *People* in London, and the *Record* and *Sunday Mail* in Scotland – for £90m. This came as a shock to its staff, who had been promised by their previous employers, Reed International, that the company would be floated on the Stock Exchange, so protecting it from falling into the hands of a single proprietor. Moreover, the proprietor in question, a buccaneer capitalist born to a family of Jewish peasants in Ruthenia, which was then in Czechoslovakia, had been the subject of a famous judgement by inspectors from the Board of Trade, in 1970, that he was someone who could not be 'relied on to exercise proper stewardship of a publicly quoted company'.[6] Both of these moguls' careers ended in scandal. Maxwell avoided going to prison for looting the pension funds under his control by drowning at sea, in November 1991; Black was sentenced in 2008 by a US court to six-and-a-half years for fraud. From this it might be deduced that they were the worst people to have been allowed to own newspapers; yet, curiously, when they were eventually replaced by less egotistic and more cost-conscious owners, their former employees wished the old rogues were back.

In Maxwell's case, though, what virtues he had as a proprietor were well disguised in the first year, as he wallowed in his new status, forgetting his promise not to interfere in the paper's political line. He altered editorials to make them more hostile to Scargill and the miners, and promoted himself as if the fact that he was proprietor was inducement enough to *Sun* readers to switch to the *Daily Mirror*. The *Daily Mirror* gave him coverage wherever his private jet touched down, whether it was in Ethiopia, to deliver famine relief, or in one of the East European Communist states, where he had business interests. A month after he had bought the paper, television viewers were treated to advertisements, fronted by Maxwell, promising that its new game 'Who dares Wins', a variant of bingo, would result in someone soon winning £1m. Frustratingly for Maxwell, within less than a week, the *Sun* proclaimed its own first bingo millionaire. After just over a year of this eulogistic publicity, Maxwell was shocked to learn that circulation was falling and the previous year's profit of £1m – paltry for a business of that size – had been converted to a £6m loss.

Despite Maxwell's megalomania, he grasped that it did not serve his interests to have his newspaper run by people too cowed to stand up to him. He moved Mike Molloy, the malleable editor of the *Daily Mirror*, upstairs and replaced him with Richard Stott. Unlike other executives, Stott was not in awe of Maxwell; indeed, there was one occasion when the proprietor was dining with his three editors and Joe Haines, Harold Wilson's former chief press secretary whom Maxwell promoted to the post of the Group's political editor, when one of them made a speech in praise of the boss and, raising his glass, told Maxwell: 'You're a genius.' Stott retorted by raising his glass to the speaker to say, 'And you're a fucking creep.'[7]

With fewer pictures of Maxwell adorning its pages, the circulation of the *Daily Mirror* rapidly recovered. Maxwell also introduced colour printing and embarked on tempestuous negotiations with the print unions. It was notorious that, because of the strength of the print unions, newspapers employed more staff than were needed to bring out the newspapers. Through sheer hard-nosed negotiation, Maxwell managed to get the shop stewards to accept new technology and tighter working conditions, which enabled him to cut 2,000 jobs, saving the company £40m a year, which even Maxwell's highly critical biographer, Tom Bower, acknowledged was 'an overwhelming victory'.[8] On the day after Maxwell's death, before his thievery had been uncovered, the front page of his newspaper was filled with a tribute signed by Stott under the headline 'The Man Who Saved the Daily Mirror'.[9] Four weeks later, a different headline filled the front of the same newspaper: 'Maxwell: £526 million is missing from his firms'.[10]

While Maxwell was a former Labour MP, Conrad Black was an unqualified admirer of Reagan and Thatcher, and believed that the UK should leave the EU. This caused no internal problems with the *Sunday Telegraph*, whose editor, Peregrine Worsthorne, was of the same mind, but Max Hastings, appointed editor of the daily in February 1986, was a maverick liberal Conservative, under whose control the newspaper was in the unusual position of being slightly to the left of *The Times*. Hastings also earned himself the nickname 'Hitler Hastings' by sacking a large number of journalists he had inherited from the old regime, including Carol Thatcher, the prime minister's daughter, who had been employed in the features department. Her mother took this as a personal insult. It was the moment at which a well-disposed Tory MP, Jock Bruce-Gardyne, decided that Hastings must have gone mad. He told Hastings, 'You can't go around sacking prime minister's daughters. I'll add this: if it had been Mark you ditched, you wouldn't still be editor of the *Daily Telegraph*.'[11]

The *Daily Telegraph* opposed the use of British air bases for the bombing of Libya, rebuked Thatcher for failing to protect the underclass, opposed the restoration of hanging when Thatcher and other cabinet ministers voted for it, and criticized the shootings of three IRA members in Gibraltar. This provoked a number of long memos from Black, or from Andrew Knight, chief executive of the Telegraph group. Black used the letters pages of the *Telegraph* to write in, as a reader, opposing the line taken by his own newspaper. And it earned Hastings the enmity of Thatcher acolytes, including the furious Paul Johnson, who had edited the *New Statesman* in the 1960s and defended Thatcher with the fervour of a convert. Seeing him at a party one evening Hastings asked: 'Are we on speakers at the moment, or not, Paul?', whereupon 'the great sage gnashed his teeth – the only occasion outside the pages of P.G. Wodehouse that I have known this feat physically accomplished – and snarled: "No, we are not. You are a swine and a guttersnipe of the lowest sort. And what's more, if you weren't a coward as well, you'd hit me for saying that!"'[12] Yet for all the apoplexy the *Daily Telegraph* must have provoked among core readers, it retained a circulation healthily above 1m, while the ideologically pure *Sunday Telegraph*'s circulation fell.

Rupert Murdoch was already the dominant figure in the tabloid end of the market through his ownership of the mass-circulation newspapers, the *Sun* and the *News of the World*. His company, News International, like all newspaper companies, was in thrall to highly organized trade unions, particularly the elite National Graphical Association (NGA). Their power came from the nature of their work. Before the arrival of computers, newspaper pages were made up ready for the printing press 'on stone' – the stone being basically a shelf the size and shape of a page, upon which the text was inserted, letter by letter, in the form of thin metal slats. The metal letters were cast back to front, and the entire page was set in the form of mirror-writing. A skilled compositor could perform this task in minutes, without mistakes. That skill was so valuable, in an industry where speed of production was everything, that proprietors were prepared to pay very high rates and accept short working hours, provided the pages were ready. When Andrew Neil was appointed editor of the *Sunday Times* in 1983, his annual salary was £50,000, which was what the best paid compositors on the *Sun* were said to be receiving. A strike by the compositors inevitably meant a day's edition lost, unless it could be resolved speedily. This gave the print unions' chapels a power that they sometimes used altruistically. Early in the miners' strike, in May 1984, the *Sun* sought to publish a front-page picture that had caught Arthur Scargill with his arm raised in what looked deceptively like a Nazi salute, under the headline 'Mine Fuhrer'. In later editions, the picture and headline were gone, replaced by an announcement in bold type that they had had to be withdrawn because the print unions refused to handle them.[13] For the most part, though, the NGA's mission was to protect the high wages and agreeable working practices of its members in a manner that made it unpopular with other unions, as well as driving management to exasperation.

Yet Murdoch had one reason to be grateful to these militant 'inkies'. By the early 1980s, the NGA printers were caught in a dilemma that has confronted successive groups of skilled workers since the eighteenth-century days of Ned Ludd: their skills had been rendered useless by advancing technology. It was no longer necessary for newspaper pages to be put together by assembling metal blocks on stone. It could all be done by computer and journalists could input their copy directly, cutting out the need to employ NGA members at all. In the late 1970s, Kenneth Thomson, owner of *The Times* and *Sunday Times,* proposed to bring the new technology to his newspaper offices in Gray's Inn Road, near King's Cross. This led to a confrontation so serious that many people feared that *The Times* and its associated titles would not survive. During the last months of the Labour government, Tony Benn even called the unions to put them a proposition that the BBC should buy the titles – only to be ordered by Jim Callaghan to stay out of a dispute that was not part of his remit.[14] Soon afterwards the unions struck, and stayed out for more than a year, costing Thomson £40m. The strike ended with an agreement that no one except a member of the victorious NGA could lay a finger on the new computer keyboards. A few months after the return to work, journalists on *The Times* went on strike, whereupon Thomson lost heart and on 12 October 1980 he put both titles up for sale. Murdoch made a late entry into the bidding war that followed, and by sheer charm convinced Harold Evans, the highly regarded editor of the *Sunday Times*, that joining the Murdoch empire was the least-worst option on offer. The NGA also made the mistake of thinking that their members' jobs would be safe with Murdoch. Michael Foot fought a rearguard battle to have the sale referred to the Monopolies Commission, but Margaret Thatcher was grateful for the support Murdoch's newspapers had given her in 1979 and did not propose to stand in his way. In January 1981, Murdoch bought the two national newspapers, and their supplements, and the building in Gray's Inn Road, whose combined worth was several times the £12m he paid for them.

Harold Evans, who was moved from the *Sunday Times* to edit *The Times,* enjoyed a good relationship with Murdoch for a time – better certainly than his successor on the Sunday title, Frank Giles, whom Murdoch classed as a Communist, 'and his wife too'. However, for Evans, trouble was not long in coming. Murdoch was in the office on the night that Egypt's President Sadat was assassinated, and overheard a journalist querying a cartoon on the grounds of taste. The conditions attached to the sale of *The Times* supposedly prevented Murdoch from giving a direct instruction to a journalist, but that did not deter the new proprietor, who – according to Evans – said: 'Bugger taste. We want to sell newspapers. Print it!'[15] Soon, Evans had gone.

Andrew Neil, who edited the *Sunday Times* from 1983 to 1994, wrote:

> When you work for Rupert Murdoch you do not work for a company chairman, you work for a Sun King. All life revolves around the Sun

> King: all authority comes from him. He is the only one to whom allegiance must be owed and he expects his remit to run everywhere.[16]

Neil was just thirty-four when Murdoch plucked him from a reporter's job on the *Economist* to put an end to what they both saw as the left-liberal ethos of the *Sunday Times.* The main casualty was the political editor, Hugo Young, who left to become chairman of the trust that owns the *Guardian.* Neil was right wing in his beliefs about trade unions and the free market, but did not altogether share his boss's admiration for Margaret Thatcher. In March 1984, the *Sunday Times* filled its front page with the revelation that Mark Thatcher had arrived in Oman soon after his mother had paid an official visit, using her name to tout for business for a British construction company. The proceeds were paid into a bank account of which Denis Thatcher was a co-signatory. Challenged about this in the Commons, Thatcher attacked the *Sunday Times* for using subterfuge to obtain details that 'are not in any sense a public matter'.[17] Neil was never permitted to meet Mrs Thatcher socially.

The first challenge to the power of the NGA since the dispute that took *The Times* out of circulation came not from Fleet Street but from a man named Selim 'Eddie' Shah, a British-born self-made businessman of Iranian descent who owned a number of giveaway newspapers that he wanted to print on a second-hand press on an industrial estate in Warrington. With the new computer equipment he had installed, Shah believed that it needed only six people to operate the presses; the print unions insisted on eight each from the NGA and Society of Graphical and Allied Trades (SOGAT) unions, so Shah hired non-union staff. When six NGA members at his Stockport plant went on strike in protest, he sacked them. The NGA made it a national dispute, placing pickets at each of Shah's plants, and warned firms that if they took advertising in a Shah newspaper where there was an NGA closed shop they would be boycotted.

This was secondary action, which had been illegal since 1980, but no employer had ever dared try to enforce the law. Shah, however, proved to be an obstinate enemy. He went to the High Court and obtained an injunction under which the NGA was heavily fined and ordered to keep its actions within the law. The union called a two-day national strike, which meant that there were no newspapers over the last weekend of November 1983. On the following Tuesday, hundreds of printers and sympathizers, including a contingent of Welsh miners, picketed Shah's Warrington plant. That also was illegal. In the early hours, Cheshire police called in the Manchester riot squad to disperse the crowd. On 9 December the NGA was fined £550,000 for organizing an illegal mass picket. Four days later, the TUC General Council met in a long, tense session. The NGA wanted their support for a second national strike, which would put the TUC in direct confrontation with the government, but they voted 31 to 20 not to risk it. The NGA action in Warrington petered out.

During 1985, Shah followed up this victory by launching *Today,* the first national newspaper produced with the new technology and by members of the electricians' union, the Electrical, Electronic, Telecommunications and Plumbing Union (EETPU), who agreed to a no-strike clause and did not insist on a closed shop. The paper never took off, having no obvious identity, and Shah ended up selling it to Tiny Rowland, who sold to Murdoch, who closed it in 1995. One of the first people to forecast that it would not succeed was Andreas Whittam Smith, City editor of the *Daily Telegraph*, a canon's son who 'seemed permanently swathed in a long dark grey overcoat [and] looked like an old-fashioned bishop, or possibly archdeacon'.[18] He was asked his opinion by an American magazine and without much thought fell back on the accepted wisdom that the crowded national newspaper market was too expensive for any new entrant to survive. On reflection, though, he realized that this need not be true, if the new technology was put to use. He sounded out people he knew in the City, enlisted two colleagues from the *Daily Telegraph*, Matthew Symonds and Stephen Glover, and between them they laid secret plans to launch a new national daily. It is a moot question whether or not this plan could ever have succeeded, if it had not had unexpected, unplanned help from Rupert Murdoch.

In 1979, Murdoch had invested £100m in new printing facilities in Wapping, on the edge of London's Docklands, where he had 'some of the finest Georgian warehouses in Britain' ripped down and replaced by 'one of the ugliest modern factories in London'.[19] He had intended to move his two tabloid newspapers there, but could not reach agreement with the print unions. He devised a stratagem to lure the print unions into a trap. In February 1985, he announced that he was planning a new London evening newspaper, to be printed in Wapping, as a competitor for the *Evening Standard.* This newspaper was even allotted an editor, who interviewed other possible recruits. This was just a smokescreen to conceal the arrival of specialists from an American IT company to set up a computer system capable of bringing out all four of Murdoch's titles, on which journalists would write their copy directly into the computer, without any input from NGA linotype operators. Eric Hammond, leader of the EETPU, was brought into the secret and helped recruit maintenance staff. Hammond expected his union to get negotiating rights in return, but they were never granted. After he had served his purpose Murdoch refused even to return his calls. Murdoch also arranged for an Australian firm, TNT, to deliver his newspapers by road in order to head off the risk that the rail unions would refuse to handle them. Late in the year, the unions were informed that when the new London newspaper went into production, it would operate with half the normal level of SOGAT members and there would be direct inputting of copy by journalists. Murdoch was counting on provoking a strike, and got what he wanted. When 5,000 NGA and SOGAT members walked out, in January 1986, Murdoch sacked them all.

The print unions were accustomed to winning their industrial disputes, because they could usually afford to keep their members out longer than the employers could afford to have their newspapers out of circulation. But this time they had thousands of strikers picketing a compound fortified by razor wire, behind which the newspapers were being produced by hundreds of strike-breakers, even when the streets outside were blocked by protestors. Inside Wapping, Murdoch's flying visits generally had the effect of making a tense situation worse as – to quote Andrew Neil – 'he had become increasingly unsympathetic and fractious . . . terrorising his senior managers and making them too scared to take any decisions'.[20] The Labour Party announced that journalists working for Murdoch would not be admitted to press conferences at Labour headquarters. Journalists on the *Sunday Times*, who felt they had been railroaded into being part of a dispute that would never end and who had very nearly voted as a National Union of Journalist chapel to refuse to enter Wapping (the vote was sixty to sixty-eight), threatened to strike. Murdoch ignored the threat, until he learnt that journalists on the *Sun* were also in a mutinous mood. He gave them all a 10 per cent pay rise.

In the East End of London, the Wapping dispute was the local equivalent of the miners' strike. It had the same divisive effect on the working-class community and veterans of the dispute remember it with the same unforgiving clarity. In London, there were near neighbours who would not speak to each other, twenty-four years later, because they were on different sides in the Wapping dispute. The Wapping compound was under siege day and night from pickets, with reinforcements coming in from far afield, including the Yorkshire mining villages, but they never once stopped the TNT lorries from taking the newspapers out for distribution. Since they could not halt production, the unions had to acknowledge, eventually, that they could not win. After more than a year, they surrendered and took a pay offer worth between a third and a half of what Murdoch would have had to pay in redundancy if they had not gone on strike. Not only was the power of the print unions broken, but every union and every management in the private sector took note that, with a sympathetic government behind it, any firm with enough funds to bear temporary losses could defeat a union, no matter how well organized. After Wapping, no shop steward in any private firm ever wielded the influence that the fathers of the NGA chapels used to have. This was the most significant victory by a private employer in any industrial dispute in post-war Britain.

Victory allowed Kelvin MacKenzie, the new editor of the *Sun*, to give free rein to what one of his former protégés, Piers Morgan, described as his 'particular form of dangerous genius'.[21] MacKenzie's origins were middle class; his parents and both his brothers were journalists; he was educated at Alleyn's in Dulwich, a direct grant school that later became a private school; but he aped the mindset of a working-class Tory, even to the extent of professing to support Millwall Football Club. When entertaining senior staff, he offered lager from the can; when angry, he used streams of foul language. The *Sun*'s political editor, Walter Terry, left in 1983 having had the words 'crap', 'cunt' and 'fucking' hurled at him more often than he could stand. No one was more sorely tested by the boss's mercurial moods than Stuart Higgins, on the news desk, who drove MacKenzie to heightened fury by sitting through a torrent of abuse, smiling. On one occasion, *Sun* hacks heard demonic laughter coming from the editor's office, and in the morning, on page five of the newspaper, they saw a photograph of Higgins under the heading: 'Want someone to yell at? Scream at? Fume at? – Ring Higgy the Human Sponge, He'll Soak It Up'. Under this, Higgins's direct line number was printed in large type. Around 1,000 readers took up the invitation to ring and be abusive, a response triumphantly recorded in the next day's paper under the heading 'We Hate Higgy'.[22] The resilient Higgins survived to take MacKenzie's job in 1994.

Between high jinks, the *Sun* was a pillar of support for Margaret Thatcher, preaching for the free market, strong defence and mistrust for foreigners, particularly the French. In 1984, during a dispute over the export of British lamb, the *Sun* distributed badges bearing the slogan 'Hop Off You Frogs'.[23] When Jacques Delors produced a report in October 1990, proposing the launch of the single European currency, the *Sun* had a front-page graphic showing two fingers to the EU president under the headline 'Up Yours Delors'.[24] This ferocious popularism, combined with the *Sun*'s huge circulation, which reached 4.3m in February 1989, gave it a reputation for being able to make or destroy politicians. When the Conservatives were re-elected in 1992, the newspaper boasted that it was 'The *Sun* wot won it'. The defeated Labour leader, Neil Kinnock, who had refused to communicate with the *Sun* except through libel lawyers, seemed to agree. Detailed research suggested that about 11 per cent of *Sun* newspapers readers, or 116,000 voters, had switched from Labour to Conservative, enough to make a difference in some marginal seats.

Meanwhile, Andreas Whittam Smith's secret had been rumbled. On 27 December 1985, the *Financial Times* accurately reported that a quality daily newspaper produced on new technology was to be launched in 1986, the *Independent*. Whittam Smith and his confederates had raised only £2m out of the £18m they needed for the launch, but circumvented this problem by bluffing, attracting other investors by giving the impression that the project was more developed than it actually was. In April, they announced that they had the necessary money and would launch in the autumn, causing a rush of job applications from journalists on *The Times* and *Sunday Times* eager to escape Wapping. This was a lucky circumstance that meant that when the newspaper appeared for the first time, on 7 October 1986, it had one of the best teams of writers in the industry. The first day's main story was written jointly by Sarah Hogg, who went on from journalism to be head of the Downing Street Policy Unit under John Major, and Andrew Marr. There was no self promotion on the front page, as if the appearance of a new national newspaper was not news in itself, and the design was unexpectedly conservative, so that instead of appearing to break the mould of British journalism, it looked like a newspaper that had been coming out for years.

Despite the huge goodwill that it attracted, the new venture was in a parlous financial condition for months and it would have been a bold punter who would have bet on its surviving for much more than a year. Sales started at around 330,000, but by January they were down to 257,000 and the venture was estimated to be losing £20,000 a day. Then, for no obvious reason, the figures improved, and by March 1987 were at 291,000. The following month, the newspaper had a sensational scoop, when Phillip Knightley, a former *Sunday Times* journalist, turned up from Australia with a manuscript of *Spycatcher*, the memoirs of the embittered former MI5 employee Peter Wright. The government had deployed the Official Secrets Act to prevent publication in the UK, but, try as it might, was unable to have the ban extended to Australia. The *Independent* published a long extract on a Monday morning, focusing on Wright's allegation that MI5 had tried to prove that Harold Wilson was a Soviet agent. This helped launch the forbidden book as the publishing sensation of the year – though after the excitement had died down, people who had spent money on it were left wondering why so much attention had been paid to the unreliable memoirs of an angry, weird old man obsessed about his pension. It also landed the *Independent* in court. The case drifted inconclusively through the legal system while performing wonders for the newspaper's reputation. Circulation climbed above 400,000 and a copy of the day's *Independent* almost had the status of a fashion accessory.

Then its founders heard that a group including David Lipsey, editor of *New Society* and a former Downing Street adviser during Callaghan's premiership, was planning a similar venture. This would be a new quality Sunday newspaper to be called the *Correspondent*. Mainly on Stephen Glover's initiative, the *Independent* rushed to launch its own Sunday title in competition. Thus two new Sunday newspaper entered the same market, the *Correspondent* in September 1989, and the *Independent on Sunday* in January 1990 – just as the economy headed into recession. The *Correspondent* went out of business after fourteen months and the *Independent* titles failed to achieve the profitability and circulation that had almost been in their grasp.

After Wapping, it was always likely that one of the broadcasting unions would be the next target of a union-busting operation. The camera crews and other technicians were protected by agreements dating from the 1950s, which had not changed as technology improved, and could be tiresome for those trying to make programmes. However, owning a television franchise was so profitable that managements preferred to keep paying rather than risk a strike. In September 1987, fired by her third election victory, Margaret Thatcher summoned television executives to Downing Street for a lecture, stating that they had allowed their industry to be the 'last bastion of restrictive practices'.[25] The practices of which she complained were mostly to be found in the large, profitable regional television companies, but it was within two smaller ones that confrontations began. The management at Tyne Tees Television, in Newcastle, told its technicians that staff costs were too high and then sacked the thirty-four members of the EETPU who walked out in protest. David Reay, the managing director, refused an offer from the men to return to work while talks continued, and insisted on bringing programmes out without them.

However, the main battle was at TV-am. Early in 1984, the Australian media mogul Kerry Packer bought into the company and installed a fellow Australian, Bruce Gyngell, as managing director. The company had such heavy debts hanging over from its first loss-making months that it was not even certain that it could pay that month's wages, until Gyngell arranged an unusual £1.2m advance payment for an advertising campaign for toys and applied himself with great energy to pushing up the ratings. Until then, it was assumed that television viewers wanted their weather forecasts delivered by people with some understanding of meteorology. Gyngell decided that anyone who could read an autocue and smile would do, and turned his attractive Swedish secretary, Ulrika Jonsson, into the nation's first celebrity weather girl.

Even that stroke of genius did not stop Gyngell obsessively worrying that the company would lose its franchise unless it could reduce costs. The showdown began over something seemingly trivial. *Good Morning Britain* ran a 'Caring Christmas' roadshow that, under the union agreement, required six support staff. Gyngell insisted that four would be enough. The main broadcasting union, the Association of Cinematograph Television and Allied Technicians (ACTT), fired a shot across his bows by calling its 229 members out on a one-day strike in November 1987. It had a shock when Gyngell refused to allow them back. Gyngell had decided to 'do a Wapping': 'I don't want to see another ACTT man in this building ever again,' he told his senior staff.[26] The union was thus manoeuvred into an unwanted, prolonged dispute as Christmas approached. The example of Wapping made victory unlikely, and public opinion was bound to be against them when popular television presenters such as Lorraine Kelly were seen crossing picket lines in a dispute over a Christmas charity drive. 'The public relations battle is a no-hoper for us. We might as well forget it,'[27] their shop steward, Tim Wight, confessed ruefully. Meanwhile, *Good Morning Britain* continued to broadcast, on an annual wage bill that fell from £8m to £2m, with executives or secretaries handling the cameras. Audience figures went up and up, and Bruce Gyngell won a place in Margaret Thatcher's heart because there was no one she loved more than a union-buster. As a mark of favour, she agreed to be interviewed several times on David Frost's Sunday morning programme. The dispute was settled after 22 months when Gyngell in effect paid the ACTT members £700,000 to go away. By 1989–90, TV-am had a strong claim to be the world's most successful television company, showing an annual profit of £24m and having taken 70 per cent of breakfast TV audience.

Just before Thatcher was brought down, her government passed the 1990 Broadcasting Act, which set out new rules for the ownership and regulation of the mass media. Its avowed intention was to make regulation lighter and choice greater. It also restricted cross-media ownership by stipulating that no newspaper company could own more than 20 per cent of a television company – though, of course, there was no question of this rule applying to

Rupert Murdoch. For the purposes of this piece of legislation, Sky was defined as a non-UK service. The Act also laid down that television franchises would be awarded in blind auctions to the highest bidder. Under this much criticized clause, Thames Television lost its franchise to Carlton, in what looked like revenge for their documentary *Death on the Rock*, about the killing of three IRA members in Gibraltar. An unintended consequence was that when the broadcasting authority was presented with a bid for the breakfast franchise from GMTV, which was so extravagant that it later had to be revised downwards, they had no option but to accept. All Gyngell's union-busting was to no avail. TV-am went out of business on 31 December 1992. One of the letters of commiseration he received was from Margaret Thatcher. She wrote, 'When I see how some of the other licenses have been awarded I am mystified that you did not receive yours, and heartbroken. I am only too painfully aware that I was responsible for the legislation.'[28]

The decade's final addition to the airwaves was the satellite company Sky, which started broadcasting on 5 February 1989, after Rupert Murdoch had emerged victorious from a war of nerves with Richard Branson, who planned a rival channel called BSB. It was very uncertain that any satellite television could make a profit in Britain, competing against four well-established terrestrial channels; two rival satellite channels would have been doomed to fail. Before Sky was launched, twenty-four-hour rolling news bulletins were unknown and there was a great deal of scepticism about whether or not the public needed the service, but Sky was blessed in its early years by such events as the collapse of communism, the release of Nelson Mandela, the World Cup and the fall of Thatcher, all of which suited the twenty-four-hour format well.

As the press barons and television companies thrived, so did members of an unloved profession that feasted off them – the libel lawyers. Britain's libel laws have been the recipient of endless criticism, because it is so much easier to sue than to defend a libel case. In the latter half of the 1980s, they had the additional cachet that juries were awarding higher and higher damages so that, in the absence of a national lottery, one of the most obvious ways to get rich quickly was to be libelled. In 1987, a former naval commander, Martin Packard, sued a Greek newspaper that had accused him of betraying the resistance movement during the years when Greece was ruled by a junta. The offending newspaper sold forty copies in the UK. A jury awarded Packard £450,000. The following year, Koo Stark, a thirty-two-year-old former soft-porn actress who had been seen in the company of Prince Andrew, was awarded £300,000 from the *People* for a report that wrongly implied that she had been to bed with him. These sums, like all libel awards, were tax free. It seemed as if no one could ever lose a libel case until an elected politician, Michael Meacher, sued Alan Watkins of the *Observer* for implying that Meacher had falsified his background to make him appear more working class than he really was. Uniquely, the jury found for Watkins, as if MPs were the only class of human being that libel juries held in lower esteem than journalists.

It also seemed that the race was on to set new records in damages. In October 1986, the millionaire thriller-writer Jeffrey Archer had to resign from his position as deputy chairman of the Conservative Party after the *News of the World* photographed him at Victoria station, in London, meeting a prostitute named Monica Coghlan, to hand her £2,000 in cash. Archer denied the obvious inference. 'I have never, repeat never, met Monica Coghlan, nor have I ever had any association of any kind with a prostitute,'[29] he said.He claimed he was giving her money so that she could escape journalists who were trying to get her to say that she had sold him her services. The next day, the *Daily Star* went further than the *News of the World* by alleging that Archer had paid for sex. Archer sued the *Star*. In court, Coghlan gave a detailed description of meeting Archer for sex in a hotel room, while he persisted in his denials. One of the extraordinary aspects of the case was the number of people who either knew or suspected that Archer was committing perjury. While the *Daily Telegraph's* coverage of the case seemed to take Archer's side, its editor, Max Hastings, privately 'did not venture to anticipate that in reality Jeffrey would end up in prison', but 'never doubted that he deserved to'.[30] Woodrow Wyatt noted in his diary: 'I think that the prostitute was telling more of the truth than Archer.'[31] But the judge was more impressed by Mary Archer, a confident Oxford-educated scientist. He admonished the jury:

> Remember Mary Archer in the witness box. Your vision of her will probably never disappear. Has she elegance? Has she fragrance? Would she have – without the strain of this trial – a radiance? . . . Is there abstinence from marital joys for Archer – for Jeffrey? Is he in need of cold, unloving, rubber-insulated sex in a seedy hotel?[32] The jury took the hint, and awarded Archer £500,000.

That record sum for damages was held for less than two years, to be topped when Sonia Sutcliffe, the wife of the 'Yorkshire Ripper', sued the satirical magazine *Private Eye*. This peculiar case had its origins in the unseemly rush by tabloid journalists to buy up witnesses' stories, which began even before Sutcliffe had made his first court appearance, after someone in Yorkshire leaked his name. His father, John Sutcliffe, and two sisters, for instance, were bought up by the *Daily Mail*, with whom they entered into a £5,000 contract for an exclusive interview and relevant photographs. Olivia Reivers, who had survived being attacked by Sutcliffe, was paid £4,000 by the *Daily Star*. On 30 January 1981, three weeks after Sutcliffe's arrest, *Private Eye* alleged: 'The *Daily Mail* appears to be leading in the squalid race to "tie-up" the Sutcliffe family. While lorry driver Peter Sutcliffe is in custody, his wife Sonia had made a deal with the *Mail* worth £250,000'.[33] At first, this report, which went on to give other details about press buy-ups, produced no reaction from Sonia Sutcliffe, but had an extraordinary impact in the larger world. It triggered a furious reaction from Doreen Hill, who was in grief over her daughter Jacqueline's murder (see Chapter 2) and instructed her solicitor to send a complaint to the Press Council. Mrs Hill drew support from a vast number of influential people, including the Queen, whose private secretary wrote to say that 'Her Majesty . . . certainly shares in the sense of distaste which right-minded people will undoubtedly feel'.[34]

The *Private Eye* story was wrong in one important detail – Sonia Sutcliffe had never clinched a deal with the *Daily Mail* nor any other newspaper – but that went unchallenged until January 1987, when a solicitor's letter suddenly arrived at *Private Eye*'s offices, demanding damages. The magazine offered to apologize and make a substantial payment to Sutcliffe's victims, but Mrs Sutcliffe, who had not been able to return to her teaching job since her husband's arrest, was worried about her mortgage and wanted to go to court. In the witness stand she came across as a sincere and timid woman caught up in something she did not understand. It took the jury just an hour-and-a-half to reach a verdict in her favour, and award damages of £600,000, about ten times the total compensation paid to all Sutcliffe's surviving victims. Maureen Long, for instance, who had survived horrible injuries inflicted on her by Sutcliffe, merited £8,500. 'If this is justice, I'm a banana,' *Private Eye*'s editor, Ian Hislop, declared outside the court.[35] Other newspapers who had received writs from Mrs Sutcliffe's lawyers took the hint and settled in a hurry. Even after the *Private Eye* award had been reduced on appeal to £60,000, Mrs Sutcliffe was the richer by around £270,000. She should have quit while she was on top, but she went on to sue the *News of the World* over a story alleging that she had attempted a romance with a Greek travel agent who could pass as a Ripper 'lookalike'. The story was untrue, but the *News of the World* fielded a formidable legal team who succeeded in bringing forth evidence that Sonia Sutcliffe admired her husband 'Pete' for his campaign to clean up the streets; hated the nickname 'Ripper'; admired Hitler; had lied to Bradford Council to receive benefits when she had a large sum in the bank; and most significantly had accepted money from newspaper journalists. She lost and the legal costs must have drained all her earlier winnings. Although *Private Eye* could now claim that the thrust, if not the detail, of the original story had been proved right, it did not alter the fact that it had lost many thousands of pounds.

Soon, even the jury's eye-watering award in that case had been eclipsed in a weirdly obscure case involving an expatriate Russian historian and a former army officer. Lord Aldington, chairman of Sun Alliance insurance, had been a brigadier stationed near the Yugoslav border at the end of the Second World War, when thousands of Russians, Ukrainians and Yugoslavs who had fought on the German side were handed over to the Communists by the British. They faced near certain death. At the behest of a businessman with a grievance against Sun Alliance, Count Nikolai Tolstoy wrote a pamphlet accusing Aldington of having blood on his hands. About 10,000 copies were printed. The libel award was £1.5m, plus £500,000 costs. Tolstoy was then told that if he wished to appeal, he must pay a £124,900 advance to indemnify Aldington's costs. He declared himself bankrupt and years later won a ruling from the European Court of Human Rights that the judgement infringed his right to free speech. Aldington died in 2000, without receiving any damages.

Amid awards like these, the *Sun* rolled over and paid up without going to court to contest a case brought by the singer Elton John. He was the subject of a tale that Kelvin MacKenzie's brother, Craig, had brought into the office during the Wapping dispute. It alleged that the rock star had recruited rent boys for long orgies involving drugs and bondage, even specifying the date of one of the sessions. The story was so obviously unsound that the legal department gave the editor a written warning not to run it, but this was ignored. In no time, the *Daily Mirror* had run a counter story proving that Elton John had been aboard Concorde on the specified date. The *Sun* persisted for twenty-one months, using increasingly dubious tactics in an effort to find something sufficiently incriminating to frighten their target into dropping his lawsuit, but finally gave up in December 1988 on the eve of the scheduled court hearing. That morning's front page was dominated by an enormous headline saying 'Sorry Elton', underneath which was printed the news that the paper had agreed to pay him £1m. Christmas at the *Sun*'s office party was cheered by a tirade from Kelvin MacKenzie to all his 'fucking useless' staff, in honour of the reprimand he had just received from Rupert Murdoch.[36]

Despite the setbacks in court, the nation's media moguls and their consumers could look back on a boom decade. For the television viewer, restricted ten years earlier to a diet of three channels, there was the first glimpse of a world to come in which there would be no limit to the number of programmes beamed into the home – though whether or not more would mean better was another question. Although Fleet Street, as a geographical location, had lost the industry that made it special, the newspapers were actually enjoying a rare boom because of the dramatic fall in the cost of producing them. There were new national titles on sale in the newsagents for the first time since the war. In the long run, the computer technology that had given the failing newspaper industry this shot in the arm would threaten its continued existence, but not yet. For the time being, the industry was doing well.

Chapter 12

The Bomb and the Ballot

On the morning of 27 October 1980, prison wardens in Northern Ireland's notorious H-Block went from cell to cell delivering breakfast, as usual, to the republican and loyalist gunmen held there. Unusually, seven Irish Republican Army (IRA) prisoners, led by their commander, a hardened republican named Brendan Hughes, refused to eat. It was another development in a battle that been waged since the mid-1970s between IRA prisoners and the British government. The IRA internees demanded to be classed as political prisoners, and specifically to be allowed to wear their own clothes. This might seem a piffling cause for such a tragedy that was about to begin, but the symbolism went to the heart of the Northern Irish conflict. The republicans had never accepted the settlement of 1922 that divided Ireland. The Provisional IRA, the smaller Irish National Liberation Army (INLA) and the virtually defunct Official IRA considered themselves to be patriots fighting an army of occupation.

In the late 1970s, this demand had produced the so-called 'dirty protest', during which the men refused to wear any clothes at all, remaining in their cells wrapped in blankets. The wardens would not go in to clean the cells while the prisoners were inside, with the result that the walls became smeared in excrement and the men lay covered in maggots, looking almost Christ-like with their long, matted hair. Despite the effect of these images on opinion abroad, the Labour government did not budge and nor did the Conservatives. The best hope for the protestors was the announcement, in July 1979 that the Pope was going to visit Ireland. Cardinal Tomás Ó Fiaich, the Irish primate, who had some sympathy for the blanket protestors, went to Rome to persuade the Pope that he should include County Armagh in his itinerary. The Pope's presence in Northern Ireland might have embarrassed the government into making a concession that would end the blanket protest, but on 27 August 1979, the very day that the cardinal was in the Vatican to plead his case, eighteen soldiers were killed in an IRA ambush. On that same bloodstained day, a bomb ripped apart a small private cruiser off Ireland's west coast, killing Earl Mountbatten, the seventy-nine-year-old favourite uncle of the Prince of Wales, his daughter's eighty-three-year-old mother-in-law, his grandson, aged fourteen, and a boat boy, aged fifteen. Thomas McMahon, leader of the IRA's South Armagh Brigade, was convicted of the bombing by a special court in Dublin in December, and spent more than seventeen years in prison. Mountbatten had no connection with Ireland, other than to take his holidays there, but Bobby Sands, one of the H-Block prisoners, justified his murder because 'he knew the problem and did nothing about it. He did nothing except to exploit Ireland and its natural resources'.[1] Those bombs also killed any prospect of a papal visit to the north. Instead, speaking to a vast open-air gathering outside Dublin on 29 September, the Pope made an appeal in halting English to the IRA to turn away from violence.

If the prisoners inside H-Block had been more in contact with the outside world, they might have realized that they had picked the wrong time to step up their protest. It was unthinkable that a Conservative government, particularly one led by Margaret Thatcher, was going to be seen to make concessions to the IRA that a Labour government had denied them. Thatcher had lost a highly valued ally to Irish terrorists. On the afternoon of 30 March 1979, Airey Neave, who had so shrewdly managed Thatcher's leadership campaign and then been appointed spokesman on Northern Ireland, was driving up the exit ramp of the underground car park beneath the House of Commons when the angle of the slope set off a plastic bomb attached beneath the car, killing him. Since that day, no car has been allowed into the Commons car park until its underside has been checked. 'He was staunch, brave, true, strong, but he was very gentle and kind and loyal,'[2] Thatcher said, after visiting Neave's widow. 'Some devils got him,' she added, the same day.[3] The 'devils' in questions were the INLA.

Margaret Thatcher also had the right of the Conservative Party to take into account. Enoch Powell had left the Conservatives in 1974 to join the Ulster Unionist Party (UUP). He was back in the Commons and commanded considerable respect on the Tory right. Thatcher was also somewhat in awe of him. He and the UUP leader Jim Molyneaux argued that Northern Ireland should be treated as integral to the United Kingdom and that its six counties should be governed in the same way as Yorkshire or Strathclyde. A minority within the UUP, including the young David Trimble, believed that Northern Ireland should have special, devolved arrangements. Their rivals for Protestant support, the Democratic Unionist Party (DUP) led by the fiery Reverend Ian Paisley, were more anti-British in their rhetoric than the UUP and were also de facto devolutionists. Neave's murder inadvertently strengthened the devolutionists' position, because he had sympathized with Enoch Powell. His successor, Humphrey Atkins, was a less ideological Tory who was persuaded by civil servants in the Northern Ireland Office that retaining the Irish government's cooperation in combating republican terrorists should be their first priority, which would be put at risk if the government set about integrating Northern Ireland into the UK.

Atkins therefore called a conference to discuss devolution, which Jim Molyneaux boycotted, perhaps thinking that he could deal with the prime minister over her minister's head. This was a foolish move, based on a misreading of how pragmatic Thatcher was. Her instincts and sympathies were profoundly Unionist. She identified with the rural Protestants, whose religion and work ethic reminded her of her father. As a minister in Edward Heath's government, she had dealt directly with the old, Protestant-controlled Stormont government, and thought it worked well, though she reluctantly admitted that it was 'associated with discrimination against the Catholics.' But, above all, Airey Neave's murder, the assassination of Mountbatten and the killing of eighteen soldiers had made her decide that security had to be the first priority in the province, even at the expense of Protestant aspirations. 'I started from the need for greater security, which was imperative. If this meant limited political concessions to the South, much as I disliked this kind of bargaining I had to contemplate it,'[4] she wrote in her memoirs. 'But the results in terms of security must come through.' As a first step towards showing that she took security seriously, Mrs Thatcher resolved that nothing must happen while the H-Block prisoners were on hunger strike. There must be no suggestion that her government was 'bowing to terrorist demands'.

But the H-Block prisoners did not know that. They had no insight into the psychological make-up of the woman in Downing Street. In their isolation, encouraged by one another, they overestimated the impact of their protests. They were sure that the British would shift before anyone died of starvation. After a couple of weeks, as the British refused to move, the seven hunger strikers were transferred to a hospital wing, while Cardinal Ó Fiaich scuttled to Rome, and to London, trying to whip up a political initiative that would save their lives. On 4 December 1980, Atkins made a statement to the

Commons that offered no compromise, but out of the public eye, there seemed to be movement. In Hughes's absence, command of the IRA prisoners in H-Block had devolved to Bobby Sands, who was not on hunger strike. Sands, who was age twenty-seven, had spent almost his entire adult life in prison. There is no evidence that he had ever hurt anybody. He came from a law-abiding working-class family, but joined the IRA at the age of eighteen after Protestant violence had driven his family out of their home. He was twice caught in possession of arms – not a notably successful terrorist, therefore, but much respected by other prisoners. He was allowed to visit Hughes and the others in hospital, bringing a studiously vague thirty-four-page statement he had been given by the Northern Ireland Office. They read into it a hint of a promise of a concession and called off the hunger strike.

But still nothing happened. Hoping for the concession that never came, Sands tried to persuade his fellow prisoners to don prison clothes and re-enter the system. The IRA command outside H-Block supported him, not wanting another failure, but the men were intractable. Reluctantly, Sands devised a new plan, under which one prisoner would go on hunger strike, to be joined by another two weeks later, and then one more each week until the regime buckled. He insisted on going first, though others would have preferred him to continue acting as their negotiator and let someone else go over the top. He began his hunger strike on 1 March 1981.

Coincidentally, on 5 March, the MP for Fermanagh and South Tyrone, a rural seat with a majority Catholic population, died. The provisional Sinn Fein, the anaemic 'political wing' of the IRA, had never contested a parliamentary election and would not have won if it had. The terrorist groups had only minority support even within the Catholic minority, most of whom voted for the Social Democratic and Labour Party (SDLP), which believed in achieving Irish reunification without violence. In 1980, the SDLP was in crisis because it had parted company with its most effective leader, Gerry Fitt, who had been succeeded by the amiable but less impressive John Hume. Provisional Sinn Fein saw a unique opportunity in the emotion generated by the H-Block protests, and decided to nominate Sands. The SDLP agreed not to oppose him. The brother of the dead MP also stood aside, after a visit from Gerry Adams, Sinn Fein's vice president. As Sands approached death, Catholics in the constituency who had not voted for decades, or who would never normally have given support to the IRA, poured into the polling booths. Sands polled 30,092 votes to become Sinn Fein's first elected MP. His exuberant supporters thought that the British government could not let him die now. Michael Foot privately visited Margaret Thatcher to urge her to look for a way out, though in public he agreed that the government could not grant political status to the IRA. She told him crossly that he was a 'push-over'.[5] Sands died on 5 May, after starving himself for sixty-six days. Death made him the Provisional IRA's first martyred hero, though not in the eyes of Margaret Thatcher, who told the Commons that afternoon that 'Mr Sands was a convicted criminal; he chose to take his own life'.[6] In Derry, police and rioters fought one another for four hours and in Belfast, during similar disturbances, a fourteen-year-old boy was crushed to death.

The next hunger striker, twenty-five-year-old Francis Hughes, sentenced to life for killing a British soldier, died a week later. On 18 May, five British soldiers were killed by an IRA bomb. Two more hunger strikers died on 21 May; another on 9 July, a sixth on 13 July. Each death was answered by riots. On 18 July, Dublin experienced its worst street disturbance in nearly thirty years when 15,000 demonstrators clashed with police outside the British embassy. Each funeral was a spectacular IRA demonstration led by pipes and drums, but still there were no concessions from the British. The protest had achieved its maximum effect on the day Sands died and was producing diminishing returns. Gerry Adams was allowed into H-Block on 28 July, the day before the royal wedding, to try to persuade the men to end the hunger strikes, but they refused, driven by an intense solidarity heightened by the knowledge that two more of their number were already beyond medical help. They died on 30 July and 2 August. The death toll continued until August 20, which coincidentally was the day that Owen Carron, of Sinn Fein, was elected to Parliament in the seat left vacant by Sands' death. Ten men had starved to death and nothing had been conceded. Two days after the protest was called off, Jim Prior, the new Northern Ireland secretary, allowed the prisoners to wear their own clothes.

The short term cost to the IRA of this small concession had been immense – the lives lost, the anguish of the prisoners' families and the effort that had gone into the campaign to publicize their plight. However, its long-term effect on nationalist opinion on the Catholic housing estates, on the supply of funds from American sympathizers and on Sinn Fein's support, gained at the expense of the SDLP, gave weight to Thatcher's observation that the 'unfortunate' IRA hunger strikers were 'more use to them dead than alive'.[7] The election victory that the dying Bobby Sands scored in Fermanagh and South Tyrone was the start of the dual strategy of the ballot and the bomb. There was fierce opposition at the ensuing Sinn Fein conference, but the main leaders, Gerry Adams, Martin McGuinness and Danny Morrison, had overcome their earlier scepticism now that they saw that it was possible to win. Morrison effectively won the argument when he asked the 300 delegates: 'Is there anyone here who objects to taking power in Ireland with a ballot paper in one hand and an Armalite in the other?'[8] The argument was won and in the 1983 general election Gerry Adams was elected MP for West Belfast. No Sinn Fein MP, then or later, actually took his seat or swore the necessary oath of loyalty.

In case anyone thought that they were not serious about the 'Armalite' half of this strategy, the IRA broke with the paramilitaries' normal practice of not killing each other's politicians. On 14 November 1981 they assassinated Rev. Robert Bradford, a Methodist minister and Unionist Ulster MP who had been particularly outspoken in calling for the death penalty for terrorists. Three Catholics were murdered by loyalist paramilitaries in revenge, bringing the total of deaths from Northern Ireland's troubles in that year to 117. The IRA also advertised its presence on the British mainland once more, in July 1982, by setting off a bomb in Hyde Park as the Household Cavalry were passing. Four troopers and seven horses were killed. Stacy Bustin, an eighteen-year-old American bystander, was hit by shrapnel in the face, stomach, legs and throat, and had a two-inch hole ripped in her left thigh. She said of the bomber: 'My first reaction was I'd love to kill him, but then I realized I would be lowering myself down to his level if I did.'[9]

Throughout the decade, there was evidence that individuals in the security forces quietly agreed with the likes of Rev. Bradford about applying the death penalty to terrorists, and did so unofficially, by shooting to kill. On 11 November 1982, three unarmed IRA men were shot dead by the police at a roadblock outside Lurgan. In the same month, two teenagers with no contact with the paramilitaries innocently approached a hayshed where arms were hidden. Michael Tighe, aged seventeen, was shot dead by members of a previously secret special unit called E4A, and his nineteen-year-old friend was injured. A few weeks later, two INLA men were killed by members of the same unit. The magistrate in charge of their inquests resigned in protest at police obstruction, and under pressure the police agreed to an inquiry into allegations of a shoot-to-kill policy. John Stalker, deputy chief constable of Manchester Police, was brought in to head the inquiry, but was suspended in May 1986 before his inquiry was complete and replaced by Colin Sampson, chief constable of West Yorkshire.

Meanwhile Jim Prior, the new secretary of state, was being pursued by shouts of 'Brits out' from Catholics and Protestants alike whenever he ventured out in his bullet-proof car, feeling like 'a foreigner in another land'.[10] When he turned up at Rev. Bradford's funeral, the reaction was so hostile that he could not take the seat at the front that the family had reserved for him, and he was jostled and kicked on the way out to shouts of 'kill him'. The Unionists then refused to attend a conference Prior tried to call to discuss political solutions to the troubles, and like Humphrey Atkins before him, Prior was left sitting in a half-empty room with members of the SDLP and the tiny Alliance Party.

In the hope of steering a way out of this logjam, Prior proposed a programme of 'rolling devolution' that would begin with the election of a 78-seat assembly that had no power initially, only a right to be consulted, but which would gradually acquire power. The elections went ahead on 20 October 1982, despite opposition from Enoch Powell's supporters, who saw it as a betrayal of the Unionists, and from the SDLP, who thought it did not go far enough. The UUP secured 26 seats to 21 for Ian Paisley's DUP, 14 for the SDLP and 10 for the Alliance, but the election's real sensation was that Sinn Fein took part and won 10 per cent of the total, earning them 5 seats. It was sufficient to convince the IRA's hard-men that the strategy of 'the ballot and the bullet' might work, though it did not mean there would be any let-up in the killing. In December 1982, an INLA bomb killed sixteen people in the crowded Droppin' Well disco in Ballykelly, near Derry, where British soldiers went to meet local girls.

There was a much bigger prey in the IRA's sights: Margaret Thatcher. Her decision to let the hunger strikers die, and the remarks she made about them, had entered folklore on Northern Ireland's Catholic estates. The British police anticipated an attempt on her life, but wrongly surmised that it would take place during her twice-weekly journeys from Downing Street to the Commons for Prime Minister's Questions. Instead, a man calling himself Roy Walsh, who gave a Lewisham address, booked himself into Room 629, overlooking the sea, on the sixth floor of the Grand Hotel, Brighton, on 15 September 1984. Three weeks later, the Conservative annual conference began and at 2.54 a.m. on Friday, 12 October, the frontage of the hotel was destroyed by a massive explosion. Four people were killed, including Conservative MP Anthony Berry (whose seat in Enfield North was taken by Michael Portillo, who held it until 1997). Norman Tebbit, the party chairman, was buried under rubble for hours. His eventual rescue was shown live on television; his wife, Margaret, was paralysed. Mrs Thatcher had been working on her speech. After the bomb went off, she plunged into the dust-filled room where her husband Denis was asleep to check that he was alright, then to her secretaries' room across the way. As she entered, one of them announced: 'Mrs Thatcher, it's all right. I've still got the speech. I'm just typing it.'[11] The conference resumed at 9.30 a.m. precisely, and Thatcher delivered that speech with iron self-control.

It did not take the police long to establish that 'Roy Walsh' was a false name. Applying laser and chemicals to his hotel registration, they found a finger and palm print belonging to Patrick Magee, who had been a known IRA activist for more than a decade. He was arrested in Glasgow the following June, with three other bombers, and spent fourteen years in prison, two-fifths of the minimum sentence passed on him at the time.

Every tragedy needs a comic interlude. The IRA never knew how much confusion they caused behind the scenes, which dragged senior officials on both sides of the Atlantic into a pointless waste of time, all because the prime minister's son liked to travel. In January 1982, Mark Thatcher competed in the Paris-Dakar motor rally, with a French woman driver and their mechanic, and became lost in the Sahara for six days near the Algeria-Mali border. On the day he was reported missing, Mrs Thatcher was due to speak to the National Federation of Self Employed. She arrived red-eyed, answered questions from waiting reporters, went into the lobby and burst into tears. She managed to deliver her speech, but for the rest of the day appears to have been effectively out of action. She then cancelled other engagements. Downing Street put out a statement saying that she was 'very upset'. Denis Thatcher flew to Algeria to coordinate the search operation. Later that week, the three missing people were found by their broken-down car. When she knew that Mark was safe, Mrs Thatcher let on that her 'heart had stopped' when she first feared for his life, but now her world looked 'totally different'. Mark's sister, Carol, was not quite so euphoric. 'I hope this is the last of Mark's motor racing. Mum can do without the hassle,'[12] she said.

When Mark Thatcher returned to London, people noticed that everywhere he went a police officer was always in close vicinity, giving rise to frivolous speculation that the Metropolitan Police had been told to make sure he did not get lost again. Rumours reached the Labour MP, Willie Hamilton, an inveterate troublemaker, who penned a written question to the home secretary asking what this police presence was costing.[13]

Whitelaw refused to answer, but before he made that decision, someone in the Home Office helpfully drew up a briefing note, preserved in the archives, to ensure that the home secretary, at least, knew what was going on, even if he was not telling Hamilton. The security forces had received a tip-off the previous August that Mark Thatcher might be on the IRA's list of targets, and having seen the effect his temporary disappearance had on his mother, they could not risk anything else happening. He had been assigned a police driver and two officers who provided round-the-clock protection.[14]

This became complicated when, soon after the Brighton bombing, Mark Thatcher moved to Dallas on business. The British embassy in Washington asked the Americans to give Mark Thatcher the same twenty-four-hour surveillance that he had had in London, which at first they were willing to do, for the sake of President Reagan's friend and ally, but not permanently. It was not long before British diplomats and the officers assigned to guard Mark Thatcher were given an insight into his character. He wanted to be protected, but as a harassed British official in Dallas complained to a colleague in the Washington embassy in January 1985, 'one of the problems about Mr Thatcher is that he does not let anyone know about his movements'.[15] Their problems were by no means over when, to everyone's relief, Mark Thatcher announced that he had found a suitable house in Dallas that he liked. In exchange for shedding his twenty-four-hour protection, he wanted an estimated $18,000 worth of modifications to improve security at his new house and proposed to send the bill to the British embassy. When they said that, regretfully, they could not justify such a use of British taxpayers' money, he suggested that they appoint him 'honorary consul' in Dallas, because then the US government would foot the bill. When told that was not likely to go down well with the British public, Mark refused to move house. John Kerr, the second most senior diplomat in the Washington embassy, and his deputy Nigel Sheinwald (who, at the time of writing, is the ambassador to Washington) had to negotiate with the authorities in Texas to get Mark's twenty-four-hour protection extended as negotiations dragged on. In return, he was expected to keep Sheinwald informed of his whereabouts, but although Sheinwald tried every few days for several months to get through to him, all Sheinwald's messages were ignored.[16] Meanwhile, neighbours in the Dallas apartment that was Mark Thatcher's temporary home objected to the disruption caused by his permanent police guard, which drew attention to his presence and added to the security problem.

After almost a year, Mark Thatcher visited London and called in at Downing Street, where he was subjected to a severe lecture by Nigel Wicks, the prime minister's principal private secretary (who would achieve prominence sixteen years later as chairman of the Committee on Standards in Public Life). Wicks did not care for the young Thatcher's 'relaxed' attitude to his safety and 'I told him rather bluntly that our interest was not so much in his own personal welfare but in the effect on his mother – and therefore on the government of the United Kingdom – if anything happened to him.'

Having thus been put firmly in his place, young Thatcher promised to behave and to report to Nigel Sheinwald as soon as he was back in the USA, though Wicks warned that he would be 'surprised' if Mark kept his word.[17] He did, though. The embassy staff 'formed the impression, for the first time in our (year long) discussions, Mark intends to cooperate'.[18]

Alas, it was a false dawn. Six months later, the embassy wrote to Downing Street again, in despair, asking for the ultimate weapon to be deployed. They wanted Margaret Thatcher to speak 'firmly' to her son.[19] A few days later, he called in to Downing Street, where Nigel Wicks discovered that he was still clinging to the notion of being appointed an 'honorary consul'. Wicks put that idea to rest by pointing out to Mark Thatcher that if he became a public official, Labour MPs would be able to ask questions in the Commons about what he was doing in Dallas, and they would have to be answered. Wicks reported that the conversation was 'not altogether satisfactory'.[20]

However, in July, after this had dragged on for more than eighteen months, Mark Thatcher called at the Washington embassy and talked to his mother on a secure telephone line.[21] Apparently that sorted him out, because the Cabinet Office file contains no more anguished correspondence between London and Washington on this topic.

A month after the Brighton bomb, in November 1984, Mrs Thatcher held a joint press conference with Garret FitzGerald, the Irish prime minister. He had set up a New Ireland Forum, consisting of representatives of nationalist parties from the north, which had since come forward with three proposals, to which she replied: 'A unified Ireland was one solution that is out. A second solution was confederation of two states. That is out. A third solution was joint authority. That is out.'[22] Out, out, out – the Unionists loved the language. Here was a prime minister they thought they could trust. It did not even appear to rouse their suspicions that no one was keeping them informed about talks in progress between the British and Irish governments, so it came as a complete shock when, on 15 November 1985, Thatcher signed the Anglo-Irish Agreement, recognizing for the first time Dublin's right to a formal say in a range of matters affecting the north, including security, public appointments and even which flags were to be flown. Eight days later, between 100,000 and 200,000 Unionists demonstrated outside Belfast City Hall. In Westminster, Ian Gow, who had been Thatcher's trusted parliamentary aide, resigned from the government, a loss that she acknowledged as a 'personal blow'.[23] All fifteen Unionist MPs resigned from the Commons simultaneously to force by-elections to demonstrate the strength of opposition to the Agreement; and fourteen were re-elected on 14 January 1986, with a combined total of more than 418,000 votes.

What the votes also demonstrated was an electoral swing from Sinn Fein to the SDLP, who gained an extra seat. Sinn Fein's vote fell again in the 1987 general election. Adams, McGuinness and Morrison easily saw off another rebellion within IRA/Sinn Fein over whether or not to continue the practice of fighting elections, but perhaps for that reason, the IRA violence increased. The toll of soldiers, police and police reservists had been falling year by year from 1981, but in the first four months of 1987 the IRA killed nine police officers. They also killed Lord Justice Maurice Gibson, Northern Ireland's second most senior judge, and his wife. On 8 November, a bomb went off in Enniskillen, County Fermanagh, during a Remembrance Day ceremony, killing eleven people and injuring sixty-three others, one of whom went into a coma and died more than thirteen years later without recovering consciousness. Millions saw or heard Gordon Wilson, a devout Christian, talk about the death of his twenty-year-old daughter, Marie: 'I bear no ill will. That sort of talk is not going to bring her back to life . . . She's in heaven and we'll meet again . . . It is part of a greater plan and God is good and we shall meet again.'[24] That bomb did more damage to the IRA's reputation than any other atrocity committed in the 1980s. On Remembrance Day 1997, Gerry Adams issued a formal apology for it.

Then, as if to even the balance, the SAS presented the IRA with a propaganda gift. On 6 March 1988, they shot dead three IRA members, two men and a woman, in Gibraltar. The trio were undoubtedly preparing a bomb attack; their Semtex was found later in a car in an underground car park. However, the SAS's lethal action revived the suspicion that the authorities were conducting a policy of shooting to kill. 'Unless the government wishes Britain's enemies to enjoy a propaganda bonanza, it should explain why it was necessary to shoot dead all three terrorists,'[25] a *Daily Telegraph* leader, written personally by the editor Max Hastings, warned.

This incident had a truly horrible aftermath. As mourners gathered for the funeral of one of the dead, at Milltown Cemetery, a lone member of the Ulster Defence Force, Michael Stone, opened fire and killed three of them. Stone was lucky to escape being beaten to death by the other mourners. He was rescued by the police and sentenced to 684 years in prison, of which he served 10. As one of his victims, an IRA member, was being buried, two British soldiers driving near the cortege took a wrong turn and found their car surrounded. Television cameras and press photographers caught the moment at which they were dragged from their car. They were taken out of sight and beaten to death.

The Gibraltar shootings also drew attention again to the Stalker inquiry, and the old 'shoot-to-kill' allegations that had never been cleared up. Stalker had published a book in which he accused officers of the Royal Ulster Constabulary of tampering with evidence at the scenes of the shootings he had been detailed to investigate. The RUC issued a statement in 1990 alleging that his book was riddled with inaccuracies, but there is at least one story Stalker told that rings true, and which may help explain why he was removed from the inquiry. He recounted having a brief conversation in the Crumlin Road courthouse with a lawyer named Pat Finucane, who specialized in representing IRA prisoners and whose brothers were IRA members. Afterwards a Royal Ulster Constabulary sergeant approached him and angrily accused him of undermining the RUC by associating with Finucane. He said: 'The solicitor is an IRA man. Any man who represents IRA men is worse than an IRA man . . . I will be reporting this conversation and what you have done to my superiors.'[26] Douglas Hogg, a junior Home Office minister, may have had Finucane in mind when he told the Commons in January 1989 that some of Northern Ireland's solicitors were 'unduly sympathetic to the cause of the IRA'.[27] Three weeks later, on 12 February, Finucane was murdered in front of his wife and three children by gunmen from the Ulster Freedom Fighters (UFF). The UFF had been infiltrated by British Military Intelligence, who appear to have been in a position to avert the murder, even if they did not actually instigate it.[28] Fifteen years later, a judge recommended an inquiry into Finucane's murder and other deaths where British collusion was suspected, but the inquiry was stalled by an argument over its terms between the family and the Northern Ireland Office. The Stalker-Simpson report was unpublished and relatives of those killed in the latter months of 1982 were still demanding answers more than twenty-five years later.

However, another festering scandal was cleared up over time. The pub bombs set off with murderous effect by the IRA in Guildford, Woolwich and Birmingham in 1974, led to eighteen men and women being imprisoned on convictions that were scandalously unsafe. The best known were the 'Guildford Four' – Paul Hill and Patrick Armstrong, convicted of both the Guildford and Woolwich bombings, and Gerald Conlon and Carole Richardson, convicted of the Guildford bomb. Their innocence had long been public knowledge, after the actual bombers had confessed. They were freed on 19 October 1989 after an inquiry by an outside force had established that the Guildford police tampered with a confession by Armstrong that had been central to the prosecution's case. They had been in prison for fifteen years. The other fourteen who were wrongly convicted had to wait until 1991.

On 30 July 1990, an IRA bomb killed Ian Gow, who had once been closer to Margaret Thatcher than almost any other MP. He had been her eyes and ears in the Commons until he resigned in opposition to the Anglo-Irish treaty. He had never taken more than the most elementary precautions over his personal safety, so it was not that difficult for his killers to locate his home and attach a bomb to the underside of his car. It was a stark reminder that though the 1980s were over, the civil war in Northern Ireland continued, and it was still an open question as to whether or not British justice could hold up under the strain of a long guerrilla war.

There was impatience in parts of the British state, where individuals thought that it only required the determination to kill a sufficient number of IRA members and sympathizers in order to finish off the movement. This attitude was to some extent encouraged by a convention that required the politicians of the day to voice the platitude that the IRA was a criminal organization, not a political movement, as Thatcher had done on the day of Bobby Sands' death. This view of the IRA was not, incidentally, confined to politicians, and was popularized in the first British film of the decade, *The Long Good Friday*, involving a well-organized gang that turns out to be the IRA. It was a good plot line, but in reality, after ten men had starved themselves to death, it should have been clear enough that even if the actions of the IRA were criminal, their motives were not those of common criminals. Yet, as Ken Livingstone's treatment by the *Sun* demonstrated, it was dangerous for any politician to utter this thought.

Nonetheless, the British establishment had dealt with civil conflicts before, and had been through the business of vowing never to give way to terrorists, of trying to meet violence with military force and a show of determination, and of eventually opening up negotiations with the enemy, which usually produced a face-saving compromise. It had happened in Kenya, Cyprus, and more recently in Zimbabwe, so there was always the possibility that, sooner or later, the British would be negotiating with Gerry Adams, Martin McGuinness and their colleagues. But not while Mrs Thatcher was in charge.

CHAPTER 13

DO YOU REALLY WANT TO HURT ME?

The reformers who liberalized the law on homosexuality in the 1960s did not intend that gay men or lesbians should be treated equally with the rest of the population, nor even that they should be seen or heard. They continued to be banned from serving in the armed forces; their relationships had no legal status; the age of consent was higher for gays than for heterosexuals; and outside the home, they ran a greater risk of arrest. They were expected to do whatever they did in private, and be grateful to a society that did not patrol their bedrooms. It was not thought to be a social problem that some people were virulently, pointlessly hostile towards gays and lesbians, provided that hostility did not convert to violent or threatening behaviour. It was the government's view that the basic building block of a stable community was the family, in which heterosexual couples came together to raise children, and that homosexuality was a potential threat to that norm that had to be contained.

However, throughout the 1970s there had been a few people prepared to identify themselves in public as gay and to protest that homosexuality was a normal occurrence deserving respect. By the 1980s, such thinking had even infiltrated the Church of England. In February 1981, the General Synod was startled to hear Rev. Peter Elers, the openly gay vicar of Thaxted, Essex, put forward the proposition that there was no 'problem of homosexuality', because 'the problem lies in the dislike and the distaste felt by many heterosexuals for homosexuals, a problem we have come to call homophobia'. Thus confronted, the Synod steered a middle course between tolerance and bigotry. Archbishop Runcie warned that anyone who 'obsessively' campaigned for gay rights must be considered unfit to be a vicar; but he added: 'We are learning to treat the handicapped not with pity but with deep respect and an awareness that often through their handicaps they can obtain a degree of self-giving and compassion which are denied to those not similarly afflicted.'[1]

In September 1982, the airwaves were filled with the song 'Do You Really Want to Hurt Me?' by an unknown group from London who called themselves Culture Club in recognition of their ethnic mix. Soon, the walls of teenagers' bedrooms were decorated with photographs of Culture Club's lead singer, causing approving parents to remark on how well-turned out she looked, until they learnt that this was no 'she', this was the androgynous Boy George. George O'Dowd, as he was originally known, was the son of an Irish factory worker from Eltham, south London. He had held only one dream-like ambition since his troubled schooldays: to dress up and be photographed. When he was nineteen years old, in the spring of 1979, he admitted to his mother that he had been having an affair with an older man. After that emotional conversation, he hitch-hiked to Walsall, where he had a fearlessly gay friend named Martin, and lived for a time in a kind of gay teenagers' commune with Martin and two wild-looking women. Martin philosophically accepted that his way of life meant 'a whack in the face at least once a month', in addition to such hazards as being strip-searched by the police. A more open-minded police officer called around after local yobs had taken to passing slowly by the house in a van, shouting that they were going to kill the 'queers' living there. 'I think he admired us. We were the first poofs he had ever met,'[2] O'Dowd recalled.

In the autumn, George hitched back to London with no sensible ideas in his head about how he might make a living. He found a job as a cloakroom attendant at the Blitz club, caught the attention of Malcolm McLaren, and by the age of twenty-one, was living the drug-fuelled life of an international rock star. Even in the USA, his popularity was unaffected by his practice of dressing like a girl; yet he disappointed his more committed fans by not making a public statement about his sexuality. 'I wanted people to know I was gay. It went against every corpuscle of my body to deny it,' he later wrote; but 'those around me, management, record company, were worried about sales potential'.[3] Boy George was a lead vocalist on 'Feed the World', but by then drug abuse and the public's fickleness were taking their toll, and once he started to fall, he fell a very long way, until he was arrested for assaulting a rent boy. It was almost impossible to equate the sad, overweight, middle-aged man who went to prison in 2009 with the glamorous New Romantic star he had once been; but in his heyday, Boy George had helped to make it be cool to be effeminate.

His professional advisers had good reason to be wary of how the industry might treat an artist who identified himself as gay. Holly Johnson, lead singer of the Liverpool dance group Frankie Goes to Hollywood, was prepared to take that risk. In January 1984, the BBC disc jockey Mike Read was playing the group's debut single 'Relax' when he began reading the lyrics and examining the record cover; he was so shocked that he stopped the record, pronounced that it was obscene, and vouchsafed never to play it again. An outright ban in all BBC outlets quickly followed. The fans' reaction was to send the single straight to No. 1. By June, this hymn to gay sex was threatening to be an even bigger seller than Culture Club's mega hit, 'Karma Chameleon'. Meanwhile, another group, Bronski Beat, had a huge success with their debut single 'Smalltown Boy', about a young homosexual leaving his home town in frustration. Bronski Beat's lead singer, Jimmy Somerville, was part of what Boy George called the 'new gay wave', for whom it was a matter of principle that they were honest about their sexuality, but who could also be disapproving of camp behaviour that played up to heterosexual notions of what gay men ought to be like. Jimmy Somerville told the *New Musical Express*, 'For us the music comes first, not our gay image. For Frankie Goes to Hollywood, it's all like theatre, messing around with these outrageous images and shocking people.' Somerville left Bronski Beat in 1985 to form the Communards with a keyboard player, Richard Coles, another young 'out' gay who would later achieve a different kind of prominence as a Church of England priest and Radio 4 presenter.

In November 1981, *Gay News* recorded a political breakthrough when Peter Tatchell, an active member of the Gay Liberation Front, was adopted as the Labour candidate for Bermondsey in south London. The Labour majority there was so substantial that it could be assumed that Tatchell was on his way to Parliament, once he had been through the formality of being endorsed by the party's National Executive. But 1981 was the Labour Party's year of turmoil. Tatchell was a supporter of the Bennite Left, and an immigrant from Australia, whose adoption was bitterly resented by the socially conservative Labour right, including Bermondsey's sitting MP, Bob Mellish, who had intended to hand his seat to John O'Grady, the leader of Southwark Council. As a former government chief whip, Mellish was used to getting his own way. It quickly reached the ears of those who either had defected or were about to defect to the SDP that there was trouble afoot in the Bermondsey Labour Party. During Prime Minister's Questions on 3 December 1981, one recently departed Labour MP taunted Michael Foot by reading an extract from an article by Tatchell advocating a 'siege of Parliament'. Foot could have ignored the provocation, but to everyone's surprise, rose to his feet to announce that 'the individual concerned is not an endorsed member of the Labour Party, and as far as I am concerned, never will be'.[4] He repeated those words 'endorsed member' very clearly, which was odd because there was no question about whether or not Tatchell was a member of the Labour Party. Foot may have confused him with someone else. His office affirmed later in the day that the word 'member' had been a slip of the tongue, and that he was referring to Peter Tatchell.

From that day, Tatchell was hurled, unprepared, into the full glare of national publicity. Every aspect of his past was on display and there was plenty there to excite disapproval. Homosexuality was a criminal offence in Australia when Tatchell was a teenager, and the country was at war in Vietnam, so he had fled to Britain to avoid the multiple risks of prison, enforced psychiatry and the draft. His sexuality, nationality and political radicalism were gifts to the *Sun*, *Daily Mail* and other newspapers on the lookout for any evidence that the Labour Party was infested by people with alien views and lifestyles. Within hours, if not minutes, of being made aware of Tatchell's existence by that exchange in the Commons, national newspapers were on to the fact that he was gay. That evening, about 70 to 100 journalists piled into the Bermondsey Labour Party office in London's Lower Road, where Tatchell and other local party members convened a hastily organized press conference. He was asked then if he was homosexual, to which he replied that he was 'against discrimination' and 'for gay rights'. From then on, he was routinely described as having 'campaigned for gay rights'.

In September, the *Sun* ran a story headed 'Red Pete Went to Gay Olympics', falsely claiming that he had been at a gay event in San Francisco. The *Sun* knew this was not true long before it printed it.[5] Not to be outdone, the *News of the World* ran a story headed 'Gay Row Rocks Labour', complete with a retouched photograph of Tatchell which made it appear that he was decked out in eye-liner and lipstick. Writers of anonymous hate mail took up the case. One wrote to Tatchell, to say that 'the people of Bermondsey have no intention of electing a cock-sucking, arse-fucking communist poof as their MP'. Another said that 'when I lived in Bermondsey [it] was a place where men were men and women counted as "manholes" and members of the "Middlesex Regiment" would not be tolerated'.[6]

Had Michael Foot had the ruthlessness required of a major party leader, he would either have resisted the pressure to renounce Tatchell in the first place, or having renounced him would have seen the campaign against him through to the end; but after he had met Tatchell, his innate kindness prevented him from contributing to the victimization that he had inadvertently started off. As Foot relented, Mellish vengefully resigned his seat to take up a well-paid post that Michael Heseltine had offered him as vice-chairman of the Docklands Development Corporation. Mellish knew that it would plunge Labour into an extremely difficult by-election at the worst possible time, just months before a general election, with a candidate who had been subjected to twelve months of brutally hostile publicity.

Once Tatchell had been formally endorsed, despite that 'never' from Michael Foot, officials from party headquarters moved into Bermondsey to see him through the by-election. They included Monica Foot, a press officer who had married into the Foot family. One of the first discussions between candidate and press officer, in the atmosphere of cold mutual distrust engendered by a year of tension, concerned the delicate matter of Tatchell's sexuality. He wanted to make a short public statement identifying himself as gay; she persuaded him not to. He recalled:

> Although Monica said the decision was up to me, she gave me the strong impression that Labour Party head office thought it was a bad idea. The national officials were not ready for an openly gay candidate. They feared that, if I came out, the by-election would end up being all about my sexuality and not about local and national issues. A similar concern was shared by local Bermondsey party members. I had some sympathy with this view.[7]

In retrospect, it is difficult to see how an open statement by Tatchell could have made the outcome any worse for Labour. So much innuendo had been served up to the public that there can hardly have been a voter left in Bermondsey who was not in the know. Just in case anyone had missed out, John O'Grady, fighting the by-election as the 'Real Labour' candidate, allowed himself to be televised touring the constituency with a loudspeaker chanting 'Tatchell is a poppet, as pretty as can be . . . He wears his trousers back to front'.[8] Meanwhile, Liberal canvassers were seen with badges saying 'I have been kissed by Peter Tatchell.' The upshot was the worst defeat suffered by the Labour Party in any parliamentary election in the entire second half of the century, in which a swing of more than 44 per cent converted the 1979 Labour majority of 11,756 into a Liberal majority of 9,319. The victorious Liberal candidate, Simon Hughes, would hold the seat for many, many years.

He always denied rumours that he, too, was gay, until he was 'outed' as bisexual by the *Sun*, twenty-three years later. Tatchell, meanwhile, gave up any hope of becoming a Labour MP and became a militant campaigner for gay rights.

Although the Tatchell affair was a festival of homophobia, it was homophobia with a purpose, a means to an end: the real target was the left of the Labour Party. In other respects, gays and lesbians could feel that they were making progress. In November 1984, less than two years after the Bermondsey by-election, the newly elected Labour politician, Chris Smith, created a sensation when he opened a speech at a protest meeting in Rugby with the words: 'I'm the Labour MP for Islington South and Finsbury, and I'm gay'. Smith had taken the precaution of being elected before declaring himself; it would take until 1997 before an unelected candidate dared do what Tatchell had considered doing in 1982, and for all those years Chris Smith remained the only 'out' gay in the Commons, which did not stop him being re-elected in four general elections.

Something worse than homophobic prejudice was threatening gay men. In 1981, a forty-nine-year-old man who had recently returned from the USA died in Brompton Hospital, London, from a rare disease associated with a damaged immune system. A year later, on 4 July 1982, Terrence Higgins, who worked for Hansard by day and as a barman in the evening, also died after his immune system had broken down. The cause appeared to be a frightening new disease known in the USA as GRID, or 'Gay-Related Immune Deficiency'. A small group of Higgins' immediate friends met in December 1982 and founded a new organization, the Terry Higgins Trust, to raise money for research into the new disease. By then, the US Centers for Disease Control and Prevention had noted that GRID could also attack people who were neither male nor gay, and had renamed it Acquired Immunity Deficiency Syndrome, or AIDS. There were, as yet, only seven reported cases in the UK, compared with more than a thousand in the USA, but it would not be long before the very word 'AIDS' would be a trigger for panic, loathing and terror.

It did not seem to matter to a certain section of public opinion if the sexual practices of gay males opened them to the risk of a fatal wasting disease. To some people's way of thinking, it was something they brought upon themselves. In the spring of 1983, the BBC's *Horizon* programme broadcast a film called 'Killer in the Village', about AIDS in New York, which caused a sudden rise in the volume of calls to London's Gay Switchboard – from 800 a week, to 5,000 – but provoked very little reaction from the rest of the population. However, in May, it emerged that a number of haemophiliacs had developed AIDS from transfusions of infected blood. The *Mail on Sunday* greeted the news with the headline 'Hospitals using killer blood'. On the second page, there was a related piece headed 'Spread of the "Gay Plague"'.[9] The next day, the expression 'gay plague' appeared in headlines in three national newspapers.[10] Suddenly, AIDS was very big news. Its victims, by inference, were in two categories – the innocent and the guilty. 'The infection's origins and means of propagation excites repugnance, moral and physical, at promiscuous male homosexuality,' a leader in *The Times* opined as it called for any men who volunteered to give blood to be interrogated 'succinctly' about their sexual practices. It continued, 'Many members of the public are tempted to see in AIDS some sort of retribution for a questionable style of life, but AIDS of course is a danger not only to the promiscuous nor only to homosexuals.'[11] A reader of the same newspaper wrote in complaining that: 'A self indulgent minority whose practices endanger the lives of innocent people, e.g. blood recipients, highlights the inseparability of private and public morality.'[12]

By August 1984, AIDS had claimed thirty-two lives out of sixty-one known victims, including one unnamed haemophiliac.[13] A second, Terence McStay, died in a Newcastle hospital in November. By now, the renamed Terrence Higgins Trust had grasped that numbers were not important: every death of a haemophiliac had dire implications for public attitudes to homosexuality. The trust suggested that gay men should stop donating blood until a reliable method of detecting infection had been found. The Home Office concurred and put out advice not to give blood, but for some reason directed it specifically at 'promiscuous' gay men. This was pointless, because the AIDS scare was having a dramatic impact on the behaviour of gay men, who were settling into steady relationships to decrease the risk of infection, and no longer considered themselves to be promiscuous. Between July 1984 and March 1985, there was a fall of between 30 and 40 per cent in the number of cases of gonorrhoea in gay men reported at the VD clinic at St Mary's Hospital, Paddington, and no equivalent fall in the number of cases involving heterosexuals – a clear statistical indication that gay men were being more careful in their sexual habits.

But for many, it was too late. More than 90 per cent of British AIDS victims were gay men. 'In Britain, AIDS is a homosexual problem,' the head of the VD clinic at St Mary's told *The Times*.[14] Rather than invoking sympathy for the majority of sufferers, the disease was a golden opportunity for the likes of Kelvin MacKenzie, editor of the *Sun*, to give their prejudices a free run. In February 1985, the *Sun* reported on the death of a young church organist from Bournemouth, who had been a regular blood donor until he was diagnosed with AIDS, under the headline: 'AIDS donor who infected forty-one people dies.'[15] There was no evidence that the dead man named in the *Sun* had infected anyone, but a complaint to the Press Council was rejected on the grounds that although the headline could be 'misunderstood', further down there was a reassuring quote from doctors that the risk that anyone had actually been infected was 'minimal'.[16] In October 1985, when AIDS claimed its most famous victim so far, the former Hollywood star Rock Hudson, the *Sun* ran a photograph of his wasted body, along with the information that his weight had shrunk to 7st.[17]

Coverage such as this could hardly fail to have an impact on public behaviour. Though the government's chief medical officer, Donald Acheson, might protest that 'you can't get it from sitting in the same room or sharing a meal with a person with AIDS',[18] many people either did not hear or did not believe him. Early in 1985, with the Royal College of Nursing forecasting that 1m people in the UK would have AIDS by 1991,[19] the British Safety Council advised medical staff, firefighters and others not to give mouth-to-mouth resuscitation to any injured person who might be homosexual. In February, the Prison Officers Association instructed its members to refuse to transfer prisoners to or from Chelmsford prison after the prison chaplain had died from AIDS.[20] At about the same time, Rev. Saward, the vicar of Ealing, had a letter from a parishioner who was refusing to take communion, having read in a newspaper that if you had a cold sore, you could catch AIDS from an infected person's saliva. The vicar protested in vain that neither he nor anyone else officiating at his church was gay.[21] When the Gay Sweatshop arrived to put on a performance at a theatre in Swansea, the cleaners refused to work until after they had been issued with rubber gloves, disinfectant and other materials.[22]

That summer, in Hampshire, the parents of a nine-year-old boy named Peter, who had haemophilia, were informed that he had developed antibodies to the AIDS virus after being given contaminated blood. This did not mean that he had AIDS, but his public-spirited parents nonetheless informed the teachers at his primary school about his condition as the children returned to school in September 1985. As the news spread, a quarter of the school's pupils were withdrawn by their parents in a cruel, panic-induced ostracism of a blameless child. Peter's parents said they could not blame people for protecting their own children, and declared that they were touched by the attitude of the majority. The Hampshire Education Authority avoided a repeat of the story when they discovered that a three-year-old haemophiliac had also developed AIDS antibodies by pre-emptively removing him from nursery.[23] In the same month, a drug addict bled to death in a bedsit in Kennington, south London. His body was taken to Southwark mortuary, but staff there refused to handle it. Instead, staff at St Thomas' Hospital, who had enough work to do on their own patients, had to carry out the post mortem. The coroner at the subsequent inquest issued a public plea against 'hysterical reactions' to AIDS.[24] By September 1985, there had been 205 cases of AIDS diagnosed in the UK and 114 deaths. By comparison, lung cancer was killing 30,000 people a year, but it was AIDS that people feared. In November, police who escorted an AIDS victim to St Albans Crown Court insisted on wearing white plastic hoods and masks for protection.[25]

Such was the scare that heterosexuals began to consider the risks of partaking in random sex. A student visiting hospital in the summer of 1986 noticed:

> two things that made this visit different from the last. The waiting room was much busier and all the new patients were obviously gay men. And I suddenly knew precisely why they were here and it made my blood run cold. They were getting HIV tests . . . AIDS had been in the news for a while, but this unsettling glimpse of the panic that had clearly taken hold among London's gay community gave me a real scare . . . Sex didn't seem so sexy with a gravestone at the end of your bed.[26]

The government had by now realized the need to act. In February 1986, full-page advertisements appeared in newspapers bearing the slogan 'Don't aid AIDS'. They also sponsored a programme of needle exchanges for drug addicts, despite the political risk that they would be seen to be condoning the use of hard drugs. The first publicity campaign, though well intended, was weakened by the coy language; it warned, for instance, that AIDS 'can be passed by intimate contact from one person to another' – advice that was at once useless and unnecessarily alarming. In the autumn of 1986, however, Mrs Thatcher's long-serving secretary of state for health, Norman Fowler, recruited a new departmental head of publicity, Romola Christopherson. Fowler probably did not know it at the time, but as well as being a competent public servant she was also lesbian, which may have coloured her attitude to the kind of thinking that preferred to let young men die of a fatal disease rather than risk offence by warning them in plain language how to avoid it. She persuaded Fowler that the publicity budget for AIDS should be raised from £2.5m to £20m, and that the material it produced would have to be more specific.

Fowler was of the generation that had left university before the sexual liberation of the mid-1960s began, yet to his credit, he accepted her advice – and out of that came the rare humorous aspects of the grim story of the AIDS epidemic. For instance, one task that befell Fowler was to go to Margaret Thatcher to forewarn that every household in Britain was going to be sent a leaflet, paid for by the taxpayer, containing the term 'rectal sex'. 'Mrs Thatcher took a lot of persuading to let that happen. She really did not like the idea of elderly ladies in Bognor receiving such material through the post,' Christopherson said. Another story she told was that she was the only woman at a departmental meeting that was shown draft publicity containing the term 'oral sex'. She claimed that a bemused secretary of state had to ask 'What's oral sex?', whereupon every man in the room turned to her, expecting her to explain. Once enlightened, the minister exclaimed: 'Crikey!' For the sake of truth and balance, it should be recorded that Fowler disputed Christopherson's version of the story. He confirmed that he expressed surprise, but said it was at an estimate of the number of people who practise oral sex. 'There is a wonderful and totally untrue story that I had never heard of oral sex. Curiously enough, I had,' he insisted.[27]

Another government poster, warning drug addicts against sharing needles, bore the caption 'It only takes one prick to give you AIDS'. For this and other offerings, Fowler was deluged with complaints from fellow Tory MPs, but from the public there were surprisingly few. There was, however, the reported reaction of the Conservative leader of South Staffordshire Council, Bill Brownhill (whose name is perpetuated in the Bill Brownhill Room at the council offices in Codsall), to an education film about AIDS: 'Those bunch of queers that legalise filth in homosexuality have a lot to answer for and I hope they are proud of what they have done. As a cure, I would put 90 per cent of queers in the ruddy gas chamber,'[28] he said. James Anderton, chief constable of Manchester Police, was of much the same mind. He described AIDS as a 'self-inflicted scourge' and the majority of its victims as people 'swirling about in a human cesspit of their own making'. His words were applauded by the *Sun*: 'What Britain needs is more men like James Anderton – and fewer gay terrorists holding the decent members of society to ransom.'[29] Subsequently, Anderton's daughter came out as a lesbian.

Under such pressure, it was almost inevitable that political action would follow. The first blast was sounded by Margaret Thatcher when she addressed the party conference that followed the Conservative victory in the 1987 election. 'Children who need to be taught to respect traditional moral values are being taught that they have an inalienable right to be gay,' she warned, adding that those children were being 'cheated of a sound start in life – yes, cheated'.[30] The challenge was taken up a month later by a Conservative MP, Dame Jill Knight. A local government bill had been introduced in the Commons, and Dame Jill proposed to add a clause, which became Clause 28, specifying that no local authority should 'intentionally promote homosexuality or publish material with the intention of promoting homosexuality' nor 'promote the teaching in any maintained school the acceptability of homosexuality as a pretended family relationship'.

Jill Knight and those who supported her appear to have been blindly convinced that homosexuality went together with left-wing politics. Actually, there were then, and have always been, a great many right-wing gays, including Conservative MPs as eminent as Enoch Powell, all of whom felt the need to conceal their sexuality, and some of whom entered into what must be virtually sexless marriages for self-protection. In the early 1980s, Harvey Proctor, the pro-hanging, anti-EEC MP for Billericay, was one of the most right-wing politicians in the land. After the Brixton riots, he addressed an anti-immigration meeting, with known fascists in the audience, and called for 'compulsory repatriation for those foreigners who riot, loot and commit serious offences'. He suggested that 50,000 should be deported.[31] In 1981, his constituency party supported him against rumours that he was actively homosexual, but his career was brought to an end at the 1987 general election after the police called at his Fulham flat and found a near-naked youth screaming with pain. Proctor admitted that he liked to hire rent boys and cane them. Being a sadist was not a criminal offence, but gay sex with men under twenty-one was, as Proctor's solicitor, Sir David Napley, pointed out in court. 'If this man had performed equal acts of gross indecency with a female prostitute under twenty-one he would have committed no offence,' he said. Proctor was fined £1,450.[32]

By this time, the warnings and the publicity about healthy sexual practices had made an impact. The number of new diagnoses of HIV per year had fallen in 1985–8 from 3,000 to 2,000. In fact, all sexually transmitted disease was on the decline. The number of diagnoses of gonorrhoea in England and Wales, for instance, dropped from around 50,000 in 1985 to just 18,000 in 1988. This restored some confidence in the gay community, while Jill Knight presented them with a cause around which they could unite and fight. As Clause 28 passed into law in May 1988, 10,000 people turned out to protest in London and 15,000 in Manchester. One of the many events organized in opposition to the clause was a gig in Manchester on 30 May 1988 by The Stone Roses, a local band with a growing following (they released their first album in 1989, kept the fans waiting five years for the second and then disbanded). The brothers Liam and Noel Gallagher were in the audience for that gig, and were so knocked out by it that they resolved to become rock stars. The legislation also motivated Boy George, out on his own after leaving Culture Club, to produce his first solo single, 'No Clause 28', and the Shakespearian actor Ian McKellen to appear on Radio 4 and announce that he was gay. He, together with the *Eastenders* actor Michael Cashman and the former Tory MP turned TV presenter Matthew Parris, were among the co-founders of Stonewall, the gay rights lobbying group, which was set up in 1989 in reaction to Clause 28. It also inspired some stylish direct action from lesbians, who until 1988 had kept themselves largely out of sight. On 2 February 1988, as the House of Lords was in the process of voting 202 to 122 in favour of Clause 28, three women unfurled thin twine ropes that they had smuggled in and tied to the ornate ironwork, then abseiled down into the chamber shouting 'Lesbians are out!'[33] One woman reached the ground and the other two dangled uncertainly before they were whisked away by the retired naval officers in charge of Commons security. Six hours before Clause 28 officially became Article 28 of the Local Government Finance Act, Sue Lawley and Nicholas Witchell were reading the national news when lesbians burst noisily into the BBC studio in Shepherd's Bush. 'We have rather been invaded,' Lawley announced, as the viewers heard muffled shouts and thumps, and the picture began to shake. Witchell said afterwards: 'I found that one of the women had chained herself to the base of Sue's desk so I sat on her and covered her mouth with my hand.'[34]

Clause 28 was a pointless piece of legislation. No prosecution was ever brought under it because there was never any plausible evidence that any council was intentionally promoting homosexuality. Nor was it explained how they ever could 'promote' it had they wanted to. Material promoting safe sex was specifically exempted from the clause and, in the very week that the clause became law, it emerged that it did not apply to sex education in state schools either. Such was the government's distrust of elected councillors that they had already transferred responsibility for sex education from local authorities to the Department of Education, which was not covered by Clause 28.[35] Generally, it did more good than harm to the cause of gay rights, and more harm than good to the Conservative Party. The stigma of being the anti-gay party lingered for twenty years, at least until David Cameron apologized for Clause 28 at the time of Gay Pride event in 2009.

Chapter 14

Like a Ghost Town

Whatever lingering reputation the Church of England had as 'the Tory Party at prayer' was finished off just before Christmas of 1985 when the Archbishop of Canterbury's Commission on Urban Priority Areas produced a document called 'Faith in the City'. The dereliction, decay and general hopelessness in the inner part of old cities where traditional industries had withered away had been part of public discourse from the start of the Thatcher years. The worst of the desolation was to be found in northern cities, and inner London. In the twenty-first century, anyone walking south over Tower Bridge sees an array of tasteful new architecture, expensive riverside flats and commercial premises, but that was not how the area looked in 1980, after the wharves had closed down, leaving what Robert Elms aptly described as 'an endless array of disused hulks lining the old abandoned docks'.[1] Inner-city decay made its way into *Tops of the Pops* via the extraordinary song *Ghost Town*, by The Specials, with its warning of desolation and doom – 'This town's becoming like a ghost town . . . government leaving youth on the shelf . . . no job to be found in this country . . . too much fighting on the dance floor'. It was this wailing, harrowing sound that topped the charts in the week that Toxteth went up in flames. Another cultural phenomenon that focused attention on inner-city life was the highly acclaimed six-part television drama series *Boys from the Black Stuff*, by Alan Bleasdale, which followed the adventures of a group of Liverpool bricklayers in their search for work. They included the immortal anti-hero Yosser Hughes, played by Bernard Hill, whose catchphrases 'gizza job' and 'I can do that' passed into everyday language.

But by 1985, the Conservatives believed they were entitled to some recognition for having got over the worst. Unemployment would peak in spring 1986. Other economic indicators showed that recovery was under way. What people needed, in Margaret Thatcher's view, was not sympathy or public investment to help them find work, but a jolly good talking-to about pulling their socks up. Visiting the recession-ridden north-east of England, she let loose at a local television journalist who challenged her about local unemployment, to which she had contributed so much. 'Don't you think that's the way to persuade more companies to come to this region and get more jobs – because I want them – for the people who are unemployed. Not always standing there as moaning minnies. Now stop it!',[2] she said.

Then, just as Thatcher thought she had won the argument, the Church of England produced its long, meticulously argued report, with its sixty-one recommendations. Of these, thirty-eight were directed at the Church, which was exhorted to identify 'urban priority area' parishes and to direct its efforts to improving parish work there, in reaction to which the Church launched a fundraising programme that delivered £18m to the parishes in question. The other twenty-three recommendations were aimed at the government, which was exhorted to improve its record on housing, homelessness, child benefit and other forms of support for children in poverty, and to support local councils grappling with inner-city decay, instead of undercutting them by constantly reducing the Rate Support Grant.[3] Their findings were irritably dismissed by one anonymous cabinet minister, who described them as 'pure Marxist ideology'.[4] To Norman Tebbit, the party chairman, they were 'muddle-headed'. Another Tory MP, John Carlile, suggested that it was the work of 'a load of Communist clerics', whereas Sir Nicholas Fairbairn, that drunken adulterer, proclaimed that since its authors 'do not understand the Kingdom of God', it was no surprise that they did not understand the kingdom of England.[5]

Woodrow Wyatt recorded in his diary: 'Rang Margaret. She was put out by the Church's report on the Inner Cities, but I told her not to bother as it was clearly a somewhat left-wing stereotype committee that had composed it. She said "There's nothing about self-help or doing anything for yourself in the report".'[6]

Conservative politicians were not the only ones to object to the direction in which Archbishop Runcie was taking the Church. On 3 December 1987, the biennial *Crockford's Clerical Directory* – the 'Who's Who' of the Church of England – came out, complete with an unsigned editorial by an Anglo-Catholic who denounced Runcie for his 'elitist liberalism'. It accused him of systematically discriminating against Anglo-Catholics and Evangelicals in appointments to senior positions in favour of clerics from the liberal theological colleges or from the dioceses of St Albans and Canterbury. 'His clear preference is for men of liberal disposition with a moderately Catholic style which is not taken to the point of having firm principles. If in addition they have a good appearance and are articulate on the media he is prepared to overlook a certain theological deficiency,'[7] the writer alleged.

The piece went on to attack Archbishop of York John Habgood, in what looked like the opening salvo to prevent him from succeeding Runcie, who was to retire within three years. Habgood retaliated by saying: 'There is a sourness and vindictiveness about the anonymous attack on the Archbishop of Canterbury which makes it clear that it is not quite the impartial review of Church affairs which it purports to be.'[8] The controversy was all gleefully picked up by national newspapers, giving *Crockford's Clerical Directory* more publicity than it has ever had before or since. The hunt was on to identify the author of the editorial. Dr Gareth Bennett, canon of Chichester Cathedral, a historian and eminent Anglo-Catholic, was repeatedly asked about the authorship by other Christians and by journalists. He claimed to know nothing, but on Monday, 7 December, he drove to a lonely spot, attached a hose to his car exhaust and gassed himself. *Crockford's* then confirmed that he was the hunted author. Dr Bennett had been a man of great intellectual gifts, as emphasized by tributes from Runcie, Frank Field and others, and the terrible manner of his death threatened to turn opinion against Runcie and his allies. Dr Habgood tried to diffuse tension by blaming the media: 'It needs to be recognized that media pressure does seem to have been a major factor that led him to his tragic death,' he said, on BBC radio. One member of General Synod, Canon George Austin, retorted:

> This is a terrible thing to say and quite untrue. My experience of the press is that they have behaved very responsibly. I believe Dr Habgood is trying to divert attention from his earlier remarks, which were quite indefensible. What he said about the preface must have added to Dr Bennett's distress.[9]

If the late Canon Bennett's intention was to prevent Habgood from becoming the next archbishop of Canterbury, in that at least he was successful.

Thatcher's differences with Archbishop Runcie were, however, only a sideshow in her long-running battle with left-wing councils. Though she was the daughter of the former alderman mayor of Grantham, she displayed an intemperate hostility to local democracy. Her famous remark about the 'enemy within' was aimed as much at left-wing councillors from London and Liverpool as at the miners' union, and her time in office was dedicated to marginalizing local councils and accumulating power at the centre. She appeared to win every round until the introduction of the poll tax, the final pyrrhic victory that was her own undoing. In her fervour to root out left-wing radicals, her government quite missed the biggest local government scandal of all, quietly taking place under their very noses. In Conservative-run Westminster, the council leader Lady Porter, who was one of Britain's richest women (as the daughter of the founder of Tesco), was illicitly arranging for council tenants to be shipped out of marginal wards to be replaced by owner-occupiers, who were assumed to be more likely to vote Conservative. Some of the council tenants were decanted into a tower block infested with asbestos. When the scandal came to light in 1991, Lady Porter and others were ordered to pay surcharges originally set at £21m.

The government's first assault on the authority of local councillors was the legislation compelling them to sell council houses to any tenant who wished to buy. For years, there had been tension between council tenants who aspired to be property owners, and councillors – not necessarily Labour councillors – who argued that their duty to house the homeless required them not to deplete their stock of council housing. The Thatcher government cut through this argument by forcing councils to sell, at discounts of up to 60 per cent, and banning them from using the proceeds to build new council properties. They had to use it to repay debt. Norwich Council already ran a scheme that gave tenants the right to buy newly built homes, which preserved the stock of council houses, but the council's attempt to fight the legislation in the high court brought them up against the wholly unsympathetic Lord Denning, Master of the Rolls. A million and a quarter former tenants took this cheap route to homeownership, raising £18 billion for public funds and turning hundreds of thousands of Labour voters into Conservatives, while for the first time in post-war memory, homeless beggars became a fixture on city streets.

Another government tactic, condemned in the Church of England report, was to reduce progressively the amounts that councils received in government grants. This process had started before the Conservatives came to office; Labour's Anthony Crosland heralded it in 1976 with his famous warning that 'the party's over'. In 1976, two-thirds of all that councils spent came from a rate-support grant at a cost to the Treasury of more than £12.2 billion a year. The Labour government reduced the Treasury's contribution year by year, until in 1979 the state supported 61 per cent of council expenditure, and the rates made up 39 per cent. Peter Shore, the environment secretary, imagined that the process would stop there, but successive Conservative environment secretaries, starting with Michael Heseltine, carried on where he left off. By 1986, the total rate-support grant had been reduced to below £8.5 billion, and covered only 46.4 per cent of all local government spending, with the larger part covered by the rates.[10] Given the defiant mood within the defeated Labour Party, there was always a risk that a few left-wing councils would push their rates ever upwards and run a political campaign to transfer the blame to the Conservative government. Michael Heseltine, who was one of the cleverest and most ambitious members of the 1979 cabinet, foresaw this and tried to head it off with a concept called the 'grant-related expenditure assessment' (GREA). This was central government's calculation of how much an individual council ought to be spending in a given year. Above that limit, councils received no grants at all. Most councils did their best to comply and between them they reduced their budgets by £196m; but a handful went in the opposite direction and produced £211m worth of planned increases, threatening to make Heseltine look foolish. The biggest culprit was the Greater London Council.

Conservative control of the GLC was swept away on the night of 7 May 1981. Until election day, the little group of Labour councillors who made up the opposition had been led by Andrew McIntosh, a market researcher, whose politics were traditional, mainstream Labour. However, after the group had swollen to fifty out of the ninety-two seats, he was supplanted by Ken Livingstone, then thirty-six years old, and very left wing. Labour had made an election promise that it would cut the cost of London's public transport and increase the capacity. This was going to cost £69m in the first year, until it hit the penalty clause in Heseltine's GREA scheme, which pushed the price for London ratepayers up to £119m. Faced with the unpalatable choice between abandoning their manifesto or doubling the rates, the newly elected councillors went defiantly ahead with the rate increase. The Conservative-controlled borough of Bromley, in south London, objected on behalf of their ratepayers, because the London Underground system does not extend to Bromley. It was highly unusual for judges to interfere when politicians were putting into effect the manifesto on which they had been elected, but in November 1981 three high court judges, headed by the eighty-two-year-old Lord Denning, concluded that the Labour Party was breaking a law that required local authorities to protect ratepayers. 'I realize that this must cause much consternation to the GLC. They will be at their wits end to know what to do about it, but it is their own fault,'[11] Denning said, and he swept aside their excuse that the GLC had only carried out the manifesto promise on which Labour had won the election. 'A political manifesto is not to be regarded as gospel. It is not binding . . . People do not vote for the manifesto,' he added. His ruling was upheld by five Law Lords. It was eight days before Christmas, the central plank of Labour's manifesto had collapsed and they were left without any guidance as to what fares they were supposed to charge to stay within the law. After some hesitation, the councillors followed the advice of their senior staff, doubled London's fares and cut the number of buses and tubes, doing damage to London's transport system and congested streets that would last for years.

This was by no means all that Livingstone and his fellow councillors did to draw the anger of middle-class ratepayers. Having set a high rate and been prevented by the judges from using it for its intended purpose, they used some of the money to extend the reach of local government into new areas. The GLC was the first council to create a women's committee; London's Gay Switchboard received a GLC grant in 1981, the first ever 'gay grant'. The GLC staff committee also set out to make the GLC an equal opportunities employer. Its industry committee set up job-creation schemes around London. They also used the exterior of the GLC offices, located immediately south of Westminster Bridge, where it could be seen from the Houses of Parliament, to publicize unemployment. In January 1982, the first of a series of giant signs appeared above County Hall announcing that London's official unemployment figure had reached 326,238. The sign was updated every month.

Livingstone's worst offence, though, in the collective opinion of the tabloid press, was his incursion into the violent politics of Northern Ireland. With bombs going off in London's streets, it might seem bizarre that London's foremost civic leader should be expected to have nothing to say on the conflict, but councillors were expected to stay out of it and certainly not to say the things Livingstone said. He called for the IRA prisoners then on hunger strike in H-Block to be granted the political status they demanded. In July 1981, he met Alice McElwee, whose son Thomas had been sentenced to a total of 141 years for terrorist offences and who was on the forty-fourth day of a hunger strike. Speaking to Alice, Livingstone appeared to agree that British soldiers had been killing innocent Catholics in Northern Ireland. The next day, Mrs Thatcher told the Commons: 'It is the most disgraceful statement that I have ever read. It is a totally unwarranted slur on our security forces, both the police and the Army.'[12]

From there on, it was open season on Ken Livingstone in the tabloids, but instead of capitulating under pressure, he kept his detractors generously supplied with reasons to be angry. In August, he moved on to the dangerous topic of gay rights. 'Almost everyone has the sexual potential for anything,' he told the Harrow Gay Unity Group in August 1981.[13] In October, after the IRA had exploded a nail bomb outside the Chelsea barracks, killing one woman (who had a nail driven through her heart) and injuring thirty-nine others, Livingstone's endless round of public engagements took him to Cambridge, where he told the Tory Reform Group: 'If they were just criminals and psychopaths, they would be crushed. But they have a motive force which they think is good.'[14] The next day's issue of the *Sun* set aside half of its front page to a commentary under the headline 'This Damn Fool says the Bombers Aren't Criminals', in which Livingstone was described as 'the most odious man in Britain'. There was an unusual follow-up at Christmas, when a *Sun* photographer snapped Livingstone dressed as Santa Claus, which the tabloid then published under the heading 'The Most Odious Santa in Britain'.

Early in 1982, Mrs Thatcher set a group of advisers and ministers the task of writing the next Conservative manifesto. One of the first ideas they threw up was to abolish the GLC outright, along with six metropolitan counties that had been created in the previous Conservative reform of local government in 1974, which had never attracted much popular support. Both ideas went into the 1983 Tory manifesto. The GLC fought back in style, showing a flair for presentation and making the most of the fact that the council's demise would mean the creation of a series of unelected boards to run London-wide functions like the fire brigade. They conducted opinion polls, which showed that most Londoners, whether they approved of Ken Livingstone or not, wanted there to be an elected London authority. One poll showed that 73 per cent of respondents were opposed to abolition. Another was taken solely of voters in Margaret Thatcher's constituency, Finchley, and showed 66 per cent opposed to abolition. Another clever move was to invite Buckingham Palace to send a member of the royal family to the formal opening of the new Thames Barrier in May 1984. The GLC suggested Princess Diana, but the message came back that the Queen herself would be delighted to officiate. Her highly publicized appearance alongside Ken Livingstone fed rumours that the Queen privately did not like Margaret Thatcher. 'By inaugurating this particular project at this particular time, the Queen is feeding every lurid persecution fantasy in Conservative central office,'[15] the *Economist* commented.

When the bill to remove the GLC went before the Commons for the first time, in April 1984, thirty-nine Conservative MPs opposed their own government. When it eventually reached the House of Lords, a year later, a group of peers tried to amend the bill to create a new, slimmed-down elected council to replace the GLC, and were defeated by only 213 votes to 209. Given the huge Conservative majorities in both Houses of Parliament, there was never a realistic chance of saving the GLC, still less the other six doomed authorities, but as its power slipped away its defenders had claimed a kind of moral victory. The GLC went out of existence at midnight on 31 March 1986 in style. About 250,000 crowded on to the South Bank to join festivities that included a firework display costing £250,000. The government had hoped that this would mean about 7,000 of the GLC's 22,000 employees would be out of work, but most actually found jobs with the London boroughs or other agencies.

There had been nothing in the Conservative manifesto about abolishing the Inner London Education Authority, but the electorate had the impertinence to make it a Labour-led ILEA and therefore it, too, disappeared, on 31 March 1990. County Hall, which had been the headquarters of both the GLC and ILEA, became the property of a government agency called the London Residuary Body, who sold it for £90m to a Japanese property company, which converted it into a hotel, restaurant and aquarium. These elected authorities were replaced by quangos, quangos and more quangos. In London alone there were fifty, including the London Residuary Body, set up in 1985 to sell off GLC assets, which was headed throughout by a former Tory councillor. The new London Fire and Civil Defence Authority, which had a budget of more than £180m a year, was coordinated by a government office for London. All this demonstrated, to quote the journalist and occasional quangocrat Sir Simon Jenkins, that 'it was not less government that Thatcherism wanted, just less local government'.[16]

The GLC was by no means the only council that the government regarded as obnoxiously left wing. Even before Livingstone's head was above the parapet, a determined character named Ted Knight, who in his youth had been a member of the Trotskyite group that became the Workers' Revolutionary Party (WRP), was elected leader of Lambeth Council. His administration faced the disagreeable choice between cutting services or running up the penalties imposed by Heseltine. Lambeth's rates went up by more than 49 per cent in 1980, with an even greater rise in prospect for the following year, though in March the Labour councillors relented somewhat and settled for a rate rise of 37.5 per cent.

In May 1983, Labour took control of Liverpool Council from the Liberals. The new, nominal leader of the council was a man named John Hamilton, who had once been expelled from the Labour Party for being too left wing, but was soft-hearted and easily bullied – a 'nowhere man', in the ungenerous opinion of his flashy deputy, Derek Hatton: 'With his V-necked pullovers, his overcoat, battered trilby, and specs, John looked every inch the retired bachelor schoolmaster . . . bumbling his way through life'.[17] The real leaders of Liverpool were Hatton, its finance committee chairman, Tony Byrne, and a political operator named Tony Mulhearn.

What happened in Liverpool in the early 1980s is a rare example of Trotskyists having an impact on British public life – not people who were crudely accused of being 'Trots' by their opponents, but Marxists whose ideology was genuinely drawn from the writings of Leon Trotsky. In the 1940s, there had been only one British Trotskyite party; thirty years later, three main offshoots had sprung from its disintegration – the WRP, the Socialist Worker Party and Militant, each with a leader old enough to be drawing a pension, respectively Gerry Healy, Tony Cliff and Ted Grant.

The WRP, of which Ted Knight was a former member, had a large following among the actors' union, Equity, including Vanessa and Corin Redgrave, and in its propaganda the party lauded Colonel Gaddafi of Libya and Saddam Hussein in Iraq as great progressive leaders. It had access to large sums of money, which allowed it to run a daily newspaper, called *Newsline*, a printing press and a publishing company. Ted Knight and Ken Livingstone used its press to bring out a weekly newspaper called *Labour Herald*. After the party imploded in 1985, in circumstances that added greatly to the gaiety of the nation, internal documents came to light demonstrating, to no one's surprise, that the WRP had been receiving subsidies from Libya and had solicited money from the Iraq government. The rift that destroyed the organization burst into the open in October 1985, when it was sensationally announced that the WRP's seventy-one-year-old founder, Gerry Healy – one of the original nineteen apostles of Leon Trotsky who had launched the British movement almost fifty years earlier – had been expelled from the party for having breached 'the revolutionary morality governing the conduct between men and women comrades'.[18] He had bedded at least twenty-six female comrades, possibly many more. 'He stood hardly an inch above a naggin bottle,' one former WRP member, Brian Behan (brother of Brendan Behan), wrote after Healy's death in 1989:

> He was bald with the little sore eyes of a newborn pig. Yet . . . I understand that seventy-six women in all were asked to embrace the erect forces of Healyite labour. His winning line was to ask the women not to withstand the onward and upward thrust of the progressive masses but to adopt a revolutionary position on this matter.[19]

The WRP split into pro- and anti-Healy factions, with the Redgraves on the pro-Healy side. Each claimed to be the official party; each brought out a newspaper called *Newsline* and claimed that theirs was the only *Newsline*.

Another offshoot of the same 1940s party was Militant, led by Ted Grant, who turned seventy in 1984. One weary leftist recalled:

> You are at a meeting and someone with a fake Liverpool accent makes a speech demanding the nationalisation of the principle 253 monopolies. Well, what's wrong with that? Why is everyone groaning? You'll soon see. Half a dozen other people stand up and make the same speech, with the same fake accent and the same curious hand movements. Are they clones? No, you just met the 'Militant'.[20]

Both groups had set out to infiltrate the Labour Party in the 1950s, but whereas Healy's faction, including Ted Knight, was detected and expelled, Grant's followers were not noticed until the 1970s, by which time they were so entrenched that they ran the Labour Party Young Socialists, giving them an automatic place on the national executive. In 1982, Michael Foot temporarily overcame his distaste for purges and expulsions and led an attempt to decapitate Militant by expelling Ted Grant and four others from the Labour Party. Yet in 1983, two members of Militant, Dave Nellist in Coventry and Terry Fields in Liverpool, were elected Labour MPs. More significantly, from 1983, Militant was a powerful presence on Liverpool Council. Hatton boasted: 'The influence of, and input from Militant's headquarters in London was immense. There is no getting away from the fact that the battles and campaigns being waged in Liverpool embodied Militant's aims and objectives nationally.'[21]

Liverpool's grant from central government was coming down year by year and the new administration was supposed to choose between cutting costs or imposing a huge rate increase. They adopted the unique strategy of doing neither. They set a budget that increased the rates by no more than the rate of inflation, but made no cuts, making it inevitable that after a few months the council would run right out of money. In 1984, the tactic worked. Patrick Jenkin, who had replaced Heseltine as environment secretary, 'handled the situation with a mixture of bluster and concession',[22] but eventually stumped up an extra £20m, leaving Liverpool's jubilant councillors in no doubt that they, and they alone, had found a way to beat the government.

Actually, the government's tactic of cutting off the money supply was not preventing voters anywhere from using local elections to register their dislike of the government. In Sheffield the rates went up by 41 per cent in 1980 and 37 per cent in 1981; yet Labour was returned with a larger number of councillors than before, and in 1980 elected a new, more left-wing leader. This was the young David Blunkett, who had overcome the disadvantages of being blind from birth and losing his father in a nasty industrial accident when he was very young to become Labour's leading authority on local government matters. He, too, was identified with the Bennite Left, though he never attracted the notoriety of Ken Livingstone or Ted Knight.

Unable to stop these high-spending councils by democratic means, the government decided in 1984 to pass the law to make it illegal for a council to set a rate higher than the government thought appropriate, a procedure known as 'rate-capping'. This was an act of centralization that made even Conservative councillors queasy, particularly when it emerged in June 1984 that, of the eighteen councils to be rate-capped, only sixteen were Labour controlled; the formula had been devised so carelessly that it ensnared Conservative-run Portsmouth Council. This was the summer of the miners' strike, when direct resistance was the order of the day. Leaders of the rate-capped Labour councils met in November, against a background of protest strikes by 100,000 of their staff, and agreed a tactic under which they would all hold their budget meetings on the same day, 7 March 1985, and would all refuse to set a rate. For a time, the show of unity was impressive, as hundreds of Labour councillors braced themselves for a confrontation, knowing that they risked being disqualified from office and personally surcharged, which could bankrupt them. However, as the months went by, the cracks opened up. For some council leaders, including David Blunkett, the point was to go to the brink in the hope of a better deal, but for others such as Ted Knight this was a political struggle, an opportunity to join the miners in galvanizing working-class resistance to the Thatcher government. As decision day drew closer, and with the miners heading for defeat, most of the councillors involved lost their nerve or were won over by government concessions. In March, South Yorkshire, Merseyside and Bradford councils and the ILEA all set a rate within the government's cap. Then the remaining councils gave in one by one, until Lambeth was the only rate-capped council left fighting. Ted Knight's majority was very thin, and one councillor's resignation was enough to upset the balance; on 3 July the remaining councillors voted 32 to 31 in favour of setting a rate. David Blunkett thought that 'Ted Knight's tactical achievement in prolonging the resistance for so long had been remarkable.'[23] The district auditor was not so impressed; the councillors were each individually surcharged £126,000, and disqualified from office.

It was victory for central government over local government, for Thatcherism over municipal socialism and, by the by, helped Neil Kinnock to secure victory over the Bennite Left. Kinnock had emerged from the Left and was trying to steer the Labour Party back to the political centre. He had a miserable time during the miners' strike, pushed this way and that, condemned by the Left for not supporting the NUM without reservations, and by the Right for not condemning picket-line violence often enough. That he came from a mining family did not make his dilemma any simpler; but when the strike was over and the councils had capitulated, the more pragmatic members of the Bennite Left, such as David Blunkett, decided that there was no future in direct engagement with the government and that the Labour Party would have to start making the compromises necessary to win a general election. The break-up of the Bennite Left was first announced in *New Socialist,* a magazine published by the Labour Party, which had been seen as an intellectual vehicle for the Bennites. In May 1985, the academic Patrick Seyd announced that 'a profound realignment of the Labour Left is taking place' in which a 'New Left' was emerging that placed a 'heavy emphasis on party unity', and rejected 'the constant search for Judas figures' and 'the Bennite conception of laying the foundations for socialism in one country through the alternative economic strategy'.[24] This 'New Left', he added, believed that Militant and other Trotskyite groups could not be left unchallenged, an observation that did not bode well for the Militant caucus on Liverpool Council.

In June 1985, the council had raised Liverpool's rates by 9 per cent, in line with inflation, without attempting to reduce their costs, leaving them with a £30m hole in the budget. This time, Patrick Jenkin refused to stump up, and as summer turned to autumn the cash duly ran out, and 31,000 staff were declared redundant. At this point, the main public-sector union, NUPE, turned decisively against Militant. Neil Kinnock seized the opportunity with a theatrical touch, during his long speech to the Labour Party conference in Bournemouth, when without warning he switched from attacking the Conservatives to exhorting supporters to promise only what they could deliver. He said:

> I'll tell you what happens with impossible promises. You start with far-fetched resolutions. They are then pickled into a rigid dogma, a code, and you go through the years sticking to that, out-dated, misplaced, irrelevant to the real needs, and you end with the grotesque chaos of a Labour council – a *Labour* council – hiring taxis to scuttle

> round a city handing out redundancy notices to its own workers. I am telling you, no matter how entertaining, how fulfilling to short-term egos, you can't play politics with people's jobs.[25]

As he spoke, the packed hall erupted. Derek Hatton rose to his feet, shouting 'liar'. Two members of the National Executive who were on the platform behind Kinnock – Eric Heffer, a Liverpool MP, and Frances Curran, a member of Militant – walked off in protest; but the majority broke into prolonged applause. It was a turning point in Labour's history. When the conference was over, the machinery was set in motion that led to the expulsion of Derek Hatton, Tony Mulhearn and other known Militants from the Labour Party. As in Lambeth, the district auditor imposed personal surcharges on the Labour councillors who had voted for a deficit, all of whom were barred from public office. A few years and dozens of expulsions later, Militant gave up trying to operate within the Labour Party and became the tiny Socialist Party.

The drama set up Derek Hatton for a career in local radio and inspired Alan Bleasdale to write another television drama series, called *GBH*, broadcast by Channel 4 in 1991. It had been ten years since another notable television play about local government, the last work written for television by Jim Allen, the master of socialist-realist drama, whose work was too left-wing for the Thatcher years. *United Kingdom* went out simply because the money the BBC invested in it had already been spent before the 1979 election, though it was held up while the corporation nervously negotiated with the new government over a proposed increase in the licence fee. It was shown, belatedly, on 8 December 1981, an experience that its director Roland Joffe (who was thirty-five in 1981) found so frustrating that he gave up on television and went on to direct two extraordinary films, *The Killing Fields* (1984) about the Khmer Rouge regime in Cambodia, and *The Mission* (1986) about the destruction of a Jesuit mission in South America. *United Kingdom* was the story of council tenants organizing a rent strike, shot on an estate in Newcastle upon Tyne using mostly unknown actors recruited locally. The lead was played by Val McLane, whose brief fame would be eclipsed by her luckier and more ambitious brother, Jimmy Nail. The most daring piece of casting was to hire someone known to the police, the prison authorities and MI5 as a political subversive to play her husband. He was a former builder, who had served a prison sentence for intimidation on a picket line outside a building site in Shrewsbury in the early 1970s, and whose MI5 file classed him as 'a political thug prone to violence'.[26] On emerging from prison, he had been adopted by the revolutionary Left as one of their own despite a brief dalliance with the National Front when he was 'politically naïve and poorly educated'.[27] *United Kingdom* was his first opportunity to demonstrate a remarkable acting talent. He was Ricky Tomlinson, who went on to household fame in the television soap *Brookside*, and as the feckless father in *The Royle Family*. *United Kingdom* followed the pattern of left-wing drama in that the sympathetic characters were working-class activists, while the least sympathetic character was the Labour MP. In *GBH*, ten years later, the comic villain was the ultra-left revolutionary poseur, loosely based on Derek Hatton and played by Robert Lindsay; the hero, played by Michael Palin, was a school teacher whose politics were mainstream Labour. That cultural shift was one of the many changes that the 1980s had wrought.

The balance sheet so far was that Thatcherism had abolished the largest councils in England, taking over their powers centrally, and had set severe limits on how those councils that remained could raise or spend money, and yet that was not enough. An Education Act was also passed, enabling schools to transfer themselves from council to government control by taking on direct grant status, but surprisingly few were enticed to take this option. Local government still functioned after a fashion, and because voters tended to vote against the government between general elections, fewer and fewer councils remained under Conservative control. Domestic and business rates were still set, collected and spent at the behest of locally elected Labour councillors. Some might call this local democracy, but Mrs Thatcher and those of like mind knew better. Thatcher's friend Woodrow Wyatt told her in one of their many telephone conversations, after the 1987 general election, 'Local government is not democratic at all. It should all be run by Whitehall with local administrators with a fixed budget from Whitehall.'[28] She thought his solution might be a step too far, but did not dispute the premise.

The argument that local government was 'not democratic' was based on the fact that there were people who could vote but did not pay the rates, because they lived in shared accommodation or were too poor, and there were others who paid rates but had no vote, because they ran businesses but did not live in the same local government district. Thatcher stated in her memoirs: 'Many people had no direct reason to be concerned about their council's overspending, because somebody else picked up all or most of the bill. This lack of accountability lay behind the continued overspending.'[29] A Conservative MP, Cecil Franks, stung by having been voted off Manchester Council, expressed the same thought more bluntly during a Commons debate on local government. He complained: 'We have experienced the virtual death of democracy in local government. Those who were the dross of society, who contributed nothing to, but took everything out of society, had a vote, whereas those who were putting something into society did not.'[30]

In Scotland, a quirk in the law required that every five years all properties had to be revaluated for the purposes of the rates. The revaluation went ahead in 1985, producing a huge shift in the burden from businesses to householders, with the latter seeing their bills go up by about 20 per cent, for which they squarely blamed the government. At the 1987 general election, the number of Conservative MPs in Scotland dropped from twenty-one to ten, out of seventy-two, the lowest number ever. It was a ghastly warning of what might happen if a rates revaluation were conducted further south. 'We can't have a revaluation in England, it would wipe us out,'[31] Mrs Thatcher told her ministers.

Instead, at a meeting at Chequers in March 1985, the elderly Victor Rothschild, a veteran political adviser, arrived with a new idea. Instead of sending bills of different sizes, one to each householder, they would bill everyone on the electoral register for the same amount, regardless of income. Everyone would then have an equally powerful motive to vote for a council that would keep the bills down. The only person at that meeting who was against the idea was the minister from the Treasury, speaking on behalf of Nigel Lawson. There were other Conservatives besides Lawson who saw that the idea might go seriously wrong, including Michael Heseltine and Peter Walker, but generally the Conservative party loved it and wanted the reform introduced straight away, particularly in Scotland. Originally, it was proposed to make the change gradually, but at the Conservative annual conference in 1987 Thatcher listened to an impassioned contribution from Gerry Malone, an ex-MP who had attributed the loss of his Aberdeen seat to the rates. She saw the audience's reaction, leant over to her friend Nicholas Ridley, the secretary of state for the environment, and whispered: 'We shall have to look at this again, Nick.'[32]

As the new tax reached Scotland, with effect from 1 April 1989, legislation went through to extend it to England and Wales. It was piloted by Ridley's deputy, Michael Howard, with great encouragement from the new Scottish secretary, Malcolm Rifkind, who reported back to the cabinet that in Scotland 'it was all working out pretty well'.[33] Almost as an aside, the government also abolished the local business rate, replacing it with a standard levy paid to central government. Simon Jenkins observed: 'The centralizing of the business rate in 1990 was the biggest single act of true nationalization ever undertaken by a British government. Yet it passed almost unnoticed.'[34]

What followed took Thatcher and her senior ministers quite by surprise. They set out expecting that the average bill would be around £278 per head; by March 1990, when inflation had started rising again, wage settlements were higher than before, and council treasurers seized a one-off opportunity to put their accounts in order – they were forced to revise that figure up to £370. The official name, 'community charge' never caught on; everyone called it the 'poll tax'. The public failed to see it as a 'charge'; they saw it as a profoundly unfair tax, under which 'the duke paid the same as the dustman'. The Duke of Westminster, whose inherited fortune was reckoned to be about £3 billion, saw the rate bill of £11,745 on his two large homes near Lancaster and Chester replaced by a charge of £1,187. He found this so embarrassing that he paid all his tenants' bills as well.[35]

The poll tax produced the biggest protest movement since CND, with thousands pledging to go to prison rather than pay. Terry Fields, the Militant MP for Liverpool Broadfields, actually did a spell in jail in 1990. When Haringey Council, in London, set a figure of £572, fighting broke out in the town hall. In Norwich, Southampton and Thamesdown protestors invaded the council chambers. In Nottingham, they came dressed as Robin Hood and his Merry Men and prevented the council from meeting by hurling imitation custard pies made from shaving cream; the meeting resumed after the police were called, and set a poll tax of £390.[36] Outside the Bristol council chambers, there was an ugly fight between demonstrators and police, which ended with twenty-one arrests; after a five-hour debate, councillors set a poll tax of £490.[37] More than 3,000 people turned up to protest outside Hackney town hall, where a riot broke out and shops were looted. In March, there was a by-election in Mid-Staffordshire, after the sitting Tory MP John Heddle had committed suicide; he left behind a majority of 14,654, which was swept away in a wave of popular feeling, handing the seat to Labour with a swing of 21 per cent.

On Saturday, 31 March 1990, the day before the Poll Tax was officially introduced, the Anti Poll Tax federation organized a protest march that attracted such a vast turnout that the last marchers were starting out five hours after the first had left. However, one group of about 200 turned into Downing Street to stage a sit-down protest and refused to move. As mounted police moved in, the protest degenerated into the worst riot since 1985. One witness saw rioters 'on a blind path of destruction. They were not threatening people and were only interested in destroying property. They wrecked loads of cafes in Covent Garden.' Another saw police drive vans into the crowd to clear a path: 'They were hitting people and people were getting swept along.

There was an old man who had his back to the van and it just pushed him away.'[38] Scaffolding was dismantled, missiles thrown, fires started and cars wrecked; about 400 policemen were injured and 339 people were arrested. Thatcher recalled, 'It was a mercy that no one was killed. I was appalled at such wickedness.'[39]

What must also have appalled her was that, as the devoted diarist Alan Clark noted fretfully, Tory MPs were 'talking openly of ditching the Lady to save their skins,'[40] now that she had surpassed her own record, set early in the 1980s, as the most unpopular prime minister since polling began. But when the council elections came in May 1990, the results were not as bad as some Conservatives had feared, partly because Lady Porter's gerrymandering delivered an unexpected Tory victory in Westminster. 'Kinnock Poll Axed' was the headline on the front page of the *Sun.* Margaret Thatcher had won a reprieve, though it was to last only another seven months.

CHAPTER 15

HERALDS OF FREE ENTERPRISE

For all his long career as the nation's favourite weather forecaster, Michael Fish is fated to be remembered for that one occasion, on 15 October 1987, when he turned to the camera, looking reassuringly smart, bespectacled and balding, to tell the viewers: 'Earlier on today apparently a woman rang the BBC and said she had heard that there was a hurricane on the way. Well if you are watching, don't worry – there isn't.'[1] The very next morning, southern England awoke to the aftermath of the worst storm since 1703. Over London, there were 94 miles per hour winds; over the Channel Islands, they were 110 mph. At least thirteen people died, including two seamen who drowned in Dover harbour and two firemen who were killed in Dorset while answering an emergency call. There were 600 distress calls just in Ealing, in west London, from people whose homes or cars had been struck by falling trees. Shanklin Pier on the Isle of Wight was smashed to driftwood, a caravan park in Jaywick, Essex was flattened, and six of the seven oaks in Sevenoaks, in Kent, came down. Twenty years later, Fish denied saying the words attributed to him, but, unfortunately for him, the record shows that he said exactly what he is alleged to have said, in the most celebrated weather mis-forecast of all time.

The worst storm for centuries was followed on Monday, 19 October, by the worst stock market crash since the war. It began that morning in Hong Kong and spread westward, time zone by time zone, through the City of London to Wall Street. On that one day, 'Black Monday', the value of shares on the London Stock Exchange fell by £50.6 billion. In other parts of the world, the collapse was even more spectacular; Hong Kong's stock market lost more than 45 per cent of its value, compared with London's 24 per cent. Why the stock market fell so far so suddenly is still a subject of debate. Stock values had shot up in August 1987, on the back of good economic news in the USA, but the US administration then became embroiled in a public dispute with Germany over exchange rates, which may have made investors nervous. That might explain why stocks fell, but not why the fall was so precipitous. The speed of the fall, ironically, seems to have been largely caused by the recent introduction of computer technology. A particular culprit seems to have been 'portfolio insurance'. As the traders arrived at work, they set their computers to sell shares at whatever price they could get, in the expectation that prices would continue to fall. The strategy depended, of course, on someone else being prepared to bet that shares would rise, but there were no takers, so the computers had to set share prices ever lower to attract buyers. After the crash 'portfolio insurance' was deemed to be a bad idea.[2]

Thus it appeared that both God and Mammon had signalled that capitalism was collapsing, as revolutionary Marxists had been predicting for so long. In that same month, October 1987, a coroner's jury brought in a verdict of unlawful killing in the inquest into 188 people who had died in Britain's worst peacetime disaster at sea for nearly seventy years, when a roll-on roll-off car ferry capsized just outside the Belgian port of Zeebrugge on 6 March 1987. The crew had allowed the ship to set sail with its bow door open. To the victims' disgust, the law did not allow a charge of manslaughter to be brought against the company that owned the ship, but only against named members of its crew. The doomed ship was called *The Herald of Free Enterprise*. But the concept it heralded was not dead. The Conservatives had just secured their third consecutive election victory, under the same extraordinary leader, who showed not the least sign that eight years in her gruelling job was wearing her down. On the contrary, she returned from the 1987 campaign full of an almost maniacal zeal in which no sector of public life escaped her attention. The director of the National Theatre, Richard Eyre, noted in his diary on 12 June 1987: 'Thatcher's back, speaking not as if she thought she was in absolute control for ever but as if she knew she was . . . Day One of the Fourth Reich.'[3] Capitalism had experienced a convulsion in October 1987, but it was socialism that all but died in the next two years.

The immediate problem confronting the chancellor, Nigel Lawson, in autumn 1987 was that he had been lumbering up for the biggest share sale in history at the very time when the stock market collapsed. The government was committed to selling its remaining 31.5 per cent shareholding in British Petroleum (BP). As usual, the date and share price had been announced well in advance. The sale was to be on 30 October and the price was to be £3.20 a share, making a total share offer worth £7.5 billion. As usual, the big City and Wall Street banks had committed themselves to underwriting the sale, for a generous fee; and an advertising campaign had encouraged members of the public to join the bonanza by investing their savings into BP shares. But since BP was only part-privatized, its shares were already on sale, and like all other shares, their value had dropped like a stone. By 30 October, they could be bought for £2.85.

The banks that had underwritten the sale were now faced with having to buy hundreds of millions of shares at more than 10 per cent above their market value. Though they had been paid to take this risk, the banks thought it quite wrong that they should be expected to stand by the commitment and demanded that Nigel Lawson call off the sale. To his credit, he faced them down, though he threw them a concession under which, for two months, the Bank of England bought back shares from any underwriters who wanted to be rid of them quickly. Even so, the bankers were outraged that they should be facing a loss. At an emergency meeting at Salomon Brothers, on Wall Street, one trader who had flown in from London found that he was the only Briton on a committee of angry Americans.

> He became a punch bag for the Americans, who pinned the blame for the crash squarely on the British government. Why were the limeys insisting on continuing their sale? . . . A few of the Americans were jumping all over the Brit for the behaviour of his countrymen. One said sneeringly, 'You guys did just this sort of thing after the war too, you know.' . . . The xenophobia was by no means limited to Salomon Brothers. An American partner of Goldman Sachs, a firm also stuck with a 100 million dollar loss on its shares in BP, called a senior Brit at Salomon and blamed him for the problem. But why? It turned out the Goldman partner wasn't thinking of his Salomon counterpart as a representative of Salomon, but as a Brit. 'Your people damn well better pull it,' he shouted. 'If it wasn't for us, you'd all be speaking German.'[4]

Perhaps the oddest aspect of the whole affair was that, despite all the publicity given to the government's problems, thousands of members of the public bought the overpriced shares, content with the thought that they would make money eventually. And in the end everyone did, when share prices recovered.

This near-miss did not in the least put off the government from selling public assets. What was left of British Steel went private in December 1988. The next privatization, of the water industry one year later, was the biggest since British Gas, raising more than £5 billion. This was the most unpopular sale of the lot, because the public generally thought it wrong that water should be a private monopoly. It did not escape Labour's attention when the new owners of Thames Water showed their gratitude for their rapidly rising salaries by donating part of their company's income to the Conservative Party. Actually, there was a case for selling the water companies that was as strong as any argument for privatization. Water and sewage pipes badly needed investment, which the privatized companies could raise on the money market. There was also the anomaly that the publicly owned water companies had been their own regulators, responsible for checking levels of pollution in the rivers as well as for cleaning them up. Nicholas Ridley, the environment secretary, also used the sell-off to separate these responsibilities by creating the National Rivers Authority.

Lawson's successful handling of the BP crisis seemed to convince him that he could do no wrong. In spring 1988 he produced a Budget that exuded confidence, cutting taxes by £4 billion a year, most of which flowed straight into the economy as extra spending money. He cut the tax rate for small businesses, raised the threshold for inheritance tax, raised income tax personal allowances by twice the rate of inflation and reduced the basic rate of income tax from 27p to 25p in the pound. He also produced the biggest gift to the highest paid since Sir Geoffrey Howe's first Budget by abolishing four of the five higher rates of income tax, leaving only the lowest, which was 40p in the pound. This reduced the tax rates of the very wealthy by a third. As these announcements tumbled out, the House of Commons became increasingly rowdy. The Scottish Nationalist, Alex Salmond, shouted: 'This is an obscenity. The Chancellor cannot do this.' The deputy speaker warned him to be quiet, but he went on shouting that it was an 'obscenity', and was ordered to leave.[5] A few minutes later, the Militant MP Dave Nellist was on his feet demanding to speak and there was so much noise that the session descended into what *Hansard* euphemistically recorded as 'grave disorder'. The deputy speaker suspended commons for ten minutes so that everyone could calm down.

Lawson also scrapped a rule that allowed married couples, if both were earning, to claim two lots of tax relief on their mortgage payments; henceforth, only the higher earner of the two could claim. However, instead of introducing the change immediately, he announced that it would come into effect on 1 August 1988, giving every couple who might be thinking of buying their first home an incentive to rush ahead and complete within six months. That summer, the season of the 'Lawson boom', house prices rose almost vertically and the government rode a wave of astonishing popularity. Two MORI polls taken ten months apart, in November 1987 and September 1988, both showed that an astonishing 50 per cent of those asked identified themselves as Conservative supporters, while Labour's support dropped from 38 to 36 per cent.

Some Labour MPs wondered if these poll ratings might improve if they ousted Neil Kinnock and Roy Hattersley and elected a new leadership. The only credible alternative to Kinnock was John Smith, the shadow chancellor, but he refused to consider running and probably would not have won anyway because he had been a minister in Jim Callaghan's cabinet when Kinnock was a left-wing rebel, and old left-right divisions lingered. Hattersley was more vulnerable, because he, too, had been a cabinet minister. In 1988, John Prescott challenged Hattersley and came close to winning. The only person to contest Kinnock was Tony Benn, who was a spent force in parliamentary politics, and he lost heavily.

However, the Lawson boom, which made the government so popular and confident, and left the opposition floundering, proved to be unsustainable. After the fun came the long hangover. House prices, which went up and up until the 1 August deadline was reached, suddenly tumbled because everyone who had thought about buying their first home had now done so. Suddenly, young couples were introduced to a new and unpalatable phenomenon called 'negative equity', something that no one had ever experienced in the old days when building societies had refused to lend to anyone who had not saved up a substantial deposit on their first home. During 1988, many couples had borrowed 100 per cent of the cost of their first home, and as prices fell they owed more than their property was worth. To make it worse, all that spending money sloshing around in the economy had set off inflation. On 8 August, Lawson was compelled to raise interest rates from 10.5 per cent to 11 per cent. A few days later, he put them up to 12 per cent, and later still to 13 per cent, which meant that the interest people were paying on their mortgages had leapt up just as their homes were falling in value. In 1991 alone, 75,000 homes were repossessed.

As months passed, thousands of couples gave up trying, lost their homes and acquired a credit rating that was going to make it difficult for them ever to raise another mortgage. One anonymous couple living in St Albans with two very young children heard through the husband's family that there was an old farmhouse in a remote part of Northumberland, with very basic amenities, being offered for very low rent. They packed all their belongings, posted their house keys and an explanatory note through the door of the local

Abbey National office, and set off for a new life, free from their mortgage, 300 miles to the north. They therefore avoided the bailiffs, whose sudden arrival to turn debtors out of their homes could be a frightening experience. Suzette Janczykowski, a graphic designer, returned to her rented flat in Bristol at midnight one evening in June 1990 to find that bailiffs had forced their way in with a crowbar, changed the locks and left a message that the property had been repossessed by the Halifax Building Society. 'I was left locked out in the middle of the night. I could have been attacked or raped or worse,' she said. In the morning, she contacted her landlord, who denied being in arrears. She was homeless for another two days, until it transpired that the bailiffs had gone to the wrong flat.[6]

The thousands who were caught out included an Iranian exile named Farzad Bazoft, who had been unable to return home since the 1979 revolution. He had taken out a 100 per cent mortgage on a £69,000 one-bedroom flat in north London before the jump in interest rates forced him to move into cramped shared accommodation. The loss of his flat seems to have increased his determination to establish himself at the *Observer,* where he was working six or seven days a week, but could not get his name in the paper. He volunteered to go on a press trip organized by the Iraq government, and there he went alone to a secret missile plant near Baghdad, where there had recently been an explosion that killed a large number of workers. Bazoft made sketches and collected soil samples, in the hope of proving that it was a nuclear plant. He was arrested and after six weeks in the hands of Iraq's police, he appeared on television confessing to being a spy. At 6.30 a.m. on 15 March 1990, Bazoft was hanged.

Recession also claimed its inevitable victims among businesses that had borrowed too much in the boom years. The effect was often delayed so the most famous casualties, such as the Middle East-based bank BCCI or the Maxwell publishing empire, were brought down early in the 1990s. Robert Maxwell fell off his yacht in unexplained circumstances on 5 November 1991. A month later, it was discovered that he had looted £526m from Mirror Group newspapers and from pension funds he had controlled, in a final desperate attempt to avert bankruptcy.

There were also properly run businesses that suffered as their customer base shrank. Amstrad, created by Alan Sugar, had been one of the great success stories of the 1980s. The son of a tailor, brought up in a council flat in Hackney, he started in business as a teenager selling electrical goods from the back of a van, and set up the firm in 1968, when he was aged twenty-one. The name Amstrad was short for 'Alan Michael Sugar Trading'. The merchandise that made him rich and famous was the PWC home computer, which he started marketing in 1986. Until then, the tiny but growing home computer market had been dominated by Clive Sinclair, who was highly inventive but not a great businessman. Sugar bought Sinclair's business in 1986 for £5m. He did not pioneer any startlingly new technology, but he organized the business effectively and offered the purchaser a reassuringly simple product. An Amstrad arrived in one box, at a reasonable price of £399, and its new owner was not required to do anything but plug it in and switch it on. Its technology was primitive by contemporary standards. You could not, for instance, connect an Amstrad to the Internet; and if you wanted to write a document of more than about 3,000 words you had to break it into parts because the machine's memory could not cope with anything of that length. However, it was the marketing sensation of 1986, when it captured 25 per cent of the European home computer market. This created a new brand of consumer, the Amstrad owner, and a sub-species, the 'Amstrad bore', who could talk about nothing but his new toy. The craze ended, almost as swiftly as it began, when more sophisticated computers came on to the market and giant firms such as Hewlett Packard did deals with high-street chains that effectively elbowed Amstrad off the shelves. 'It is possible – at certain dinner parties – for the word-processor bores to get into a state of combative one-upmanship which lasts all night. All those who eagerly bought their first Amstrads five or six years ago, now boast of having exchanged them for something else,' one writer observed in 1989.[7]

Sugar diversified by striking a deal with Rupert Murdoch to construct the dishes needed to receive satellite television, but by the end of the 1980s Amstrad's rapid growth had gone into reverse. Misfortune stimulated Sugar's interest in politics. Noticing that Labour was proposing to increase tax for the highest paid, whereas the Conservatives proposed to remove all legal protection from the wages of the lowest paid, he came out openly for the Conservatives. He then heard that an up-and-coming Labour politician named Gordon Brown had said that businessmen who were backing the Tories had prospered in the recession while others suffered. This produced a furious riposte, which filled an entire page of the *Sun*:

> I don't know who Gordon Brown is. Excuse my ignorance, but I don't. Whoever he is, he has not done his homework . . . How he has the audacity to say that Amstrad, or Alan Sugar, has flourished in the recession is a complete mystery to me . . . the value of my shares collapsed from £500 million to £100 million more or less overnight.

> The salary I have been taking in the company is pretty meagre – about £170,000 . . . So this talk that I have prospered in the middle of recession is total nonsense.[8]

Years later, after he had discovered who Gordon Brown was, he switched his support to the Labour Party and Brown awarded him a peerage.

The business community forgave the government for piloting them into recession and continued to support the Conservatives, if only for lack of a suitable alternative, but other sections of society were not so forgiving. Though Mrs Thatcher was never again as unpopular as she had been in 1981, the reforming zeal that she brought back from the 1987 election made her new enemies among middle-class professionals, notably those who worked in health or education, as she tried to create a better managed NHS, restore traditional methods of teaching in schools and cut the cost of higher education, ending the old distinction between universities and polytechnics. She had never been liked by what could broadly be called the intelligentsia. Oxford University had already let Mrs Thatcher know what it thought of her in a famous incident in January 1985 when dons voted by 738 to 319 not to award her an honorary degree, making her the first Oxford-educated prime minister since the Second World War not to receive the honour. This rejection hurt her. In one rare, reflective moment she even thought that she may have brought it upon herself. 'Many distinguished academics thought that Thatcherism in education meant a philistine subordination of scholarship to the immediate requirements of vocational training,' she lamented, while insisting that actually it was 'no part of my kind of Thatcherism'.[9]

Her first priority on returning to office in 1987 was to attack what she saw as the rot in the state education system, especially the new 'child-centred' teaching techniques, the emphasis on stirring children's imaginations rather than making them learn facts, and the blurring of subjects into wider entities like 'humanities'. She believed that too many children were leaving school without a proper grasp of reading, writing and arithmetic. She was convinced, on slim evidence, that they were being indoctrinated by left-wing teachers. She told the 1987 Conservative annual conference:

> Too often, our children don't get the education they need – the education they deserve. In the inner cities, where youngsters must have a decent education if they are to have a better future, that opportunity is all too often snatched from them by hard left education authorities and extremist teachers. Children who need to be able to

> count and multiply are learning anti-racist mathematics – whatever that may be. Children who need to be able to express themselves in clear English are being taught political slogans.[10]

What she would really have liked to do was take schools out of the control of local authorities altogether so that each could run itself like an independent school. The government would issue parents with means-tested vouchers with which to buy places for their children, thereby creating a lively market in education which, she assumed, would drive up teaching standards. However, after her old mentor, Sir Keith Joseph, retired from the cabinet in May 1986, she was never able to find another education secretary who agreed with this idea. Joseph's successor, Kenneth Baker, was not greatly interested in policy detail, but had a suave persuasiveness, which convinced her that once there was a policy, Baker was the man to sell it to the public. It was during his tenure that the state education system underwent the greatest upheaval since the introduction of comprehensives. The national curriculum, the Schools Examination, inset days, grant-maintained schools run directly by the Department of Education and other innovations all date from Baker's time as education secretary. However, Baker – who complained in his memoirs about being surrounded by officials who were 'rooted in "progressive" orthodoxies, in egalitarianism and in the comprehensive school system'[11] – took the advice of these same officials far too compliantly for Thatcher's taste. He was, for instance, content to accept recommendations from a History Working Group that emphasized enquiry and interpretation; to Thatcher, learning history was about facts and dates.

In this short period, the intrigue and political manoeuvring that was part of everyday life in Thatcher's cabinet centred on a man named John Moore, an ambitious Thatcherite whom she promoted in 1987 to replace Norman Fowler as secretary of state for health and social security. Moore was strikingly good looking, physically fit and had an interesting biography. His father was a factory worker turned publican. He had lived for a time in the USA, had an American wife and brought American corporate culture to the Commons. Nicholas Ridley, who knew Thatcher well, wrote (after she had lost her favourite, Cecil Parkinson, who was felled by a sex scandal), 'her second choice of heir apparent was John Moore'.[12] Inevitably, in this position Moore attracted dangerous enemies, some of whom, including the future prime minister John Major, wanted him out of the way so their own ambitions could be fulfilled, and others who were just plain jealous. 'Are you aglow with excitement at the prospect of actually setting eyes on this legendary creature?'

Alan Clark heard a fellow Tory MP say. In his diary, Clark reflected: 'Why is everyone so beastly? John was literally golden . . . He has gold kiss curls like a babyfood ad. He is athletic, he "trains" . . . ' Clark's verdict was that Moore was 'shallow but amiable'.[13]

During his short period of ascendancy, Moore fired up Thatcher with the idea that all the ills of the NHS could be cured by injecting a powerful dose of free-market discipline. The first move was to induce people to buy private health care by making it partially tax deductible, which Moore introduced against resistance from the Treasury. Beyond that, he suggested two possibilities: either abolish the NHS and switch to universal health insurance, or retain the NHS but overhaul it to create an internal market. The latter idea had already been worked on by various think tanks and appealed to Thatcher as the less politically dangerous.

The outcome was a reorganization that separated the 'purchaser' from the 'provider' within the NHS' new 'internal market'. The main 'purchasers' were GP practices, which were allocated budgets that they used to 'buy' hospital care for their patients. The hospitals became self-governing trusts, selling their services to GP practices and other primary care organizations. There was a veritable explosion in the number and the pay of NHS managers, as every trust needed its separate accounts department, personnel department, and so on. In five years, from 1985–91, the cost of administering the NHS rose, after inflation had been taken into account, by 23 per cent[14] while the number of NHS managers multiplied from 510 to 12,420. Their combined salary bill rose from £25.7m to £383.8m. In that period, the number of nurses fell by 20,000 (though that was partly the result of nurses having their jobs redesignated). By the turn of the decade, the best-paid NHS managers were on six-figure salaries.

John Moore did not survive in office long enough to see these reforms to fruition. The strain of being heir apparent, and of facing the formidable Robin Cook, in the Commons was too much. He lost his voice, in what seems to have been a sympathetic illness, and had his department cut in half before he was dropped from the cabinet. The new health secretary, appointed in May 1988, was the more robust Kenneth Clarke. He was no Thatcherite. She would have kept him out of the government if she felt she could, but in her mind she bracketed him and Peter Walker as more dangerous outside than in. She also respected Clarke's skills as a communicator, which were sorely needed because, after so many years in which the government had feasted on privatization, the public suspected that all these separate NHS trusts were being set up with a view to selling them to private interests, a suspicion that the Labour Party assiduously encouraged. Clarke also had to cope with a pay dispute with NHS ambulance drivers, a rare example of a strike during which public opinion was on the side of the strikers throughout.

Aided by the clouds of political dust thrown up by the health reforms, the Labour Party's political fortunes picked up in 1989, after the previous year's low, and it began to score convincing wins in parliamentary by-elections. However, electoral success was not accompanied by any revival of intellectual confidence. The party threw overboard almost the entire political programme on which it had fought two general elections, conceding so much political ground to its opponents that, over time, it was difficult to tell what separated the two main parties. The first symbolic move was for Labour to abandon the policy of unilateral nuclear disarmament that it had adopted in a blaze of publicity at the start of the decade. Neil Kinnock, who had been a unilateralist all his political life, announced a change of mind during 1988, then apparently reneged when the giant TGWU threatened to give John Prescott its block vote in the deputy leadership contest. However, he returned to the fray and put a resolution to the 1988 party conference, which was only narrowly defeated. The unilateralist policy was dropped a year later.

Labour's next move was to cull many policy documents, removing almost anything that might increase public spending. Before the 1987 general election, Conservative researchers had gone through Labour policy documents adding up what they reckoned the many pledges would cost, and came up with a figure of £35 billion, which would have represented a substantial rise in taxes. Neil Kinnock put the powerful combination of John Smith and Gordon Brown in charge of the opposition Treasury team. Brown had just been elected the youngest member of the shadow cabinet, only four years after entering Parliament, and performed so effectively that the next year he topped the poll; in 1989 he was promoted to the trade and industry portfolio. In the comprehensive policy review that reached its first set of conclusions in 1989, only two clear spending commitments remained, which were to increase state pensions and child benefit. They stayed because Robin Cook, whose brief covered social security, had fought successfully for their inclusion. There was a rule, known as 'Beckett's Law' – so named after Margaret Beckett, who had replaced Brown in the treasury team – that any other bid for public money would be dealt with 'as resources allow'. Unfortunately for Labour, the two surviving commitments were expensive, and were used effectively and ruthlessly by the Conservatives during the 1992 election to convince the public that Labour was still the party of high tax. It was this experience that drove Tony Blair and Gordon Brown to make the extraordinary promise in 1997 that for two years they would respect every departmental spending limit left behind by the Conservatives.

Another sign that the Labour Party was breaking from its roots as the political wing of the trade union movement was its renunciation of the trade union closed shop. In the early 1980s, Labour had successively committed to repealing each new piece of trade union legislation introduced by the Conservatives; but since then the mining and print unions had been broken, and others had been weakened. It was illegal under European law to make union membership a condition of employment. As early as August 1981, three former British Rail employees had won a £145,000 compensation award in a European court for being dismissed for not belonging to a union. This was not a problem for Labour then, because until 1983 the party was committed to pulling Britain out of the EU, but that policy had been dropped and Labour was now pro-EU.

In 1988, Tony Blair was elected to the shadow cabinet, supplanting Gordon Brown as its youngest member. He was first made energy spokesman, to deal with the last great privatization, of the electricity industry, then in 1989 replaced Michael Meacher as shadow employment secretary. In one of his first Commons appearances in this new role, Blair was defending the new Social Charter proposed by the European Commission to protect employment rights across the EU, when a Tory MP interrupted to ask the short, lethal question – did Blair support the clause in the charter that protected a worker's right not to join a union? Blair could only splutter: 'If it has that meaning, it also has the meaning that one has a right to be a member of a trade union.'[15] Thus caught out, Blair acted with great speed. After consulting the two people whose advice he most trusted even then – Alastair Campbell of the *Daily Mirror* and Peter Mandelson – and after forewarning some key union leaders, he delivered a statement to his Sedgefield constituency party on 17 December, which he dressed up as a 'clarification'. He announced that Labour was supporting the Social Charter in its entirety, including the clause protecting individual workers against the closed shop.[16] Calling this a 'clarification' was at best disingenuous; it was one of Tony Blair's first major contributions to the future direction of the Labour Party and, appropriately, it involved a break in the link with the unions.

More than ten years before they came to power, it was clear that Gordon Brown and Tony Blair were going to be dominant figures in the Labour Party. As early as December 1984, only twenty months after they had first entered the Commons, the Tory MP Alan Clark, who was struggling to get an Employment Bill through Parliament against well-led opposition, noted the presence across the gangway of 'two very bright boys called Brown and Blair'.[17] They were then sharing an office in the crowded premises of the Palace of Westminster, helping to write one another's speeches, and were so close that the Labour Party staff called them 'Pushmepullyou', after the two-headed llama in *Doctor Dolittle* (1967). Both were treated with suspicion that grew into hostility by the Bennite left and those in the Labour Party for whom being faithful to their principles mattered more than winning elections. Neil Kinnock was sensitive to criticism from this quarter. He reacted angrily to being accused of 'selling out' for the sake of office. Brown, Blair and those who supported them were not so easily put off course. In 1990, the *Sunday Times* columnist, Robert Harris, who was well-connected to the Kinnock brigade, used the word 'careerist' to describe them, not as an insult but in praise. He wrote: 'What we are witnessing in the Labour party at the moment is something one had despaired of ever seeing again: the return of the careerist. If that sounds pejorative, it is not meant to be. Ambition for power is the purest and most honest motive in politics'.[18] He named the four most prominent careerists – Jack Straw, Robin Cook, Gordon Brown and 'little baby-boom face himself, Tony Blair' – who happened to be the quartet who moved into the four most important positions in the Labour government seven years later. Harris' insight into Labour's future came from his very close friend, Peter Mandelson. It was widely assumed that Brown would be the next Labour leader but one, with Blair running his leadership election campaign.[19] It was not until after the 1992 general election that anyone, except possibly Cherie Blair, thought that the younger and less experienced half of 'Pushmepullyou' might be the first into 10 Downing Street.

Another change that came over the Labour Party during the Kinnock years, possibly the one that excited most comment at the time and has clung longest in the public perception of what came to be known as 'New Labour', was the dramatic improvement in the party's handling of the mass media. It began from a very low base. During the 1983 election, the party's full-time staff laboured under the crippling disadvantage that they were expected to campaign around a manifesto that their employers on the National Executive Committee vehemently opposed. The result was aptly described by Ken Livingstone as 'the worst campaign of any major political party in a Western democracy in the post-war world'.[20] When the disparate factions of the party met again, after their defeat, the one thing they agreed upon was that party policy, whatever it might be, would have to be better presented next time around.

Peter Mandelson became the party's director of communications in October 1985, coincidentally on his thirty-second birthday. With his arrival, the quality of the party's presentation took a giant leap. There were sympathetic professionals in advertising and public relations who had been willing for some time to offer their services for nothing, if only there had been someone to act as their point of contact. Soon after Mandelson had taken office, they formed a shadow agency, in which professions whose services commanded large salaries on the open market produced well-designed leaflets and logos. The traditional logo, depicting a torch, was ditched in favour of a red rose. The usual red backdrops at press conferences were replaced by a soft grey.

Mandelson also enlisted the help of Philip Gould, who was the first to introduce to British politics the marketing tool known as 'focus group research'. Previously, when political parties hired polling organizations it was to conduct conventional polls in which a thousand people or so were asked to give a yes or no answer to questions about political issues. These polls routinely produced the finding that health was the issue that people cared about most, and that they trusted Labour more than the Conservatives to run the NHS – and yet, they voted Conservative, which suggested that opinion polls were an imperfect guide to winning elections. Focus-group polling involved questioning fewer people, but doing it during a lengthy discussion monitored by a professional pollster, which gave a more detailed picture of what they really thought.

If all that Mandelson had done was enlist professional advice, it would have been enough to establish his reputation as one of the most effective department heads the party had ever employed, and would have kept to a minimum the number of people who resented his activities. But that was the less important part of his work. While the Prince of Wales referred to him in conversation as 'the Red Rose man',[21] newspapers compared him with Machiavelli, implying that he was up to something more controversial than organizing focus groups and backdrops for press conferences, but his role was not properly explained because there was not a word or phrase that described his particular activity. The phrase 'spin doctor', now so well established in the language, drifted over the Atlantic during the 1988 US presidential election. In that campaign, the professionals had to cope with hundreds of news outlets that reported events almost as they happened – and not only reported but instantly interpreted them, each event being a potential triumph for one candidate and a disaster for another. Spin doctors were needed to put their side's 'spin' before the other side got theirs in. Mandelson was the first person in the Labour Party to understand the importance of spin. For years, the Labour Party had been the underdog, constantly attacked, ridiculed and misrepresented in hostile newspapers, and given only a slightly better showing in the broadcast media. When Margaret Thatcher visited Washington, her personal rapport with President Reagan dominated the coverage. When Kinnock went, in 1987, the young Alastair Campbell, travelling with the press corps as the political correspondent of the *Sunday Mirror*, was so incensed by their behaviour that he wrote a scorching attack in the *New Statesman*, accusing a 'cynical, cowardly and corrupt Tory press' of colluding with a Republican-controlled White House to denigrate Kinnock.[22] For a lobby journalist to attack so publicly the people he worked with every day was unusual; it marked the start of an eight-year trajectory that took Campbell out of journalism and into Tony Blair's service.

After Mandelson's arrival, journalists who were used to Labour being a soft target discovered that they had to be more careful in reporting its affairs. A television journalist broadcasting live about the Labour Party might find that by the time he had come off air, his programme editor had already had Mandelson on the phone complaining. The relentless effort that the new communications director put into combating hostile coverage made him immensely valuable to those whose careers he helped to advance, such as Kinnock, Brown and Blair, and feared and loathed by others. Any politician who ran foul of Neil Kinnock might suddenly find themselves being ridiculed and denigrated in the media, and would suspect that Mandelson had been at work. After the 1987 election, the Labour Party's rising star was a now half forgotten figure named Bryan Gould, who topped the poll in the shadow cabinet elections and looked to be better positioned than anyone else to be the next party leader. Then, in his role as shadow secretary for trade and industry, he fell out with both Kinnock and John Smith because he stuck by the old party policy of opposition to the EU, and in 1989 began a political descent that eventually caused him to leave British politics altogether. In his memoirs, he blamed Peter Mandelson and his spin-doctoring:

> It was becoming increasingly clear to me over this period that Peter Mandelson was working to his own agenda – on what I and others began to call the 'Mandelson Project'. The 'project' was to ensure that Peter's protégés – Gordon Brown as the prime contender, but with Tony Blair as a fall-back – should succeed to the leadership.[23]

Because the word 'spin' came into the language of politics just when the Labour Party had learnt how to do it well, it is often mistakenly said that 'spin' was a New Labour invention. Actually, the practice is much older than New Labour; it is just that before 1988 there was no word for it. Margaret

Thatcher's press secretary, Bernard Ingham, was a skilled spin doctor years before Mandelson entered the scene; the only reason that he could deny ever being a spin doctor was that the expression had barely entered the language when he stopped. The Queen also employed an effective spin doctor in Michael O'Shea. When the Institution of Professional Civil Servants held their annual conference in May 1998, they heard from two members how civil service press officers were being pressured to spin, rather than give out information. Civil servants were required to 'expound untruths on behalf of the government, produce dodgy material, or leak documents in the government's interest,' Peter Dupont of the Central Office of Information complained. Peter Cook, of the Department of Employment, added that some of his colleagues had 'written articles of a party political nature on behalf of ministers to be inserted in the press' or 'have worked on the Action for Jobs campaign – a campaign that said little or nothing about Department of Employment services and much about the Conservative Party's views on unemployment'.[24]

The practice of 'burying bad news' was drawn to public attention by an infamous email written on 11 September 2001 by Jo Moore, a Labour spin doctor. Although she made the device famous, she did not invent it; it had been practised for years. John Major was an outstanding exponent. When he was minister for social security in the mid-1980s, one of his self-appointed tasks was to conceal how poverty had increased under Margaret Thatcher's premiership. One authoritative way to measure it was to compare the number of people who qualified for supplementary benefit, who by the governments own definition were living in relative poverty. These figures had stayed constant at around 2m until the late 1970s, then rose so rapidly that the Thatcher government decided not to publish them annually any more, but to bring them out once every two years. By the summer of 1985, publication of the 1981–3 figures was long overdue and Major devised a plan, as cunning as any that was ever dreamt by Blackadder's sidekick Baldrick, to slip them out without anyone noticing. His difficulty was that he was being pestered by written questions tabled by the Labour MP Frank Field, who had a specialist's knowledge of social security and who demanded to know when the figures were to be made available. Parliament's rules compelled Major to answer. His way round was to enlist fellow Tory MP Edwina Currie, who was also his lover (though their affair remained secret until she published her diary fourteen years later),[25] who agreed to table a written question asking for exactly the same information that Frank Field had requested. Major then had the statistics slipped into the House of Commons library when everyone's attention was distracted by Prince Andrew's wedding to Sarah Ferguson, on the afternoon of the last day in July before the Commons rose for the summer. On the same day, he wrote to Edwina Currie telling her that the figures were in the library, and wrote to Frank Field referring him to the answer he had given Currie, knowing that there was no way that he would see it before the library closed for the long summer recess. It was a master plan, worthy of a future prime minister, but Frank Field was too sharp to fall for it. He had a scout posted in the library just in case. His scout seized the statistics as they arrived and ran them through a photocopier, enabling Field to release them to the press. They showed that government policy had driven up the numbers living in poverty by around a third, to 2.64m.[26]

Perhaps the most significant development in the Labour Party during these years, though it passed almost unnoticed, was that at some point late in the 1980s or very early in the 1990s the Labour Party ceased to be socialist. In the dictionaries in print at the time, the word 'socialist' had a precise meaning, namely someone who believed in the common ownership of the main sectors of the economy. Whether the Labour Party was ever really a socialist party is a moot point, but it certainly fought the 1983 election on a socialist manifesto, replete with sweeping proposals for transferring industries to state or cooperative ownership, and on every party member's card there was an extract from Clause IV, Part IV of the party constitution, calling for the common ownership of the means of production. (Tony Blair had the clause removed in 1995, but that was several years after socialism had vanished from any Labour policy document.) Even after the 1983 defeat, each time an industry was privatized, Labour routinely promised to renationalize it. That promise was still to be found in policy documents passed by the Labour Party conference in 1989, but in the preceding year, when Tony Blair was shadow energy secretary, the main item he had to confront was electricity privatization. Uniquely for a Labour shadow cabinet minister, he made no commitment to renationalize the industry if it was sold off. The sale was delayed because of complex problems about who would pay the cost of cleaning up after the nuclear power generators; by the time it came about, in 1991, socialism had been reversed in all the former Soviet satellite states of Eastern Europe and had begun to collapse even in Russia. Neil Kinnock, once an enthusiast for state ownership, then declared that the majority of the Labour Party had never really believed in it, 'but they were the tunes of glory that were coming out. Well, we've stopped that nonsense,'[27] he pronounced.

CHAPTER 16

THE HAND OF GOD

Sometimes, a sporting contest breaks its boundaries to become a political event, not necessarily with happy consequences. Sometimes, minor sports that do not normally attract a mass following throw up performers who create such a sense of drama that suddenly there are millions watching their progress. The 1980s began and ended with political controversies that tore into the world of sport. One was stressful, but did no actual harm: that was the argument over whether or not to boycott the 1980s Olympics in Moscow. The other was the disaster at the Hillsborough stadium in Sheffield, in which ninety-six football spectators were crushed to death. These and other events on the pitch or track threw up questions about whether sport is just popular entertainment or has wider significance.

Denis Thatcher gave his view when, at the age of seventy-one, he received an unexpected accolade from the Central Council for Physical Recreation (CCPR), who elected him Spectator of the Year because of his enthusiasm for golf and his past services as a rugby referee. Interviewed by the BBC after the award ceremony in May 1986, where he was presented with what was claimed to be the world's largest bottle of champagne, Mr Thatcher remarked: 'We need money for everything, but sports for kids happens to be my desire in my advancing years. I believe that perhaps we can increase the belief in the Christian ethic, because that is what sport's about.'[1]

This was a different take on what sport is 'about' to that of the marketing director of Slazenger sports rackets who, when explaining why his company invested so much and so consistently in making its brand name visible during

Wimbledon fortnight, said: 'Sport is about winning, so it makes sense to link our products with an event that is all about winning.'[2]

The champion jockey Peter Scudamore had yet another definition. Sport, he said, was about 'making the most of it when things are going well'.[3] More directly self-aggrandizing, an early 1980s television commercial carried the slogan 'Nike – What Sport is About'.

But the athletes who had spent years training to compete in the 1980s Olympics regretfully discovered that sport was also about world politics. On 27 December 1979, the Soviet Union's elderly leaders dispatched the Red Army into Afghanistan, where the government (friendly to the Soviets) had collapsed. Their troops were soon caught up in a guerrilla war, which would last ten years and end in humiliation for the invaders. Some of their opponents were volunteer fighters from other parts of Asia, including the young Osama bin Laden. Before the invasion, a number of well-known Soviet dissidents, such as Vladimir Bukovsky, had been urging the western democracies to boycott the Moscow Olympics because of the USSR's disregard of civil rights. After the invasion, President Jimmy Carter called for an international boycott and ordered US athletes not to go. More than sixty governments issued similar instructions to their athletes, including a few such as China and Iran, who had quarrels of their own with the Kremlin.

In London, Mrs Thatcher had not been in office long. She was beset with economic problems, her government was deeply unpopular and she accepted that she could not start banning British citizens from travelling to Moscow, though her views were clear enough. To her, this was the story of the 1936 Berlin Olympics again. When a delegation from the CCPR, who met her in February 1980, protested that they should not be put under political pressure, Mrs Thatcher retorted: 'When did the defence of freedom become a political issue?'[4] One of her ministers, Angus Maude, declared on another occasion: 'Trying to prevent a nuclear Third World War is not politics, in the conventional sense of the word, and it is childish and perverse to pretend that it is . . . Let us hear no more of this nonsense about sport and politics.'[5]

What Thatcher wanted, as she told the House of Commons on 14 February, was for the sports associations to arrive voluntarily at a decision to pull out. The next day, the British Olympics Committee and each of the bodies representing an Olympic sport was sent a letter setting out the government's position. The British and American governments were considering whether they could organize a rival Games in the USA or Canada, and were prepared to put money into it, but that would have destroyed years of painstaking work that had gone into building up the number of nations participating in the Olympics. There were also travel agencies who had sold thousands of holiday packages to Moscow, who feared being beset by customers wanting their money back, and the sporting organizations had to take heed of what the athletes thought, and the athletes wanted to compete, after their years of training. In March, seventy-eight of them signed a petition delivered to Mrs Thatcher saying that they were prepared to boycott the opening and closing ceremonies, but not the games themselves, because 'we are not prepared to preside over the destruction of the Olympic movement'. The official who passed the petition to Margaret Thatcher added a note pointing out that it was not signed by the athletes most likely to bring gold medals home – Geoff Capes, Sebastian Coe, Brendan Foster, Tessa Sanderson, Daley Thompson, etc.[6] – but that turned out to be false comfort. Even Seb Coe, who would later rise to prominence in the Tory party, did not want to take part in a boycott.

There was no meeting of minds when Sir Denis Follows, chairman of the British Olympic Association (BOA), was called before the Commons Foreign Affairs Committee. Some of its members could barely comprehend how the BOA could consider sending athletes to the heart of the Communist empire, particularly when the organization was party to an international boycott of South African athletes. (Conversely, it mystified Zambia's president, Kenneth Kuanda, that the governments now demanding a boycott were the same ones who, when African states were calling for a boycott of South Africa in protest against apartheid, had told them that sport and politics should not mix.) All attempts to get Sir Denis to express a personal view on communism, apartheid or world affairs met with the response that in his official capacity he had no such opinions. He said, 'I firmly believe we must keep politics out of sport. You either accept the world as it is, or quit it.' After prolonged, hostile questioning, Sir Denis finally brought God into the discussion in an unexpected way. He told his interrogators, 'I am just not on the same wavelength as you, and that is how God made me.'[7]

Since the government would not lay down a policy, the House of Commons held a free vote, which, given the preponderance of Conservative MPs, predictably came down in favour of the boycott. Nicholas Winterton, whose long parliamentary career would come to grief during the MPs' expenses scandal thirty years later, thought a boycott of the Games was 'totally inadequate', and that they should be voting for a complete ban on trade and cultural exchanges with the Soviet Union. Jill Knight, the future champion of Clause 28, asked whether 'if one had arranged to play bridge on Wednesday with an acquaintance who had spent the previous weekend overpowering and murdering a neighbour's family, one would still do so'. Whether to go to the Moscow Olympics or not was 'essentially the same question,' she maintained.[8] Archbishop Runcie even threw in his ha'penny worth by telling the athletes that in this instance, 'it is an illusion to suppose that you can separate sport from politics'.[9] The novelist Arthur Koestler described those who thought otherwise as 'innocents'.[10] Yet when the BOA met, on 26 March, hockey was the only sport whose representative supported the boycott – though the Royal Yachting Association, the Joint Shooting Committee and the British Equestrian Federation later joined the British Hockey Board in refusing to go – but the majority was for taking part. 'We believe that sport should be a bridge, not a destroyer,' said Sir Denis.[11] Their decision effectively saved the Moscow Olympics.

One good reason for ignoring Thatcher was the very high chance that the nation's athletes would return festooned with medals. Britain's middle-distance runners were then the fastest in the world. Track racing was dominated by the rivalry between Sebastian Coe, then aged twenty-three, and Steve Ovett, who was twenty-four. They were rivals, but not friends. Coe was a university graduate who trained lightly by world standards, using unorthodox techniques designed for him by his father, and found time in his life for literature, jazz and other interests; Ovett had dropped out of art school to devote himself single-mindedly to the track. In Oslo, three weeks before the Moscow Olympics, Coe became the first athlete ever to hold world records over four distances simultaneously, the 800 m, 1,000 m, 1,500 m and one mile, but the distinction lasted for less than an hour. Ovett ran the mile and clipped a fifth of a second off Coe's record. In Moscow, Ovett came from behind and won the 800 m, with Coe coming second. Six days later, Coe came from behind to win the 1,500 m. Daley Thompson, a twenty-two-year-old Londoner, took the gold medal in the decathlon, but Jamaican born Tessa Sanderson, who was just 0.26 m short of achieving a world record for the javelin a few weeks earlier, was off form and did not qualify for the final round. In all, Britain took five golds, more than any other country outside the old Soviet block. Uniquely, not one of the gold medallists featured in the New Year's Honours list six months later. They were not forgiven for being there, though the most famous of them, Seb Coe, went on to be elected as a Conservative MP twelve years later.

After that, British interest transferred to the 1980 Winter Olympics. That year, in Lake Placid, USA, a couple of young newcomers from Nottingham gained a respectable fourth place in the ice-skating competition. They were Jayne Torvill and Christopher Dean, an insurance-book clerk and a police officer who retained their day jobs so that they could compete as amateurs in the next Winter Olympics in Yugoslavia in February 1984. There they performed a routine lasting four minutes twenty-eight seconds to an abridged version of Ravel's *Bolero*, with an estimated 24m Britons watching on television. The routine was eighteen seconds longer than Olympic rules permitted, but they circumvented that problem by performing the first eighteen seconds on their knees, having established that the performance did not officially begin until their skates touched the ice. They achieved 12 out of a possible 18 perfect scores of 6.0, the highest score in the history of the sport. By April 1984, the late Maurice Ravel (1875–1937) had a tune in the British Top 10: not the full seventeen-minute *Bolero*, but the shortened version sold in the shops as 'Torvill and Dean's *Bolero*'. In Nottingham, there is now a Torvill Drive and a Dean Close, and the public area in front of the city's National Ice Centre is called Bolero Square.

The fame they achieved by being the best in the world was soon eclipsed by another British athlete who achieved lifelong notoriety at a Winter Olympics by being the worst competitor. Britain had never produced a world-class ski-jumper. Eddie Edwards, a twenty-four-year-old plasterer from Cheltenham, was not world class either; he did not even look like a champion, with his thick glasses, protruding chin and general air of ineptitude; there was no one to train or sponsor him, nor any suitable ski slope on which to train. At one international event, the Italian team gave him a helmet to replace the one he had fastened on with string. However, he refused to give up and, in recognition of his dogged persistence, the British Federation told him that he could go to the Winter Olympics in Calgary in 1988 as Britain's first and only Olympic ski-jumper, if he could jump seventy metres. He achieved 69.5, but they decided to enter him anyway. When the news reached him, he was living in a spare room in a mental hospital in Finland, where he had gone to train.[12] In Calgary, Eddie 'the Eagle' secured a well-deserved 86th place out of 86 and was the only competitor singled out for a mention in the closing speech of the Olympics, when the crowd of thousands took up the chant 'Eddie, Eddie, Eddie!' He was so famous that when Ronald Reagan's press spokesman Marlin Fitzwalter called his first press conference in four months, and was asked why there had been such a long silence, he replied that they had been waiting for Eddie the Eagle to get a medal.[13] The Olympic authorities did not get the joke and amended the rules so that no competitor of his standard would ever be allowed to bring the sport into ridicule again.

There were moments when the England cricket team appeared to be competing for an Eddie the Eagle award, particularly during the notorious 'summer of four captains' in 1988. The English had good reason to dread playing host to the West Indies, who had beaten them humiliatingly 5–0 in the 1984 test series. When Mike Gatting led the team back to the Caribbean in 1986, he was hit on the nose by a bouncer from the fast bowler Malcolm Marshall. The ball bounced from his nose on to the stumps and was returned to Marshall with added bits of bone and cartilage. After 1988's First Test in Nottingham ended disappointingly in a draw, the *Sun* published a raunchy story about Mike Gatting and a hotel barmaid, the truth of which he denied. The selectors, however, seemed glad of an excuse to rid themselves of a captain who had already annoyed them in different ways. He was replaced by John Emburey, who was five years older and had never captained England. He led the team to defeat by 134 runs in the Second Test, and in the third by an innings and 156 runs. On that dismal occasion, no English batsman managed to score as many as 35 in either innings. Emburey was then dropped in favour of Chris Cowdrey, who had also never captained England before, and never would again, but he was the son of one of the greatest batsmen of the 1950s, and the chairman of the selectors, Peter May, was his godfather. England lost by ten wickets. Cowdrey injured his foot in a county match and dropped out of the series. The honour of completing England's dismal 'summer of four captains' went to the veteran opening batsman Graham Gooch, who presided over an eight-wicket defeat.

But not all was ignominy. The treat of the decade for English cricket fans was the legendary 1981 Ashes, or 'Botham's Ashes'. Ian Botham was the new cricket superstar, who had made his test debut in 1977 when he was twenty-one. He was one of the great all-rounders, a world-class bowler who was also formidable as a batsman. The test series that bears his name did not begin well. Despite his sporting prowess, Botham was not a good captain and the quality of his performance on the field suffered while he held the captaincy. As the First Test against the visiting Australians opened at Trent Bridge in June 1981, the *Daily Telegraph* recorded ruefully that he was 'not the bowler . . . that he was two years ago'.[14] His batting also declined. The Australians won with four wickets in hand, and the Second Test, which was a draw, was such poor entertainment that the players were assaulted by enraged spectators. England had gone twelve matches without a victory, equalling their longest-ever run of failure.[15]

Botham resigned the captaincy on 8 July and the old stager Mike Brearley was recalled to see England through the Third Test, at Headingley, where the same dismal story continued. The Australians declared at 401, troubled only by Botham's improved bowling, which accounted for six wickets. England were then all out for 174, again with only Botham showing any spirit at the crease by scoring 50. The English were subjected to the humiliation of being sent in to bat again at 3.53 p.m. on the third day and at 3.55 p.m. lost their first wicket, when Gooch was caught for a duck, having lasted just four balls in two innings. By the end of the day, England had scored 6 runs, 2 from no balls. In the morning, the bookies offered odds of 500–1 to anyone stupid enough to put money on an English victory.[16] At 2.13 p.m. the next afternoon, the Australian bowler Dennis Lillee notched up a new record for England-Australia matches by taking his 142nd wicket. England had lost 5 men for 105, and needed 122 runs just to prevent themselves going down to an innings defeat, when Botham came in as seventh man. Suddenly there began one of those stories usually only found in boys' comics. While other English wickets fell, one after another, no one, not even the ferocious Lillee, could stop Botham scoring runs and, after all the other English wickets had fallen, he was not out for 149. No English player had ever previously scored a century and taken even as many as 5 wickets in an innings against Australia. The visitors now had 339 minutes in which to score 130. They did not make it. The fast bowler, Bob Willis, took 8 Australian wickets for just 43 runs, the England wicket-keeper, Bob Taylor, achieved a world record by catching his 1,271st victim behind the stumps and Australia were all out for 111. England not only won the test, but went from there to win the series 3–1. When the Australian captain Kim Hughes was asked what had been the chief difference between the sides since the Second Test, he replied instantly: 'Simple – Ian Botham.' Mike Brearley concurred: 'What Kim says is fair. Take Botham out of our side and it would make us look ordinary.'[17]

The 1980s was possibly the worst decade English football ever endured, not for what happened on the pitch, but for the events in the stands that permanently changed the game. In 1982, England qualified for the World Cup in Spain, after an absence of twelve years, and got through to the second round, which was also as far as Northern Ireland progressed, while Scotland went out in the qualifying round. Four years later, in Mexico, England reached the quarter-final, while the other two were knocked out in the opening round; and in 1990, England achieved fourth place, losing to West Germany in the semi-final, the best outcome since 1966. The incident that stuck hardest in the memories of English fans took place in Mexico. As the English squad set off for the 1986 World Cup, they could see their way clearly through the early rounds, up against weaker teams. The first major problem was the quarter-final against Argentina. The Argentine team had suffered an unforeseen humiliation in Spain in 1982. They had gone there thinking the World Cup was theirs. They had won on home ground in 1978 and had a new star player in Diego Maradona, then twenty-one years old, who promised to be the greatest footballer since Pele. However, they had not even reached the semi-finals when Maradona was sent off for kicking a Brazilian player in the testicles, and they were beaten 3–1. The Argentines were not likely to go out so easily in 1986. Their match against England, on 22 June 1986, was never going to be a simple sporting contest. Cheerleaders for both sides were hyping it up as if it were a rerun of the Falklands War. 'Argies here we come' was the headline in one British tabloid, while its nearest Argentinian equivalent, *Cronica*, ran a headline that translated as 'We're coming to get you, pirates!'[18] The two governments became anxious about the possibility of serious trouble, and agreed to advise their respective team managers to warn the players not to inflame the situation. On the whole they did as asked. 'Look, mate, I play football. About politics, I know nothing,' Maradona insisted. In the sell-out crowd of 114,580 in the Azteca Stadium there was, surprisingly, just one fist fight, after an Argentinian ripped up a Union Jack. The real controversy was on the pitch.

Five minutes into the second half, a defender, Steve Hodge, succeeded in taking the ball off an attacking Argentinian player, just aside of the penalty area, but miscued it, sending it high in the air back into the penalty area, when the English goalkeeper, Peter Shilton, and Maradona both jumped for it. A confused second later, the ball was in the net and Maradona was running off to celebrate with his team-mates, while an outraged Shilton signalled a foul. The linesman and referee allowed the goal. Maradona followed it later with a superb run that began beyond the halfway line, went past three defenders and outsmarted Shilton. As the game drew to a close, Gary Lineker scored what the English regarded as the equalizer, but the official score was 2–1, England were out and Argentina went on to win the World Cup. Afterwards, Bobby Robson paid an unqualified tribute to Maradona's second 'miracle' goal. 'It's wonderful when the world can produce great players of his calibre,'[19] he said. But even without having seen the film or stills photographs, he was sure that the first should have been disallowed because 'Maradona handled the ball into the goal'.[20] And that was, indeed, what had happened, as the photographic evidence proved. When the English players saw Maradona in the dressing room, they thought he might acknowledge that the goal was at least dubious, but he was having none of it. Challenged in public, he made what is probably the most famous remark ever uttered by a footballer. His actual words, recorded by one of the more reliable and dispassionate news agencies covering the event, were: 'That goal was scored a little bit by the hand of God and another bit by Maradona's head.'[21]

Years later, Maradona admitted that the now infamous goal should never have been allowed; but if his behaviour at the time seems unsporting, it should be judged against what it meant to the Argentinians to be up against England four years after the war in the South Atlantic.' Maradona said later:

> Before the match, we said football had nothing to do with the Malvinas war but we knew a lot of Argentinian kids had died there, shot down like birds. This was revenge. Bollocks was it just another match! It was more than winning a game, and it was more than knocking England out of the World Cup. We blamed the English players for everything that had happened, for all the suffering of the Argentine people.[22]

Off the pitch, three tragedies changed the nature of English football as a spectator sport. The first was on 11 May 1985, as 11,000 spectators watched Bradford City play at home against Lincoln City. The wooden stadium in Bradford's Valley Parade ground had been built in 1908. West Yorkshire County Council had written to the football club twice in 1984 warning that 'the timber construction is a fire hazard, and in particular there is a build-up of combustible materials in the voids beneath the seats. A carelessly discarded cigarette would give rise to a fire risk.'[23] Just before half-time, a match or a cigarette stubbed out in a polythene cup fell through the wooden slats on to the accumulated rubbish. Within about four minutes, the roof and stands were ablaze. Pictures broadcast live on television showed fans frantically scrambling to escape and a policeman running on to the pitch with his hair on fire. A shocking 56 people died and 255 were injured.

It should have been plain that this was a ghastly accident for which the club was at fault, and that the spectators were the victims, but the government's instinctive reaction was to assume that, somehow, football hooligans were responsible. The century-old link between football and casual violence was reckoned to have worsened during the 1970s, when English football fans developed an international reputation for bad behaviour. By 1985, after the miners and other 'enemies within' had been dealt with, football hooligans became a national obsession, the number one receptacle of public disapproval.

Thus, when Thatcher and Leon Brittan, the home secretary, met to discuss the Bradford tragedy, they decided that any inquiry should take heed of rumours – unfounded rumours, but never mind – that the fire had been started by spectators throwing smoke bombs. Brittan appointed a High Court judge, Sir Oliver Popplewell, to investigate the fire. Controversially, the remit of his investigation also included trouble that had broken out on the same day during a match in Birmingham, where a fifteen-year-old boy had been killed and 125 people had been arrested. It was alleged by one of the more eminent spectators, Lord Mishcon, that when one of the Birmingham supporters, a young Asian, was arrested, about fifty Leeds fans made the Nazi salute and shouted 'Seig Heil'.[24] When Brittan announced his decision to the House of Commons, his Labour shadow, Gerald Kaufman, said that lumping the two incidents together was 'deeply offensive to the bereaved and deeply offensive to the victims'. Brittan argued that it would be 'wholly artificial' to treat crowd behaviour and safety standards as separate issues.[25] The Popplewell inquiry produced no evidence of bad behaviour in the Bradford tragedy. His report tried to dispel the beliefs that hooliganism was something new, that it was restricted to football matches or that it was specifically English, all without effect.

However, there was an aspect of Popplewell's findings that received enormous publicity. It identified what seems to have been a new phenomenon that football hooligans were not all drawn from the rough end of the working class. These 'new hooligans', as Popplewell called them, 'often hold down good jobs during the week, dress stylishly and detach themselves from those fans with club scarves who travel on official coaches or trains. They plan their violence as a recreation in itself to which football is secondary or a mere background.'[26] They were actually more organized than Popplewell realized, forming gangs with names like the Inter City Firm (ICF), which followed West Ham, so named because its members – who dressed smartly to avoid the attention of the police – travelled to away matches on the Inter City service. Then there were the 'Service Crew' attached to Leeds, the 'Gooners' from Arsenal, the Millwall 'Bushwhackers', the Leicester 'Baby Squad' and the Chelsea 'Headhunters'. A member of the ICF, interviewed by Thames Television in August 1985, explained: 'I think I fight, like, so I can make a name for meself and that, you know, hope people respect me for what I did.'[27]

This phenomenon was neatly captured in a drama shown on BBC2 in February 1989. Written by Al Hunter and directed by Alan Clarke, *The Firm* was one of the best television films of the decade. It starred Gary Oldman as an estate agent named Bex, who leads one gang of hooligans in pitched street battles against another. One critic wrote:

> Bex is a new breed thug, of the kind now earnestly identified by sociologists ('Why don't we just tell him we like hitting people,' he jeers, when one such appears on TV). He is thirty, earns good money, has a family and a neat new house. He and his 'firm' dress smartly,

> drive BMWs and travel first class to their bloody battle grounds. To his gang he is 'a visionary'. He does it all, he tells his wife, 'because I need the buzz'.[28]

By mischief or coincidence, the film was broadcast the day after Colin Moynihan, the sports minister, appeared on BBC1's *Going Live!*, optimistically explaining how ID cards would bring hooliganism under control. The one and only conclusion that Mrs Thatcher had drawn from the Popplewell report was that all football clubs should issue ID cards, so that troublemakers could be banned from matches, along with anyone who had not had the foresight to order a ticket in advance. Luton Town Football Club, chaired by an abrasive right-wing Conservative MP named David Evans, admitted no visitors at all; from August 1986, all home matches were played before an exclusive audience of registered Luton supporters living within twenty-five miles of the town.

It was to no avail that Judge Popplewell emphasized that most people who went to football matches deplored the violence and wanted only to enjoy the game. By the time his report was published, the horror at Bradford had been overshadowed by the worst incidence of English football hooliganism in living memory, when Liverpool met the Italian club, Juventus, for the European Cup final at the Heysel Stadium in Belgium on 29 May 1985. About an hour before kick-off, Liverpool fans, who were already in belligerent mood, reputedly saw a banner at the far end of the stadium saying 'Red Animals', which sent them into a frenzy. They smashed through the inadequate barriers and laid into the Italians with fists, pieces of concrete and planks of wood, driving them back against a wall. Some of the victims had already been trampled to death before the wall gave way. Others were buried or trampled or crushed as it collapsed. When the police intervened, they were attacked. The Juventus players did not want to come on to the pitch, but were persuaded that cancelling the game would make the violence worse. It ended only as the teams appeared, an hour late and flanked by riot police. There were thirty-nine Italians and Belgians dead, and hundreds injured.

The chairman of the Football Association, Bert Millichip, was in Mexico that day, discussing the impending World Cup and, because of the time difference, was asleep as the catastrophe unfolded. He was awoken by the British ambassador, who had received a message from Margaret Thatcher suggesting that he come back to London at once. He did and was called in to meet the prime minister. Mrs Thatcher then said at a press conference: 'It isn't that we're numb, we're worse than numb. We witnessed that agony and it's even worse after nearly twenty-four hours than it was when we saw it, because the full enormity is coming home as we saw those scenes on television. Everything, but everything, must be done.'[29] Two days later, the Football Association decided to pull all English teams out of all European competitions for a season, a decision that Margaret Thatcher applauded, but which did not go far enough for the Union of European Football Associations (UEFA), who banned all English clubs indefinitely. The ban lasted five years for all except Liverpool, for whom it lasted seven years.

This ban did not extend to the England squad, though many British politicians thought it should. During the European Championship in June 1988, English hooligans rioted in Stuttgart, Düsseldorf, Frankfurt and Cologne. The damage ran to hundreds of thousands of pounds, there were 800 arrests and one man was drowned in the River Main in Frankfurt. The Germans called it 'the new British disease', and a Dutch newspaper called them 'the scourge of Europe'. During a match in Frankfurt, all the English supporters stood for the national anthem and some directed Nazi salutes at the Germans and chanted 'two world wars and one world cup'. The news so disgusted Margaret Thatcher that at the G8 summit of world leaders in Toronto, she took Helmut Kohl, the West German chancellor, aside to apologize.

The worst football tragedy of the decade – indeed the worst in British football history – came ten months later, on 15 April 1989, at the Hillsborough stadium in Sheffield, the venue for the FA Cup semi-final between Liverpool and Nottingham Forest. Liverpool supporters were allocated the Leppings Lane end of the ground. They arrived in Sheffield in their thousands. About 12,000 were in the stands before the 3 p.m. kick-off, but most were reluctant to take their places in the stadium early because there was no entertainment inside. At 2.45 p.m., 5,000 supporters were outside trying to get through 12 turnstiles. The senior police officer on the spot grew alarmed and pleaded over the radio for the turnstiles to be opened before someone was crushed to death. It took three increasingly desperate appeals before Chief Superintendent David Duckenfield, who was supposedly running operations from the control room, arrived at a decision. It was the first major football match Duckenfield had handled; he had been transferred to his new job only a month earlier. Eventually, he gave the order to open the gates, but did not think to warn the officers inside the grounds to expect a sudden flood of 5,000 impatient supporters.

The Leppings Lane end was divided into pens; in some there was ample room, but Pen 3 and Pen 4 were full to capacity. The fans did not know that;

all they could see was the high walls of the terrace and a tunnel, above which was written the word 'Standing', and through which they could see the pitch. Undirected, they poured through the tunnel and into the two pens that were already full. The tunnel had a one-in-six gradient. Some people were lifted off their feet and carried forward by the crush. As it worsened, people shouted for help and begged for connecting gates to be opened so they could escape into other pens, but the teams were on the pitch by now and the police could not hear in the general din. Fans managed to push one gate open, but the police closed it and forced the desperate spectators to get back into the crush. A few climbed the fences. They were spotted from the control room, where it was assumed that they were hooligans out to disrupt the match; the dog handlers were summoned to keep them in place. A strong perimeter fence had been constructed to prevent a pitch invasion, and now those who had arrived early for the game were being squeezed to death against it. Police on the spot frantically signalled to those in the middle to move back, but they could not. The late arrivals at the back were watching the players, unaware of what was happening in front of them, and did not see the need to move. As people had their lives crushed out of them, the game began. At 3.04 p.m., Peter Beardsley, the forward whom Liverpool had bought two years earlier for £1.9m (then the highest transfer fee ever paid by an English club), struck the crossbar at the far end and the exultant Liverpool fans surged forward, causing a crash barrier in Pen 3 to snap, sending those it supported tumbling forward. At this point, Ground Commander Superintendent Greenwood ran on to the pitch and told the referee to stop the game. It was 3.05 p.m. and ninety-six people were being crushed to death.

As the desperate fans tried to escape, many of the officers who could have helped seemed to stand by, paralysed. This was not entirely their fault. To quote the findings of the official inquiry: 'They had been summoned in response to what was thought to be a threat to public order. What they found was a horrific scene of carnage and some young officers were shocked into impotence. It was truly gruesome. The victims were blue, cyanotic, incontinent; their mouths were open, vomiting; their eyes staring'.[30] Shocking images filled that evening's television bulletins. On Sunday morning, staff at the *Liverpool Echo* turned up to work voluntarily to produce a special edition of the paper with a graphic close-up picture on the front page of a man and woman crying in distress in the crush, under the headline 'Our Day of Tears'.

There was, inevitably, a hunt for someone to blame. The Liverpool fans on the spot had blamed the police; some had abused, spat and even assaulted the stunned officers. It was not long before the police were retaliating by blaming the fans, taking their cue from the top. Within ten minutes of the game being stopped, the chief executive of the Football Association, Graham Kelly, visited the control room and was told by Chief Superintendent Duckenfield that the problem had been caused by a gate being forced by the fans, when Duckenfield was the man who had given the order to open the gates only half-an-hour earlier. Interviewed on television, Kelly said, correctly, that there appeared to be two versions of what happened, that of the police and the fans.[31] As the bodies arrived at Northern Hospital, the police collected evidence to prove a thesis that drunkenness was the cause of the tragedy. Corpses were meticulously tested for the alcohol level in their blood. Liverpool supporter Les Aspinall had gone to the match with his wife and two sons, but the parents were separated from the boys and afterwards spent several hours searching for their son Philip at the local hospital. At around 9.30 p.m., Les went back to the ground, and was shown his son's body, but he was not immediately allowed to go and break the news to his wife and his other son, because the police insisted on questioning him about the route they had taken to the ground and whether or not they had stopped for a drink. 'Eventually I thought they were trying to get something out of me. They were on at me for about half an hour when eventually the nurse came and said "This man's wife's waiting there and he's in no fit state to talk to you".'[32]

The local Liverpool media managed the difficult feat of covering the event in its full horror without offending a city that was moving from shock and grief to anger. The disaster had added 500,000 to the sales figures of the Sunday newspapers, and Liverpool was teeming with national newspaper reporters hunting for grieving relatives or anyone else out of whom they could winkle information. The first to catch the backlash was the *Daily Mirror*, which on Monday morning carried horrific pictures of crushed, dying fans in full colour. Some could be seen to be going blue for lack of oxygen, and the *Mirror* was roundly and unanimously condemned by callers to a local radio phone-in programme. But the next day, Tuesday, all the pent-up anger in Liverpool found another target. For once, the *Daily Mirror* could thank Kelvin MacKenzie for coming to its rescue.

Sun journalists had been hearing the unofficial police version of what happened. They were told that there had been a conspiracy by drunken Liverpool fans to arrive late, en masse, so that a large number of ticketless fans would be able to get through in the confusion. The stench of vomit and urine was taken as evidence of drunkenness, rather than a body's natural tendency to empty itself when squeezed hard enough. The angry reaction of the traumatized fans immediately afterwards was thrown into the mix, with other yet more colourful tales, and the whole concoction filled the whole of Wednesday's front page of the *Sun,* under a two-word headline written by MacKenzie in person: 'The Truth'. The only story that was attributed to a named witness came from Irvine Patrick, a Tory MP from Sheffield, who had heard from a police officer that fans had molested the body of a dead girl. *Sun* journalists were not the only ones to have heard these tales; they also appeared in the *Star,* the *Sheffield Star* and in Murdoch's other papers, but the *Sun* went further than the others in treating the story as authoritative. The reaction in the north-west that Wednesday was something the *Sun* had never before experienced. Newsagents either refused to sell the paper, or put it under the counter. In Kirkby, near Liverpool, there was a spontaneous public meeting in the shopping centre, and a television crew was invited in to see copies of the paper being set on fire. Everywhere around Liverpool, copies of the *Sun* were torn up or burnt; people seen reading it had it torn out of their hands. All attempts by local media to solicit a comment from anyone at the *Sun* were met with silence. The broadcaster Brian Hayes, who hosted a television show in front of a studio audience in Manchester, had a photograph of Kelvin MacKenzie, a red telephone and an egg timer on the table before him, and taunted the *Sun*'s editor by daring him to ring before the timer ran out. Sales of the *Sun* in the Liverpool area crashed. The management admitted that circulation in central Merseyside fell from 140,000 to 100,000; in the whole Merseyside region, it is estimated to have gone down from 320,000 to 204,000.[33] The boycott endured for years, eventually forcing a begrudging apology from the *Sun* and, later still, from Boris Johnson after the *Spectator* magazine, which he then edited, accused Liverpool of 'wallowing in grief',

In the immediate aftermath, the Hillsborough tragedy did nothing to shift the government's firmly held belief that the sole problem with football was the hooligans who followed it. Five months afterwards, in September 1989, the England team travelled to Stockholm for a World Cup qualifier, followed by a press corps who were expected to file stories of English hooligans on the rampage. Unusually, they included a thirty-three-year-old Arsenal fan, Colin Ward, a former hooligan and serial chronicler of hooligan violence, who was hired by the *Today* newspaper to travel undercover with the fans. He returned convinced that the real story was not English hooligans looking for trouble but journalists looking for English hooligans, and reinterpreting minor incidents as riots.[34] However, the government was soon armed with fresh statistics that the Swedish police had arrested 206 people and that 102 of them were English. In fact, 101 of those 102 people had been released for lack of evidence, but this provoked a protest from the British sports minister,

Colin Moynihan, who thought that they had been let off too lightly and would 'regard it as a battle honour to be kept overnight and kicked out of a country'.[35] Home Secretary Douglas Hurd announced that he was setting a national police intelligence unit to combat the hooligans, a move that his Labour opposite number, Roy Hattersley, welcomed as long overdue.[36] A friendly international against Holland, scheduled to take place in Rotterdam in December, was cancelled at Moynihan's request; the Football Association refused to handle tickets for the next England match in Poland; and the Polish Tourist Board was asked by the British government to stop selling tickets to the English.[37]

Meanwhile, as normal, the government had appointed a High Court judge to conduct an inquiry into the Hillsborough disaster. Their choice, Peter Taylor, had one of the finest minds in the British courts and went about the task with exemplary seriousness. His interim report, published four months after the catastrophe, came as a shock to the police. Lord Taylor did not accept that drunkenness had played any significant part in the tragedy, or that there had been an abnormally high number of fans arriving without tickets, or that the thousands who arrived at around 2.30 p.m. for a 3.00 p.m. kick-off, on a hot day, were unreasonably late. Of the fans' behaviour after the catastrophe, he said that instances of police being abused, spat at or assaulted were 'comparatively small', adding that 'in deploring them, one must recognise the uniquely horrifying experience which those responsible had just suffered'. He dismissed all the other salacious stories that had turned up in the *Sun* with the comment that 'those who made them, and those who disseminated them, would have done better to hold their peace'.[38]

By contrast, the judgement he passed on the senior police officers involved was scorching. The evidence he heard from the police, he said, was mostly 'in inverse proportion to their rank'. Where young constables were 'intelligent and open', many of their superiors were 'defensive and evasive',[39] as indeed they might well have been, because Taylor's blunt conclusion was that the immediate cause of the catastrophe was the 'blunder' the police had made by opening the gates without making themselves ready for the inevitable rush of thousands of fans that followed. He was also unsparing in his criticism of the way football grounds were managed. He drew a picture of an industry in which annual ticket sales had fallen from 77m a year in the late 1950s to 20m, run in many cases by businessmen who did not appear to have the slightest care for the comfort or safety of their dwindling clientele. Perversely, the tax system encouraged the clubs to spend vast sums on players, and none at all on the comfort and safety of the fans, because transfer fees could be offset against tax, but improvements to a stadium could not. The result was filthy, unsafe grounds, filled with the stench of cheap food and urine because the toilets were so bad that it was, in effect, accepted that men would relieve themselves against a wall, if they could get to one, or into empty drink cups or any other convenient receptacle. The ways the pens were designed invited another disaster, and yet, he complained:

> Amazingly, complacency was still to be found after Hillsborough. It was chilling to hear the same refrain from directors at several clubs I visited: 'Hillsborough was horrible – but, of course, it couldn't have happened here.' Couldn't it? The Hillsborough ground was regarded by many as one of the best in the country.[40]

One aspect of the industry that Taylor was not asked to investigate was the spreading corruption in football. The omission is understandable because not much was known in 1989 about the under-the-counter deals done when players were bought and sold. The public was given its first major insight after Terry Venables, the manager of Tottenham Hotspur, teamed up with Alan Sugar to buy the club from a property owner who had run it from his tax exile in Monaco. Their partnership came to grief after Venables bought Teddy Sheringham from Nottingham Forest, whose manager was Brian Clough. The deal included £50,000 in cash, allegedly handed over in a motorway cafe. Sugar, innocently assuming that this was a legitimate payment, added VAT, which was mysteriously returned. Venables cleared up the misunderstanding by saying, 'Cloughie likes a bung', whereupon a furious Sugar made the whole scandal public, only to find that the world of football was more interested in protecting its two most loved club managers than in the complaints of a rich outsider.[41] To the end of his days, Clough denied that any part of that unexplained £50,000 was ever meant for him. This cowboy attitude to money had corroded Tottenham's finances so much that the club had to sell an injured Paul Gascoigne to Lazio. Gascoigne was a much-flawed character, a child in a man's body, but he was the nation's favourite footballer. He had provided the most memorable moment of the 1990 World Cup, during the semi-final that England lost to Germany, when he burst into tears after receiving a yellow card. That England had come so close to reaching the final was a bright note to the end of what was not a good decade for British football.

Because of the Taylor Report, there is no standing room at Premier League grounds any more. Taylor did not accept the protests of those who said that the experience of going to a football match – standing and swaying in a crowd – would never be the same again. Taylor believed that fans could sit and watch, and still lose themselves in the shared excitement, and be safe. He seems to have been vindicated on the last point because in more than twenty years since Hillsborough there have been no other catastrophes on anything like that scale. Hooliganism and racism have also declined. But there are those who believe that Hillsborough and its aftermath allowed the money men to take over the game and hike up admission prices until, in the opinion of at least one fan, 'football has ceased to be the people's game, in any meaningful sense. It's become a game defined by egoism, rapacity and greed, and by a grotesque mercantile, neo-liberal winner-takes-all ethos'.[42]

CHAPTER 17

STAND DOWN, MARGARET

MARGARET THATCHER was in fine form when she delivered her annual speech to the Conservative Party conference in Bournemouth on 12 October 1990. She was the undisputed mistress of her party; her enthusiasm for the job was undimmed; she had weathered two political crises, one concerning relations with the EU, the other over the poll tax; and a week earlier, she had knocked the final day of the Labour Party conference off the top of the news by announcing that, after much deliberation, the UK had joined something called the Exchange Rate Mechanism (ERM), a preliminary move towards the creation of a single European currency. Moreover, her scriptwriters had thought of a good joke. Her capacity to misunderstand jokes was legendary, but evidently this one had been patiently explained to her, and she delivered it with aplomb. It was a joke at the expense of the Liberal Democrats.

The third party had been enduring such a dire time that there was a serious question mark over its long-term survival. In 1987, the Liberal-SDP Alliance, under the joint leadership of David Owen and David Steel, had fallen victim, again, to a disproportionate election system that allotted them only 22 MPs – 17 Liberals and 5 for the SDP – on 23 per cent of the vote. Most members of both parties thought it was time to end the Alliance and merge, which they duly voted to do; but a minority, including David Owen, refused to be bound by the result and insisted on maintaining a separate SDP. The two parties went into direct competition, replacing the old electoral pact with something resembling a suicide pact. The Alliance's greatest strength had been its capacity to win parliamentary by-elections, but they were not able to do this when they fought each other. In the by-election in Richmond, Yorkshire, in February 1989, the candidates of the SDP and Democrats (as the merged Alliance was briefly called before they became the Liberal Democrats in October 1989) took a combined total of nearly 28,500 votes, but because they were divided the winner, with just over 19,500, was the twenty-seven-year-old Conservative, William Hague. In the election to the European Parliament, in June 1989, the Green Party came third, with nearly 2.3mn votes, 1.3m more than the Democrats. By now, the Democrats' new leader, Paddy Ashdown, was in despair. He wrote in his diary: 'I can't snap out of the depression. We seem to be on the edge of oblivion. I don't think I have ever been so miserable in my entire life.'[1] The SDP's final humiliation was a by-election in Bootle in May 1990, in which they came sixth, behind Labour, the Conservatives, the Liberal Democrats, the Greens and Screaming Lord Sutch of the Monster Raving Loony Party. The party then wound itself up, leaving the field to Paddy Ashdown, who began the long, slow task of rebuilding the Lib Dems as a credible third party.

Their travails greatly amused Thatcher's speechwriters, and soon she had the Conservative Party faithful roaring with laughter as she declared:

> Politics is a serious business, and one should not lower the tone unduly. [Here the official transcript records 'laughter'.] So I will say only this of the Liberal Democrat symbol and of the party it symbolises. This is an ex-parrot. [Loud laughter and applause.] It is not merely stunned. It has ceased to be, expired and gone to meet its maker. [Laughter and applause.] It is a parrot no more. [Laughter.] It has rung down the curtain and joined the choir invisible. [Laughter.] This is a late parrot.[2]

It was surely Margaret Thatcher's funniest moment. A week later, others could laugh, too, because the parrot she had pronounced dead revived and gave her a nasty peck. There was a by-election in Eastbourne on 18 October 1990, which the Conservatives had every reason to be confident of winning. It was not just that they had won this very middle-class seat in 1987 with a majority of nearly 17,000, but this was Ian Gow's old seat, and it was confidently expected that the awful circumstances of his assassination would bring out the Conservative vote. To general astonishment, the Lib Dems won comfortably, with a 20 per cent swing. The Conservatives had thought that the worst was behind them, but as Parliament reassembled after the long summer break, they realized that could yet lose the next general election.

Thatcher might have survived the domestic disaster of the poll tax had her attitude to the world beyond Britain's shores not looked so inward. Her views on race belonged to a different decade, as she demonstrated time and again in her indulgence of the apartheid system. Though she had once been keen enough to see British athletes boycott the Moscow Olympics, she resolutely refused to see a case for sanctions against white-dominated South Africa. 'Sanctions only work by causing unemployment and starvation and misery,'[3] was her fixed view. She did, however, see a need for apartheid to reform itself, and when at last South Africa had a reforming political leader in President F.W. de Klerk, she hailed him as the new Gorbachev. The great symbolic event of February 1990 was the release of Nelson Mandela after more than twenty-seven years in prison, which did not mean that the apartheid system had been dismantled, but was a sign that the end was near. Thatcher had scheduled a press conference on the steps of Downing Street to mark Mandela's release, but was so shocked to learn that as he emerged from prison he said that the ANC should not disarm while apartheid continued to exist that she cancelled her appearance.[4] She wrote to President George Bush Sr and other world leaders suggesting that the ban on new investment in South Africa be lifted without delay. When the twelve EU foreign ministers met, ten days later, no one supported her. Even George Bush rang to say that he could not support her either because of opposition from the US Congress.

The collapse of communism in Eastern Europe ought to have reinforced Mrs Thatcher's stature on the world stage because no democratically elected leader had been more staunchly anti-Communist than the one the Russians called the Iron Lady. To listen to her acolytes it was as if she and Ronald Reagan had brought down the whole system, yet she was curiously diminished by the loss of a convenient enemy. 'Too often the democratic peaceful nations let slip their guard because they assumed that the danger had gone, assumed that the future would be one of peace and progress,'[5] she told the Young Conservatives' conference on the eve of Mandela's release. She was not to be lulled into thinking that tearing down the Berlin Wall meant that the Communist danger had passed, as she demonstrated when she told an astonished House of Commons that Neil Kinnock was a 'crypto Communist'.[6] He burst out laughing.

By the spring of 1990, it was obvious that the East German people wanted to share western prosperity, and the West German government, led by Helmut Kohl, was determined to see through reunification, despite the immense cost. This prospect revived all Thatcher's wartime prejudices. She lectured the Germans on why the future of their country was not a matter for them alone; they must take into account 'the sensitivities and interests of others in Europe as well' because, as she explained to the Board of Deputies of British Jews, 'it is understandable that, for some, bitter memories of the past should colour their view of the present and the future'.[7] Her fears were echoed in Poland, whose borders had been shoved westwards at Germany's expense in 1945. The West Germans had never recognized the Oder-Neisse line (the Polish-German border drawn after the Second World War), which had been an academic question while East Germany was in the way, but not anymore. No one leant the Poles a more sympathetic ear than Margaret Thatcher, and on 23 March 1990, as East Germany held its first free election in fifty-eight years, she gave an interview to *Der Spiegel* in which she claimed: 'I've heard Helmut say, "No, I guarantee nothing, I do not recognize the present borders." I heard it myself after the dinner in Strasbourg.' As soon as this was reported to Chancellor Kohl, he ordered his press spokesman to deny that he had ever said any such thing. The *Sunday Times* accused her of 'consummate folly to give the Germans the impression that the British government is, at best, grudging in its support for the reunification of the two parts of their nation and, at worst, hostile'.[8] Even the normally chauvinist *Daily Express* weighed in two days later: 'Surely, forty-five years after the end of World War Two . . . we can accept this momentous event with something more imaginative and generous than public foreboding?'[9] When Helmut Kohl arrived on a visit at the end of the week, a slightly chastened Mrs Thatcher told him: 'I do not think that it will come as a great surprise to anyone that I am not always the world's greatest diplomat and thank goodness for that!'[10]

Indeed, her diplomatic style did not come as a surprise to Germany's leaders. They had been on the receiving end of it for more than ten years. Mrs Thatcher had set the tone of her relations with Britain's EU partners at the start of her term in office when she launched a highly publicized campaign to claim back what she called 'our' money from the EU. Membership had become annually more expensive for the UK, whose net contribution to the EU was £800m in 1978, and threatened to be £1 billion in 1979, until she embarked on a ferocious campaign to have it reduced. It took four years to reach a satisfactory agreement. While Thatcher was undoubtedly justified in doing battle on behalf of British taxpayers, her diplomatic style shocked some of the Europeans. In May 1980, EEC Commissioner Christopher Tugendhat was told by a German official that her manner had hurt Helmut Schmidt, the chancellor, 'in his male pride'. 'If things are to be put right between our two countries, she must find a way of making it up to him,'[11] he added.

In the middle of the decade, Thatcher seemed to settle down and recognize that there were benefits to EU membership. She believed in free trade and, late in 1985, after only a relatively minor fracas with the Germans, she signed the Single European Act, believing it would accelerate progress towards a single market, although it contained the phrase 'Economic and Monetary Union', which clearly committed the signatories to work towards abolishing their separate currencies, sublimating them in what is now known as the euro. She seems to have believed that this objective lay so far in the future that it could be ignored, but in the second half of the 1980s it became clear that the German and French governments, and the president of the Commission Jacques Delors, meant business. Two new sets of initials entered political discourse. There was the EMS, or European Monetary System, and the ERM, the Exchange Rate Mechanism. The EMS was relatively uncontroversial; the UK had joined that when Jim Callaghan was prime minister. The ERM was the new element. EU states that joined it were required to limit currency fluctuations within the system. Since the Deutschemark (DM) was the strongest currency in the system, it was against the DM that others measured their performance; if the value of a currency slipped too many pfennigs below the DM, the government concerned had to raise interest rates until its currency was back within the accepted limits; conversely, the government had to lower interest rates if its currency rose too far.

This appalled Margaret Thatcher. There were rational reasons for not wanting to tie sterling to the DM because of the structural difference between the British and German economies, but there was also a powerful irrational reason. Thatcher's teenage years were the war years; she married a much older man partly because the generation who might have been her boyfriends went off to fight. This was behind what Nigel Lawson bluntly described as her 'saloon bar xenophobia'.[12] That the Germans were urging other EU nations to merge their currencies with the DM exacerbated her hostility to the whole project, until she believed that Europe, to quote Sir Geoffrey Howe, was 'a continent that is positively teeming with ill-intentioned people, scheming, in her words, to extinguish democracy'.[13] Nicholas Ridley, who was loyal to her to the end, recorded sitting beside Mrs Thatcher in Strasbourg as she addressed the European Parliament. 'You could feel the waves of hostility emanating from her,' he wrote. Ridley, of course, blamed the Europeans. 'Her forthrightness and her tenacity were alien to Latin politicians . . . Deep down they resented her because she was so utterly unmanoeuvrable.'[14]

Ridley, who had been moved from running local government to the job of secretary of state for trade and industry, had his own thoughts on the

Europeans, which he confided one day in July 1990 to Dominic Lawson, editor of the *Spectator*. Having seemingly forgotten that he was giving a taped interview to a journalist, rather than chatting with the son of a colleague (Nigel), he opined that the proposed single European currency was 'a German racket designed to take over the whole of Europe' and that the French were 'poodles'. 'You might just as well give in to Adolf Hitler,' he continued.[15] It was no surprise to the elder Lawson that Ridley felt free to make these comments, since Ridley 'had many times heard Margaret utter precisely the same sentiments in private – as, indeed, had I'.[16] However, when they became public there was a predictable scandal and Mrs Thatcher had to find a new trade secretary, and lost one of the last reliable supporters she had in the cabinet.

Her isolation in the cabinet arose from the fact that Howe and Lawson, the two most important of her ministers, were Thatcherite in domestic economic policy only. Neither shared her aversion to Germany; both believed that sterling should join the ERM, and both were men of great intellectual confidence who were not going to accept that Thatcher or her favourite adviser, Sir Alan Walters, knew better. Of the two, she had more respect for Lawson, because Howe's sheep-like manner made him easy to underestimate, whereas Lawson had a manner that left others in no doubt of his superior intellect. On meeting him, Max Hastings noted that 'where some ministers flattered editors, the Chancellor's courtesy could not mask his amazement that so callow a figure as myself had by some reckless misdeal of fate been elevated to the chair of the *Telegraph*'.[17] Lawson had tried to persuade Thatcher that joining the ERM would discourage runs on the pound in 1985, when a sudden rise in the value of the dollar had forced him to put up interest rates. She consulted Alan Walters, who told her that, on the contrary, ERM membership would actually make currency speculation at sterling's expense more likely. Since Lawson was not proposing to enter the ERM straightaway, that seemed to settle the matter.

However, on a Friday in November 1987, Thatcher granted an interview to journalists from the *Financial Times*, who asked her why it was Treasury policy to fix sterling at a parity of 3DM to the pound. They produced charts demonstrating that when Lawson had raised interest rates in August, it was because the pound was falling below 3DM, and when he had cut interest rates twice in quick succession after the stock market crash in October, it was because the pound was getting ahead of the DM. She was not expecting the question and flatly denied it was happening. She has maintained ever since that Lawson had secretly changed government policy to bounce her into agreeing to join the ERM. 'How could I ever trust him again?' [18] she demanded. But he claimed: 'It was always an implausible insult to her formidable intelligence to suggest that she could possibly have been unaware of it, even if I had wished to keep her in the dark, which, of course, I did not.'[19] Whichever version is true, relations between the prime minister and the chancellor never recovered.

The issue came back in dramatic fashion in June 1989 during the run-up to a summit of the EU nations in Madrid, to which European Commissioner Jacques Delors had submitted a paper setting out a programme for merging all the EU's currencies, into what was later called the euro. Thatcher and Lawson were united in opposing monetary union, but Lawson continued to believe that sterling would benefit from joining the ERM and thought that the UK would be better placed to oppose monetary union from inside rather than out. In that month's elections to the European Parliament, the Conservative Party had campaigned on a slogan that: 'If you don't vote Conservative next Thursday, you'll live on a diet of Brussels'. The reaction was not the one they expected: 5.3m votes were cast for the Conservatives, and 6.1m for Labour, making it the first national election that the Conservatives had lost since 1974. The result convinced Sir Geoffrey Howe, who had just become Britain's longest-serving foreign secretary for more than seventy years, that Thatcher's antagonism to the EU was bad policy and bad politics. He persuaded Lawson to join him in presenting a common front over the more immediate question of membership of the ERM. Thatcher reluctantly agreed to see Howe and Lawson together in her office on 20 June and agreed to ponder what they had said. Once they were out of sight, she turned to Alan Walters, who came up with a counter-proposal, which she forwarded to her two ministers without revealing its authorship. They insisted on seeing her again and, with even more reluctance, she agreed. Early on Sunday morning, 25 June, the day they were due to fly out to Madrid, the two ministers presented her with a bald ultimatum: either she agree a date by which the UK would join the ERM, or they would both resign. She blamed Sir Geoffrey Howe for this 'nasty little meeting', as she called it, and became convinced that 'this quiet, gentle, but deeply ambitious man – with whom my relations had become progressively worse as my exasperation at his insatiable appetite for compromise led me sometimes to lash out at him in front of others – was now out to make trouble for me'.[20] She was so angry that she refused to speak to Howe on the flight to Madrid. Once there, she followed the course suggested by Alan Walters, laying down conditions for Britain's entry to the ERM without any mention of a date, but she did clearly utter the words: 'I can reaffirm today the United Kingdom's intention to join the ERM.' That was good enough to satisfy Howe, who called it 'as close to the outcome for which Nigel and I had been pressing as we might have hoped',[21] but in Thatcher's mind, it was game, set and match to her. She could not resist rubbing it in by standing at the door as ministers arrived for the following Thursday's cabinet meeting, so that she could whisper gloatingly to Howe and to Lawson 'no date'.

She took her revenge a month later, on 24 July 1989, as the Commons was about to rise for the summer break, when she called an unsuspecting Howe to Downing Street and told him he was being removed from the Foreign Office. She offered him the alternative jobs of home secretary or leader of the House of Commons, with the chairmanship of a clutch of cabinet committees. He went away, shell-shocked, and later in the day agreed to be leader of the Commons provided the job came with the title of deputy prime minister. Despite the title, once the news was out, everyone knew that Howe had been demoted, especially since Thatcher's press secretary Bernard Ingham briefed lobby journalists that the title of deputy prime minister had 'no constitutional significance'.[22] It also emerged that Howe might lose his grace-and-favour residence at Chevening to his young successor, John Major. According to the *Sun* on 26 July, he was reduced to nothing but a flat in the Old Kent Road. When Howe made his first Commons appearance in his new capacity, the Conservative benches erupted in cheering, which ought to have warned Thatcher to take care.

These events were against the background of changes in the Labour Party. The promise to pull Britain out of the EU had disappeared from party policy documents midway through the decade, and Labour was repositioning itself to be more pro EU than the Conservatives. John Smith, the shadow chancellor, had only one act of indiscipline on his long parliamentary record when, in 1972, he was one of the group of Labour MPs that had included Roy Jenkins and David Owen who broke the whip to vote in favour of Britain joining the EU, or Common Market as it was then called. His deputy, Gordon Brown, was also committed to ERM membership; so was Neil Kinnock, after being persuaded of the case for membership by his economic adviser, John Eatwell. When Eatwell and Kinnock's former press secretary, Patricia Hewitt, set up a new think tank, the Institute for Public Policy Research (IPPR), in July 1989, its first publication was a paper by the Goldman Sachs economist, Gavyn Davies, a future chairman of the BBC. He argued that sterling should join the ERM without delay. There was one important dissenter in the shadow cabinet – Bryan Gould, the shadow trade and industry secretary. He headed the committee in charge of revising the party's economic policy, which was presented to Labour's annual conference and formally adopted as party policy on 4 October 1989. It announced, baldly: 'We oppose moves towards a European Monetary Union' and that 'substantial changes would be required before the next Labour government could take sterling into the Exchange Rate Mechanism'.[23]

Within three weeks, what had been party policy, was party policy no more. John Smith and Gordon Brown went on a tour of three European capitals, which convinced them that the plans for a single currency were serious. They were in mid-air, between capitals, when they read an article written by Thatcher's adviser Alan Walters months earlier and reprinted in the *Financial Times* on 18 October, which described the EMS as 'half-baked', and they guessed how irritating that must be for Nigel Lawson. On 24 October, there was a Commons debate on the economy, called by Labour, which Smith used to announce casually that Labour was committed to joining the ERM under the right conditions. Challenged by Tory MPs to say when this had become party policy, Smith blithely acted as if it always had been.[24] Gould, who was out of the loop, had taken to the airwaves to defend what he thought was party policy, only to learn that party spin were quietly advising journalists that he had got it wrong. In November, he was shifted to the less sensitive job of shadow environment secretary and replaced by Gordon Brown, whose position as one of the half-dozen most influential figures in the party was thus publicly confirmed.

That was by the by, however. Smith's and Brown's immediate aim was to bait Lawson: 'I advise the Chancellor to make an early decision on the important question of whether he will jump or be pushed,'[25] said Smith. Later, Brown chimed in to assure Lawson that he was not paranoid because 'they really are out to get him'. Television cameras had just been introduced to the Commons for the first time and caught Lawson's scowl as Labour MPs jeered: 'Go on – smile!'

That was Tuesday. On Thursday, Lawson told the prime minister that it was impossible for them to work together while Alan Walters remained in place as her adviser, and he resigned. Interviewed the following day, Mrs Thatcher seemed unable to comprehend why he should have done such a thing. 'To me, the Chancellor's position was unassailable. I always support him,' [26] she said.

The more interesting question now, though, was whether or not Margaret Thatcher's position was 'unassailable'. Under Conservative Party rules, it was remarkably easy for anyone to challenge the incumbent leader. Only two nominations from fellow MPs were required, and their names were not made public. However, the opportunity came round only once a year, at the start of the new parliamentary term in November. A number of pro-EU Tory MPs thought that November 1989 provided an opportunity to remove Thatcher. The obvious challenger was Michael Heseltine, who had flounced out of the cabinet in 1986 over the Westland affair, a seemingly obscure row ostensibly about the future of a small firm that manufactured helicopters. The argument, which ended two cabinet careers, one permanently, was given edge because the dispute over Britain's future in Europe lay at its heart. Heseltine, who was then defence secretary, wanted the ailing Westland company to be taken over by a European consortium to ensure that Europe had the independent capacity to produce military helicopters. Thatcher preferred the bid from the US company, Sikorsky. After a titanic personality clash, Heseltine resigned. Leon Brittan, the trade secretary, also had to go, for authorizing the leak of a confidential document to undermine Heseltine. Ever since, Heseltine had been a formidable presence on the backbenches, with an undisguised ambition to be prime minister. But he was not interested in implicating himself in a bid to remove Thatcher unless he could be sure of success.

The conspirators then turned to the former cabinet minister, Ian Gilmour, but he also did not want to impale himself in a contest he was sure to lose. At this point, a little-noticed MP named Sir Anthony Meyer stepped forward. Meyer was an old Etonian, a former diplomat, and a man whose pro-Europeanism meant that he had never been considered for a government post. His decision to challenge Thatcher ended his parliamentary career, when his constituency party sacked him. It also prompted the tabloids to uncover his long affair with a black blues singer, which came as no surprise to his forgiving wife. Despite these handicaps, he drew 33 votes to Thatcher's 314. Though the figures looked decisive, George Younger, a former cabinet minister who had been part of Thatcher's campaign team, warned her that it was a sign of discontent within the party.[27]

The most sensible conclusion that Thatcher could have drawn from this warning, as it related to personnel management, was not to risk offending Sir Geoffrey Howe any further. He was the person most likely to follow Lawson out of the cabinet and was a much respected figure on the Conservative backbenches. In the early 1980s, he had done more than anyone, apart from Thatcher herself, to put Thatcherism into effect. By summer 1990, he was the only member of the original 1979 cabinet still there, again apart from Thatcher. Unfortunately, she could not resist humiliating him. During the Conservative Party conference, Patrick Nicholls, the transport minister in charge of lecturing the public on the dangers of drinking and driving, had been stopped by the police, drunk at the wheel, and had to resign. Mrs Thatcher was very distressed to learn that Nicholls would not receive redundancy to compensate him for having to live off an MP's salary instead of the higher pay and perks of a government minister, because the appropriate legislation had not yet been passed. She also discovered that the House of Lords had very little legislation to debate. All this she blamed on Geoffrey Howe, to whom she delivered a dressing down in front of the rest of the cabinet, one of whom described the scene later: 'It was as if she was hitting him round the head: boom, boom, boom. And he just sat there, soaking it all up.'[28]

As mentioned in Chapter 1, the most famous comment ever made about Howe was Denis Healey's observation that being attacked by him was like 'being savaged by a dead sheep'. Possibly, Thatcher calculated that the sheep had no bite. Besides, he seemed to have no further cause for complaint over the main issue that had divided them when, in October 1990, she allowed her new chancellor, John Major, and her new foreign secretary, Douglas Hurd, to persuade her to join the ERM – a decision that would bring catastrophe to the Conservative government two years later.

Thatcher spent the last weekend of October 1990 at an EU summit in Rome, where she clashed with European Commissioner Jacques Delors over his blueprint for EU integration. On her return, she delivered a report to the Commons, where Neil Kinnock accused her of setting the rest of Europe against her and dividing the Conservative Party. This set Thatcher off. Delors, she said, 'wanted the European Parliament to be the democratic body of the Community, he wanted the Commission to be the Executive and he wanted the Council of Ministers to be the Senate. No! No! No!'[29] Some minutes earlier, Kinnock had suggested that since there appeared to be an underhand campaign by her acolytes to denigrate Geoffrey Howe she should say something in his defence. She answered dismissively that Howe was 'too big a man' to need a 'little man' such as Kinnock to speak for him.[30] Howe listened to all this and decided that he could take no more. Two days later, on 1 November, he resigned.

That resignation was damaging enough for Thatcher in itself, but there was worse the next week. Howe was entitled by parliamentary convention to make a resignation statement, to which MPs had to listen in silence, without interrupting. He did so on 13 November, speaking in the usual sheepish mumble, so that Thatcher had to press her ear against the speaker on the back of her seat to hear him. The content belied the delivery. He delivered a long, articulate argument for better relations with Europe; he blamed the high rate of inflation, which would soon tip the UK into recession, on Thatcher's obstructiveness over the ERM; and ended with the devastating exhortation: 'The time has come for others to consider their own response to the tragic conflict of loyalties with which I have myself wrestled for perhaps too long.'[31]

This was in that brief period of the year when the rules allowed a leadership contest; Howe's words were a direct invitation to someone to have a go. That obvious someone was Michael Heseltine, who emerged from his Belgravia home the following morning to announce that he was a candidate. There followed one of the most frenetic weeks in recent parliamentary history as the corridors, tea rooms and lobbies became full to bursting with Conservative MPs plotting, taking sides and trying to find out what was going on. Having easily seen off the previous year's challenger by ignoring him, Thatcher seemed to think that the same tactic would work again. The commentator Alan Watkins wrote: 'It is difficult to know whether Margaret Thatcher and her advisers realized they had a fight on their hands. The answer is probably that they did realize this, but misjudged its seriousness.'[32] Another mystery is who, if anyone, actually ran her campaign. It was an inconvenient time for George Younger, who was busy as chairman of the Royal Bank of Scotland; other experienced whips refused to be implicated, and it seems that the job devolved to a minor player named Sir Peter Morrison, who grossly overestimated her support. She, meanwhile, thought that it would show her up in a good light if she was away from London, acting the world leader, while Heseltine was grubbing in the Commons, looking for votes. She was in Paris on 20 November, when news reached her that though she had beaten Heseltine 204-152, the margin was not enough, under the rules, to prevent a second ballot. She immediately bounced down the steps of the Paris embassy, pushed aside the BBC correspondent John Sergeant, who was broadcasting live, and announced that she would fight on.

The proclamation created serious problems for her cabinet ministers, who saw her authority slipping away and feared that unless a new candidate such as Hurd or Major entered the contest, Heseltine would win. That evening, when she was back in London, John Wakeham, the chief whip, shrewdly arranged for her senior ministers to see her one at a time in her office behind the Speaker's Chair. First in was Kenneth Clarke. 'His manner was robust in the brutalist style he has cultivated: the candid friend,'[33] Thatcher recalled. He promised her his vote if she went ahead, but advised her to pull out to avoid humiliation. That advice was repeated, in varying forms, by the majority of those who trooped in behind him. Others, meanwhile, led by Norman Tebbit and Michael Portillo, were organizing a campaign to persuade her to hang on. She thought about it overnight, and resigned in the morning, 22 November 1990. It had taken exactly three weeks from Geoffrey Howe's resignation, and eight days from his resignation speech, to bring her down.

The next week was taken up with choosing her successor in a contest between Heseltine, Hurd and Major. John Major was the youngest, least experienced and least impressive of the three. He had served for a few months as foreign secretary, during which he had put in a mediocre performance at a Commonwealth Summit; then had followed Lawson as chancellor, in which capacity his main achievement was to get the UK into the ERM. On the crucial day when Thatcher was deciding whether to run or not to run, he was shut away in his Huntingdon home recovering from an operation on his wisdom teeth. During the week's campaigning, he somehow gave the impression that he was the least pro-European of the three candidates and the one least likely to abolish the poll tax. Once elected, he gave Heseltine the job of abolishing the poll tax and proved to be more pro-EU than those who had voted for him realized. Shortly before his election, Mrs Thatcher told a private meeting of party staff who had gathered to bid her goodbye that she would be 'a very good back seat driver'[34] but it did not take her long to discover that her back-seat advice was neither sought nor wanted. All that was left was the long years of inactivity, nursing her sense of betrayal and thinking bitterly about 'the candid friend Ken Clarke, the candid minister Malcolm Rifkind, the candid loyal friends all with the same message.' What hurt most of all, she added, warming to the theme of personal betrayal, 'was that this was treachery – while I had been away, signing a treaty for my country, for the end of the cold war! It was treachery with a smile on its face. Perhaps that was the worst thing of all.'[35]

She was not alone in thinking that she had been betrayed. The brutal manner of her dispatch served its purpose in the short term in that it delivered another Conservative general election victory, but after that the memory lingered like a festering wound that took more than a decade to heal. Yet there was a sense in which she need not have felt betrayed. Early on, she had declared that her mission was to 'roll back the frontiers of socialism', which she had, and after her departure they stayed rolled back even during more than a dozen years of a Labour government. Thatcher had beaten the Left. If she had been less addicted to being in power, if all that she had cared about was whether or not her set of ideological values survived, she could have settled into a contented old age.

She was not defeated because of anything in which she positively believed, but because of something in which she did not believe, best encapsulated in her famous statement that 'there is no such thing as society'. Interviewed for a women's magazine in the euphoria after her third election victory, she decried what she saw as the modern self-indulgence of expecting the government, or society, to do what people could do for themselves:

> They are casting their problems on society and who is society? There is no such thing! There are individual men and women and there are families and no government can do anything except through people and people look to themselves first. It is our duty to look after ourselves and then also to help look after our neighbour and life is a reciprocal business.[36]

And in case she had not made the point clear, she repeated: 'There is no such thing as society. There is living tapestry of men and women and people and the beauty of that tapestry and the quality of our lives will depend upon how much each of us is prepared to take responsibility for ourselves.'

This vision that there was nothing between the nuclear family and the vagaries of the capitalist system may have held no terrors for a woman brought up in conditions of economic security and who had married into money, but for most people, it was a frightening prospect. She was too blunt in telling people that in order to maximize economic efficiency, it was necessary to destroy many of the social ties that kept people in interdependency. After ten years of upheaval and bewildering change, the British decided that they would rather there was such a thing as society, and turned to less driven, more conciliatory leaders who did not alarm them with that kind of talk.

Epilogue

One of the highest grossing Hollywood films of the 1980s was *Back to the Future*, featuring the mad scientist Doc Brown and his time-travelling DeLorean car. Had someone obtained this marvellous machine in Britain in 1980 and set the controls for 1990, they would have emerged in a land profoundly different from the one they left behind, though it might on superficial examination have seemed to be much the same. The sights would be reasonably similar. Most of the landmarks, traffic jams, crowds, shopping centres and run-down suburbs were much as before, unless the visitor happened to emerge in one of the regenerated areas where relics of an industrial past had been torn down and replaced with smart new buildings, such as on the south bank of the Thames around Tower Bridge, in the old Liverpool docklands or on the north bank of the Tyne in Newcastle. They would learn that the Queen was still on the throne, the Conservatives still running the government, and they might even hear the familiar word 'recession' crop up in conversation. The British economy began and ended the decade in recession.

What had changed beyond recognition was not the physical landscape but the material circumstances in which people lived and the way they viewed the world. Money, society and politics had changed their meaning. It was a wealthier, more mobile society – except for those who were shut out of the world of work, whose numbers were higher than in 1980. The old saying 'never a borrower or a lender be' had fallen into disuse. It was considered downright perverse not to borrow from the banks or the building societies, who were free and willing to lend with an abandon that would have been out of the question ten years earlier. People did not need to go to the bank on Friday to ensure they had enough cash for the weekend. Cash was obtainable night and day in any reasonably sized town, and anyway most businesses accepted credit cards. By the end of 1989, Britain's consumers owed a grand total of £304 billion, of which about £255 billion was tied up in mortgages and about £7.6 billion was owed on credit cards and store cards.[1] Ten years earlier, total debt on everything except first mortgages and bank overdrafts came to about £5 billion; credit card debt was probably only about £750 million.[2]

As the 1990s dawned, people were more aware of their rights as citizens and consumers, and less deferential of authority, but they were less likely to be involved in any kind of political activity. They were more mobile, particularly if they were young professionals. The idea of staying with one employer throughout a person's working life, paying compulsorily into the firm's pension fund, to be presented with a gold watch and chain on retirement, was as dated as the gramophone. Ambitious people switched jobs or switched from employment to self-employment and back, taking with them their newly acquired portable pensions. The proportion of the nation's income derived from self-employment had doubled during the 1980s.[3] Overall, income from wages and salaries accounted for only 62 per cent of household income in 1990, compared with about 75 per cent in 1968. For two sections of the population, money earned through work of any kind was an insignificant portion of their income: those at the bottom, who lived off social security, and those at the top, where their real money came from investments. That was one symptom of the glaring disparity in wealth that was a legacy of the Thatcher years. Another was the continuing 'north-south divide'. In 1990, the average family in south-east England spent £251 a week; whereas the equivalent for Yorkshire and Humberside was £189.

The great state-run monopolies that had brought gas, electricity and water to the home in 1980 had either gone, or were on the way out, replaced by private companies on the lookout for new businesses into which they could diversify. The ordinary consumer may not have noticed the difference this made to the supply of the basic utilities, but they certainly felt the effect of the privatization of British Telecom. No one needed to wait for a telephone to be installed – telephones could be bought in shops (there was even a range of colours and designs to suit individual taste), and there was no longer the same exasperating delay in getting connected to the network. In 1979, 33 per cent of pensioners living alone had a telephone; the 1990 figure was 75 per cent. Only the very poor or the mildly eccentric did not have a telephone in the home.

Home computers, CD players and colour televisions were now too common to be status symbols. Vinyl records would soon disappear from the shops, except as collectors' items, as CDs took over. The next big boom forecast by the Economist Intelligence Unit in November 1990 was in the sale of 'white goods' – devices for the kitchen, including automatic dishwashers and microwaves. You could impress visitors to your home by showing them your state-of-the-art microwave, but if you really wanted the neighbours to know that you had money to spend you invested in a satellite dish. Other status symbols included car telephones, or fax machines in the home, while at work there were people who delighted in strutting about holding huge, brick-like mobile telephones.[4]

There were other technologies at the development stage that had not yet made their entry into everyday life. In November 1990, the same month that saw Margaret Thatcher brought down, it was reported that Japan's Nippon Telegraph and Telephone company was developing a mobile phone that would work anywhere, weigh no more than about four ounces, be small enough to fit in a pocket, cost less than £100 and be capable of running for a month on a rechargeable battery.[5] A more significant but less publicized development took place at the European Organization for Nuclear Research (CERN), in Switzerland, where a British scientist, Timothy Berners-Lee, wrote a proposal in 1989 to create a means by which scientists across the world could exchange information by computer. At that time, the fashion in physics was to give new inventions names drawn from classical mythology, but Berners-Lee insisted, rather prosaically, that he would call his invention the World Wide Web. The first successful communication between a server and an HTTP client took place at CERN on 25 December 1990.

However, the most significant transformation had nothing to do with new inventions. It was the change in the political and social landscape. Anyone growing up in 1980 was entering a dangerously divided world, the long-term future of which seemed uncertain. The words 'capitalist' and 'capitalism' cropped up in conversation, even among people who were only remotely interested in politics, because it was apparent to anyone that the capitalist system was not the only possible way of ordering human affairs. In 1980, the journalist and future Labour MP Chris Mullin began work on a novel entitled *A Very British Coup*, which imagined a left-wing Labour prime minister coming to power on the back of a series of corruption scandals, and having his plans to take Britain down the parliamentary road to socialism halted by a politely organized Whitehall coup that forced him to resign. Mullin claimed at the time of the book's publication in 1982: 'Britain is ripe for destabilisation. It would not be necessary for the United States government to resort to military coups, invasions, assassinations or any of the other strong arm stuff tried out on its Third World clients. There is a wide range of other options.'[6] Instead of laughing at him for peddling fantasies, Mullin's real-life protagonists paid him the compliment of denouncing his novel as subversive propaganda, because there still appeared to be an outside possibility that Mullin's friend, Tony Benn, might be the next prime minister. One critic pronounced: 'Presumably this cautionary tale is meant to further the cause of the Left in British politics by exposing the dastardly nature of its opponents. In fact, the insight it provides may ensure that the reader votes Conservative, or Social Democrat, for the rest of the century.'[7]

In 1988, the novel was stylishly adapted for television by Alan Plater; the only complaint heard was that it could be construed as a libellous depiction of the Labour Party, whose leaders were so obviously not radical socialists, like Mullin's characters. The whole story was 'littered with implausibilities', Hugo Young declared magisterially in the *Guardian*. He conceded that 'in 1981, when it was written . . . a tremor of belief rumbled round', but added: 'Seven years on, it doesn't look quite like that any more'.[8] It was one of many signs that the contest was over; Britain's political future was settled. People no longer talked about capitalism or its alternatives, because they expected the capitalist system to last forever.

Class also seemed to disappear as a subject of political or sociological discussion. The days were gone when any politician seriously seeking election would promise to defend the interests of one social class to the exclusion of others. The only polite way to talk about class at all was to promise to ignore or abolish it. During the leadership contest that followed Margaret Thatcher's downfall, John Major made a much acclaimed and widely quoted promise that he would bring about 'changes to produce across the whole of this country a genuinely classless society'.[9] The trade unions, which for so long had functioned as the most effective promoter of working-class economic interests and social aspirations, were in chronic decline, their power broken not just by the succession of employment laws passed by the Thatcher government and the set-piece confrontations with the miners and print unions, but also by the changing pattern of work and property ownership. People in what had been working-class occupations now owned cars and televisions and had mortgages on their properties. The typical union member was increasingly likely to be an office worker, employed by the state, rather than a factory worker with a capitalist boss. Membership of TUC-affiliated unions fell by nearly a third, from just under 12.2m in 1980 to 8.4m in 1990.[10] Strikes had become rare; mass pickets unheard of – a thing of the past.

The largest working-class crowds to trouble the police, away from football matches, were the followers of a new craze, acid-house music, which attracted hundreds or even thousands of people to what became known as 'rave' parties. The organizers quickly ran out of venues where they could hold these events legally, so took to hiring out-of-the-way sites such as warehouses and keeping the venue secret until the last minute, in the hope that the party would be well under way before the police located it. The first rave parties were held on the outskirts of London, near the newly opened M25, but soon spread. In July 1989, there was chaos on the M4 after a landowner near Swindon suddenly withdrew permission for his land to be used, presumably after being spoken to by the police. One would-be participant recorded:

> We had paid £16 each in London record stores for tickets with no address, just a telephone number. From 8.30 p.m., a recorded voice directed us to Membury service station on the M4: 'You will receive further instructions there'. The police were faster. As we arrived they closed the service station. Most people never reached the hangar nearby. At the airfield, we found police Land Rovers standing guard, lights off, beside locked hamburger vans. Other party-goers, stretching miles back, halted in mid-motorway. Horns blasted in frustration. At 3 a.m. the Peugeot received instruction and we swarmed to Chievely services, eighteen miles away. 'Keep calling this number,' the voice said. The convoy circled the forecourts but, minutes later, the police caught up. By 4 a.m. most people were demoralised.[11]

Six months later, the authorities were alerted to a plan to hold a New Year's Eve rave party in a warehouse in Rugby, which was expected to draw a crowd of 10,000. Warwickshire police brought in officers from all over the county and set up a roadblock on Junction 1 of the M6, but 200 revellers were there ahead of them. In the resulting scuffles, a police van and two cars were overturned, and five people were arrested.[12] In April and May 1990, thousands flocked to warehouse parties in Blackburn every Saturday night. When the police located the venues, the organizers moved to Cheshire, West Yorkshire and Barrow-in-Furness in Cumbria. In June, 231 people were arrested at an illegal party in Wakefield. In July, it was reported that a regular party held on waste-ground in Birkenhead was attracting between 2,000 and 3,000 people most Saturdays.[13] In times past, concerts organized in defiance of the authorities were usually associated loosely with left-wing politics. Rave parties were a form of rebellion without any obvious ideological clothing, though at least some of the organizers followed the libertarianism associated with the Federation of Conservative Students. The first-known organizer was a public schoolboy named Tony Colston-Hayter; one of his helpers was Paul Staines, another public schoolboy who achieved prominence, years later, as the right-wing blogger, Guido Fawkes.[14] Those parties were a harbinger of a period when it seemed that the only prevailing ideology was a belief that people have a right to consume what they want to consume.

A character in Jonathan Coe's *The House of Sleep* says:

> Everybody gets it wrong about the 1980s, don't they? They think it was all about money, and maybe it was, for some people, but for the people I used to hang about with, the students and people like that, there was a different set of values, just as severe, just as intolerant, really. We were so obsessed with politics all the time.[15]

It would not be at all contradictory to say that the decade was 'about' money and 'about' left-wing politics, since much of it was taken up with a titanic struggle between those two forces; but, really, Coe's character is describing the first half of the decades. There is little evidence of many students being 'obsessed with politics' after the miners' defeat. Though the mass pickets outside Wapping and the fight against the poll tax would demonstrate that the British had not lost the taste for protest, the protests had become conservative. People were taking to the streets to prevent change and put some sort of brake on the triumphal advance of money, rather than in the hope of creating a brave new world.

One symptom of changed times was that it became progressively harder to distinguish the main political parties one from another. Anybody who followed the news even cursorily in 1980 knew what distinguished Labour from the Conservatives. By 1990, it took a specialist to tell you where Conservative and Labour policies diverged. Voting became less a matter of deciding where you stood on the great issues of the time, and more of a consumer choice between personalities. Consequently, the character or behaviour of politicians started to seem more important than the causes they championed. It is noteworthy that during the 1980s there was only one headline-grabbing political sex scandal, when Cecil Parkinson had the misfortune to have his extra-marital activity exposed in the week of a Conservative annual conference. Otherwise, the sexual and financial peccadilloes of MPs was barely reported – not because they were all behaving themselves, but because such things did not seem important against the background of huge events like the miners' strike or the Falklands War. But a time was coming when sex and money were the surest ways to get a politician into the news. After the great upheavals of the 1980s, there were no more big political causes to be fought. 'Nowadays, there is a clear tendency to proclaim the death of all ideologies in the name of the victory of capitalism,' the novelist Carlos Fuentes lamented, writing in the *Guardian* in the last week of 1990.[16]

However, to proclaim that history has ended, that all ideologies have been routed by the final victory of liberal capitalism is itself ideological. It was to be the prevailing ideology of the 1990s. British history did not end during the 1980s, but it did slow down, because the events of that turbulent decade had settled the way that Britons would be ruled and the way they thought about the world for at least the next quarter of a century.

Notes

Introduction

1. According to Frank Field, Labour MP for Birkenhead, a visitor to a Merseyside Jobcentre would see 'jobs advertised at £1.20 an hour, £1 an hour, £57.25 a week', while the best paid ones would offer 'princely sums of £70 and £91 a week'. *Hansard*, 17 July 1985, col. 330.
2. *People*, 14 July 1985.
3. Bob Geldof, with Paul Vallely, *Is That It?*, Macmillan, 1986, p. 301.
4. Brenda Polan, *Guardian*, 3 October 1985.
5. Bob Geldof, *Is That It?*, p. 300.
6. David Pallister, 'The arms deal they called the dove: how Britain grasped the biggest prize', *Guardian*, 15 December 2006.
7. *Financial Times*, 17 November 1986.
8. By far the best primary source for any words attributed to Margaret Thatcher is the comprehensive archive held at Churchill College, Cambridge, almost all of which is available on the website of the Margaret Thatcher Foundation. The telegram from Milton Friedman, dated 5 May 1979, and her reply, dated 11 May, was included in a collection released on 30 January 2010.
9. During an interview with Douglas Keay, 'AIDS, education and the year 2000!', *Woman's Own*, 31 October 1987.
10. Handwritten draft by Margaret Thatcher for a speech to be delivered. This was also among the batch of documents released on 30 January 2010.
11. John Hills et al., *An Anatomy of Economic Inequality in the UK – Report of the National Equality Panel*, Government Equalities Office, London, 2010, p. 41, p. 27.

12. *The Times*, 14 October 1981.
13. Francis Fukuyama's essay 'The End of History?' first appeared in the magazine *The National Interest* in 1989.
14. She used this expression in a valedictory interview with ITN, broadcast 28 June 1991.

CHAPTER 1

1. Kenneth Williams, *The Kenneth Williams Diaries*, edited by Russell Davies, HarperCollins, London, 1993, p. 581.
2. Lee Hall 'Adaptation', from the programme notes to *Billy Elliott; The Musical*, Victoria Palace Theatre, London, 2005.
3. Tony Benn, *Conflicts of Interest: Diaries 1977–80*, Arrow, London, 1990, p. 494.
4. Sir Nicholas Henderson, 'Britain's Decline; its causes and consequences', *Economist*, 2 June 1979.
5. Obituary, Sir Nicholas Henderson, *Daily Telegraph*, 20 March 2009.
6. Nicholas Henderson, *Mandarin, The Diaries of an Ambassador 1969–1982*, Weidenfeld and Nicolson, London, 1994, p. 269.
7. Jim O'Donoghue, Carol McDonnell and Martin Placek, *Consumer Price Inflation 1947–2004*, Office for National Statistics, London, 2006, p. 41.
8. *The Times*, 16 April 1980.
9. *The Times*, 9 July 1980.
10. *Hansard*, 9 March 1970, col. 892.
11. *Flight International*, 1 March 1980.
12. Factsheet M5, 'Member's pay, pensions and allowances', House of Commons Information Office, London, May 2009.
13. Factsheet M6, 'Ministerial Salaries', House of Commons Information Office, London, May 2009.
14. Obituary, Lady Barnett, *The Times*, 21 October 1980.
15. Kenneth Williams, p. 619.
16. *The Times*, 21 October 1980.
17. Richard Littlejohn, *Daily Mail*, 24 November 2006, quoted in Mark Garnett, *From Anger to Apathy – The British Experience since 1975*, Jonathan Cape, London, 2007, p. 92.
18. *Together We Can Win, the Story of Two NUPE Branches Involved in the Council and Hospital Workers Pay Dispute, Winter 1978/9*, National Union of Public Employees, Northern Division, 1979, p. 26.
19. MacGregor was the most expensive public servant the British government had ever hired. His basic pay was £48,000 a year, and in addition, Lazard Frères was to receive a fee of £675,000 if MacGregor proved to be good at the job, with the

possibility of an extra £1,150,000 if he could make British Steel profitable, a large chunk of which would go direct to MacGregor, as a partner in the bank. When Sir Keith Joseph revealed the figures in the Commons his words were drowned in derisive laughter, combined, no doubt, with a touch of envy, given that he was being paid more than the prime minister, even without the bonus.

20. *The Times*, 2 November 1981.
21. *The Times*, 5 June 1980.
22. Sir Keith Joseph, speech at the Grand Hotel, Birmingham, 19 October 1974. The full text of the speech is available on the website of the Margaret Thatcher Foundation, at www.margaretthatcher.org.
23. I heard her make this boast during a speech at a Conservative rally in Slough, shortly before the general election of February 1974.
24. *Daily Express*, 3 February 1975.
25. Gordon Greig, the political editor of the *Daily Mail*, was even instructed by English to ring Thatcher at home on a Sunday, on the eve of the declaration of her candidature, to ask her how anyone with a voice like breaking glass could ever lead the Conservative Party. Years later, he would regale younger journalists (such as me) with a vivid description of the noise that came down the telephone in reply.
26. Margaret Thatcher, *The Downing Street Years*, HarperCollins, London, 1993, p. 26.
27. Edward Heath, *The Course of My Life: My Autobiography*, Hodder & Stoughton, London, 1988, pp. 573–4.
28. Information from Heath's long-serving adviser, Michael McManus, reveals that that day Heath had been complaining about the chairs on which they were expected to sit. However, when he and Lady Thatcher finally met backstage, and she remarked, 'Hello Ted, have you seen those awful chairs?', he replied, 'Can't see what is wrong with them.'
29. Margaret Thatcher, *The Downing Street Years*, p. 14
30. Nigel Lawson, *The View from No. 11: Memoirs of a Tory Radical*, Bantam, London, 1992, p. 64.
31. *Observer*, 26 September 1982, quoted in Robert Leach, *Political Ideology in Britain*, Palgrave Macmillan, London, 2002, p. 112.
32. Maurice Cowling, *Conservative Essays*, Cassell, London, 1978, p. 9.
33. Margaret Thatcher, *The Downing Street Years*, p. 11.
34. John Campbell, *Margaret Thatcher – Volume Two: The Iron Lady*, Jonathan Cape, London, 2003, pp. 251–2.
35. *Observer*, 15 January 1984.
36. The text of the draft statement is in the Cabinet Offices. It is undated, but is likely to have been drafted in February 1984.
37. *Hansard*, 29 February 1984, col. 218W.
38. Letter to Peter Shore MP, 12 April 1984. Full text at www.margaretthatcher.org.

39. Neil Hamilton MP 'Getting the Joke', in Iain Dale (ed.), *Margaret Thatcher: A Tribute in Words and Pictures*, Daily Telegraph/Weidenfeld & Nicholson, London, 2005, p. 216.
40. My first face-to-face encounter with her came as I was hurrying along a narrow corridor behind the Speaker's chair when Prime Minister's Questions had just ended. Ahead of me, that diminutive, familiar figure was coming in the opposite direction, but for a moment I was too startled to stand aside. With a pleasant enough smile on her face, she raised a finger and moved it from side to side, like a windscreen wiper, telling me that I had a choice of flattening myself against the wall to my left or right, so long as I made way for her. It was the gesture of someone accustomed to being obeyed.
41. On one of her trips abroad, late in her premiership, I was among a small group of journalists permitted to go to the front of the aircraft, where she was holding court. It was rather like flirting with someone's grandmother. The party included Gordon Greig, the veteran political editor of the *Daily Mail,* whom she knew well. He made a teasing remark about her relations with Sir Geoffrey Howe, which were then at breaking point, whereupon she poked his lapel and told him: 'You must rearrange your ideas, Gordon.' This flirty, easily amused side of her personality was never displayed in public.
42. *Hansard*, 14 June 1978, col. 1027.
43. Alan Clark, *Diaries – Into Politics*, Weidenfeld & Nicolson, London, 2000, p. 147.
44. Kingsley Amis, *Memoirs*, Vintage, London, 1991, pp. 315–9.
45. Woodrow Wyatt, *The Journals of Woodrow Wyatt, Volume One*, edited by Sarah Curtis, Pan, London, 1998, p. 206.
46. Hugo Young, *One of Us: A Biography of Margaret Thatcher*, Pan, London, 1990, p. 383.
47. *Hansard*, 25 January 1985.
48. John Campbell, *Edward Heath: A Biography*, Jonathan Cape, London, 1993, p. 711.
49. Tony Benn, *Against the Tide; Diaries 1973–76*, Arrow, London, 1990, p. 616.
50. *The Times*, 29 September 1976.
51. Quoted in Jim Prior, *A Balance of Power*, Hamish Hamilton, London, 1986, p. 167.
52. Ian Gilmour, *Dancing with Dogma: Britain Under Thatcherism*, Simon & Schuster, London, 1992, pp. 22–3.
53. *Daily Mail*, 26 April 1979.
54. Margaret Thatcher, speaking at a general election press conference, 23 April 1979. BBC Sound Archive. Full text at www.margaretthatcher.org.
55. Speech to Conservative rally at Darlington, 23 April 1979.
56. *Guardian*, 4 January 1981. See also, Phillip Knightley, *The Rise and and Fall of the House of Vestey*, Time Warner, London, 1993.
57. Elizabeth Bailey, 'The Vestey Affair', *New York Times*, 2 November 1980.

58. Ian Gilmour, *Dancing with Dogma*, p. 6.
59. Jim Prior, *A Balance of Power*, pp. 119–20.
60. Speech to the Conservative Party conference, 10 October 1980. Full text at www.margaretthatcher.org.
61. Hugo Young, *One of Us*, p. 215.
62. *The Times*, 9 October 1981.
63. Andy McSmith, *Kenneth Clarke: A Political Biography*, Verso, London, 1994, p. 72.
64. *Hansard*, 26 November 2008, col. 768.
65. Nigel Lawson, *The View from No. 11*, p. 686.

CHAPTER 2

1. Lawrence Byford, HM Inspector of Constabulary, 'The Yorkshire Ripper Case – Review of the Investigation of the Case, pp. 95–6. This report was presented to the Home Office in December 1981, but was never published. Since 2006, however, it has been possible to access on the Home Office website at www.homeoffice.gov.uk.
2. Sheila Rowbotham, Lynne Segal and Hilary Wainwright, *Beyond the Fragments – Feminism and the Making of Socialism*, Merlin, London, 1979, p. 41.
3. Rosalind Carne, 'Feminist theatre divides to rule', *Financial Times*, 4 January 1982.
4. Quoted in Rosemary Betterton (ed.), *Looking On, Images of Femininity in the Visual Arts and Media*, Pandora, London, 1987, p. 153.
5. Bertolt Brecht, *Threepenny Novel*, translated by Desmond I. Vesey, Penguin, London, 1961, p. 115.
6. Brian Masters, *Killing for Company: The Case of Dennis Nilsen*, Coronet, London, 1986, pp. 14–15.
7. Lawrence Byford, 'The Yorkshire Ripper Case', p. 13.
8. Michael Bilton, *Wicked Beyond Belief: The Hunt for the Yorkshire Ripper*, HarperCollins, London, 2003, p. 32.
9. Lawrence Byford, 'The Yorkshire Ripper Case', pp. 9–11.
10. *The Times*, 3 December 1980.
11. Associated Press, 3 December 1980.
12. Margaret Thatcher, 'Speech to Conservative Women's Conference', 25 May 1988. Full text at www.margaretthatcher.org.
13. Hugo Young, *One of Us: A Biography of Margaret Thatcher*, Pan, London, 1990, p. 237.
14. Letter from Clive Whitemore, Principal Private Secretary, 10 Downing Street, to John Halliday, Principal Private Secretary, Home Office, 25 November 1980.

15. Letter from L.E. Emmentt to the Chief Constable, West Yorkshire Police, December 1980. John Humble, from Sunderland, was identified by DNA evidence in 2005 as the hoaxer and sentenced to eight years for perverting the course of justice.
16. Letter from S.S. Kind to Dr Alan Curry, Forensic Science Service, 6 January 1981.
17. *Yorkshire Post*, 27 December 2007.
18. Richard McCann, *Just a Boy: The Story of a Stolen Childhood*, Ebury Press, London, 2003.
19. Richard McCann, interviewed by Michael Buerk, *The Choice,* BBC Radio 4, 2 September 2008.
20. International Prostitutes Collective, *Some Mother's Daughter: The Hidden Movement of Prostitutes Against Violence*, Crossroads Books, London, 1999, pp. 49–51.
21. *The Times*, 19 January 1982.
22. *Daily Mail*, 19 January 1982.
23. *Hansard*, 21 January 1981, col. 428.
24. *Hansard*, 21 January 1981, col. 426.
25. Simon Calder, *Hitch-Hikers' Manual: Britain*, Vacation Work, Oxford, 1979.
26. *The Times*, 6 January 1982.
27. United Press International, 11 December 1982; see also Jennifer Temkin, *Rape and the Legal Process*, Sweet and Maxwell, London, p. 10.
28. *Guardian*, 13 March 1986.
29. Her story can be accessed on the BBC website at www.bbc.co.uk/stoke/insidelives/2004/06/jill_saward.shtml.
30. *Guardian*, 4 February 1987.
31. *Hansard*, 24 January 1986, col. 126.
32. Clare Short, *Dear Clare . . . this is what Women Feel about Page 3*, Letters edited and selected by Kiri Tunks and Diane Hutchinson, Hutchinson Radius, London, 1991.
33. *Hansard*, 12 March 1986, col. 938.
34. Peter Chippindale and Chris Horrie, *Stick it up Your Punter – The rise and fall of the Sun*, Mandarin, London, 1992, p. 201.
35. Andy McSmith, *Faces of Labour, The Inside Story*, Verso, London, 1997, pp. 224–5.
36. Helena Kennedy and Jennifer Nadel, *Sara Thornton, the Story of a Woman who Killed*, Gollancz, London, 1993.
37. Jennifer Temkin, *Rape and the Legal Process*, p. 1.
38. *Independent*, 11 April 1990.

CHAPTER 3

1. Margaret Thatcher, *The Downing Street Years*, HarperCollins, London, 1993, pp. 239–48.
2. *The Times*, 25 January 1980.
3. *The Times*, 30 January 1980.
4. *The Times*, 7 February 1980.
5. *The Times*, 14 February 1980.
6. John Minnion and Philip Bolsover (eds), *The CND Story: The First 25 Years of CND in the Words of People Involved*, Allison & Busby, London, 1983, p. 35.
7. E.P. Thompson, *Protest and Survive*, Penguin, London, 1980, pp. 18–19.
8. *You Can't Kill the Spirit: Yorkshire Women Go to Greenham*, Bretton Women's Book Fund, Wakefield, 1983, quoted in Kate Hudson, *CND, Now More Than Ever*, Vision, London, 2005, p. 138.
9. *Financial Times*, 13 November 1985.
10. Walter Patterson, 'Futures: A dramatic change in attitudes', *Guardian*, 13 December 1985.
11. 'I regret nothing, says Stasi spy', BBC, 20 September 1999, at http://news.bbc.co.uk/1/hi/special_report/1999/09/99/britain_betrayed/451366.stm.
12. *Hansard*, 2 November 1998, col. 628.
13. *Hansard*, 17 January 1989, col. 299.
14. *The Times*, 9 March 1985.
15. Stella Rimington, *Open Secret – The Autobiography of the Former Director-General of MI5*, Arrow, London, 2002, p. 176.
16. In 1978, Martin Linton, a journalist on *Labour Weekly*, surveyed constituency parties and estimated that the true membership figure was 284,000. The exercise was repeated in 1981 by Harold Frayman, another *Labour Weekly* journalist, who arrived at a figure of 300,250. Patrick Seyd, *The Rise and Fall of the Labour Left*, Macmillan, Basingstoke, 1987, p. 40.
17. John Silkin, *Changing Battlefields: The Challenge to the Labour Party*, Hamish Hamilton, London, 1982, p. 35.
18. Interview with Dr David Hubbard, 'The Press Gang', *World in Action*, Granada TV, 5 March 1984.
19. David Owen, *Time to Declare*, Michael Joseph, London, 1991, p. 418.
20. On Jim Murray, see Andy McSmith, 'The Shoppie on the Scotswood Road', in *Faces of Labour, The Inside Story*, Verso, London, 1997, pp. 189–212. David Owen, *Time to Declare*, p. 477.
22. Statement issued by Shirley Williams, Bill Rodgers, David Owen and Roy Jenkins to the Press Association, 25 January 1981. The full text can be found at www.liberalhistory.org.uk/uploads/LimehouseDeclaration.pdf.
23. *Hansard*, 26 March 1981, col. 1074.

24. *The Times*, 19 September 1981.
25. David Owen, *Time to Declare*, p. 520.
26. Sadly, even Gerald Kaufman cannot recall where or when he first made this aphorism, but there is no dispute that he was its author. He says that he wishes he had taken out a copyright on it, because it has been quoted so often that it could have made him rich.
27. Original copies of the manifesto 'New Hope for Britain' (Labour Party, 1982) are now difficult to obtain. The full text was reproduced in *The Times Guide to the 1983 Election*, *The Times*, London, 1983, pp. 304–33, and is available on the internet at http://labour-party.org.uk/manifestos/1983/1983-labour-manifesto.shtml.
28. John Golding, *Hammer of the Left, Defeating Tony Benn, Eric Heffer and Militant in the Battle for the Labour Party*, Politico's, London, 2003, p. 289.
29. Ian McAllister and Richard Rose, *The Nationwide Competition for Votes: The 1983 British Election*, Frances Pinter, London, 1984, p. 5.
30. *The Times*, 26 May 1983.
31. David Owen, *Time to Declare*, p. 577.
32. *The Times*, 27 May 1983.

CHAPTER 4

1. Sally Bedell Smith, *Diana: The Life of a Troubled Princess*, Aurum Press, London, p. 83.
2. Quoted in Tina Brown, *The Diana Chronicles*, Century, London, 2007, p. 64.
3. Nigel Dempster, *Daily Mail*, 19 May 1993.
4. *The Times*, 25 February 1981.
5. Tim Clayton and Phil Craig, *Diana: Story of a Princess*, Atria, London, p. 62.
6. Andrew Morton, *Diana, Her True Story – In Her Own Words*, Chivers Press, Bath, 1998, pp. 37–8.
7. Tina Brown, *The Diana Chronicles*, p. 111.
8. Sarah Bradford, *Diana*, Viking, London, 2006, p. 114.
9. Andrew Morton, *Diana, Her True Story – In Her Own Words*, p. 31.
10. Michael Shea, *A View from the Sidelines*, Sutton, Stroud, 2003, pp. 121–2.
11. Andrew Morton, *Diana, Her True Story – In Her Own Words*, p. 42.
12. Tina Brown, *The Diana Chronicles*, p. 148.
13. Andrew Morton, *Diana, Her True Story – In Her Own Words*, pp. 53–4.
14. Andrew Morton, *Diana – Her True Story*, BCA, Swindon, 1992, pp. 73–4.
15. *The Times*, 30 July 1981.
16. Andrew Morton, *Diana: Her True Story – In Her Own Words*, p. 43.
17. Harold Evans, *Good Times, Bad Times*, Atheneum, London, 1984, p. 316.

18. For this account of the state of the music industry in the early 1980s, I have drawn heavily on Simon Garfield, *Expensive Habits: The Dark Side of the Music Industry*, Faber and Faber, London, 1986.
19. Steve Malins, *Duran Duran Notorious: The Unauthorised Biography*, Sevenoaks, London, 2005, p. 10.
20. James Maw, *The Official Adam Ant Story*, Futura, London, 1981, pp. 118–9.
21. Peter York and Charles Jennings, *Peter York's Eighties*, BBC Books, London, 1995, p. 36.
22. Midge Ure, *If I Was . . ., the Autobiography*, Virgin, 2004, p. 59, p. 57.
23. Boy George with Spencer Bright, *Take It Like a Man: the Autobiography of Boy George*, Pan, 1995, pp. 56, 138.
24. Robert Elms, *The Way We Wore: A Life in Threads*, Picador, London, 2005, p. 197.
25. Martin Kemp, *True – The Autobiography of Martin Kemp*, Orion, London, 2000, p. 54.
26. Robert Elms, *The Way We Wore*, p. 197.
27. Steve Malins, *Duran Duran Notorious*, p. 16.
28. Boy George, *Take It Like a Man*, p. 212.
29. Andrea Ashworth, 'Once More With Feeling', *Observer*, 20 March 2005.
30. Simon Garfield, *Expensive Habits*, p. 13.
31. *Daily Mirror*, 21 July 1983.
32. *Daily Mirror*, 16 April 1985.
33. Interview on *TV-am*, 17 April 1985.
34. Woodrow Wyatt, *The Journals of Woodrow Wyatt, Volume One*, edited by Sarah Curtis, Pan, London, 1998, p. 38.

CHAPTER 5

1. *The Times*, 8 October 1980.
2. Quoted in Andrew Roth and Byron Criddle, *Parliamentary Profiles 1997–2002 A–D*, Parliamentary Profile Services, London, 1998, p. 157.
3. 'Note for the Record: Vietnamese Refugees', 9 July 1979, NA Prem 19/130.
4. TV interview for *World in Action*, 27 January 1978. Full text at www.margaretthatcher.org/speeches/displaydocument.asp?docid=103485.
5. Lord Scarman, *The Scarman Report: the Brixton Disorders 10–12 April 1981*, Penguin, Harmondsworth, 1983, p. 27.
6. 'Policing Britain's Police', *Economist*, 8 May 1982.
7. Lord Scarman, *The Scarman Report*, pp. 83–4.
8. *Final Report of the Working Party into Community/Police Relations in Lambeth*, Public Relations Division, London Borough of Lambeth, Brixton, January 1981, pp. 2–7.

9. BBC News, 14 May 2001.
10. *Guardian*, 15 May 1981.
11. *Evening Standard*, 25 May 2004.
12. 'Violence as West Indians march in Protest', *The Times*, 3 March 1981; *Sun*, 3 March 1981; *Daily Express*, 3 March 1981; 'Why black unrest brings out the banner headlines', *The Times*, 4 March 1981.
13. Sukhdev Sandhu, *London Calling: How Black and Asian Writers Imagined a City*, HarperCollins, London, 2003, p. 279.
14. Lord Scarman, *The Scarman Report*, p. 95.
15. An eyewitness account by the 'We Want to Riot, Not to Work Collective' (1982), reproduced at www.urban75.org/brixton/history/riot.html.
16. Ibid.
17. Lord Scarman, *The Scarman Report*, p. 75, p. 65.
18. William Whitelaw, *The Whitelaw Memoirs*, Headline, London, 1989, p. 243.
19. Lord Scarman, *The Scarman Report*, p. 71.
20. *The Times*, 6 July 1981.
21. William Whitelaw, *The Whitelaw Memoirs*, pp. 246–7. Whitelaw was not always so calm. A year later, when a harmless vagrant named Michael Fagan broke into Buckingham Palace and found his way to the queen's bedroom, where he talked quietly to her until police arrived, Whitelaw experienced such 'utter shame and misery' that he wanted to resign. Mrs Thatcher had to talk him out of it.
22. *Hansard*, 16 July 1981, written answers col. 430.
23. *Hansard*, 6 July 1981, col. 24.
24. Margaret Thatcher, *The Downing Street Years*, HarperCollins, London, 1993, p. 145.
25. *The Times*, 16 October 1981.
26. Michael Heseltine, *Life in the Jungle, My Autobiography*, Hodder & Stoughton, London, 2000, p. 216.
27. *Financial Times*, 1 May 1986.
28. *ITN News at 10*, 30 September 1985; *Guardian*, 1 October 1985.
29. *Guardian*, 8 October 1985.
30. *The Times*, 9 October 1985; *Guardian*, 9 October 1985.
31. David Rose, 'They Created Winston Silcott, the Beast of Broadwater Farm', *Observer*, 18 January 2004.
32. Information from Paul Boateng. See Andy McSmith, *Faces of Labour, The Inside Story*, Verso, London, 1997, p. 233.
33. *The Times*, 30 April 1987; *Financial Times*, 30 April 1987.
34. *The Times*, 1 May 1987.
35. *Financial Times*, 15 November 1985.
36. Hanif Kureishi, *The Buddha of Suburbia*, Faber and Faber, London, 1990, p. 78.
37. *The Times*, 18 April 1984.
38. *Hansard*, 23 July 1997, cols 998–1,000.

39. Inter Press Service, 7 October 1988; *Independent*, 6 October 1988.
40. *New York Times*, 13 July 1991.
41. Quoted in *Washington Post*, 29 September 1990.
42. John Torode, 'Illiberal liberalism', *Independent*, 3 October 1989.
43. Christopher Hitchens, 'Not yet Dead Yet', in *Unacknowledged Legislation, Writers in the Public Sphere*, Verso, 2000, p. 127.
44. Quoted in Andrew Roth, *Parliamentary Profiles 1987–1991, vol.II, E–K*, Parliamentary Profile Services, London, 1989, p. 534.
45. Dan Fisher, 'Split between Britain, U.S. seen as inevitable', *Los Angeles Times*, 19 April 1990.
46. *Guardian*, 11 October 1989.
47. *Sunday Times*, 9 December 1990.
48. *Observer*, 18 November 1990.
49. *Independent*, 24 January 1990.
50. *Sunday Times*, 16 December 1990.
51. Sarah Helms, 'Census will include question about race', *Independent*, 14 November 1989.

CHAPTER 6

1. Simon Weston, *Walking Tall, An Autobiography*, Bloomsbury, London, 1989, p. 131.
2. *Hansard*, 17 December 1980, written answers col. 225.
3. *Hansard*, 2 December 1980, col. 651.
4. Quoted in Max Hastings and Simon Jenkins, *The Battle for the Falklands*, Michael Joseph, London, 1983, p. 24.
5. Peter Beck, *The Falkland Islands as an International Problem*, Routledge, London, 1989.
6. *Hansard*, 2 December 1980, cols 129–34.
7. Pierre F. de Villemarest, *The Strategists of Fear – Twenty Years of Revolutionary War in Argentina*, Voxmundi, Geneva, 1980. The bookshop where I was working in 1980 was one of the recipients of a free copy of this book.
8. *Whitley Bay Guardian*, 9 January 1981.
9. Henry Leach, *Endure No Makeshifts, Some Naval Recollections*, Leo Cooper, London, 1993.
10. John Nott, *Here Today, Gone Tomorrow – Recollections of an Errant Politician*, Politico's, London, 2003, pp. 213–4.
11. Admiral Sandy Woodward, with Patrick Robinson, *One Hundred Days – The Memoirs of the Falklands Battle Group Commander*, HarperCollins, London, 2003, p. 82.

12. Alan Clark, *Diaries – Into Politics*, ed. by Ion Trewin, Weidenfeld & Nicolson, London, 2000, p. 305.
13. Hugo Young, *One of Us: A Biography of Margaret Thatcher*, Pan, London, 1990, p. 275.
14. John Nott, *Here Today, Gone Tomorrow*, p. 257.
15. David Colville, 'Invasion and Occupation – The Story of a Stanley Resident', 2000, at www.falklands-malvinas.com/forum/viewtopic.php?t=679.
16. *The Times*, 5 April 1982.
17. *Daily Star*, 3 April 1982.
18. Margaret Thatcher, *The Downing Street Years*, HarperCollins, London, 1993, p. 183.
19. *Hansard*, 3 April 1982, cols 639, 641.
20. Alan Clark, *Diaries – Into Politics*, pp. 312–13.
21. *Hansard*, 3 April 1982, col. 661.
22. *Hansard*, 3 April 1982, cols 654–5.
23. *The Times*, 6 April 1982.
24. James Reston, 'A Matter of Honor', *New York Times*, 7 April 1982.
25. *Hansard*, 7 April 1982, col. 994.
26. Margaret Thatcher, *The Downing Street Years*, p. 208.
27. This exchange is posted on YouTube at http://uk.youtube.com/watch?v=rGxsLbK9F0A.
28. *Sun*, 4 May 1982.
29. Peter Chippindale and Chris Horrie, *Stick it up Your Punter – The rise and fall of the Sun*, Mandarin, London, 1992, pp. 117–19.
30. David Hart-Dyke, *Four Weeks in May – A Captain's Story of War at Sea*, Atlantic Books, London, 2008, pp. 84–5.
31. Robert Harris, *Gotcha! The Media, The Government and the Falklands Crisis*, Faber and Faber, London, 1983, pp. 66–7.
32. Sandy Woodward, *One Hundred Days: The Memoirs of the Falklands Battle Group Commander*, Naval Institute Press, London, 1997, p. 27.
33. *Private Eye*, 9 April 1982.
34. *Sun*, 29 April 1982.
35. Robert Harris, *Gotcha!*, p. 72.
36. *Hansard*, 6 May 1982.
37. *Sun*, 7 May 1982.
38. *Daily Mirror*, 8 May 1982.
39. *Daily Star*, 22 May 1982.
40. Giles Radice, *Diaries 1980–2001: From Political Disaster to Election Triumph*, Weidenfeld & Nicolson, London, 2004, p. 71.
41. Nicholas Henderson, *Mandarin: The Diary*, Weidenfeld & Nicolson, London, 1994, p. 461.

42. Andy McSmith, 'The Popular Reaction', *The Empire Strikes Back – Some Views on the Falklands War*, Tyneside Ad Hoc Committee for Peace in the Falklands, Newcastle, 1982, p. 21.
43. Carol Thatcher, *A Swim-on Part in the Goldfish Bowl – A Memoir*, Headline, London, 2008, p. 106.
44. David Hart-Dyke, *Four Weeks in May*, p. 150.
45. 'Factsheet No.16', *Statistical Digest of By-election Results in the 1979–1983 Parliament*, House of Commons Public Information Office, London, 1983.
46. Max Arthur, *Above All Courage – First-Hand Accounts from the Falklands Front Line*, Sphere, London, 1985, p. 139.
47. Simon Weston, *Walking Tall*, p. 147.
48. *Guardian*, 17 October 2007.
49. Letter from HM Treasury Information Rights Unit, 19 December 2008, received in response to a Freedom of Information request.
50. Figures taken from Table 2.1, 'Defence', March 1983.
51. *Hansard*, 23 December 1982, written answers col. 632.
52. Along with all Margaret Thatcher's speeches, the speech to the Conservative Rally at Cheltenham, 3 July 1982, is available in full at www.margaretthatcher.org/speeches/.
53. Sir Rex Hunt, 'A Welcome Visit', in Iain Dale (ed.), *Margaret Thatcher, A Tribute in Words and Pictures*, Weidenfeld & Nicolson, London, 2005, p. 90.
54. *The Times*, 27 July 1982.
55. *Guardian Weekly*, 1 August 1982.
56. *Hansard*, 25 June 1986, written answers, cols 161–2.
57. 'Report of the Board of Inquiry into Loss of an Army Airs Corps Gazelle over the Falkland Islands on 6 June 1982', 6 November 1986, unpublished. This and other unpublished inquiry reports can be found in the Freedom of Information Publication Scheme on the Ministry of Defence website.
58. 'Report of the Inquiry into the Death of Argentine Prisoner of War Suboficial Primero (SIMQ) Felix Artuso', 30 April 1982, unpublished.
59. 'Board of Inquiry (Report) – Loss of SS Atlantic Conveyor', 21 July 1982, unpublished.
60. 'Loss of HMS Sheffield – Board of Inquiry', 28 May 1982, unpublished, Annex J 'Analysis of Attack and Response', pp. J2, J3 and J5.
61. Sandy Woodward, *One Hundred Days*, pp. 237–8.
62. *Daily Mirror*, 9 August 1982.
63. Philip Williams, with M.S. Power, *Summer Soldier, The True Story of the Missing Falklands Guardsman*, Bloomsbury, London, 1991.
64. Press Association, 11 November 1991.
65. *Sunday Mail* (Glasgow), 29 January 1989.
66. *Guardian*, 26 May 1988.
67. *The Times*, 1 June 1988.

68. Margaret Thatcher, speech on Pinochet at the Conservative Party Conference, 6 October 1999, at www.margaretthatcher.org/speeches/displaydocument.asp?docid=108383.

CHAPTER 7

1. *The Times*, 9 August 1984.
2. *The Times*, 20 October 1981.
3. *The Times*, 21 January 1984.
4. Chris Dunckley, *Financial Times*, 10 February 1982.
5. Sean Hardie and John Lloyd, *Not The Nine O'Clock News*, BBC, London, 1980, p. 11.
6. Lewis Chester, *Tooth & Claw, the Inside Story of Spitting Image*, Faber and Faber, London, 1986, p. 52.
7. Lewis Chester, *Tooth & Claw*, p. 68.
8. Roger Law, with Lewis Chester, *Still Spitting at Sixty: from the '60s to my Sixties, a Sort of Autobiography*, HarperCollins, London, 2005, p. 137.
9. Bryan Appleby, 'The Infamous Puppeteers are Brought to Book', *The Times*, 30 September 1985.
10. Chester Lewis, *Tooth & Claw*, pp. 108–9.
11. Michael Church, *The Times*, 14 February 1981.
12. Decca Aitkenhead, 'What Are You Looking At?', *Guardian*, 19 June 2004.
13. *Hobart Mercury*, 24 June 1989.
14. This quotation appears in a BBC obituary of Spike Milligan, 2 April 2002, posted at www.bbc.co.uk/dna/h2g2/A710047. I have been unable to find the original.
15. Christopher Dunkley, *Financial Times*, 22 July 1987.
16. *Independent*, 29 September 1989.
17. *Independent*, 17 November 1989.
18. *Campaign*, 10 November 1989.
19. Andrew Collins, *Heaven Knows I'm Miserable Now: My Difficult 80s*, Ebury Press, London, 2004, p. 241.
20. Wally the dog was much talked about during a free rock concert in Windsor, which I covered as a journalist in 1975.
21. Paul Manning, *How to be a Wally*, Futura, London, 1983.
22. Steve Clark, *The Only Fools and Horses Story*, BBC, London, 1998, p. 11.

CHAPTER 8

1. David Douglass and Joel Krieger, *A Miner's Life*, Routledge & Kegan Paul, London, 1983, pp. 2–5.

2. Francis Beckett and David Hencke, *Marching to the Fault Line, the 1984 Miners' Strike and the death of Industrial Britain*, Constable, 2009, pp. 47–8.
3. J. Wake, interview with David Akerman of ITN. See Michael Crick, *Scargill and the Miners*, Penguin, Harmondsworth, 1985, p. 98.
4. V.L. Allen, *The Militancy of British Miners*, Moor Press, Shipley, 1981, p. 140.
5. *Hansard*, 3 April 1984, col. 808.
6. Johann Hari, 'Comrades up in arms', *New Statesman*, 10 June 2002.
7. *Financial Times*, 22 January 1982.
8. *The Times*, 21 March 1984.
9. *The Times*, 7 March 1984.
10. The report was leaked to the *Economist*, 27 May 1978. It is quoted at length in Huw Beynon (ed.), *Digging Deep, Issues in the Miners' Strike*, Verso, London, 1985, pp. 35–56.
11. Margaret Thatcher, *The Downing Street Years*, HarperCollins, London, 1993, pp. 140–41.
12. Nigel Lawson, *The View from No. 11: Memoirs of a Tory Radical*, Bantam, London, 1992, p. 140.
13. Ibid., p. 154.
14. Ibid., p. 157.
15. Kim Howells, 'Stopping Out, the Birth of a New Kind of Politics', in Huw Beynon (ed.), *Digging Deep*, pp. 143–6.
16. Stella Rimington, *Open Secret, The Autobiography of the Former Director General of MI5*, Arrow, 2002, p. 163.
17. *Hansard*, 20 March 1984.
18. Francis Beckett and David Hencke, *Marching to the Fault Line*, p. 61.
19. *The Times*, 24 March and 26 March 1984.
20. *Guardian*, 19 November 1984.
21. The full speech notes are on the website of the Margaret Thatcher Foundation at www.margaretthatcher.org/speeches/displaydocument.asp?docid=105563.
22. Ian MacGregor, *Enemies Within. The Story of the Miners' Strike*, HarperCollins, London, 1986, p. 220.
23. I should know: I was the press officer in charge of issuing passes at that conference. I had to explain to the Conference Arrangements Committee (CAC) how a solicitor had been in possession of a *Daily Express* press pass and did not know the answer until the next day. The CAC then announced, to loud cheers from the conference hall, that they had invalidated the pass issued to Sir Larry Lamb, the editor of the *Daily Express*.
24. Margaret Thatcher, *The Downing Street Years*, p. 366.
25. Francis Beckett and David Hencke, *Marching to the Fault Line*, p. 141.
26. *Hansard*, 30 October 1984, col. 1158.
27. Arthur Scargill, 'We could surrender – or stand and fight', *Guardian*, 7 March 2009.

28. *The Times*, 29 October 1984.
29. For an exhaustive account of Windsor's involvement with the NUM and the 1990 allegations against Scargill and Heathfield, see Seumas Milne, *The Enemy Within, The Secret War Against the Miners*, Verso, London, 2004.
30. Roy Greenslade, 'Sorry Arthur', *Guardian*, 27 May 2002.
31. *Sunday Express*, 21 May 2000, 7 July 2002.
32. Stella Rimington, *Open Secret*, pp. 163–4.
33. *Guardian*, 8 September 2001.
34. Jill Miller, *You Can't Kill the Spirit: Women in a Welsh Mining Village*, Women's Press, London, 1986, quoted in Francis Beckett and David Hencke, *Marching to the Fault Line*, p. 172.
35. Francis Beckett and David Hencke, *Marching to the Fault Line*, p. 205.
36. IRV/8 and IRV/9 from the documents headed 'The Cost of the Miners' Strike in 1984–5', released by the Treasury on 30 June 2008.
37. Figures for the total workforce are from the Coal Authority. Current membership figures for the NUM and UDM are from the Certification Officer.
38. Barrie Clement and Ian Herbert, 'Still Fighting, 20 Years On', *Independent*, 5 March 2004.

CHAPTER 9

1. Bob Geldof (with Paul Vallely), *Is That It?*, Guild Publishing, 1986, pp. 213–4, 215.
2. BBC News, 15 November 1984.
3. This information comes from an unpublished memorandum presented to a ministerial meeting held at the Foreign Office, 28 October 1984, now in the Cabinet Office archives.
4. Note by Charles Powell, private secretary to the prime minister, 29 October 1984; Cabinet Office archives.
5. Bob Geldof, *Is That It?*, p. 10.
6. Midge Ure, *If I Was . . ., the Autobiography*, Virgin, 2004, p. 132.
7. Boy George with Spencer Bright, *Take It Like a Man: the Autobiography of Boy George*, Pan, 1995, pp. 303–4.
8. Martin Kemp, *True – The Autobiography of Martin Kemp*, Orion, London, 2000, pp. 113–4.
9. Midge Ure, *If I Was . . .*, p. 145.
10. Bob Geldof, *Is That It?*, p. 218.
11. *Daily Mirror*, 7 June 1983.
12. John Wilson, 'Chasing the Blues Away', *New Statesman*, 15 May 2008.
13. *The Lady's Not for Spurning*, BBC Four, 25 February 2008.

14. Michka Assayas, *Bono on Bono – Conversations with Michka Assayas*, Hodder & Stoughton, London, 2005, p. 112.
15. *The Times*, 27 September 1980.
16. Alexis Petridis, 'Ska for the madding crowd', *Guardian*, 8 March 2002.
17. Testimony of General Sharon to the Israeli Commission of Enquiry, 25 October 1982, quoted in David Gilmour, *Lebanon: The Fractured Country*, Sphere, London, 1984, p. 176.
18. Andrew Collins, *Still Suitable for Miners – Billy Bragg: The Official Biography*, Virgin, London, 1998, p. 116.
19. *Report of the Annual Conference of the Labour Party 1985*, p. 178. A party researcher named Tony Manwaring and I originally had the job of trying to convince Smith that Billy Bragg would be an asset to the Jobs and Industry Campaign. He was notably reserved in his reaction until he had been home to Edinburgh, but came back enthused.
20. *Daily Express*, 29 May 1986.
21. Andrew Roth, *Parliamentary Profiles, vol. II E–K*, Parliamentary Profile Services, London, 1989, p. 437.
22. *Liverpool Echo*, 7 January 1985.
23. Joe Haines, *Maxwell*, Guild Publishing, London, 1988, p. 399.
24. Midge Ure, *If I Was . . .*, p. 151.
25. Bob Geldof, *Is That It?*, p. 257.
26. Ibid., p. 258.
27. Ibid., p. 261.
28. Laura Jackson, *Bono, The Biography*, Piatkus, London, 2001, p. 70.
29. Interview for *Weekend World*, London Weekend Television, 16 January 1983. The full text is on the website of the Margaret Thatcher Foundation at www.margaretthatcher.org/speeches/displaydocument.asp?docid=105087.
30. Bob Geldof, *Is That It?*, p. 314.

CHAPTER 10

1. Peter Chippindale and Chris Horrie, *Stick it up Your Punter – The rise and fall of the Sun*, Mandarin, London, 1992, p. 240.
2. Peter York and Charles Jennings, *Peter York's Eighties*, BBC Books, London, 1995, p. 117.
3. *Economist*, 23 July 1983.
4. *Financial Times*, 10 August 1983.
5. *Guardian*, 28 October 1991.
6. The figures are taken from a letter dated 21 October 1983 from the Inland Revenue, addressed to John Moore, the financial secretary of the Treasury. It was

one of a batch of Treasury documents released after a Freedom of Information request on 3 November 2009.

7. Letter from the chancellor of the exchequer to the prime minister, 6 February 1984.
8. Letter from John Moore to John Driscoll, Inland Revenue, 15 February 1984.
9. Letter from Andrew Turnbull, private secretary to the prime minister, to an official of the Inland Revenue, 1 March 1984; Inland Revenue press release, 13 March 1984.
10. Information from Nigel Farage, MEP, son of Guy Farage.
11. Michael Lewis, *Liar's Poker*, Hodder & Stoughton, London, 1989, p. 184.
12. Margaret Thatcher, speech to the Institute of Socio-Economic Studies, New York, 15 September 1975. Full text on the website of the Margaret Thatcher Foundation at www.margaretthatcher.org/speeches/displaydocument.asp?docid=102769.
13. Keith Joseph, *Stranded in the Middle Ground?*, Centre for Policy Studies, London, 1976.
14. Mark Garnett, *From Anger to Apathy, The British Experience since 1975*, Jonathan Cape, London, 2007, p. 233.
15. *Tatler*, July/August 1986, quoted in John Rentoul, *The Rich get Richer, The Growth of Inequality in Britain in the 1980s*, Unwin, London, 1987, p. 11.
16. Geoffrey Howe, *Conflict of Loyalty*, Macmillan, London, 1994, p. 143.
17. Adrian Hamilton, *The Financial Revolution*, Penguin, Harmondsworth, 1986, p. 33.
18. *Financial Times*, 11 December 1982.
19. Michael Lewis, *Liar's Poker*, pp. 163–4.
20. *Financial Times*, 18 September 1985.
21. *Hansard*, 11 December 1979, written answers cols 565–6.
22. Interview with the author.
23. Christopher Hird, 'New Mirror Fades: Interview with Clive Thornton', *Marxism Today*, August 1984.
24. Midge Ure, *If I Was . . ., the Autobiography*, Virgin, 2004, pp. 75–6.
25. I was also in Newcastle for that by-election and was privileged to borrow this wondrous new machine, which I took into a pub where the Geordies crowded around to examine it. One woman, curious about the correct positioning of its thick black aerial, inquired innocently: 'Do you do it with it sticking straight up?'
26. Margaret Thatcher, speech to Conservative Party Conference, 10 October 1986. Full text at www.margaretthatcher.org/speeches/displaydocument.asp?docid=106498.
27. *The Times*, 3 June 1985.
28. *Washington Post*, 24 November 1980; Harry Whewell, 'Word Wise', *Guardian*, 6 September 1981.

29. *Drinking in Great Britain, IAS Factsheet*, Institute of Alcohol Studies, St Ives, Cambridgeshire.
30. Ann Barr and Peter York, *The Official Sloane Ranger Diary: The First Guide to the Sloane Year*, Ebury, London, 1983, p. 82.
31. *Financial Times*, 16 April 1983.
32. Peter York and Charles Jennings, *Peter York's Eighties*, p. 98.
33. *Guardian*, 13 November 1986.
34. 'The Social Reportage of Dafydd Jones', *Professional Photographer*, 26 June 2009.
35. Toby Young, 'Let me tell you the secret behind the Bullingdon posturing of David and Boris: Oxford contemporary looks behind that decadent image', *Daily Mail*, 23 July 2009. See also Toby Young, 'Class', in Rachel Johnson (ed.), *The Oxford Myth*, Weidenfeld & Nicolson, London, 1998.
36. *Financial Times*, 31 July 1986.
37. The photograph first appeared in Francis Elliott and James Hanning, *Cameron, The Rise of the New Conservative*, Harper Perennial, London, 2009. The writers say that Cameron's invitation to join the Bullingdon Club came at the end of his first year in university, i.e. around July 1986. The photograph, which is not dated, must have been taken between then and when Johnson left Oxford a year later.
38. Andrew Gimson, *Boris, The Rise of Boris Johnson*, Simon & Schuster, London, 2006, p. 63.
39. Francis Elliott and James Hanning, *Cameron*, pp. 59–60.

CHAPTER 11

1. *Hansard*, House of Lords, 30 November 1982, col. 1198.
2. Chris Dunkley, 'The Morning After Channel Four', *Financial Times*, 3 November 1982.
3. *New York Times*, 19 October 1984.
4. *Financial Times*, 29 December 1982.
5. Anna Ford was neither the first nor the last woman to take exception to Aitken, who had wealth, charm, connections, good looks and a dubious character. He had dated Carol Thatcher, whom he allegedly treated so badly that her mother resolutely refused to give him a job in government. She showed better judgement than John Major, who made him a cabinet minister, putting him on the road to becoming the only ex-cabinet minister in the post-war years to go to jail.
6. Joe Haines, *Maxwell*, Guild Publishing, London, 1988, p. 310.
7. Joe Haines, 'Richard Stott: the Man Who Loved the Mirror', *Daily Mirror*, 31 July 2007. In this version, Haines quoted Stott as saying 'effing', which is not likely to have been what he actually said.
8. Tom Bower, *Maxwell, The Outsider*, Mandarin, London, 1988, p. 400.
9. *Daily Mirror*, 6 November 1991.

10. *Daily Mirror*, 5 December 1991.
11. Max Hastings, *Editor, An Inside Story of Newspapers*, Pan, London, 2003, p. 78.
12. Ibid., p. 85.
13. David Jones, Julian Petley, Mike Power, Lesley Wood, *Media Hits the Pits – the Media and the Coal Dispute*, Campaign for Press and Broadcasting Freedom, London, undated, p. 9.
14. NA Prem 16/2213.
15. Harold Evans, *Good Times, Bad Times*, Atheneum, London, 1984, p. 304.
16. Andrew Neil, *Full Disclosure*, Macmillan, London, 1996, p. 160.
17. *Hansard*, 6 March 1984, col. 732.
18. Stephen Glover, *Paper Dreams*, Jonathan Cape, 1993, p. 8.
19. William Shawcross, *Rupert Murdoch, Ringmaster of the Information Circus*, Pan, London, 1993, p. 335.
20. Andrew Neil, *Full Disclosure*, p. 154.
21. Piers Morgan, 'You Ask the Questions', *Independent*, 10 March 2005.
22. Peter Chippindale and Chris Horrie, *Stick it up Your Punter – The rise and fall of the Sun*, Mandarin, London, 1992, p. 207.
23. Peter Chippindale and Chris Horrie, *Stick It Up Your Punter!*, p. 170.
24. *Sun*, 1 November 1990.
25. *Financial Times*, 22 September 1987.
26. *Daily Telegraph*, 30 November 1987.
27. *Financial Times*, 28 November 1987.
28. *Independent*, 18 October 1991.
29. *Daily Telegraph*, 27 October 1986.
30. Max Hastings, *Editor*, p. 200.
31. Woodrow Wyatt, *The Journals of Woodrow Wyatt, Volume One*, edited by Sarah Curtis, Pan, London, 1998, p. 395.
32. *The Times*, 24 July 1987; *Guardian*, 24 July 1987. One person who knew for a fact that Archer was lying was his friend Ted Francis, whom he had bribed to give him an alibi for the night he was with Coghlan. In 1999, when Lord Archer of Weston-super-Mare, as he had since become, was Conservative candidate for the post of mayor of London, Francis told all. Archer was sentenced to four years in prison for perjury.
33. This account of the Sonia Sutcliffe libel case is drawn from Paul Foot, *Ripping Yarns – Sonia Sutcliffe, The Press and the Law*, Private Eye, London, 1991.
34. *The Times*, 7 May 1981.
35. BBC News, 24 May 1989.
36. Peter Chippindale and Chris Horrie, *Stick It Up Your Punter!*, p. 271.

CHAPTER 12

1. Patrick Bishop and Eamonn Mallie, *The Provisional IRA*, Corgi, London, 1994, p. 313.
2. Margaret Thatcher, 'Remarks After Leaving Airey Neave's widow' 30 March 1979, see the website of the Margaret Thatcher Foundation www.margaretthatcher.org/speeches/displaydocument.asp?docid=103991.
3. BBC Radio News, 30 March 1979.
4. Margaret Thatcher, *Margaret Thatcher, The Downing Street Years*, HarperCollins, London, 1993, pp. 385–8.
5. Ibid., p. 391.
6. *Hansard*, 5 May 1981, col. 17.
7. Letter to Cardinal Tomás Ó Fiaich, 15 May 1981. Full text on the website of the Margaret Thatcher Foundation at www.margaretthatcher.org/speeches/displaydocument.asp?docid=104650.
8. Ed Blanche, 'IRA Claims It Is Stronger Because of Hunger Striker', Associated Press, 4 December 1981.
9. Associated Press, 28 July 1982.
10. Jim Prior, *A Balance of Power*, Hamish Hamilton, London, 1986, p. 182.
11. Carol Thatcher, *A Swim-on Part in the Goldfish Bowl – A Memoir*, Headline, London, 2008, pp. 172–3.
12. *Daily Express*, 15 January 1982.
13. *Hansard*, 8 November 1982, written questions, col. 32.
14. All the details about Mark Thatcher's protection are in unpublished Cabinet Office documents made available after a Freedom of Information request. The references to the IRA threat and resulting police protection are contained in an unsigned Background Note drawn up as Home Office officials considered how to answer a written question tabled in the House of Commons in November 1982 by the Labour MP Willie Hamilton on the cost of protecting Mark Thatcher.
15. Letter from David Hollamby, British Consul in Dallas, to Sarah Gillett, British Embassy, Washington, 10 January 1985.
16. Letter from John Kerr, head of chancellery, British Embassy in Washington, to Frederick Butler, principal private secretary to the prime minister, 13 May 1985.
17. Letter from Nigel Wicks, principal private secretary to the prime minister, 15 October 1986. The addressee is not identified but can be assumed to have been John Kerr.
18. Letter from John Kerr to Nigel Wicks, 6 December 1985.
19. Letter from John Kerr to Nigel Wicks, 6 June 1986.
20. Letter from Nigel Wicks to John Kerr, 16 June 1986.
21. Letter from Mark Pellew, British Embassy, Washington, to Nigel Wicks, 18 July 1986.

22. Press conference, 19 November 1984. Full text on the website of the Margaret Thatcher Foundation www.margaretthatcher.org/speeches/displaydocument.asp?docid=105790.
23. Margaret Thatcher, *The Downing Street Years*, p. 403.
24. BBC interview, 9 November 1987.
25. Max Hastings, *Editor, An Inside Story of Newspapers*, Pan, London, 2003, p. 135.
26. John Stalker, *Stalker*, Harrap, London, 1988, p. 49.
27. *Hansard*, 17 January 1989.
28. On the Finucane murder, see Kevin Toolis, *Rebel Hearts, Journeys within the IRA's Soul*, St Martin's Press, New York, 1996.

CHAPTER 13

1. *The Times*, 28 February 1981.
2. Boy George with Spencer Bright, *Take It Like a Man: the Autobiography of Boy George*, Pan, 1995, p. 129, p. 127.
3. Ibid., p. 208.
4. *Hansard*, 3 December 1981, cols 388–9.
5. Peter Chippindale and Chris Horrie, *Stick it up Your Punter – The rise and fall of the Sun*, Mandarin, London, 1992, pp. 136–7.
6. Quoted in Peter Tatchell, *The Battle for Bermondsey*, Heretic Books, London, 1983, p. 72.
7. Peter Tatchell, email to the author, 28 February 2009.
8. Peter Tatchell, *The Battle for Bermondsey*, p. 132.
9. *Mail on Sunday*, 1 May 1983.
10. '"Gay Plague" May Lead to Blood Ban on Homosexuals', *Daily Telegraph*, 2 May 1983; 'Alert over "Gay Plague"', *Daily Mirror*, 2 May 1983; 'Watchdogs in "Gay Plague" Probe', *Sun*, 2 May 1983.
11. *The Times*, 21 November 1984.
12. Dr Roger Watson, letter in *The Times*, 28 February 1985.
13. *Guardian*, 31 August 1984.
14. *The Times*, 6 March 1985.
15. *Sun*, 23 February 1985.
16. *The Times*, 17 July 1985.
17. *Sun*, 3 October 1985.
18. *The Times*, 7 February 1985.
19. *The Times*, 10 January 1985.
20. *The Times*, 6 February 1985.
21. Letter from Michael Saward, *The Times*, 21 February 1985.

22. 'Gays Put Mrs Mopps in Panic on Aids', *Sun*, 19 February 1985; 'Mrs Mopps rebel over a gay play', *Daily Mirror*, 19 February 1985; 'Mrs Mopps in a Fury', *Daily Express*, 19 February 1985.
23. *Guardian*, 20 September 1985.
24. *The Times*, 28 September 1985.
25. *The Times*, 9 November 1985.
26. Andrew Collins, *Heaven Knows I'm Miserable Now: My Difficult 80s*, Ebury Press, London, 2004, p. 254.
27. Andy McSmith, 'Crikey! How Aids flustered the Tories', *Observer*, 3 January 1999.
28. *Guardian*, 18 December 1986. Bill Brownhill was interviewed by LBC on 18 December 1986 about his comments and refused to retract them. A recording of the interview is retained by the British Universities Film & Video Council, Bournemouth University.
29. *Guardian*, 12 December 1986; *The 1980s Aids Campaign*, BBC, 16 October 2005.
30. Margaret Thatcher, 'Speech to Conservative Party conference', 9 October 1987. Full text on the website of the Margaret Thatcher Foundation at www.margaretthatcher.org/speeches/displaydocument.asp?docid=106941.
31. Andrew Roth, *Parliamentary Profiles L–R*, Parliamentary Profiles Services, London, 1984, p. 650.
32. *Daily Telegraph*, 21 May 1987.
33. *Guardian*, 3 February 1988; *The Times*, 3 February 1988.
34. *Guardian*, 24 May 1988.
35. *Sunday Times*, 29 May 1988.

CHAPTER 14

1. Robert Elms, *The Way We Wore: A Life in Threads*, Picador, London, 2005, p. 189.
2. Remark to Tyne Tees TV, 11 September 1985. Transcript can be accessed on the website of the Margaret Thatcher Foundation at www.margaretthatcher.org/speeches.
3. *Faith in the City, A Call to Action by Church and Nation – The Report of the Archbishop of Canterbury's Commission on Urban Priority Areas*, Church House Publishing, London, 1985, pp. 361–2.
4. *Sunday Times*, 1 December 1985.
5. Associated Press, 3 December 1985.
6. Woodrow Wyatt, *The Journals of Woodrow Wyatt, Volume One*, edited by Sarah Curtis, Pan, London, 1998, p. 22.
7. *Guardian*, 3 December 1987; *The Times*, 3 December 1987.
8. *Guardian*, 4 December 1987.

9. *The Times*, 14 December 1987.
10. David Blunkett and Keith Jackson, *Democracy in Crisis: The Town Halls Respond*, Hogarth Press, London, 1987, p. 153.
11. *The Times*, 11 November 1981.
12. *Hansard*, 23 July 1981, col. 492.
13. *Sun*, 19 August 1981, quoted in John Carvel, *Citizen Ken*, Chatto and Windus, London, 1984, pp. 91-2.
14. *The Times*, 13 October 1981.
15. *Economist*, 24 March 1984.
16. Simon Jenkins, *Thatcher & Sons, A Revolution in Three Acts*, Penguin, London, 2007, p. 131.
17. Derek Hatton, *Inside Left: The Story So Far . . .*, Bloomsbury, London, 1988, p. 68.
18. *The Times*, 30 October 1985.
19. *Independent*, 21 December 1989.
20. Prunella Kaur, *Go Fourth & Multiply: The Political Anatomy of the British Left Groups*, Dialogue of the Deaf, Bristol, no date, p. 1.
21. Derek Hatton, *Inside Left*, p. 71.
22. David Blunkett and Keith Jackson, *Democracy in Crisis*, p. 156.
23. Ibid., p. 183.
24. Patrick Seyd, 'Bennism without Benn: realignment on the Labour left', *New Socialist*, no. 27, May 1985.
25. *Report of the Annual Conference of the Labour Party 1985*, p. 128.
26. The existence of Ricky Tomlinson's file was revealed by Peter Taylor in the BBC documentary *True Spies* in August 2002; see *Guardian*, 22 August 2002.
27. Ricky Tomlinson, *Ricky*, Time Warner, London, 2004, p. 105.
28. Woodrow Wyatt, *The Journals of Woodrow Wyatt, Volume One*, p. 382.
29. Margaret Thatcher, *The Downing Street Years*, HarperCollins, London, 1993, p. 645.
30. *Hansard*, 30 July 1984.
31. Kenneth Baker, *The Turbulent Years: My Life in Politics*, Faber and Faber, London, 1993, p. 116.
32. Nicholas Ridley, *My Style of Government*, Hutchinson, London, 1991, p. 125.
33. Nigel Lawson, *The View from No. 11: Memoirs of a Tory Radical*, Bantam, London, 1992, p. 900.
34. Simon Jenkins, *Thatcher & Sons*, p. 174.
35. *Guardian*, 6 March 1990.
36. *Independent*, 6 March 1990.
37. *Financial Times*, 7 March 1990.
38. *Independent on Sunday*, 1 April 1990.
39. Margaret Thatcher, *The Downing Street Years*, p. 661.

40. Alan Clark, *Diaries – Into Politics*, edited by Ion Trewin, Weidenfeld & Nicolson, London, 2000, p. 290.

CHAPTER 15

1. BBC News, 15 October 1987.
2. Annalena Lobb, 'Looking Back at Black Monday: A Discussion With Richard Sylla', *Wall Street Journal*, 15 October 2007.
3. Richard Eyre, *National Service – Diary of a Decade*, Bloomsbury, London, 2003, p. 21.
4. Michael Lewis, *Liar's Poker*, Hodder & Stoughton, London, 1989, p. 288.
5. *Hansard*, 15 March 1988, col. 1008.
6. *The Times*, 23 June 1990.
7. Jane Ellison, *Guardian*, 15 June 1989.
8. *Sun*, 23 March 1992.
9. Margaret Thatcher, *The Downing Street Years*, HarperCollins, London, 1993, p. 599.
10. Margaret Thatcher, 'Speech to Conservative Party Conference', 9 October 1987. Full text at www.margaretthatcher.org/speeches/displaydocument.asp?docid=106941.
11. Kenneth Baker, *The Turbulent Years, My Life in Politics*, Faber and Faber, London, 1993, p. 168.
12. Nicholas Ridley, *My Style of Government*, Hutchinson, London, 1991, p. 40.
13. Alan Clark, *Diaries – Into Politics*, Weidenfeld & Nicolson, London, 2000, p. 197.
14. *Hansard*, House of Lords, 25 November 1993, col. 345.
15. *Hansard*, 29 November 1989, col. 727.
16. *Guardian*, 18 December 1989; John Rentoul, *Tony Blair, Prime Minister*, Warner, London, 2001, pp. 155–6.
17. Alan Clark, *Diaries*, p. 54.
18. *Sunday Times*, 28 October 1990.
19. When I first went to meet Gordon Brown in 1986, when I was working as Labour Party press officer, I mentioned this to Peter Mandelson, who said to me: 'You are going to meet a future Labour prime minister.'
20. Ken Livingstone, *Livingstone's Labour: a Programme for the Nineties*, Unwin Hyman, London, 1989.
21. *Independent on Sunday*, 10 February 1991.
22. Alastair Campbell, 'You Guys are the Pits', *New Statesman*, 3 April 1987.
23. Bryan Gould, *Goodbye to All That*, Macmillan, London, 1995, pp. 225–6.
24. *Guardian*, 20 May 1988.
25. Edwina Currie, *Diaries 1987–1992*, Little, Brown, London, 2002, p. 49. John Major is the person referred to as 'B' in the entry for 20 March 1988.

26. John Rentoul, *The Rich Get Richer, The Growth of Inequality in Britain in the 1980s*, Unwin, London, 1987, pp. 34–5.
27. 'We Are the Managers Now', *Director* magazine, September 1991.

CHAPTER 16

1. *The World At One*, BBC Radio Four, 22 May 1986.
2. *Financial Times*, 7 July 1984.
3. *The Times*, 14 November 1988.
4. Minutes of the meeting between the prime minister and the Central Council for Physical Recreation, held at 10 Downing Street, 4 February 1980. The minute is in the Cabinet Office archives and was released after a Freedom of Information request in March 2006. Mrs Thatcher's words are reported in indirect speech in the original.
5. Statement by Angus Maude, Paymaster General, 24 January 1980, held in the Cabinet Office archives.
6. The petition and the appended note, dated 3 March 1980, are in the Cabinet Office archives.
7. Minutes of Evidence taken before the Foreign Affairs Committee, 5 March 1980, questions 537, 539 and 601.
8. *Hansard*, 17 March 1980, cols 66 and 110.
9. *The Times*, 12 March 1980.
10. *The Times*, 18 March 1980.
11. BBC, 24 March 1980.
12. Brian Viner, 'Eddie "the Eagle" Edwards: "It was while I was in a mental hospital I heard I was in the Olympic team"', *Independent*, 8 December 2008.
13. *The Times*, 27 February 1988.
14. *Daily Telegraph*, 12 June 1981. Quoted in Michael Melford, *Botham Rekindles the Ashes, The Daily Telegraph Story of the '81 Test Series*, Daily Telegraph, London, 1981, p. 32.
15. Michael Melford, *Botham Rekindles the Ashes*, p. 131.
16. *Economist*, 25 July 1981.
17. *Guardian*, 23 August 1981.
18. Jimmy Burns, *Hand of God, The Life of Diego Maradona*, Bloomsbury, London, 1996. p. 156.
19. Associated Press, 23 June 1986.
20. *The Times*, 23 June 1986.
21. United Press International, 23 June 1986.
22. Diego Maradona, with Daniel Arcucci and Ernesto Cherquis Bialo, *El Diego, the autobiography of the world's greatest footballer*, translated by Marcela Mora Y Araujo, Yellow Jersey Press, London, 2005, pp. 127–8.

23. Associated Press, 14 May 1985.
24. *Hansard*, House of Lords, 24 July 1985, col. 1221.
25. *Guardian*, 14 May 1985.
26. Quoted in *The Hillsborough Stadium Disaster 15 April 1989, Inquiry by the Rt Hon Lord Justice Taylor, Final Report*, Home Office, London, 1990.
27. Quoted in Patrick Murphy, John Williams and Eric Dunning, *Football on Trial, Spectator Violence and Development in the Football World*, Routledge, London, 1990, p. 87.
28. Fiona Maddocks, *Independent*, 27 February 1989.
29. Margaret Thatcher, press conference, 30 May 1985. Full text on the website of the Margaret Thatcher Foundation at www.margaretthatcher.org/speeches/displaydocument.asp?docid=106060.
30. Lord Justice Taylor, *The Hillsborough Stadium Disaster 15 April 1989, Inquiry by the Rt Hon Lord Justice Taylor, Interim Report*, Home Office, London, 1989, p. 15.
31. Lord Justice Taylor, *The Hillsborough Stadium Disaster*, pp. 16–17.
32. Phil Scraton, *Hillsborough, The Truth*, Mainstream Publishing, Edinburgh, 2009, p. 99.
33. Peter Chippindale and Chris Horrie, *Stick it up Your Punter – The rise and fall of the Sun*, Mandarin, London, 1992, p. 292.
34. Colin Ward, *All Quiet on the Hooligan Front, Eight Years that Shook Football*, Headline, London, 1996, pp. 23–58.
35. *Guardian*, 8 September 1989.
36. *Hansard*, 11 September 1989.
37. *Independent*, 22 September 1989.
38. Lord Justice Taylor, *The Hillsborough Stadium Disaster*, p. 44.
39. Ibid., p. 49.
40. Ibid., p. 4.
41. Tom Bower, *Broken Dreams – Vanity, Greed and the Souring of British Football*, Simon & Schuster, London, 2007, pp. 61–8.
42. Jason Cowley, *The Last Game – Love, Death and Football*, Simon & Schuster, London, 2009, p. 270.

CHAPTER 17

1. Paddy Ashdown, *The Ashdown Diaries, Volume 1: 1988–97*, Allen Lane, London, 2000, p. 50.
2. Margaret Thatcher, 'Speech to Conservative Party Conference', 12 October 1990, full text on the website of the Margaret Thatcher Foundation, www.margaretthatcher.org/speeches/displaydocument.asp?docid=108217.
3. Margaret Thatcher, interviewed in the *Sunday Times*, 21 February 1990.

4. *Daily Telegraph*, 12 February 1990.
5. Margaret Thatcher, 'Speech to Young Conservative Conference', 10 February 1990. The full text is available on the website of the Margaret Thatcher Foundation, www.margaretthatcher.org/speeches/displaydocument.asp?docid=108011.
6. *Hansard*, 18 November 1990, col. 1375.
7. Margaret Thatcher, 'Speech to the Board of Deputies of British Jews', 18 February 1990. The full text is available on the website of the Margaret Thatcher Foundation at www.margaretthatcher.org/speeches/displaydocument.asp?docid=108017.
8. *Sunday Times*, 18 February 1990.
9. *Daily Express*, 20 February 1990.
10. Margaret Thatcher, 'Speech to the Konigswinter Conference', 29 March 1990. The full text is available on the website of the Margaret Thatcher Foundation at www.margaretthatcher.org/speeches/displaydocument.asp?docid=108049.
11. Christopher Tugendhat, *Making Sense of Europe*, Viking, London, 1986, p. 122.
12. Nigel Lawson, *The View from No.11: Memoirs of a Tory Radical*, Bantam, London, 1992, p. 900.
13. *Hansard*, 13 November 1990, col. 463.
14. Nicholas Ridley, *My Style of Government*, Hutchinson, London, 1991, p. 160.
15. *Spectator*, 13 July 1990.
16. Nigel Lawson, *The View From No.11*, p. 900.
17. Max Hastings, Max Hastings, *Editor, An Inside Story of Newspapers*, Pan, London, 2003, pp. 107–8.
18. Margaret Thatcher, *The Downing Street Years*, HarperCollins, London, 1993, p. 701.
19. Nigel Lawson, *The View From No.11*, p. 789.
20. Margaret Thatcher, *The Downing Street Years*, p. 701.
21. Geoffrey Howe, *Conflict of Loyalty*, Macmillan, London, 1994, p. 583.
22. *Daily Telegraph*, 26 July 1989. Although Ingham's remarks were reported here, he was not named because of the convention all his lobby briefings were off the record. I was present at Ingham's briefing, in 10 Downing Street on the morning of 25 July, as a correspondent of the *Daily Mirror*. He was named in the *Independent* on 26 July as the source of the disparaging comments about Howe, but not quoted verbatim, because the *Independent* did not go to his briefings.
23. 'Competing for Prosperity', report of the Policy Review Group on A Productive and Competitive Economy, *Meet the Challenge, Make the Change: A New Agenda for Britain*, Labour Party, London, 1989, p. 14.
24. Andy McSmith, *John Smith: A Life 1938–1994*, Mandarin, London, 1994, pp. 197–200.
25. *Hansard*, 24 October 1989, col. 689.

26. *The Walden Interview*, LWT, broadcast 29 October 1989. The full text is available on the Thatcher Foundation website at www.margaretthatcher.org/speeches/displaydocument.asp?docid=107808.
27. Margaret Thatcher, *The Downing Street Years*, p. 830.
28. Bruce Anderson, *John Major*, Headline, London, 1992, p. 207.
29. *Hansard*, 30 October 1990, col. 873.
30. *Hansard*, 30 October 1990, col. 865.
31. *Hansard*, 13 November 1990, cols 463, 465.
32. Alan Watkins, *A Conservative Coup: The Fall of Margaret Thatcher*, Duckworth, London, 1992, p. 178.
33. Margaret Thatcher, *The Downing Street Years*, p. 852.
34. *Independent*, 27 November 1990.
35. Margaret Thatcher, interview in *Thatcher: the Downing Street Years*, BBC1, 10 November 1993.
36. *Women's Own*, 31 October 1987.

EPILOGUE

1. *Financial Times*, 19 November 1990.
2. *Economist*, 9 December 1979.
3. This statistic and others that follow are drawn from the *Annual Expenditure Survey 1990*, Office of National Statistics, London, 1992.
4. For me, the image of these huge devices will always be associated with a heroic little immigration official at Heathrow who was on duty when Margaret Thatcher returned from an overseas trip in 1990 in a plane full of civil servants, advisers and political journalists. This man insisted that the whole party, apart from Margaret and Denis Thatcher, must go through passport control, on the far side of the airport, to check that there were no illegal immigrants on board. No amount of pleading by Thatcher's staff would budge him. We all had to be driven across Heathrow by coach so that we could file through passport control, watched by a bored officer who sat with arms folded and feet up. The official who showed such zeal in enforcing the rules had a huge mobile phone that he held close to his left ear all the time, in case it rang. It seemed to give him confidence.
5. *Independent*, 12 November 1990.
6. *Guardian*, 5 September 1982.
7. *Financial Times*, 11 September 1982.
8. *Guardian*, 21 June 1988.
9. *The Times*, 24 November 1990.
10. TUC annual reports, 1980 and 1990.
11. *Independent*, 3 July 1989.
12. *Birmingham Evening Mail*, 2 January 1990.

13. *Independent*, 22 July 1990.
14. The standard source on acid house is Matthew Collin, *Altered State: The Story of Ecstasy Culture and Acid House*, Serpent's Tail, London, 1997.
15. Jonathan Coe, *The House of Sleep*, Penguin, London, 1998, p. 216.
16. *Guardian*, 27 December 1990.

Index